Accession no.
36163050

D1766684

FAMILY
COMMUNICATION

To my family, Graham, Huw, Jake, and Rachel, who provide me with a living laboratory for experiencing family life, and without whose support, inspiration and stories, this book would not have been possible. But especially to Graham, who continually lights my fire in all the right ways.

To my students, past, present, and future, you continue to bring joy to my life through your continual willingness to share the intimacies and intricacies of your own family lives. May you find something relevant to your lives within these pages.

FAMILY COMMUNICATION
Nurturing and Control in a Changing World

Beth A. Le Poire
University of California, Santa Barbara

LIS LIBRARY

Date 15/06/12   Fun... R-fore

Order No. 2364697

University of Chester

WITHDRAWN

SAGE Publications
Thousand Oaks ■ London ■ New Delhi

Copyright © 2006 by Sage Publications, Inc.

All rights reserved. No part of this book may be reproduced or utilized in any form or by any means, electronic or mechanical, including photocopying, recording, or by any information storage and retrieval system, without permission in writing from the publisher.

For information:

 Sage Publications, Inc.
2455 Teller Road
Thousand Oaks, California 91320
E-mail: order@sagepub.com

Sage Publications Ltd.
1 Oliver's Yard
55 City Road
London EC1Y 1SP
United Kingdom

Sage Publications India Pvt. Ltd.
B-42, Panchsheel Enclave
Post Box 4109
New Delhi 110 017 India

Printed in the United States of America on acid-free paper.

Library of Congress Cataloging-in-Publication Data

Le Poire, Beth A.
Family communication: nurturing and control in a changing world / Beth A. Le Poire.
    p. cm.
Includes bibliographical references and index.
ISBN 1-4129-0406-4 (pbk.)
   1. Communication in the family. 2. Family. I. Title.
HQ734.P736 2006
306.87—dc22

                                             2005014504

05 06 07 08 09 10 9 8 7 6 5 4 3 2 1

Acquiring Editor:	Todd R. Armstrong
Editorial Assistant:	Deya Saoud
Production Editor:	Sanford Robinson
Typesetter:	C&M Digitals (P) Ltd.
Copy Editor:	Linda Gray
Indexer:	Jeanne R. Busemeyer
Cover Designer:	Glenn Vogel

Brief Contents

Contents

Acknowledgments

Several groups of individuals need to be acknowledged as true contributors to this work. First, the work and dedication of the reviewers of various stages and parts of this manuscript were first-rate. The final version of this book is dramatically different in structure, content, and overall quality because of the time, dedication, insightfulness, and thoroughness of the reviewers, including Tamara Afifi, Pennsylvania State University; Nancy J. Eckstein, Bethel University; Kory Floyd, Arizona State University; Daena J. Goldsmith, University of Illinois at Urbana-Champaign; Paulette Grotrian, Washtenaw Community College; Jon A. Hess, University of Missouri–Columbia; Chris Segrin, University of Arizona; Cindy H. White, University of Colorado, Boulder; and Steve Wilson, Purdue University.

Second, a highly competent group of scholars in the family communication research arena provided work or review pieces that were highly instrumental in the writing of several areas of this book. First, Anita Vangelisti needs to be highly commended for her edited *Handbook of Family Communication*, also published by Sage. Several of the authors (and their coauthors) from this handbook also deserve specific acknowledgment; their conscientious, thorough, and thoughtful reviews provided the groundwork for several areas of this book. Specifically, I'd like to acknowledge the work of Catherine Surra (on mating), Ted Huston (on parenting), Laurie Van Egeran (on communication in infancy), Laura Stafford (on middle childhood), Brett Laursen (on adolescent-parent communication), John Caughlin (on privacy and demand withdrawal), Allan Sillars (on conflict), and Steve Wilson (on violence in parent-child relationships). In addition, several researchers took the time to provide me with important and timely research reports and should be acknowledged for their collegial spirit. Special acknowledgment goes to Tammy Afifi (nee Golish), Dawn Braithwaite, John Caughlin, Denise Solomon, and Anita Vangelisti.

Third, all my students deserve recognition. My undergraduates in family communication classes continually inspire me with their enthusiasm for the topic and their willingness to share very intimate family information in large classes. In addition, my undergraduate honor's students and my graduate students continually teach me about issues related to family communication. Special acknowledgment goes to Lauren Ponsford and Emily Moyer-Guse for their independent work on sexual communication between parents and adolescents. Rene Dailey continually taught me about confirmation and disconfirmation in family relationships and provided me with important foundations in the parenting styles literature. Finally, Ashley Duggan, Margaret Prescott, Beth Kono, Mimi Wang, Jennifer Stroufe, and Carolyn Shepard provided me with important insights into communication surrounding depression, eating disorders, and violence. Many of their ideas appear in this text. A special added thanks to Margaret Prescott for providing feedback on the first two chapters.

Fourth, I must acknowledge the incredible group of editors I was fortunate to work with at Sage. Todd Armstrong, the acquisitions editor, made this book happen and became a good friend and an adopted member of my family. Deya Saoud provided amazing artwork and graphics to bring the work to life through art, pictures, and pictorial representations of abstract numbers. Copy editor Linda Gray made astute editorial adjustments during the production of the book.

Fifth, my colleagues at UC Santa Barbara provided me not only with the sabbatical to allow the time to write this text, but also supported this teaching endeavor in a highly research-oriented department. I therefore would like to acknowledge Andrew Flanagin, Howard Giles, Miriam Metzger, Anthony Mulac, Robin Nabi, James Potter, Dave Seibold, Ronald Rice, Cynthia Stohl, Michael Stohl, and Scott Reid. I'd especially like to acknowledge Jimmy Bradac, who died during this time and who still continues to provide inspiration to us all to pursue our academic goals.

Finally, although I dedicated this book to them, I would be remiss not to acknowledge my family again. My husband, Graham, provided support beyond the call during the writing of this book. Quite literally, he provided the structural (e.g., guest house where I did my writing), computer (networking all our computers and providing computer support for frantic calls), and motivational support throughout the process. It can quite honestly be said that this book would not have happened without him. My stepsons, Huw and Jake, have provided me with a rich forum for learning about step- and blended families and continually enrich my opportunities to learn through real-life family communication experiences. They, along with their mother and stepfather truly provided me with a living laboratory to bring the family communication text to life with examples from their own lives. In this same vein, my daughter, Rachel, brought a rich learning experience as well, as we all learned how the blended family could be enriched through the addition of a biological connectedness to her brothers. She also continues to help me learn about adding infant children to families and, along with Huw and Jake, shows me the true joy that only parenting can add to your life. My extended and family of origin also provided me with many examples to bring this book to life, and I thank them for their inspiration as well.

Preface

Family communication has been of interest to researchers, teachers, and students for decades. As we transition into a time when traditional nuclear families (biological mother, biological father, and children all living in the same house) represent only one in four families, those interested in family communication are as interested in the effects of divorce, single parenting, remarriage, newly reconstituted families (stepfamilies and blended families), and adoptive families as they are in the traditional processes of relationship development, marriage, and adding children. As I introduce the topics in this book, I'm hoping you can think of this text as another lesson that you've learned in your family communication class from an additional teacher instead of thinking of it as another dry, boring textbook! To help put us both in the right frame of mind, I'd like to give you some idea of the perspective I bring to the topic of family communication. In concert, I'd like you to find the ways in which this book applies to your current and future lives within families. If you call your parents, siblings, or friends to tell them about something you've read in this book, then it will have been a success.

Families and Communication

What does your family look like? If you are like many of my students, you probably think your family was different from the norm. You probably assume that most families have two parents with a mother who works part-time or not at all and a father who works outside the home. Even though this family form is traditional and *nuclear*, most folks your age were raised in alternative family forms. In fact, only about 24% of kids are raised in the traditional nuclear home (only 10% if you consider only families where the mom stayed at home full-time to be "traditional" nuclear homes). My stepsons (Huw, 19, and Jake, 15), my daughter (Rachel), my husband (Graham), and I are all part of what scholars in family communication call a "binuclear blended" family. The boys live with their mom and their stepdad 6 days every 2 weeks and they live with their dad and me 8 days every 2 weeks. So this form approximates a true nuclear family because the children live in a traditional configuration (one female parent and one male parent in each family unit) in both homes. The difference would be that they live with only one *biological* parent in each home at any one time. This is consistent with the latest U.S. census, which reports that 69% of children are currently living with two parents even though the census also reports that only 24% are living with married couples (U.S. Census Bureau, 2002). Our family is blended because my husband and I have one biological child and we live with two of my husband's biological children. Thus, there are bloodlines connecting all the children in the family. One of the things you will find surprising from this book is that although you might assume that the majority of folks are raised in traditional nuclear homes, a majority of us were actually raised in alternative family forms. This book explores definitions of families that will allow us to consider the full complement of family forms, including cohabitating couples, single-parent homes, stepfamilies, binuclear families, families including one or two gay parents, couples with no children, and extended families (in Chapter 2).

No doubt some of you will be curious about why we would include all those forms within our definition of the family. Most definitions of families (biological, legal, and sociological) revolve in some way or another around procreation or regulation of sexual conduct. We will consider the assumptions inherent in such definitions and where we get those assumptions from. We will investigate governmental, religious, and societal impacts on our current assumptions about what a family should or should not look like (in Chapter 1). Alternatively, our definition will revolve around marriage-like commitment and the two primary functions of *nurturing* and *control* carried out in all family forms, regardless of a couple's decisions about having children.

Theories of Family Communication

We will also consider theories about family communication in this book (in Chapter 3). Don't stop reading!! Let me show you how you can apply them to your own life. Take me, for instance. I'm 41 years old, and I just had my first biological baby 3 years ago. As you can imagine, this put me in a quandary when I decided to sign the contract to write this book. I wasn't sure whether I should add the role of "textbook author" to my new role of "mother" and to my expanding repertoire of roles. I say "expanding roles" because I added "wife" 6 years ago. Although this new role in and of itself can be an exciting and frightening addition, I simultaneously assumed the role of "stepmother." I sound quite nontraditional, but I am merely an illustration of the growing complexity experienced by all of us entering family configurations in various forms as we traverse the 21st century. Given all the changes our society has undergone with regard to family forms, these unique and challenging roles are becoming quite ordinary and normative.

One perspective that will be introduced throughout this textbook is *roles theory*. Roles theory will help us to understand the demands and prescriptions placed on us by our roles within families. No doubt, some of you have already been surprised (almost shocked) by my disclosure that I would simultaneously mother a toddler and attempt to write a textbook. What type of mother fails to devote most of her time and attention to feeding, bathing, and cuddling her small child? Others of you might be shocked that a newly minted full professor in communication with many publications and graduate students would even attempt to become a mother at this late stage in her life. Still others among you will believe (as I did) that it is possible for women to do it all. This book explores these gender role assumptions (why men feel extreme pressure to be the resource providers and women feel extreme pressure to be the nurturers) in families and the types of internal and external conflicts they cause within and across family members. We will also consider all the roles that family members can hold and how they affect communication within families.

Families are also systems with many members who work interdependently with one another and continually affect one another. As such, *family systems theory* will help us to understand how families adapt to change and mobilize collective action toward goals. This perspective assumes that all families will have hierarchical goals, with larger goals (e.g., health and welfare) subsuming more short-term goals (e.g., education, good job, health care benefits). All these goals help direct the behavior of family members toward attainment of those goals. This approach proves especially helpful when trying to understand families that include alcoholics or drug addicts (or any other member with behavior that is seemingly out of control). In these families, all members are affected by the drunken and out-of-control behavior of the alcoholic. Simultaneously, many of the children raised in this family understand only unpredictability because it has been the only constant in their family lives. Thus, family systems theory helps us to understand why families may inadvertently and unintentionally work to maintain status quo in families that seem to be highly problematic.

Finally, *rules theory* will help us to understand the verbal and nonverbal rules of communication that exist in families. Within each of your families, you probably have one other to whom you can disclose. For many of you, it will be your mother. For others, it will be your siblings. What are the factors that promote these rules and how you learn them? Who do you go to for comforting? Who do you turn to for security? What topics are taboo? In my family of origin, for instance, we were not allowed to talk about my grandmother's first husband. What secrets will you uncover about your own family?

Family Development

What about you? Where do you fall in this process of family life? The majority of you who are traditional students will be moving from your family of origin into your newly formed family (sometimes called family of procreation, but again, this assumes that families are about organizing sexual conduct and procreation). This means you will take the lessons you learned in the family you grew up in into the family you will make for yourself. This is an exciting time for you because many of you will be dating, and although not all of us will admit it, much of the dating process is spent in mate selection—trying to differentiate between marriageable and nonmarriageable mates. In this text, we will explore both sociopsychological and psychoanalytic approaches to why you are attracted to the partners you are attracted to. The psychoanalytic approaches are my favorite because these fit most squarely within the communication arena. *Attachment theories* examine how you attached to your primary caregiver (still generally the mother figure) and how this affects how you subsequently attach to romantic significant others in your life. Specifically, most of you will have had warm and available caregivers who made you feel loved and who you learned were trustworthy. For those 50% of us raised this way, we grew up to be securely attached to our parents. The other 50% were not so lucky in that we attached in insecure ways. We either were anxious-ambivalent or avoidant in our attachment to our parents (depending mainly on our parents' availability and consistency). These styles then result in various tendencies to approach or avoid relationships. In general, those with secure attachments will approach others with low fears of intimacy and abandonment because they know they are lovable and others are trustworthy. Those who were anxious-ambivalents or abandoned by their caregiver in some way (through physical or psychological abandonment) will enter relationships with higher-than-average fears of abandonment and moderate fears of intimacy. These are the people who badger their partners with love. They're overly attentive and overly jealous and get their self-esteem from their romantic partners. They're the ones who call you in the middle of the night to see if you will go drive by their partners' house with them to "see if they're okay" (read, to see if they're dating someone else, dead, angry with them, breaking up with them, etc.). These romantic partners are called *preoccupieds*, for their obvious preoccupation with their romantic partners. The last category of individuals, *avoidants*, were probably role reversed by their caregivers. In other words, they had parents who were immature or needed attention and assistance in childlike ways that forced the child to grow up too soon and basically parent the parent. Because these folks learned that attachment meant loss of identity (their identity revolved around caregiving others), their greatest fears are of intimacy while they are simultaneously afraid of abandonment (their caregivers were not available to parent them while they were taking care of their parent). Ultimately, these styles attract each other in a multitude of ways (although preoccupieds and avoidants drive each other nuts, they are particularly well suited to each others' childhood attachment styles) and play out in various ways. This book explores (in Chapter 4) how these attachment styles play out. Never fear, we will talk about ways in which romantic partners' attachment styles can ultimately override the parents' influence.

Besides focusing almost exclusively on families and communication, this book also talks a lot about children and their role in the development of the family. What happens when we add children to the married couple (Chapter 5)? Is it true that most couples experience a decrease in marital satisfaction following the birth of a child? How do marital partners manage the sixfold increase in workload that accompanies the birth of a baby? In what ways do new communication patterns with the infant develop? What happens when we add new siblings? How does a family deal with the unique challenges of adolescent children? My two stepsons are 19 and 15. They have taught me a lot about what it means to parent teenage boys. They have both given their permission for me to use their stories to bring life to this book.

How do we raise our children to be socioemotionally competent individuals who contribute to society (Chapter 6)? In what ways do parenting styles contribute to the physical, socioemotional, and academic development of the children? In keeping with the theme of this book on nurturing and controlling communication, parents are typically seen to vary along the two dimensions of *responsiveness* (nurturing) and *demandingness* (control). Authoritative parents are both responsive and demanding, providing high standards for their children in a loving environment. These parents foster many positive socialization outcomes in their children in terms of self-esteem, social competence, and academic development. Authoritarian parents, by contrast, are highly demanding but not highly nurturing. These parents place many structured demands on their children under the auspices of "parental authority." As you might suspect, children often chafe under this harsh form of parenting and do less well on socialization outcomes. Finally, permissive parents are highly responsive but not very demanding. In this way, they exert little control over their children but provide a warm and nurturing environment. Again, children of permissive parents do not thrive as well on socioemotional outcomes.

_____ The Unique Role of Communication in Families

Highlighting communication specifically, this book also considers the unique role of communication in helping to maintain intimacy and closeness in the family in the face of opposing needs for autonomy (Chapter 7). Although closeness and intimacy have been related to greater marital satisfaction, individual members of a family also have a need for self-directed behavior. These two needs often oppose one another and cause conflict, which is discussed in Chapter 8. This chapter examines the inevitability of conflict and the role that communication plays in either escalating or de-escalating conflict and conflict outcomes. Conflict styles and their relationship to the stability of marriage are also considered. Furthermore, constructive conflict (leading to more positive outcomes such as closeness) is differentiated from destructive conflict (leading to harmful outcomes) through the use of various interpersonal models of conflict. This chapter also explores the growing tendencies for violence in our society. This chapter presents profiles for the batterer and battered as well as the reasons why folks stay in these highly destructive relationships.

Chapter 9 considers the role that important family members can play in trying to get their family members to stop problematic behavior. Many families currently face challenges with substance abuse, eating disorders, and depression. All these problems promote internal stress within the family unit. Inconsistent nurturing as control theory explains the paradoxes that exist in the relationship between the healthy family members and the unhealthy family member and how these relationships play themselves out in ways that might not promote the most effective behavioral resistance strategies. In other words, family members of substance abusers, those with eating disorders and depression may behave in inconsistent ways surrounding the problematic behavior. Finally, Chapter 10 attempts to integrate the material across the topics discussed in the book: definitions, family forms, family theories, mating, adding children, socializing children, intimacy and autonomy dialectic, conflict and violence, and assisting problematic behavior. Following a review of the literature presented throughout this book, it is concluded that family communication research offers two principles of family communication: (a) perception is reality (or how you perceive your family members affects how you communicate with them and how they communicate with you and, ultimately, reinforces your original perception) and (2) the golden rule of communication (or how you communicate profoundly affects the ways in which others in your family communicate with you).

1 Introduction: Families, Communication, and Family Communication

Families are primarily composed of involuntary relationships that are often rife with emotional intensity, subtle innuendo, and histories of both great pleasure and intense grievances. The reason families are so interesting to most of us is that we all come from some sort of family (our **family of origin**), and most of us are moving toward some sort of family (our newly formed family or, potentially, our **family of procreation**). Many of us came from family situations that were highly satisfying, and we report feeling nurtured, loved, and supported. Some of us were less fortunate and came from families where we experienced high levels of control with less nurturing, and we were dissatisfied with our experiences. Almost all of us want to know how to "do" family communication in the future so that we can have the most satisfying family lives and communicative experiences. In addition, many groups or agencies (governmental and religious) attempt to weigh in on issues relevant to family life, and debates abound regarding what type of family form is best (for children and adults) and what types of families should be recognized legally (or not).

To lay the groundwork for understanding family communication, it is first necessary to come to a common understanding of notions of *family*, *communication*, and *family communication*. The danger in defining such terms is that as you read each term just now, you quickly referenced your understanding of each. This is wonderful for learning because you already have the cognitive foundation (i.e., basic idea), but it's also potentially problematic for learning in that you might feel you understand family, communication, and family communication so well that you might be less receptive to new ways of thinking about them.

Ideas of family, communication, and family communication are not as straightforward as they first appear. For instance, families have become so diverse that any definition is likely to be found wanting in that it might be so narrow as to exclude certain types of families. Many definitions, for instance, include biological or legal ties that exclude both cohabiting couples and gay couples with children. To compensate, authors on the topic frequently define families so broadly that they potentially include other types of relationships that are not familial in nature. Thus, definitions of perceived kinship can include best friends and individuals who "feel" like your brother or sister. This is problematic in that many of the communicative processes that operate in your family are in evidence *because* of the involuntary nature of most familial relationships (besides your spouse or partner, all other familial relationships are inherited). You didn't get to *choose* your dad, for instance, but your best friend was definitely a choice.

In an attempt to grapple with these thorny issues, this text not only defines families in terms of **relatedness** (biological, legal, or marriage-like commitment) but also in terms of how family members *function* for one another (in line with a task performance definition of families). Family members are often strong socializing agents for one another, and thus **nurture** (i.e., encourage, provide the foundations for) the development of the various family members in differing ways (physical, socioemotional, and intellectual development, for instance). In addition, the very nature of the involuntary relationships in families places powerful constraints on each individual member's behavior. Thus, family members tend to **control** each other's behavior through discipline, guidance, teaching, complex patterns of psychopolitical negotiation (struggles of competing wills and needs), interpersonal influence, conflict, dominance, and sometimes violence. This text proposes a definition of family that includes relatedness, nurturing, and control.

To further complicate the issue, many individuals classify any type of information transmission as **communication**. This leaves communicators responsible for sending messages that were purely unintentional behavior. For instance, eating, sleeping, and walking might be considered communicative even though the person was just behaving and did not want to send any message at all. Many of my students would make the claim that if I were to sleep in the front of the classroom, I would be communicating that I am tired. As a nonverbal scholar, I'd prefer to be more exact about which nonverbal behaviors should count as communication and which behaviors should not. In this text, we will differentiate between behaviors that are truly *communicative* and those that are purely *informational*. The main way we will differentiate communication and information is through intent.

Finally, family communication is the most complex notion of all; families serve as the cornerstone for our lives and provide a rich forum for every type of communication, from affection to conflict. Because families are primarily composed of involuntary relationships, they can be characterized by greater levels of emotional intensity, subtle relational messages, and histories that range from warm and affectionate times to periods of intense conflicts. This rich context promotes the tendency to hold family members responsible for their behavior—even when they did not intend to communicate at all. For instance, I tend to be grumpy (subtle understatement!) if I'm forced to wake up too early in the morning. This is not a sign of how I'm feeling about my spouse that day. Regardless, my behavior can often have unfortunate communicative consequences. In this text we will try to distinguish between true communication (where both the sender intended to send a message and the receiver perceived the intention of the communication), communication attempts (where the sender intended to send a message but it was not received), attributed communication (where the receiver attributed communicative intent where there was none), and behavior (actions that were not intended to communicate and no intention was perceived). While all the categorizations can provide **information**, only the first three include some level of **communicative intent**. In my example, my grumpiness would be an example of attributed communication in that my husband perceived lack of affection from my behavior, even though I did not intend to communicate disaffection. **Family communication,** then, is defined as messages that are typically sent with intent, that are typically perceived as intentional, and that have consensually shared meaning among individuals who are related biologically, legally, or through marriage-like commitments and who nurture and control each other.

Families

All of us come from families, and therefore most of us feel we understand fully what a family is. For some of us, our families were **nuclear** (with two parents, who may or may not be working outside the home, and children residing together) and included our mother, our father, and our siblings. Although experience (and a show of hands in the classroom) demonstrates that a number of us in the classroom will have come from this situation, only about a quarter (24%) of the total U.S. population will have grown up in nuclear families (see Figure 1.1). Alternatively, many of us were raised in **single-parent homes** (about 28% of children) by our mothers (about 84% of those raised in single-parent homes were raised by single mothers), or in **stepfamilies** that included stepparents, stepsiblings, half-siblings (about 14%). Many of us had parents who divorced when we were young (about 31% of early baby boomers report being divorced), and we now live in **binuclear families**—sharing our time relatively equally between our mother

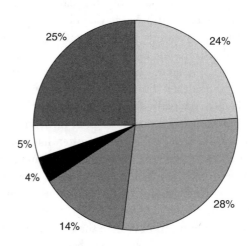

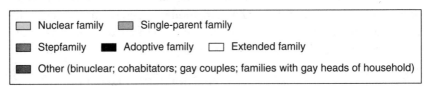

Figure 1.1   Family Type (in % of U.S. population)

SOURCE: U.S. Census Bureau (2003).

and stepfather's and father and stepmother's houses. Some of us live with a **cohabiting parent** (with one parent who is now cohabiting but not married—about 40% of cohabitants report living with children)—and that parent might be gay as well. Some of us were **adopted** (about 4% of us), and some of us live in **extended families** (about 5% live with grandparents). All these types of families illustrate the complex network of relationships that might constitute a family. Finding a definition to include all these **family forms** is challenging.

All these families also help illustrate that no definition of family incorporating biological or legal ties includes *all* types of families, because not all families include individuals with blood or legal connections. To add to the complexity, not all individuals include all family members with biological or legal ties in their *self-defined* family configurations. Many individuals consider their stepfathers to be their "Dads," whereas they consider their biological fathers to be their "sperm-donors." Thus, families also include complex levels of emotional ties and self-definition that include some family members and exclude others. In this first section of the book, we will explore these thorny issues in detail as we attempt to come up with a definition of family that includes complex patterns of procreation, legal ties that bind, and self-defined commitments for some family forms that are not socially sanctioned by the laws of the state.

Biological Definitions

Many of us, when asked who is in our family, describe those to whom we are biologically related. For instance, 5- to 7-year-olds asked to draw family trees drew representations with biological mothers and fathers even when they co-resided with parents and stepparents across households (Dunn, O'Connor, & Levy, 2002). For these children, **biological ties** defined family more than **legal ties** did. This biological relatedness criterion is central to many definitions of the family based on bloodlines, genetics, or biological connectedness. This is also consistent with court-approved definitions of families, which frequently rely on biological blood tests to determine paternity in contentious child support cases. In addition, children who are adopted often refer to their "birth mother and father" as separate from their adoptive parents—the first delineation referring to their bloodline and the second referring to the legal relationship. Many adopted children, even though their adoptive family relationship experience was highly successful in that it nurtured them fully and provided for them, still feel driven to establish their "roots" through a greater understanding of their biological connections. Even though their adoptive mothers functioned legally and within the family as their nurturing and controlling "mother," they still refer to their biological mother as their "birth mother." This distinction is important to them because it recognizes the complexity and the strength of the biological connectedness.

This is consistent with many definitions of family that place procreation and all related behaviors as central to the definition of family. Mary Anne Fitzpatrick and John Caughlin (2004), both prominent researchers in the family communication arena, argue that many definitions of family are "thinly veiled political or ideological statements rather than scientifically neutral views" (p. 727). They review three classes of definitions in the extant literature on family—the first of which is family structure definitions. **Family structure** definitions presuppose clear criteria for family membership in that the family of origin "is the extended family or any group of individuals who have established biological or sociolegal legitimacy by virtue of shared genetics, marriage, or adoption," whereas the family of procreation, "usually called a 'nuclear family,' is further restricted to those living in the same house" (p. 727). Fitzpatrick and Caughlin note the limitation of these definitions in the failure to incorporate the social changes of high divorce rates and new birthing technologies. For instance, these definitions exclude children who split their time between two households and children who were physically carried by a mother who did not provide the genetic materials for these conceptions. This perspective assumes that the primary motivation for marriage is to produce offspring. This is obviously not the case for 29% of all family forms, including those who are married with no children and cohabitants without children, but regardless, it is a societal expectation that families revolve around producing and rearing children.

This perspective is central to the religious and governmental hotbed of debate surrounding the recognition and legalization of gay marriages. Many religious conservatives vehemently oppose the legalization of gay marriages. The evidence for their convictions lies in biblical citations indicating that sexual intercourse should be for the purposes of procreation only. They thus oppose all nontraditional familial practices of premarital sex, cohabitation, married couples with no children, recreational sex within marriage, and "married" gays. For these conservatives, definitions of the family revolve around regulating sexual practices. We will discuss the nature of these policy reforms and laws in Chapter 2 in the sections on governmental and religious influences on the family.

Legal Definitions

The legal system is another governmental agency that plays a large role in helping us to define the family. Individuals allow the courts to make familially defining decisions, such as where their child will reside and who will get visitation rights, how long those visits should be, and whether those visits should be supervised or unsupervised. The courts also make judgments (frequently based on tests of biological connectedness) as to who will and will not have to pay child support. In addition, the courts can decide who is and who is not a "fit" parent. Courts frequently make decisions with regard to living arrangements of the children who are born with drugs or alcohol in their systems. In many states (California, for instance), mothers are legally obligated to fulfill sobriety requirements before custody is resumed. There are also clear laws about the legal obligations of stepparents to their children even though they have very few legal rights. Even though I am obligated to provide adequately for my stepsons, if anything were to happen to my husband, I would have no legal rights to custody or visitation with them (Mason, Harrison-Jay, Svare, & Wolfinger, 2002; Mason & Zayac, 2002). However, some stepparents have been given visitation rights after the disso-lution of the family due to third-party visitation laws.

Sociological Definitions

Sociological definitions of the family typically place reproduction as central to the definition of family, yet also include self-definition as a type of a loophole for including all types of family forms that don't fit neatly within the two dimensions of biological (birth) or legal connectedness (marriage/adoption).

Self-Definition. One commonly accepted definition of family within the discipline of communication is this:

> Networks of people who share their lives over long periods of time bound by ties of marriage, blood, or commitment, legal or otherwise, who consider themselves as family and who share a significant history and anticipated future of functioning in a family relationship. (Galvin, Bylund, & Brommel, 2003, p. 5)

Although this definition does well to include many diverse family forms that do not fit neatly within biological or legal lines, it does not do well to exclude other types of relationships that do not include "relatedness." One can imagine many friends who "feel" like family in that you have known them "donkey's years" (since kindergarten, grad school, or the like) and you anticipate their acting as an auntie to your children (a sustained lifelong relationship), yet legally, this person would not be recognized as your family member by any legal court. To further complicate the issue, in emer-gency situations, many hospitals and school systems do not recognize these relationships either.

One can also imagine several problems with the importance of "antici-pated future functioning of a family relationship" as defining the family. Given the frequency of divorce, it is likely that divorcing parents (or parents considering divorce) might not anticipate future functioning of a family rela-tionship. Regardless, they *will* continue to coparent the children long after the ink has dried on the divorce papers. The lack of anticipation of future family functioning, in and of itself, does not guarantee that the members will discontinue family membership, as will be evident at their children's weddings and their grandchildren's graduations. For example, the introduction I usually use for my husband's ex-wife is, "This is my stepsons' mother." While I'm not genetically or legally related to her in any way, the familial relationship is evident in that she is the *biological* mother and I am the *stepmother* of the same sons. We are in essence part of the same family and anticipate being related through the communicative actions of our children well into the future.

Other family definitions include the notion of shared living arrangements. For instance, one governmental agency that continually struggles with defining families for purposes of counting them is the U.S. Census Bureau. In 2002, it defined family as "a group of two people or more (one of whom is the householder) related by birth, marriage, or adoption and residing together; all such people (including related subfamily members) are considered as members of one family" (U.S. Census Bureau, 2002, p. 4). Their primary criteria for inclusion are biological *or* legal ties plus common residence. According to the definition, parents not residing with their children are not considered a family. This is problematic for several reasons. First, not sharing residences does not ensure that one is no longer a member of a particular family. Although some family members vehemently wish that moving out would ensure that they had cut all familial ties, unfortunately, the involuntary nature of biological and legal ties ensures that your mother is still your mother even while you are away at college and that the dad who owes child support but lives three states west still has to pay your college tuition. Second, not all of us live with both parents simultaneously. This does not mean that neither parent is in your "family" when you are in the custody of the other family. Third, many families are extended, and because your grandparents, aunts and uncles, and cousins don't live with you, this does not mean they are not biologically related to you.

Fitzpatrick and Caughlin (2002) also review two other types of definitions that guide social science research in communication. These definitions highlight goals within families and the unique role that communication plays in fulfilling these functions within the family. They deserve special mention here because they underscore the approach to defining families used throughout this book. *Psychosocial task definitions* focus on the performance of certain tasks of family life. Task definitions typically describe the functions of family where the family is a psychosocial group made up of one adult member and one or more others, where fulfillment, nurturance, and development are the central goals of the group. They provide an example of a task definition of family as the "social unit that accepts responsibility for the socialization and nurturance of children" (p. 727). As they point out, this definition, while doing a fair job of including stepparents and even cohabitants with children, excludes families without children and therefore excludes cohabiting couples and married and gay couples with no children.

However, this definition does a nice job of highlighting the importance of family members' fulfilling certain functions for each other within the family. Finally, *transactional process definitions* define family as "a group of intimates who generate a sense of home and group identity, complete with strong ties of loyalty and emotion, and an experience of a history and a future" (Fitzpatrick & Caughlin, 2002, p. 728). Although these definitions highlight the importance and centrality of communication to the definition of family, they suffer from the problems of self-definition that we referred to earlier. However, they highlight the two processes of interdependence and commitment inherent in families—characteristics that serve us well to distinguish friendship and nonkinship relations from family relationships.

All Family Forms Include
Nurturing and Control Functions

It is clear at this point that not all families include birth or regulation of procreative activities (biological relatedness). It is also clear that legal definitions of the family do not recognize all family forms as political and that religious debates abound surrounding many familial issues and definitions. Also, self-definitions are faulty as well, because they frequently fail to recognize biological relations as familial members. We are therefore forced to consider a broad range of relatedness among family members along with the functions that all family members fulfill for one another in order to qualify as a family.

As the above delineation of biological, legal, and self-definitions demonstrates, the criteria of relatedness in a family is complex; not all family members fulfill all the relatedness criterion. It is therefore possible to create a logical inclusion string that includes all types of relatedness that might be evidenced across family types. We can therefore determine membership in a family to necessarily include the following:

1. Relatedness (biological relatedness *or* legal ties *or* commitment similar to marriage). Relatedness refers to the involuntary nature of families in all their various forms of connectedness. This includes biological families where genetic ties are evidenced (families including a biological father, a biological mother, and their offspring). This also includes families with legal relatedness (marriages with no children present, adopted children, and stepparents). Finally, this includes heterosexual and homosexual cohabitation where the partners see this relationship as similar in commitment level to marriage. This commitment is thus limited to romantic pairing units (married couples, cohabiting couples, gay couples) and does not extend to close friends and the like. We will exclude the concept of self-definition here because many individuals might include close friends and others who provide warmth and joy in their lives but who are not objectively recognized as "related" or as family by organizations with resources. These friends are not related in biological, legal, or marriage-like-commitment ways.

2. Nurturing. Although not all family forms include procreation or even attempts at procreation, all family forms (biological, legal, or marriage-like commitment) include some forms of nurturing behaviors. Nurturing behaviors include all attempts to encourage the development (e.g., physical, socioemotional, intellectual) of the other family members. In other words, growth is encouraged (and sometimes discouraged) within the family. This recognizes that not all family members are equally nurturing. In fact, some family members fail to nurture altogether (e.g., abandoning parents), but in general, a family is composed of members who have an influence on one another's personal development. It is therefore possible for this nurturing function to cut across all family forms and family relationships in that spouses nurture each other, parents nurture children, siblings nurture each other, and gay couples nurture each other's and sometimes their children's development as well. Therefore, this perspective can include "sperm-donor" fathers (they contributed to your physical and, potentially, to your psychological development) and stepfathers (they contributed to your intellectual, educational, and socioemotional development). This perspective can also include married couples and cohabitants with no children (they encourage each other's growth as individuals across the various dimensions of development). In addition, members of your extended family can also be seen to be contributing to your physical development through your biological connections to them (e.g., you may have the same sociological and psychological tendencies as your fifth cousin in Idaho even though you have never met him and were socialized in dramatically different ways). Thus, nurturing cuts across all family forms and all family relationships.

3. Control. Finally, while assisting your development as human beings in general (*nurturing*), members of your family will also try to influence or control your behavior in ways that promote your competence across the aforementioned domains of development. *Control* in the family begins as children grow (when you began crawling and walking, your caregivers had to begin to control your behavior to protect your safety). It can be argued that control began even before children were added to families in that the struggles that couples experience during their transition to living together include many struggles over control. Decisions abound in families and therefore so do opportunities for control struggles. Seemingly simple decisions regarding when to eat dinner, which social engagements to attend, and how much sexual activity to engage in can be fertile ground for control struggles among couples. Larger decisions are even more compelling in this regard as couples struggle with where to live, whether both spouses or partners will work, and how many children to have. Many issues of control couples face in their struggle to get the other primary partners' desires to match their own. Issues of control play out within families as family members try to negotiate joint outcomes. Control can be seen through discipline, intimacy negotiation, conflict, violence, and interpersonal influence attempts at changing undesirable behavior in the family (e.g., to get the alcoholic to stop drinking or the eating disordered daughter to eat).

Communication

Settle those spats in nothing flat with a Home Court Reporter!

SOURCE: Real Life Adventures © GarLanco. Reprinted with permission of Universal Press Syndicate. All rights reserved.

Communication is central to the family and to its functioning. This is especially true for the two primary functions of nurturing and control. Nurturing includes communication that is central to encouraging development, including both verbal and nonverbal behaviors that are encouraging and supportive. Control includes communication that is central to guiding, influencing, and limiting the types of behaviors evidenced by family members. Communication is central to the two primary functions of nurturing and control that occur within families.

At this stage, many of you may feel as though you have a more advanced understanding of what constitutes communication. If asked, most of you will list sender and receiver, intentionality, messages, encoding and decoding, and transmission as central to any definition of communication. You would be right to include all these elements, and we will explore them further here. Like families, however, definitions of communication are complex in that some definitions of communication include all types of behavior, even when no communicative intent was included. Thus, we will wrestle not only with the elemental parts of communication but also with the fundamental *nature* of messages that make them communicative—or not.

Let's begin with the elements of communication. John Bowers and James Bradac (1982), two of the pioneering researchers in communication, review the literature in communication with regard to which issues researchers in communication find important to include in communication definitions. First, and most important, they argue that communication is *the transmission and reception of information*. This includes notions of sender and receiver and the importance of including both in any communication transaction. Second, they also argue that *communication is the generation of meaning*. Thus, consensually shared meaning among members of a particular language community is also important. Third, although some argue that communication is situated within the individual, it is argued here that *communication is the relationship behaviors of interacting individuals*. Senders and receivers interact in ways that include simultaneous transmission of information so that both communicators are senders and receivers simultaneously. Fourth, although some would argue that animals can communicate, this text subscribes to the notion that *human communication is unique* in that humans are the only symbol-using creatures and thus are the only ones able to represent the nature of the universe in abstract concepts in their minds (through language use).

Fifth, the definition of communication offered here subscribes to the notion that communication is *ongoing and processual*. This implies that communication is dynamic and fluid and that communicators continually influence each other through their communication behavior. Sixth, some scholars find it important to recognize *communication as contextualized*— that is, communication within the family is different and distinct from other communication events *because* it is occurring within the family structure. While the arguments are a bit complex for an intro-level textbook, I believe that many of the communicative processes occurring outside the family also occur inside the family. This is not to say that father-daughter communication is not influenced by the unique processes operating in families; it simply means that many of the characteristics of this father-daughter communication will be similar to communication within other types of relationships. Finally, and most central to the following discussion, some scholars in communication like to assert that human beings cannot not communicate. In this text, however, it is argued that human beings can *not* communicate. In other words, it is possible to behave in ways that are not communicative.

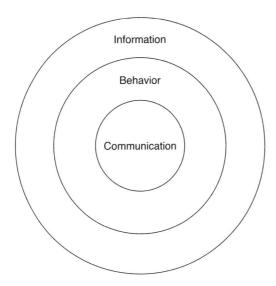

Figure 1.2   The Relationship Between Information, Behavior, and Communication

Information, Behavior, and Communication

Those who espouse this last premise that human beings cannot *not* communicate make the argument that all behavior is informational and thus communicational in nature. This ignores the most important element of communication—the communicators' intent or desire to communicate. It is clear that some behaviors have no communicative intent. For instance, as mentioned earlier, eating, walking, and sleeping are all behaviors with potential information value but that have no communicative intent. Thus, while many students of communication might argue that my eating in front of the classroom is communicative because it informed them that I was hungry, I would contend that it *informed* them of my hunger without any intention on my part to *communicate* that information. Consider the model shown in Figure 1.2.

All behaviors are informative in that they reduce one's uncertainty by half. As illustrated in Figure 1.2, information, behavior, and communication can be conceptualized as three concentric circles with information being the largest and most subsumptive, behavior being the next largest circle within information, and communication fitting neatly within behavior, which fits within information (Burgoon, Buller, & Woodall, 1996). Thus, communication is always behavioral and behavior is always informational. Therefore, all behavior is informational, but not all behavior is communicational. It is therefore possible to not communicate. To most fully consider this debate, consider issues surrounding intentionality to communicate.

Source Versus Receiver Versus Message-Centered Orientations

The earliest conceptualizations of communicator intent assumed that it was most relevant to communication that the communicator (or sender) intended to communicate—the so-called **sender orientation**. This came from the "magic bullet" era, where it was assumed that communication was all-powerful and that all a source had to do was to "put a message out there" and it would have strong and clear impact. However, as became clear from the media studies of the 1950s and 1960s, many messages indeed did *not* have the effect they intended. In fact, they sometimes had the opposite effect.

Along with these findings, and the advent of the "me" generation of the 1960s, communication transitioned into more of a **receiver orientation** in that what became more important than the sources' intent to communicate was the receivers' perception of intent. Therefore, if individuals as senders were pre-occupied, tired, or distracted, other individuals perceiving the messages as intentional communication of disregard were given precedence over the actual sender of the message. Messages that were perceived as intentional were classified as communication. This is problematic in that many behaviors that were not intended to communicate at all were perceived as communication. Individuals as senders became responsible for a large number of behaviors that might have been rude or inconsiderate but that definitely did not fit within the realm of communication. Therefore, scholars moved toward a more complex model of intentionality (see Table 1.1) that considered both the sender's intent and the receiver's perception of intent (Burgoon & Ruffner, 1978).

True communication occurs only when both the receiver and the sender perceive an intention to communicate. A **communication attempt** occurs when a sender intends to send a message but the receiver does not perceive the intention. On the other hand, when the sender does not intend to communicate, but the receiver perceives the intention to communicate, this is an example of **attributed communication**. Finally, when neither the sender intends nor the receiver perceives an intention to communicate, **behavior** has occurred.

For example, suppose that I am getting ready for class and walking at a jogging pace through the halls of the communication department as I scurry to

Table 1.1   The Role of Sender and Receiver Intention in Defining Communication

	Receiver Perceives Intent to Communicate	*Receiver Does not Perceive Intention to Communicate*
Sender Intends to Communicate	**Communication**	**Communication Attempt**
Sender Does Not Intend to Communicate	**Attributed Communication**	**Behavior**

get the last-minute details of my lecture prepared. You see me, but I absentmindedly fail to see you and therefore do not acknowledge your head tilt, eyebrow flash, and smile. Generously attributing my lack of social graces to absentminded professorism, you correctly interpret my actions as behavior and do not take offense. However, as often is the case in power-differential situations, you might perceive that I am blowing you off on purpose given some long-ago-forgotten-on-my-part comment or other you made in class. In this case, your perception of my intent combined with my own lack of intent would qualify this interaction as fitting within attributed communication, because you attributed intention to communicate to my behavior even though there was none. It might also be possible in this case that I was blowing you off because I was really busy and thus "acted" busy to communicate that I could not talk right now. If you still perceived my actions as unintentional and actual busyness, then this communication behavior would be classified as a communication attempt. Finally, if I *did* intend to blow you off, and you perceived my actions as blowing you off, then true communication would have occurred.

As a nonverbal scholar, however, I would be remiss to fail to consider the often messy messages that we send nonverbally. Consider the case of depression. Depressed individuals rarely have the motivation to get out of bed let alone communicate their depression to others. Regardless, they nevertheless communicate in ways that do give rise to the conclusion that they are depressed. Their dejected nature communicated through lack of facial affect, slumped posturing, and flat vocalic affect clearly communicates that they are feeling depressed. It might be argued that although they don't have a conscious intent to communicate their depression, they might have an unconscious intent to communicate this depression in order to receive much-needed social support. Therefore, their behavior might still be classified as communication if the receiver perceives their intent to communicate. It is important to consider the nature of the message along with intentionality when defining behavior as communication. Thus, it is possible to include a *message-centered* definition of intentionality, such that communication is defined as messages "that (a) are typically sent with intent, (b) are used with regularity among members of a given social community, society, or culture, (c) are typically interpreted as intentional, and (d) have consensually recognized meaning" (Burgoon et al., 1996, pp. 13–14).

This definition allows us to include nonverbal messages such as nonverbal accommodation (which are not intentional at a conscious level) to be included in our definition of communication.

Family Communication

All these definitions allow us to define family communication. Combining the earlier definition of family with our current definition of communication allows us to define family communication in the following way:

Messages that are typically sent with intent, that are typically perceived as intentional, and that have consensually shared meaning among individuals who are related biologically, legally, or through marriage-like commitments and who nurture and control each other.

Why Communication Is Central to Families _____

Because families are primarily composed of involuntary relationships (besides the primary couple unit), family communication can be fairly intense. Power struggles frequently occur as members struggle to attain different goals. Spouses argue over how to spend money, the best way to discipline the children, and whether to switch jobs or move to another house. Adolescents struggle against their parents' conceptions of them as children as they strive to develop their own unique sense of self as separate from their parents. The warmth and affection experienced in families can also be a source of great sustenance as individual family members go out into the world to do the business of their daily lives. Furthermore, the push and pull between warm nurturing behaviors and disciplinary or controlling behaviors can put communicators in complex dilemmas regarding the best way to communicate with their family members.

On a day-to-day basis, and to facilitate task completion, family communication can be quite mundane. Much of the morning communication between parents or marital partners often revolves around coordination of child care, transportation of the children to and from school and to various activities, preparation of the evening meal, and organizing necessary activities around the house (who will call the "bug man" or the apartment supervisor?). At the same time, communication can be affectionate to hostile (verbally or nonverbally). Each message contains both content (the verbal "stuff" of the interaction) and relational (implied messages about the nature of the relationship) dimensions (Watzlawick, Beavin, & Jackson, 1969). I can discuss the daily tasks with warmth and good humor or with coolness and seriousness and communicate very different messages regarding how I am feeling about my spouse and the relationship on any particular day.

Both Nurturing and Control Require Communication

Nurturing communication includes communication that encourages the social, emotional, and intellectual development of family members. Through nurturing and supportive communication, children can be encouraged to grow, learn, and integrate well with their friends. Nurturing and supportive communication between spouses can provide a "safe haven" from the demands of the external working world and can cement the intimate bonds between the primary marital or couple unit. Quizzing your child in the car on the way to school in final preparation for his or her spelling test can encourage intellectual achievement, for instance. Alternatively, talking with your child about the importance of including all his friends in the morning "pickup" game of football can encourage social development. Inquiries regarding the final stages of your husband's cold can encourage his health maintenance and simultaneously function to nurture him. Thus, communication within families can be very nurturing.

Nurturing communication can be the source of much satisfaction with family life. When asked what made their families "happy," most of my students replied that they knew their parents loved them, they continually felt encouraged by their parents, their parents were affectionate, and they really enjoyed talking with and "hanging out with" their parents. In addition to the communication of nurturing, children also experienced satisfaction with their families because of what their parents *did*. Many children reported that their parents always attended their games, recitals, or school plays and that they were involved in their lives. This type of nurturing is central to the physical, socioemotional, and intellectual development of children. Nurturing communication is central to this experience.

Controlling communication can also be positive in that it can function to encourage the development of family members (e.g., parents might see grounding errant children as a way to ensure that they are not too tired to learn in school the next day), but control may also be the source of conflict, influence attempts, and sometimes violence. Controlling communication is in evidence when family members limit the options of other family members. My stepsons continually fight over the satellite remote. They both have TVs in their rooms, but there is only one satellite remote that they must share in order to watch the premium channels. Each feels controlled by the other's choices and thus (often intense) conflict results.

While parents attempt to control their children, spouses simultaneously and frequently control each other. Some of the earliest (and most uncomfortable) stages of relationship integration are when each spouse attempts to control the other's behavior in an attempt to integrate behavioral routines (e.g., Solomon & Knobloch, 2004). They also try to control each other through interpersonal influence attempts to sway them to their point of view, through conflict over competing goals, and sometimes through violence.

Changing Family Forms
Require Communication for Coordination

As noted earlier, the forms the family can take are widely diverse. Many of the treatments of family communication assume that the family includes one father figure, one mother figure, and children. Thus, communication is assumed to surround the traditional nuclear roles of nurturer (mother) and resource provider (father). However, we know that mothers are now reentering the workforce, with many mothers working within the first year after giving birth (51%; U.S. Census Bureau, 2001), so many families are considered "dual-earner" households. Communication in these families is more complicated as parents try to negotiate both breadwinner and nurturing roles simultaneously. Such simultaneous role holding requires more communication for coordination of household tasks and child care (e.g., Ehrenberg, Gearing-Small, Hunter, & Small, 2001).

Such nontraditional nuclear families are not the only change on the family landscape. Nuclear families are rapidly being matched by single-parent homes (28% of children are raised in single-parent homes), especially within the black community (45% of black children are raised in single-parent homes). Most of these families are headed by mothers (84%), and thus women are fulfilling the roles of both parents simultaneously within these families. They must both provide communication that *nurtures* (facilitates growth) and *controls* (e.g., disciplines) their children. Thus, these families are likely to experience more stress. Of single-parent homes headed by mothers, 39% live below the poverty line (Dunifon & Kowaleski-Jones, 2002). Living below the poverty line simultaneously provides fewer amenities to the children with growing needs for resources over the life span of school attendance and provides the single mother or father with fewer opportunities for support (e.g., day care for children, help with household maintenance). These greater burdens on the single parent result in less time for communication with children and greater reliance on children for household assistance and emotional support. As a result, children may grow up faster in single-parent homes.

Cohabiting single parents are also more common now, especially fathers (33% of single fathers are cohabiting) (U.S. Census Bureau, 2003a). Communication is even more complicated as single parents communicate with both children and significant others in their home. In addition, cohabiting adults try to take on "stepparent" roles without the legal bonds of marriage. Stepparenting is difficult enough, but stepparenting without the legal institution of marriage complicates things further. The biological parent and the cohabiting adult use communication to try to negotiate nurturing and controlling roles with children who may be confused about their relationship to the cohabiting adult. Stepfamilies—families that include some legal and some biological connectedness—and **blended families**—families that include legal-only (e.g., stepparents) and some biological-legal (e.g., half-siblings) relationships—are equally complex, even with the legal bonds of family. To add more to the communication complexity, new stepparents may bring their own children with them. Biological parents may nurture and control their biological and stepchildren in diverse ways, leading to competition and conflictual communication between the stepsiblings and their new stepparent.

Gay couples and gay couples with children face their own communication difficulties. Not only are they not recognized by the legal system (see more in the governmental regulation section in Chapter 2), they also have difficult decisions with regard to deciding to disclose their sexual identity to their children or to individuals external to the family. Families may lose custody of their children if external members find out they are gay. In addition, children may be embarrassed to communicate their parents' sexual orientation to outside family members because there are many assumptions made in general society about the children's own sexual orientation based on their parents and their upbringing. Thus, there may be a certain amount of closedness in families that include gay parents. Finally, although less represented in society at large, there may be additional difficulties in communicating within adoptive families and extended families. Adoptive children may feel less a part of the family than biological children, and children being raised by their grandparents may feel like this family structure is atypical and may refrain from talking about their family much at school. Issues surrounding family communication, therefore, are highly affected by the form the family takes.

Roles, Systems, and Rules Require Communication

All these changes in family form manifest themselves communicationally through the roles that various members hold. In addition, the entire family system is affected by the loss or addition of family members, and thus the form of the family may affect the balance within the family. Finally, rules for communication may be very different for those in nuclear families than they are in single-parent families or in families with gay parents.

This text explores the various roles that family members negotiate through communication with **roles theory**. Roles theory assumes that the roles one holds are powerful dictators of the behaviors one enacts. Mothers and fathers play roles of nurturer, provider, disciplinarian, health maintainer, financial adviser, and so on. Having parents who are dual earners can also complicate the traditional gender distribution of these roles and lead to quite complex communication as partners attempt to disperse family roles. As mentioned earlier, the diverse forms the family takes can also influence the roles family members take as they try to "play the role" of parent even when they are not (in the case of stepparent or cohabiting adult with a single parent). Single parents also take on a greater number of roles because there is no other residing parent to share role distribution. All these factors contribute greatly to the types of nurturing and controlling behavior that can occur in families.

Family systems theory attempts to explain the communication between family members as a function of the systems theory concepts of interdependence, balance, equifinality, and wholeness. These theories also try to explain communication behavior in families through a greater understanding of family system regulation in the pursuit of family goals. They assume that all members operate together in the pursuit of some larger goal (e.g., happiness, socioemotional development of children) and that family members communicate in certain ways within the family in an attempt to self-regulate attainment of those goals. In other words, disciplining a child through "grounding" after he or she has been caught sneaking out in the night is an example of attempting to regulate the child toward the goal of physical, socioemotional, and intellectual development by ensuring his or her safety. Thus, communication activities within the family surround goal attainment.

Rules theory attempts to explain the rules in communication. All families have verbal and nonverbal rules about how to communicate. For some families, there are clear rules about who to talk to for what. My stepsons know, for instance, that if they have a question about all-things-technical, they communicate with my husband. Anything health related goes to their mom, the nurse. Anything school related comes to me. Although these rules are not spoken or written, through experience, it has become obvious who holds expertise in which areas. There are also clear rules about topic avoidance during the teenage years. Most teens, for instance, will not talk to their parents about sex or dangerous behaviors (e.g., Guerrero & Afifi, 1995). Thus, communication rules of appropriateness and desirability are clearly operating within families. There are also nonverbal rules for communicating. I know, for instance, that if I want to talk to my oldest stepson, Huw, about anything personal or intimate, it is best done in the car in the dark so that no eye contact can occur. This kind of compensatory insurance ensures that there is no "intimacy overload" and that comfort is achieved and maintained. In sum, communication rules operate within families on verbal and nonverbal levels.

Relationship Development Leading to Coupling Requires Communication

Although all of us came from families of origin, not all of us are in newly formed families (or potential families of procreation). Many of you in this class, however, will be dating, seriously dating, or engaged as you attempt to move into your own new family. This process of mate selection is quite complex and includes communication in several ways. First, the communication of attraction and courtship is rife with verbal and nonverbal indicators of interest. For instance, nonverbal cues to attraction include head tilt, downward glance, and shy smiles (and sometimes the hair flip) (Burgoon et al., 1996). In addition, many report sociological and psychological characteristics that attracted them to their mate (like similarity on attraction and values, physical appearance, physical proximity, etc.).

Psychoanalytic factors of relationship attachment may also come into play. We learned how to be loved and whether people were trustworthy from our parents. For those of us who learned we were lovable and others were trustworthy, we learn to attach in secure ways to others. We approach romantic relationships fearlessly. For those of us who were abandoned in some way or another (physically or emotionally), we learned that people were untrustworthy and we fear that we may be unlovable. We are therefore cautious in our approach to relationships but seek fulfillment in being recognized as lovable individuals through our relationships with others. We thus become preoccupied with our partners and how they feel toward us. For those of us who were role reversed by our parents (they demanded our caregiving rather than vice versa), we learned that intimacy meant losing our own sense of self. We learned that others were untrustworthy but that we were responsible and trustworthy. We became dismissive-avoidant of relationships later in life as we keep ourselves busy to avoid too much intimacy in relationships. All these **attachment styles** have implications for the communication of approach and avoidance in relationships. We will explore these (as well as a potential interaction between parental attachment and partner attachment style) in Chapter 4.

Adding Children Requires Communication

A number of societal forces encourage married couples to have children. As you might surmise, adding children can wreak havoc on the communication between the original couple. Simply adding another individual to an already demanding communication structure changes the number of communication pathways from two to six. The communication demands have tripled simply by adding one child. The addition of children also adds new roles to the already demanding role of spouse. Furthermore, the work demands of child care add to the workload of relational and house maintenance that each individual member holds regardless of his or her external job requirements. Not surprisingly, marital satisfaction frequently diminishes after adding children because the domestic duties surrounding child care increase a typical parent's workload by sixfold (Huston & Holmes, 2004).

The demands of child rearing also vary depending on the age of the child. Infants and toddlers demand constant supervision, and school-age children require attention to homework and development of social and emotional skills. The adolescent years can be very demanding as the child attempts to develop a unique and separate identity from the parent. Such a withdrawal often involves more time spent in peer communication and a frequent amount of derogating communication aimed at parents (as their role of authority figure diminishes). In addition, parents frequently have to negotiate disciplinary action at this point. Disagreements can arise over the appropriate level of monitoring of adolescents (especially for female adolescents). Thus, communication within the family is highly affected by the addition of children.

Raising Children Requires Communication

Much time is spent communicating with children to develop their socioemotional competence. Parents are frequently concerned with encouraging positive self-esteem and positive parental identification. Both of these can be achieved through warmth and supportiveness, moderate control attempts, and consistency in control attempts (Broderick, 1993). Parents frequently control their children's behavior in an effort to provide them with the best grounds for development. Such efforts can be characterized through various parenting styles that include differing levels of control and nurturing, from high levels of control coupled with low warmth (e.g., so-called *authoritarian* parents), to high levels of control coupled with high warmth where parents negotiate with children but still provide the greatest percentage of the rules (e.g., so-called *authoritative* parents), and low levels of control and high levels of warmth (e.g., so-called *permissive* parents; Baumrind, 1966, 1996). Such varying levels of control (i.e., *demandingness*) and nurturing (*responsiveness*) are shown to be related to various outcomes for children, with authoritative parenting (or moderate levels of control) being related to what most determine to be the best outcomes (e.g., Hart, Newall, & Olsen, 2003).

In addition, parents often attempt to use learning theory to reinforce the behavior they would like to encourage and punish the behaviors they would like to discourage. Learning theory argues that following behaviors with positive consequences can encourage more long-term retention of the behavior. Positive and warm communication can be used as reinforcement for positive behavior. Communication can similarly be punishing or aversive to a child. Avoiding a scolding can be a strong motivation for a third grader. We see, then, that communication behavior can both reinforce and punish desired and undesirable behaviors in children.

Finally, parents can encourage mastery orientation or learned helplessness in their children by the way they respond to their children's successes or failures. Children who receive bad grades and are told by their parents that "It's okay—you couldn't have done better" learn that they are not very bright and acquire *learned helplessness,* or the tendency to want help in order to achieve. Children learn a *mastery orientation* by having their parents and significant others attribute their positive behavior to dispositional characteristics and their negative behavior to situational characteristics. Those with bad grades who are told they can do better when they study harder next time learn *mastery orientation.* In addition, letting the child take responsibility for achieving a clean room similarly supports a *mastery orientation.* How parents communicate about achievements can have a serious impact on the ways in which children attempt to achieve things in the future. Thus, communication is central to the socialization process.

Balancing Intimacy and
Autonomy Requires Communication

Communication in families can also be rich with messages of intimacy. Family members frequently disclose (or fail to disclose) important information to each other. Disclosure is a way to increase intimacy, but too much negative disclosure can actually be perceived negatively. Disclosure is also closely associated with nonverbal intimacy behaviors as partners display closeness through nonverbal involvement, pleasantness, expressiveness, and less social anxiety (e.g., Coker & Burgoon, 1987). These patterns of closeness and distance are likely to ebb and flow as partners experience differing needs for closeness and distance during the life span of the relationship. Such cycling in communication behavior is explained by dialectic models of communication and intimacy enhancement.

Family members can also have important conversations about sexuality and other important closeness-enhancing issues. In addition, even though very few parents discuss premarital sexuality with their children (some studies say as little as 10% of parents talk with their children about sex), those who do have children with later age of sexual initiation, consistent condom use, and less sexually transmitted diseases (e.g., Hutchinson, 2002). However, in general, teenagers avoid discussing sexuality with their parents, especially their opposite-sex parent (Guerroro & Afifi, 1995). So although communication regarding sexuality is uncommon among parents and adolescents, such communication can be associated with positive outcomes.

Managing Conflict Requires Communication

As stated throughout the earlier sections, the family environment is rich with opportunities for conflict. From a systems perspective, individual family members can have dramatically different desires for goal attainment. These goal conflicts often lead to the communication of interpersonal influence and conflict in the family. Children argue with their parents about negotiation of rules (Smetana, 1995), and couples frequently have conflict over topics ranging from finances to religious involvement of children (Newton & Burgoon, 1990). Such conversations provide a fertile environment for conflict communication.

How couples handle conflict can be highly predictive of the success of a relationship. John Gottman (1995), a social psychologist who researches communication in marital couples, argues in his book on marital success that couples who consistently exhibit criticism, defensiveness, contempt, and stonewalling are at a higher risk for divorce. He also argues that couples who match conflict styles in one of three ways have a greater probability of success in their marriage. He argues that *validators, avoiders,* and *volatiles* all have a greater probability of success in their marriage. Validators are that rare breed of individuals who can listen and affirm what their partner is saying during a conflict, even if they don't agree with their partner. They validate the concern, and the couple is able to move past the conflict. Conflict avoiders generally believe in the sanctity of marriage and avoid conflict with their spouse altogether. Although some worry that this type of conflict style might suppress anger and thus build up dangerous levels of repression, this conflict style matching seems to be functional for a good percentage of the population. Finally, volatiles love and fight intensely. These people yell, argue, and make up loudly. While many who know couples like these don't understand the tendency to stay in such a volatile relationship, this pattern of "blowing up" followed by loving works well for those who match on volatile styles. Thus, communication of conflict can have strong implications for the continuation of marriage.

Finally, although several communication models of conflict can be explored, the interpersonal model of conflict talks about distal and proximal factors promoting conflict and distal and proximal outcomes of conflict. Proximal factors promoting conflict include the eliciting event, as well as mood, current context, and the like. One student reported having a conflict with her boyfriend after he informed her that his ex-girlfriend had called and invited him to her graduation. At the same time, she had specifically *not* invited the current girlfriend. This eliciting event was the distal factor. The distal factors eliciting conflict include history surrounding the conflict. Had they had earlier conflict over this ex or had the boyfriend previously gone out with the ex during their relationship, this would constitute the proximal context. Proximal outcomes are the immediate consequences of the conflict, such as long drawn-out silences and immediate emotional hurt. More distal, or longer-term, consequences might include a lack of trust surrounding the ex-girlfriend in the future. Family communication can include conflict, which is influenced by the past and the present and which will result in outcomes in the present and the future.

Dealing With Violence Requires Communication

Violence can be interpreted as an extreme outcome of conflict. Violence can manifest itself in child abuse and neglect, partner-focused violence, and elder abuse. To further compound the issue, violence in the home can have a wide-ranging impact on the children exposed to such behavior, regardless of whether the violence is aimed at the children. Specifically, a range of children's developmental outcomes—including social, emotional, behavioral, cognitive, and general health functioning—are compromised by exposure to domestic violence (Wolfe, Crooks, Lee, McIntyre-Smith, & Jaffe, 2003). The communication of violence and the communication surrounding violence in the family are important issues to address in family communication.

In 1998, victims of violence varied by race. For every 1,000 individuals, 110 American Indians, 43 blacks, 38 whites, and 22 Asians were victims of violence (Rennison, 2001). Specific to the family, 19.6 of 1,000 women between 16 and 24 experience being a victim of intimate partner violence and the percentage of female homicide victims killed by intimate partners has remained about 30% since 1976 (Rennison & Welchans, 2000). Many communication models attempt to explain patterns of violence in the home.

Skills deficits models argue that violent partners lack the communication skills to deal with conflict, and thus, violence occurs. In a similar vein, the **frustration-aggression model** argues that when batterers become frustrated, this frustration gets channeled into violence. The **coercive communication model** argues that the batterer is attempting to coerce his or her partner and when attempts fail, violence occurs. The **interpersonal model** is perhaps the most contentious in that it argues that violence does not begin in all relationships with the batterer because the partner in this case provokes the violence. Regardless of one's explanation for violence, the communication surrounding the violent events and the consequences is likely to be intense. Chapter 8 explores the communication surrounding violence in the family.

In addition, child abuse has been estimated to affect between 2.4 million (actual reports) and 6.9 million children (Wilson & Whipple, 1995). Because control is a central communicative function of family life, it is particularly troubling that much violence against children stems from disciplinary responses to perceived child misbehavior. The communication of nurturing is central to differences between abusive and nonabusive parents in that nonabusive parents consistently display more positive verbal and nonverbal behaviors than do abusive parents (see Wilson & Whipple, 1995, for review). Exploring communication differences between abusive and nonabusive parents is imperative for improving communication in abusive parental relationships.

Changing Undesirable Behavior in the Family Requires Communication

As alluded to earlier, many families include a member who has some out-of-control behavioral tendencies. These tendencies are generally self-destructive, but they can also have a devastating impact on the other family members as well. These family members may abuse substances, have an eating disorder, be depressed, or be physically abusive. To give you an idea of how many families are affected, substance abuse has become an alarming issue in this country with as many as one in four children being exposed to the effects of substance abuse. Besides the effects on children, the partner of the substance abuser also often experiences negative consequences as a result of the substance abuse. In fact, the substance abuser's partner is often put in the difficult position of nurturing the substance abuser through substance abuse episodes while simultaneously trying to control or stop the substance abuse. Inconsistent nurturing as control theory attempts to understand the paradoxes in this relationship that make it difficult for partners to assist their partners through substance abuse, eating disorders, depression, and violence.

Partners of those with behavioral compunctions such as substance abuse, eating disorders, or depression have competing needs for nurturing and control. In fact, before labeling the behavior as problematic, partners often communicate in ways that support the behavior—encouraging the substance abuser to relax with a drink, encouraging the eating disordered individual's fixation on exercise and diet, empathizing with the symptoms of the depressed. This supportive behavior is understandable, especially in light of the research that shows that drinking has been found to facilitate marital functioning for steady drinkers (alcoholics who drink every day) in that they become better problem solvers and are simply more interactive with their partners (Le Poire & Cope, 1999). The motivation for maintaining the drinking is more obvious in this particular case. However, most partners of spouses with behavioral compulsions experience some critical incident that causes them to evaluate their partner as having a serious problem. For instance, substance abusers may be missing for several days in a row, may crash the car, or may exhibit violence. This usually promotes the partner to try to prevent future substance abuse. At this point, they begin to punish the behavior consistently by pouring out booze, calling the cops, or threatening to leave the relationship. Initially reinforcing behavior changes to punishing behavior. Eventually, however, partners of substance abusers realize that there is really very little that they can do to facilitate their partner's recovery as they come to terms with the "disease model" of addiction. This realization, combined with being tired of being a "nag" leads partners to sometimes nurture their substance-abusing partner and sometimes attempt to control the substance abuser. This mix of nurturing and controlling behavior approximates intermittent reinforcement and intermittent punishment and can actually serve to reinforce the actual behavior the substance abusers' partners want to diminish. Thus, the partners of the substance abusers find themselves in a conundrum with regard to how to communicate with their substance-abusive partner. In Chapter 9, we will consider the impacts of substance abuse, eating disorders, and depression on the family and will also consider the communicative ways in which partners can actually facilitate their partner's attempts at increased mental and physical health.

The Powerful Role of Communication of Expectations in Families

Finally, most of you will be concerned with how to communicate within your families most successfully. The family communication literature shows that there is a definite link between how you think and how you communicate within families. In other words, cognition and communication are linked in fundamental and important ways. With regard to cognition, your perceptions, attributions, and expectations provide the frame of reference within which communication episodes within the family occur. Powerful research is presented here showing that regardless of the "facts," if you perceive your family member positively, you will be more satisfied in that relationship and your relationship will be more stable. Conversely, if you see your family member negatively, you will be less satisfied and your relationship is likely to be less stable.

This is likely to translate into actual communication behavior as well. First, if you think of your family members positively, you will be more likely to communicate this expectation to them through the ways in which you communicate with them. If you expect positive communication behavior, you are more likely to be more positive, and this positivity will lead to greater reciprocation in the form of positive communication from your family members. Furthermore, this brings home the second rule of family communication: You get as good as you give. In other words, your own communication within your family is a powerful determinant of the type of communication behavior you receive. Much of the literature on family communication shows that behaviors from family members are generally matched. Heightened conflictual behavior is met with greater intensity of conflict behavior, whereas greater positivity is met with greater positivity. Conversely, greater negativity is also met with greater negativity, and unfortunately, this pattern is the hardest one to break out of.

In conclusion then, the family communication literature shows that how you think about your family members can have a powerful effect on how you communicate with them. Furthermore, how you communicate with your family members can have a powerful effect on the way your family members communicate with you. Ultimately, both thinking and communicating in more positive (or negative) ways result in greater positivity (or negativity) in family relationships. The strength of perceptions to influence actual communication behavior within the family will be explored more fully in Chapter 10.

Summary

In sum, this chapter attempts to define *family, communication,* and *family communication.* Whereas families have previously been defined in biological, legal, or self-defining ways, this text defines families through their *relatedness* (biological, legal, or marriage-like-commitment) and through their functions of *nurturing* (encouraging physical, social, emotional, and intellectual growth) and *control* (limiting the behavioral options of family members through their inclusion in the family unit). Communication is defined as *messages that are typically sent with intent between two or more persons, messages that are typically seen as intentional, and messages that have consensually shared meaning.* In addition, this chapter distinguished between behaviors that can be informative (when no intent to communicate is evidenced) and behaviors that are clearly communicative in nature (when both the sender and the receiver perceive the intent to communicate on the part of the sender).

Furthermore, family communication is defined as messages that are typically sent with intent, messages that are typically perceived as intentional, and messages with consensually shared meaning among individuals who are related biologically, legally, or through marriage-like commitments and who nurture and control each other. Family communication is especially important because of changing family forms (e.g., nuclear, single-parent, gay parent, blended families). These changes in forms result in highlighting communication as an important coping mechanism for dealing with changing family roles, rules, and systems. Furthermore, the importance of communication in the family is underscored by the all important function families have of socializing children. To further illustrate the importance of family communication, sometimes children are being socialized in families that include conflict, substance abuse, and violence. Moreover, all these issues point up the most important function that communication has in families: to simultaneously nurture and control family members. Family members facilitate individual member growth through nurturing and facilitate socialization through control. In fact, nurturing and control are the two central functions that communication serves within families.

KEY TERMS

behavior   nurturing
biological family   receiver orientation
communication   relatedness
conflict   roles theory
controlling   rules theory
family forms   sociological definitions
information   source orientation
intimacy   substance abuse
legally defined family   violence

QUESTIONS FOR APPLICATION

1. Using ♂ & for men and ♀ & for women, draw your family tree. Show links of marriage, having children, divorces, and deaths. For further description of genograms, see www.genopro.com/genogram_rules/default.htm. What terms best describe your family form?

   a. What factors affected whom you included in your family tree? Did you draw members of your family who were related to you by biology, legal ties, self-definition, or commitment? What influenced your decisions about who to include in your family?

   b. If you were to include biological relatedness, legal ties, self-definition, and commitment, what members of your family had you inadvertently excluded? Describe your reaction.

   c. Did you include only family members you lived with over a significant period of time or did you also include your extended family? Why or Why not?

2. Describe your family in terms of (a) relatedness, (b) nurturing, and (c) controlling.

3. How did your family nurture and control you? How well do these concepts describe your family situation?

2

Family Forms in
Our Changing Society

The Family Context

The form of the family is rapidly changing. Examining the last 40 years provides a remarkable picture of the changes that our parents and we ourselves have observed in our lifetimes. These changes translate into communication practices and norms that have had to adapt as quickly as our notions of family have. While popular notions of family lead one to assume that the

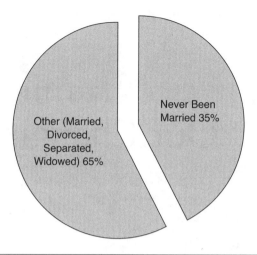

Figure 2.1   Marital Status (ages 24–34)

SOURCE: U.S. Census Bureau (1999).

nuclear family (two opposite-sex parents with biological children) was and is the norm in this culture, married couples with children constituted only 44% of all family households in 1960 and represent only one in four (24%) of all family households since 2000 (U.S. Census Bureau 1992, 2001). Furthermore, while the largest type of single-parent home in 1970 was due to an absent spouse, single-parent homes are increasingly composed of never-married parents (up from 7% in 1970 to 31% in 1990). Families who traditionally created their communication surrounding the roles of mother, father, and biological children are now communicating in increasingly complex situations where one parent assumes all the roles and communication responsibilities of two parents.

About 110.6 million adults (or 56% of the adult population) are married and live with their spouse (U.S. Census Bureau, 1999). However, about 34.7% of adults between the ages or 25 and 34 (13.6 million) have never been married (see Figure 2.1).

Those "Carrie Bradshaws" out there in their early 30s who complain of never being married are actually typical of one third of the population of adults their age! Interestingly, this percentage is even higher for African Americans in this age group (53.4%). Given this trend, it is not surprising that individuals are marrying later in life. Men are now an average of 26.8 years old when they marry (compared with 23.2 in 1970), and women are typically 25.1 (compared with 20.8 in 1970). In addition, a common myth has been perpetuated surrounding women's ability to get married at later ages, but a recent U.S. census report on the number of marriages and divorces indicates that 71% of 30-year-old women were already married and that it was likely that another 21% would get married (Kreider & Fields, 2001).

It was predicted that 92% of women would be married over their life span. A greater percentage of time in the life span is now spent in the development of relationships that can eventually lead to marriage (in the communication activities of courtship and mate selection) with lesser time actually spent communicating around the typical family issues of marriage, task distribution, and rearing children.

In addition, although the divorce rate continues to soar (up around 50% when one compares the number of marriages per year with the number of divorces per year in the United States), only 9.8% of adults are currently divorced (around 19.4 million adults). The divorce rate of 50% may be misleading because it does not consider the number of marriages entered into in the year of each divorcing couple, but we do know that 32% of men and 34% of women born between 1945 and 1954 (the early baby boomers) have been divorced (Kreider & Fields, 2001). Many family communication activities now surround relational dissolution, custody arrangements, and lessening of the impacts of divorce on children. Following divorce, a large number of individuals are now reentering the dating scene, with remarriages increasing dramatically. About half of all marriages every year are remarriages (46%; National Center for Health Statistics, 1995), about one fifth of men (22%) and one fourth of women (23%) born between 1945 and 1954 report being married twice, and the percentage of those who divorced predicted to be remarried during their lifetime is 75% (Kreider & Fields, 2001). Communication activities in the family increasingly have to do with new member integration, with stepparents and stepsiblings attempting to develop new roles within increasingly complex family forms.

Women are also playing more dual roles now; the number of married-couple families with wives in the labor force has increased from nearly 30% to nearly 60% since 1960 (see Figure 2.2).

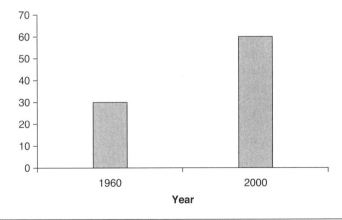

Figure 2.2   Married-Couple Families With Wives in the Labor Force (in percentages)

SOURCE: U.S. Census Bureau (2001).

To further round out this changing picture, the percentage of wives in the workforce with children under 1 year of age has gone up dramatically from 31% in 1976 to 51% in 2000 (compared with 70% of women without an infant). This figure is even higher for educated women, with 64% of women with infant children in the workforce (Bachu & O'Connell, 2001). In addition, black women with infants have relatively higher labor force participation (66%) compared with whites (57%) and Hispanics (42%). Not surprisingly, the percentage of working mothers increases as their children grow, with mothers of children under 6 (59%) and those with children aged 6 to 17 (74%) working even more than mothers of infants (U.S. Census Bureau, 2003a). A large number of communication issues surround redistribution of family roles and responsibilities as parental figures attempt to maintain both nurturing and resource provision roles.

Implications for Communication in the Family

This changing landscape creates many challenges for members of families as they communicate and live together. As is now strikingly apparent, not all of us are being raised in "traditional" nuclear families where Dad goes off to work and comes home and lays down the rules while Mom greets us at the door when we get home from school with a smile on her face and a cup of our favorite hot cocoa (with tons of whipped cream) in her hands. Some of us are living without dads, and others of us are living without moms. The communication rules regarding nurturing and control are very different in single-parent situations where one parental figure assumes all the functions of nurturing and control in the family. To complicate things even further, your mom may be living with some guy who is not your stepfather but would like to act as if he is. "What's *his* problem?" It is highly likely that role confusion and interrole conflict abound in this single-parent or cohabiting parent family situation.

Others of us do live with two parents but come home from school to find the key under the mat and instructions for how to start dinner. Children are now expected to assume the roles of nurturers in the family because their mothers are out assuming the role of providers. This not only leads to more adultlike responsibilities being assumed by the children but may also lead to difficulties in adjustment for parents who were raised in an era where fathers were the resource providers and mothers were traditionally the nurturance providers. This reciprocal (as opposed to complementary) role holding can lead to many complications as parents divide labor in the household. "Who wears the pants around here, anyway?" In addition, role confusion may abound as both parents try to fulfill multiple role demands. If Mom is working to provide resources (just like Dad), who is cleaning the house, making dinner, and making sure the kids are organized for school? If Mom and Dad divide the household and child care tasks, who is going to maintain the yard and the cars? The rapidly changing environment is wreaking havoc on what used to seem to be an orderly system of role distribution. To add to the growing complexity, many governmental and religious influences attempt to tell us that the "traditional" family form is best for stability and raising children.

Societal Influences on the Family Form

A number of societal forces contribute to our notions of family form. Many governmental and religious messages bombard us regarding notions of family, appropriateness and desirability. Many of you are familiar with the term "family values," a politically conservative term advocating the two-parent family where the husband is the resource provider and the wife is the stay-at-home mother. This perspective assumes that all other family forms (even two-parent homes where the mother works part-time) are the source of significant familial and social problems. In this section, we will explore the governmental and religious influences that contribute to our notions of the appropriateness of any family form and potentially influence the ways in which we communicate within our own families.

Governmental Regulations

The decline in marriage, combined with increases in cohabitation, divorce, and single parenting across all socioeconomic and racial groups has generated concern among policymakers (e.g., Dunifon & Kowaleski-Jones, 2002; Lichter, Graefe, & Brown, 2003; Waddan, 2003). The result has been changes in laws and welfare policies deliberately established in an attempt to encourage certain family forms over others. In addition, these policy changes have frequently resulted in a greater return of women to the workforce, which ironically, is another concern that many touting family values share. The government is creating pressure on families to be two-parent households where one parent works outside the home while the other maintains the house and raises the children. Because this is the case in only a small percentage of families, the rest of us in "alternative" family forms are left to feel insufficient in some way.

To illustrate the typical governmental response to concerns regarding the moral decline of the family, consider recent welfare reforms. The 1996 Personal Responsibility and Work Opportunity Reconciliation Act was designed to increase marriage and reduce out-of-wedlock childbearing, especially among low-income families (Dunifon & Kowaleski-Jones, 2002; Lichter et al., 2003). Policy changes included increased paternity establishment and child support enforcement, requirements that teenage parents live with their own parents (or other adults), and financial incentives for states managing to reduce nonmarital births while maintaining current abortion rates (Cancian & Reed, 2001). The assumption of this program is that increasing two-parent households will diminish dependence on public assistance and children will be better off in a number of ways. However, recent research across 7,665 women between the ages of 25 and 45 indicates that marriage alone does not offset the long-term deleterious effects associated with unwed childbearing, nor does it eliminate the existing disparity in poverty and welfare receipt among various racial and ethnic groups (Lichter et al., 2003). Early unwed childbearing significantly reduces the probability of subsequent marriage (Bennett, Bloom, & Miller, 1995; Lefebvre & Merrigan, 1998), with teen unwed mothers being more than twice as likely as other women to be never married by the time they reach 35 (Lichter & Graefe, 2001). In addition, only 30% of teen unwed mothers who later marry remain married (Graefe & Lichter, 2002). This bill is currently (2005) being reintroduced for reauthorization by both the house and senate.

Besides growing divorce rates and single parenthood, a number of other political factions purport that the difficulties families and children are facing are primarily due to the rise of women in the labor force (Giele, 2003). Remember that 53% of mothers with 1-year-olds are working outside the home, with this number increasing to 74% by the time children are between 6 and 17 years of age (U.S. Census Bureau, 2003a). This "decline" in the family is explained in various ways by these political factions. For instance, the **conservative explanation** offered by the "new family advocates" argues that the breakdown in two-parent families, which is accompanied by divorce, out-of-wedlock births, and father absence, has put children at greater risk of school failure, unemployment, and antisocial behavior. They argue that the cure for these societal ailments is a return to religious faith and family commitment. This commitment includes cutting welfare payments to unwed mothers and mother-headed families. Such policies that have been put in place (e.g., Temporary Assistance for Needy Families; TANF) have in fact resulted in an overwhelming return to the workforce by single mothers (and lesser reliance on public assistance programs) (Corcoran, Danziger, Kalil, & Seefeldt, 2000; Lichter & Graefe, 2001) but have also resulted in a greater external focus as mothers work outside the home and rely on alternative sources of child care. The return of mothers to the workforce has also served to diminish the belief that low-income single mothers lack a strong work ethic (Blank & Schmidt, 2001; Monroe & Tiller, 2001; Smith, Brooks-Gunn, & Klebanov, 2000).

The **liberal analysis of family change** argues that the negative effects of family change are the result of economic and structural changes that have placed new demands on the family while failing to provide necessary social supports (Giele, 2003). This perspective argues that women are reentering the workforce because they are having fewer children and so need to spend fewer years in their care. Women are also living longer. Thus, the family is relying on the urban workplace for economic sustenance and schools for socialization. Given this economic equality among partners, traditional economic divisions of labor between the genders are diminished, placing higher demands of emotional fulfillment on the spouse. These demands (or more likely, the inability of the partners to meet them) are at the heart of the downfall of modern marriages. The liberals argue that increasing pressures on women to join the workforce are at the heart of the downfall of the modern marriage and, thus, the modern family.

The **feminist view** lies somewhere between the conservative and the liberal view in that it supports the family as an institution, but it also has an appreciation for modernity (Giele, 2003). Traditionally, feminists try to understand women's role in society compared with the dominant male paradigm and thus attempt to understand changes in the family form as resulting from the increasing number of women in the workforce. Feminists judge family strength not by its form (e.g., two parent versus single parent) but by its functioning (Giele, 2003). They argue that families are well functioning if they promote human satisfaction and development (*nurturing*), with both women and men serving as family caregivers as well as productive workers. They attribute most difficulties of children to low-wage work of single mothers, inadequate child care, and inhospitable housing and neighborhoods.

To further illustrate this ongoing bombardment with regard to the "right" and "good" form of the family, national and legal debates surround family issues such as abortion, single-parent homes, and child custody. In addition, seven states still classify "lewd and lascivious" male-female cohabitation as illegal. Florida, Michigan, Mississippi, North Carolina, North Dakota, Virginia, and West Virginia still have laws against such unlawful cohabitation (Center for Family Policy and Practice, 2005; Fields, 2001). To further complicate issues, several states have laws on the books prohibiting same-sex marriages. Same-sex marriages gained national attention in the early 1990s when the Hawaiian Supreme Court ruled that the legislative ban on same-sex marriages violated the state's constitution (Mason, Fine, & Carnochan, 2003). In response, Hawaii passed a constitutional amendment limiting marriage to heterosexual couples, and 29 other states enacted laws barring the recognition of same-sex marriages performed in other states. At a federal level in 1996, the U.S. Congress enacted the **Defense of Marriage Act,** which gives all states the right to refuse recognition of same-sex marriages from *other* states and defines marriage as heterosexual unions for federal law purposes (Chambers & Polikoff, 1999). Regardless, Vermont passed a civil union statute that grants the benefits and responsibilities afforded to married couples under state laws (Mason et al., 2003). However, same-sex marriages remain unrecognized legally across the United States.

Given the governmental and religious resistance to acknowledging same-sex unions, it is not that surprising that gay and lesbian couples raising children have been under even greater scrutiny and public debate. In a nationally televised case, Rosie O'Donnell spoke out against the Florida courts that denied the right to adopt to a gay couple who had raised a foster child with HIV because the child no longer had HIV-positive status. Florida specifically bars the adoption of minor children by lesbian and gay adults (Patterson & Redding, 1996).

While this outright "barring" is uncommon, denial of rights to gay and lesbian couples is not. The "fundamental rights" to marry and raise children have not been extended to lesbian and gay Americans (e.g., Cain, 1993; Patterson & Redding, 1996; Rivera, 1991; Rubenstein, 1991). In fact, as late as the fall of 2004, Minnesota and 19 other states had reforms on the ballot specifically designed to forbid same sex marriages (Morris, 2004). Furthermore, many lesbian and gay adults have been denied the opportunity to become foster or adoptive parents (Patterson, 1995; Ricketts, 1991, Ricketts & Achtenberg, 1990) and have had custody or visitation with biological children denied or curtailed primarily because of their homosexuality (Cain, 1993; Rivera, 1991). Sodomy laws (like the one in Texas which was repealed in 2003) are central to denying rights to lesbian and gay parents and their children because courts often justify the denial of child custody or the curtailment of visitation based on the illegality of the parents' presumed sexual conduct (e.g., *Bottoms v. Bottoms,* 1995; Patterson & Redding, 1996; *Roe v. Roe,* 1985).

In addition to adoption, foster care, and child custody, some gay and lesbian couples rely on in vitro fertilization. Denial of rights extend here as well; much discussion within fertility clinics focuses on the withholding of infertility treatment from lesbians. In fact, 4 of 12 Dutch infertility treatment centers actually withheld such treatments from lesbian couples (Hunfeld, Fauser, de Beaufort, & Passchier, 2001), even though the Netherlands is one of only four countries that has legalized same-sex marriages (with Belgium, Spain, and Canada). There is also concern that for lesbians in particular (and the concern is shared for single-mother homes) the absence of the father is considered to increase the risk of gender identity confusion and less conventional gender role behavior (Falk, 1989; Green, 1992; Patterson, 1992).

Religious Influences

Many religious organizations have become increasingly involved in controversies surrounding the nature of the family. Statements about single parenthood, teen unwed pregnancy, gay couples and parents, and abortion are a few places where churches attempt to influence the family form. All churches and faiths (Catholic, Protestant, Jewish) appear to be similar in their belief that two opposite-sex parents should be raising children.

In response to a growing number of countries passing legislation recognizing same-sex unions (e.g., the Netherlands, Belgium, and two provinces in Canada), the Vatican published a document explaining the Catholic Church's opposition to same-sex unions. In a blatant example of religion attempting to influence government, the Pope called on all Catholic members of parliament to oppose legislation that "equates what the Catholic Church regards as normal families with gay couples" (BBC News, 2003c).

Public concern with family decline increased steadily after 1980 and is concentrated among evangelical Protestants who attend church regularly (Brooks, 2002). Regardless, there are examples of Protestant churches that do accept gays. For instance, the Australian Uniting Church became the country's first mainstream denomination to accept homosexual priests (BBC News, 2003a). And here in the states, in 2005, the United Church of Christ has approved a resolution that endorses same-sex marriages.

In another example of church influencing state, President George W. Bush recently responded to the "threat" of U.S. Anglicans appointing Gene Robinson, the first openly gay bishop, by saying that "I believe a marriage is between a man and a woman, and I think we ought to codify that one way or the other" (BBC News, 2003b). Bush declined to pass moral judgment on homosexuals, but also commented that he was "mindful that we are all sinners."

Social Science Influences

On the flip side of concerns about single-parent homes and poverty are the advocates of increased labor force participation by both parents (to reduce dependence on public assistance). To add to the complexity of the debate, much social science research explores the ill effects of day care programs on children. In 1986, Belsky's analysis of research was very controversial because he concluded that early and extensive nonmaternal care increased the probability of insecure attachments to parents and promoted aggression and noncompliance among toddlers, preschoolers, and children in early primary school (Belsky, 2001). Despite the plethora of research activity designed to refute these claims, Belsky recently defended this position. Regardless, he did provide research evidence showing that the quality of maternal caregiving mediates these negative effects and that the amount of time in nonmaternal care also affects these outcomes (Belsky, 1999). It seems that parents are criticized both for not working and then for placing their children in child care when they do work. This is especially troubling in light of the plethora of "welfare to work" reforms that exist to assist young mothers' return to the workforce.

Family Forms

Cohabiting Couples

Cohabiting couples are opposite-sex partners who live together but have not recognized the extent of their commitment through the legal institution

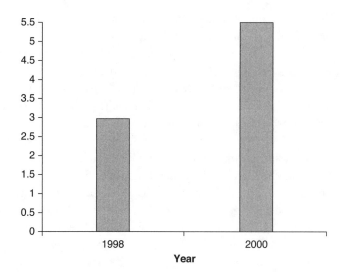

Figure 2.3   Cohabitants (in millions)

SOURCE: Zinn and Eitzen (2002).

of marriage. In recognition of the greater number of heterosexual couples choosing to cohabit instead of getting married, the relationship category "unmarried partner of the opposite sex" was added to the 1990 U.S. Census Bureau questionnaire (Kalish, 1994). The number of unmarried couple households increased from 1.3 million in 1978 to 3.0 million in 1998 as shown in Figure 2.3 (Zinn & Eitzen, 2002). This number continues to grow dramatically, with 5.5 million unmarried-partner households reported in 2000. Of these, 4.9 million reported opposite-sex partners (Simmons & O'Connell, 2003).

More than half of today's marriages are preceded by cohabitation, and a majority of adults under 40 have experienced one cohabiting union (Bumpass & Sweet, 1989, 1995). Cohabitation is arguably a family status (Brown, 2000), with 40% to 43% of cohabiting couples having residing children (Bumpass, Sweet, & Cherlin, 1991; U.S. Census Bureau, 2004) and 2.2 million children living with a cohabiting parent (Manning & Lichter, 1996).

Bianchi and Casper (2000) estimate that over half of couples who married after 1985 cohabited first. These authors offer several explanations for this increasing trend. They argue that later age for first marriages, new living arrangements following divorce (and preceding remarriage), and increasing individualism and secularism underlie the growing acceptability of living together. Most individuals, however, report that cohabitation is a precursor to (46%), or a trial, marriage (15%). Thus, cohabitation is seen as a prelude to more traditional family forms. A minority report that they cohabit as a substitution for marriage (10%) or that they are simply coresidential daters (15%). This is consistent with Bumpass (1990) who reports that couples list wanting to ensure compatibility before marriage more than any other reason for living together. Bianchi and Casper (2000) also report that after 5 to 7 years, 21% of the couples they studied still lived together, 40% were married, and 39% were separated.

Still others argue that freedoms of dormitory or apartment living, female financial independence, and less pressure on males to be married for business purposes all contribute to greater cohabitation (Goldscheider & Waite, 1991). Finally, others have argued that economic incentives (Chevan, 1996) and emotional advantages with few economic and legal restrictions promote greater cohabitation (Bianchi & Spain, 1996).

The amount of research on the effects of cohabitation on cohabitants and on children living with them is growing. Recent studies have shown that cohabiting women suffer higher rates of physical violence and emotional abuse (Brownridge & Halli, 2000; DeMaris, 2000). In addition, cohabitants are more likely to be unhappy or dissatisfied with their current situation compared with married women (Brown, 2000; Brown & Booth, 1996). Finally, cohabitants report higher levels of depression than their married counterparts (Brown, 2000). This depression is exacerbated by the presence of biological and stepchildren. Depression scores of marrieds were unaffected by the presence of children.

Couples With No Children

Married couples with no children are made up of two opposite-sex individuals who have legalized their commitment to one another through the bonds of marriage. The percentage of married couples without children is currently at 28.7%, which is down from 30.3% in 1970 (U.S. Census Bureau, 2001). As an interesting side note, this number is greater than married couples living with children. In addition, 43% of women in childbearing years (15–44 years old) were childless in 2000 (Bachu & O'Connell, 2001). Among 40- to 44-year-olds, 19% were childless, which is almost double those in 1980 (10%). Comparable rates for Hispanic women are lower, however, with only 11% of 40- to 44-year-olds remaining childless.

Although we know little about these couples (except that some are struggling with infertility issues), there is also very little research about them. We do know, however, that married individuals have higher levels of psychological well-being than nonmarried individuals (regardless of whether the nonmarrieds are never-married, separated, divorced, or widowed) (Lee, Seccombe, & Shehan, 1991). In addition, married individuals have lower rates of mortality (Rogers, 1995; Verbrugge, 1979), and they are less susceptible to dying from accidents or suicides. Marital quality is an important factor, however, in that people in unhappy marriages report lower levels of well-being than nonmarrieds (Gove, Hughes, & Briggs Style, 1983).

Interestingly, marital *status* is more strongly related to well-being among men, whereas marital *quality* is more closely tied to well-being for women.

With regard to communication among married couples with no children, we know that it is possible for them to spend more time communicating with each other and developing their careers rather than nurturing and disciplining their children. Predictable developmental patterns of stress associated with discipline and other child-rearing issues can be lower. They also do not go through the normal developmental stressors of raising (and struggling with) adolescents or experiencing the "empty nest syndrome." However, while the figures might never be known, many of these couples may not be making the choice to remain childless.

As we choose to marry later, with many of us focusing on careers and delaying childbearing, it is possible that many of these couples may not be choosing to be childless. It is estimated that as many as 5% of couples may be experiencing **infertility**, usually defined as the inability to conceive after 12 months of regular unprotected intercourse (Anderson, Sharpe, Rattray, & Irvine, 2003). It is possible that infertility issues and communication surrounding their medical treatment may be central to these couples' lives. Although the majority of women have children between the ages of 20 and 34 (around 600 births per 1,000 divided nearly equally between the ages of 20 and 24 [208 births], 25 and 29 [235 births], and 30–34 [199 births]), the numbers drop to 93 per 1,000 for 35- to 39-year-olds and 30 per 1,000 for 40- to 44-year-olds (Bachu & O'Connell, 2001) (see Figure 2.4).

Although many of these numbers reflect the choice to have children younger, it is possible that fertility rates are lower among 35- to 44-year-olds. Thus, women may be relying on costly infertility treatments or alternative ways of having families. This drive may be very damaging to relationships as married individuals place their time, attention, and efforts

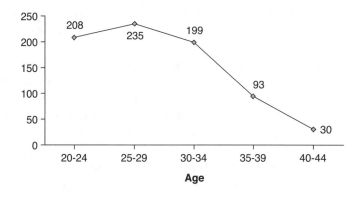

Figure 2.4   Births (per 1,000 women)

SOURCE: Bachu and O'Connell (2001).

into conceiving a child. Research suggests that infertility problems are among the most upsetting experiences in peoples' lives and that young men and women planning in vitro fertilization have more short-term social and emotional problems (Fekkes et al., 2003; Freeman, Boxer, Rickels, Tureck, & Mastroiani, 1985; Mahlstedt, Macduff, & Bernstein, 1987). While some studies indicate the lack of emotional disorder in couples seeking infertility treatment (Anderson et al., 2003), other studies support the link between the goal of biological parenthood and happiness. For those potential parents who strongly believe that having a biological child is necessary for happiness and life satisfaction, their fertility problems predicted significantly greater distress (Brothers & Maddux, 2003).

Nuclear Families

Nuclear families are families in which two biological parents (one mother and one father) raise their biological or adoptive offspring in the same living environment. Married couples with children represent one in four (24%) of all family households since 2000 (U.S. Census Bureau, 1992, 2001). In addition, if one defines nuclear families by inclusion of only families where the father goes out to work and the mother stays at home, the percentage of nuclear families is less than 10% (Cartier, 1995; Scanzoni, Polonko, Teachman, & Thompson, 1989). Even though nuclear families are the most supported form of families in terms of governmental and religious support, very little is known about their functioning. A growing literature suggests that marriage is associated with better emotional and physical health and that children, on balance, do better being raised by their married biological parents (e.g., McLanahan & Sandefur, 1994; Waite & Gallagher, 2000). Married couples also have more resources, are better networked, and are healthier (Waite & Gallagher, 2000).

Gay Couples (and Gay Couples With Children)

Gay couples are same-sex couples who are committed to one another with the same level of commitment as married individuals. They are lifetime partners who are committed to one another's socioemotional, physical, and intellectual development as individuals and who fulfill the family functions of nurturing and control. Even though gay couples have commitment similar to marriage and nurture and control each other in ways similar to more traditionally recognized family forms, there has been state- and federal-level resistance to the recognition of gay marriages. Legislation exists at both state and federal levels that prohibits the legalization of such unions (see the governmental regulation section). Of the 5.5 million unmarried partners reported in the 2000 census, 594,000 of them were partners of the same sex (301,000 male couples and 293,000 female couples). Interestingly, these

Figure 2.5   Following a 13-year commitment that spanned two countries and a separation exacerbated by the fact that Jon and Angus could not legally marry, which would have facilitated Angus's U.S. citizenship, Jon Baxter and Angus Sinclair have a commitment ceremony on July 20, 2003, in the synagogue and receive a letter recognizing their union from the state of California.

numbers represent less than .6% of all 105.5 million households reported in the United States and nearly 1% of all households maintained by couples (60 million) (U.S. Census Bureau, 2004).

> The first service I provided to the twin babies to whom I am now a mother was to drive to the lab with my partner, Jeannie, to collect a test tube with about 5cc of pink liquid at the bottom. I took the test tube from Jeannie, who was writing out a cheque at the front desk, and I went to the restroom to undo my bra and place the glass vial carefully under my left breast to keep it warm for its hectic ride across town to Pacific Reproductive Services where the contents would be poured into a syringe, pushed through Jeannie's cervix and into her uterus, there to await the descent of whatever egg might, in the next twenty-four hours, make its way from her ovaries, previously stimu-lated into hyper-activity by the use of the injectable fertility drug, Fertinex. When the sperm was duly insider her, Jeannie stood on her head in a corner of the tiny room. "It worked for that woman in *Antonia's Line*," she said. (Livia, 2000, p. 215)

Gay couples with children are same-sex couples (lesbians or gays) who are committed to one another with the same level of commitment as married individuals and assume the role of parent (*nurturer/controllers)* to at least one child. Some researchers report that there are between 1.5 to slightly over 2 million lesbian mothers and gay fathers with about 14 million children in the U.S. (Coontz, 1992; Gottman, 1989; Patterson, 1992; West & Turner, 1995). However, these numbers are difficult to confirm. For instance, we know that 594,000 couples are in same-sex households, but only 22% of male partners and 34% of female partners report living with their own or unrelated children (U.S. Census Bureau, 2003b). Others approximate that there are over 1.5 million lesbian mothers (Henry, 1990) and more than 400,000 gay fathers (Goldenberg & Goldenberg, 1991) in the United States. In Australia, even though more gay couples (20,711) report living together than do lesbian couples (17,063), only 963 gay couples (5% of all gay couples) compared with 3,276 (24% of all lesbian couples) lesbian couples declared living as couples with children (Australian Bureau of Statistics, 2001; Mikhailovich et al., 2001). Lesbian mothers and gay fathers have children in a variety of ways, including (a) heterosexual relationships before they "came out," (b) through adoption or fostering, (c) through the use of donor insemination or surrogacy, or (d) by becoming the partner of someone who already has children (Clarke, 2001).

Many individuals express concerns regarding gay couples raising children. Most of these concerns are with regard to negative effects on the development of the children. However, no studies to date have documented adverse effects of lesbian motherhood on child development or quality of parenting (Baetens & Brewaeys, 2001; Brewaeys, 2001; Falk, 1989; Golombok, 1998; Hunfeld et al., 2001). In addition, children in lesbian and gay families develop socially and academically in line with their peers in heterosexual families (Patterson, 1992). Regardless, college students asked to discuss recent media representations of lesbian and gay parents (in newspapers and on talk shows such as *Donohue, Ricki Lake,* and *Oprah*) revealed that students use the following arguments to oppose gay and lesbian parenting: (a) "The Bible tells me that lesbian and gay parenting is a sin." (b) "Lesbian and gay parenting is unnatural." (c) "Lesbian and gay parents are selfish because they ignore 'the best interests of the child.'" (d) "Children in lesbian and gay families lack appropriate role models." (e) "Children in lesbian and gay families grow up lesbian and gay." and (f) "Children in lesbian and gay families get bullied" (Clarke, 2001, p. 555). The influence of religious and governmental forces on attitudes toward gay couples with children is evidenced in the attitudes of these undergraduates.

Regardless of societal perceptions, the overall conclusions of many studies support the argument that life in homosexual families is not appreciably different from heterosexual family life (West & Turner, 1995). With regard to communication, disclosure of one's sexual identity may provide the greatest challenge to gay families. While some parents report that openness with their children about sexuality is a primary strategy for strengthening the family system (Levy, 1992; Martin, 1993), others report that they did not disclose their homosexuality to their families because they believed their family members and their co-workers posed the biggest threats in terms of rejection and discrimination (Wells & Kline, 1987). The research supports the perceptions of the first set of gay parents above in that the disclosure of homosexuality to children deepened the parent-child relationship (Clay, 1991). West and Turner (1995), however, report that disclosure of homosexuality was more a concern of lesbian mothers than gay fathers. They reported that mothers reported that one of the most stressful aspects of their family lives revolved around their children's comfort level with open disclosures to peers, with children inviting friends over to the house less often and some being concerned that their mothers might embarrass them by being openly affectionate with their partners.

Not surprising, given the potential negative ramifications of disclosure in terms of potential custody battles and the like, gay parents find disclosing their sexuality to external nonfamily members problematic—even when it is linked to their children's health. For instance, Mikhailovich et al. (2001) report that although 89% of lesbian and gay parents with children reported satisfaction with their child's health care, 49% reported being fearful to disclose their sexual orientation, and 29% reported problems with their child's health care related to their disclosure of their sexual orientation or their family constellation. Disclosure of a parent's sexuality may pose the most problems in terms of communication in families with gay parents. Very little is known regarding families in which nonparental members are gay (e.g., children, uncles, grandparents).

Single-Parent Families

Single-parent families include only one parent and at least one child residing in a similar residence. About 19.8 million children under 18 live with one parent (27.7% of children; U.S. Census Bureau, 1999). In addition, it has been estimated that given the current divorce rate, 50% of all children under 18 may live in single-parent homes for some portion of their growing-up years (Paasch & Teachman, 1991).

Of the nearly 28% of children currently living with one parent, the majority live with their mother (84.1%), and the majority of those children live with mothers who had never been married (40.3%). Numbers of children in single-parent homes are even higher for black mothers (45% of black children are being raised by their single mothers). Black women (regardless of being defined as high or low risk) are more likely to have a nonmarital first birth (54% compared with 30% for Hispanics and 15% for Caucasians), less likely to be married (34% compared with 58% for Hispanics and 67% for Caucasians), and are more likely to be below 180% of the poverty line

LIBRARY, UNIVERSITY OF CHESTER

Figure 2.6   My niece, Shelly, and her adorable son, Liam, represent the 28% of all families that are single-parent families; of these, 84% are headed by mothers.

(49% compared with 46% for Hispanics and 20% for Caucasians) (Lichter et al., 2003). This paints quite a complex understanding of the differences across black families compared with both Hispanic and Caucasian families. Regardless of these striking differences between black families and Caucasian families, the negative effects of single parenting on black children are not as evidenced as in Caucasian homes. Specifically, Dunifon and Kowaleski-Jones (2002) found single parenthood associated with reduced well-being among European American children, but not among African American children. For African American children, maternal warmth and provision of rules had the most direct effects on children's delinquency.

Consider the case of Tanya, a young black single mother who works full-time as an administrative assistant at a company that provides stock options to its employees. She is not considered "high risk" because she was raised by both of her parents in an intact home and her mother was educated and worked outside the home. She has been raising her two young sons, Andrew and Jonathon, on her own since they were very small. She married big Jonathon shortly after she became aware that she was pregnant with Andrew. Although she still considers herself married to Jonathon (she is still seen wearing her wedding ring), she has been living on her own with the boys since Andrew was 2 and Jonathon was a baby. Her religious beliefs make it difficult for her to define herself as a single mother even though from the early days of their marriage big Jonathon was "missing" several nights a week. He has been running from federal drug enforcement officers and recently physically abused her when she confronted him about a child he might have had with another women about the time "little" Jonathon was born. Through all this, she finds it difficult to proceed with the divorce documentation because it means so much to her to avoid the definition of single mother, even though she has been acting in this capacity for 3 years. She also reports that single motherhood among her black friends is more respected if it is the result of divorce as opposed to unwed motherhood. Tanya is representative of the research finding that marriages motivated by an unintended pregnancy have high rates of dissolution (Heaton, 2002; Timmer & Orbuck, 2001). In general, the black culture in the United States is different from the Caucasian culture in that it is more matriarchal, with a mother or grandmother typically seen as the "head of the household."

The numbers of children being raised by single fathers is increasing but still shy of the number of children being raised by single mothers. Children living with their single fathers (about 2 million single fathers) were more likely to be the product of divorce (44.4%) than an out-of-wedlock pregnancy (33.3%). My husband is an example of this; after Graham divorced Chris, he raised his two boys half the time (8/9 of 14 days) from the time they were 6 and 9 until they were 8 and 12. Most children being raised by single parents were raised without another adult in the home (55.7%). However, those raised with single fathers were more likely to live with a cohabiting partner (33%) than were children raised with single mothers (11%) (U.S. Census Bureau, 2003a). My husband and I, for instance, lived together during the 5 months we owned a house together before we got married. More single fathers are likely to have a mother figure in the home while they "single parent." Thus, it seems that more single fathers are trying to approximate a nuclear family by cohabiting. As you can imagine, the complexities are greater in this family situation than in the traditional nuclear family in that the cohabiting female attempts to communicate in ways similar to a mother and may experience rejection and consternation on the part of the children.

Single mothers, on the other hand, are less likely to provide their children with a father figure in the home. This may be due, in part, to the tendency for societies to see mothers as more central to the mission of raising children. However, there are a growing number of fatherhood movements (e.g., the fatherhood responsibility movement) claiming that it is dangerous to raise children (especially boys) without a father in the home (Gavanas, 2004).

In addition, those raised by single mothers were more likely to be raised below the poverty line (34%) than those being raised by single fathers (16%). It is more typical for single-mother homes to receive public assistance and food stamps because they are more likely to live well below the poverty line (less than $12,120 per year for a family of two; Connecticut Health Policy Project, 2003). This adds unique communication dimensions to the family; it is unlikely that this overworked and overburdened mother can afford the luxury of assistance in the home to allow her "quality" time with her children.

As one example of society telling us which types of family forms are preferable, the single-parent family has been widely researched in terms of its impact on children. Single-parent homes are often characterized in negative ways and are often criticized for being the shaky cornerstone of our increasingly immoral society. Single-parent families have been portrayed as the root cause of many social problems, including substance abuse, juvenile delinquency, unmarried motherhood, and school failure (Davidson & Moore, 1996). These effects are often attributed to the family structure and less to the fact that the majority of single-parent homes have a higher rate of poverty (34% for single-mother homes), move more frequently, and are headed by individuals with less education (Hanson & Sporakowski, 1986).

In addition, psychological distress and less effective parenting practices have been associated with inadequate support (Simons, Beaman, Conger, & Chao, 1993). Lack of social support is most likely a result of greater poverty and frequent geographic moves. Also, women being raised by single mothers have approximately a 20% lower probability of marriage than women raised by two parents (South, 2001). Women growing up in a nonintact family with mothers who either had low education or were never employed were roughly twice as likely to have unwed births (Lichter et al., 2003). They were also less likely to be currently married and were nearly twice as likely to be poor.

Children are not the only ones affected by divorce, however. The most frequent complaints of single parents include lack of money, role overload, lack of a social life, and ex-spouses (Richards & Schmiege, 1993). Studies also indicate that single mothers who are divorced have a higher rate of depression and anxiety than do women of other marital statuses (Spence, Najman, Bor, O'Callaghan, & Williams, 2002). Attaining much needed social support is a way for single mothers to moderate the depression and anxiety associated with their divorce and single parenting. In fact, divorced mothers with children are more likely to have contact with friends than are never-marrieds or married persons who have children (Alwin, Converse, & Martin, 1985). This more frequent contact combined with quality of friendships can significantly affect the postdivorce adjustment of single mothers (Thiriot & Buckner, 1992).

Blended and Binuclear Families

Blended families (sometimes referred to as the stepfamily) include families that typically include one biological parent, a nonbiological parent, and the biological child or children of one parent. Increasingly, they include biological children of both the original biological parent and the new stepparent. **Binuclear families** are made up of two households where children reside alternately with one biological parent and one nonbiological parent residing in both households. Numbers of children living in blended (marriages with children from former relationships and children from the newly constituted family) or stepfamily (marriages with children from former relationships only) arrangements are harder to come by using U.S. Census data. We do know that of the 2.4 million marriages in the U.S. each year, 1.1 million (or 46%) are remarriages (National Center for Health Statistics, 1995). About half these remarriages involve remarriage for both spouses (U.S. Bureau of the Census, 1993). In addition, Davidson and Moore (1996) make the claim that blended families are the third most common family form after the single-parent and two-parent household. They indicate that one third of all children will live with a biological and a stepparent for at least 1 year before they reach 18 (Dainton, 1993). However, only 32% of black, 16% of Hispanic, and 15% of white children live in stepfamilies—and nearly all live with their biological mothers (U.S. Census Bureau, 1993).

There is an increasing amount of complexity in stepfamily arrangements, which adds to the challenges of communicating within such a family form. Not only are parents, stepparents, and children struggling to define their new family form and their roles within them, but the ambiguity of stepparents' roles is further blurred by their lack of legal rights. Stepparents who do not adopt their stepchildren have no legal identity (Mahoney, 1994). Their rights and duties as a stepparent are largely undefined, and a consistent understanding of their role within the family is not reflected in any definitions that do exist (Mason, 2000). Stepparents have recently been allowed to petition for custody of children during a divorce through a definition of parents by estoppel (individuals who present themselves as parents) and are having success in obtaining visitation with their stepchildren following divorce (American Law Institute, 2000). Regardless, such changes in the law are slow in coming, with the success in visitation largely resulting from states' general third-party visitation statutes that allow individuals to petition for visitation when there is disruption in the family (Mason et al., 2003).

Furthermore, children and parents in stepfamilies are likely to have divergent perceptions of the stepparents' role in parenting (Fine, Coleman, & Ganong, 1998; Fine, Kurdek, & Hennigen, 1992). To add to the complexity, stepfamilies may experience higher rates of child-rearing conflict, lower levels of cohesion, higher levels of stress, and more problems in child adjustment than families in first marriages (Bray, 1988; Bray & Berger, 1993; Zill, Morrison, & Coiro, 1993). Afifi and Shrodt (2003) reported that uncertainty levels and avoidance of the state of one's familial relationship were higher in postdivorce and stepfamilies than in first-marriage families. Afifi and Keith (2004) report that children in stepfamilies experience "ambiguous loss" surrounding (a) the loss of one's previous family form and traditional nuclear family ideal, (b) the loss of a single-parent bond, and (c) the loss of a non-custodial parent-child bond. Taken together, these findings indicate that communication in stepfamilies may be very complex due to a variety of factors.

Regardless, monitoring levels of children do not appear to be lower in stepmother families than in nuclear families, with monitoring slightly lower in stepfather families (Fisher, Leve, O'Leary, & Leve, 2003). Thus, stepfamilies with stepmothers do not appear to be at higher risk for antisocial behavior, difficulties in school, and related problems (all outcomes associated with low levels of monitoring). Although stepfathers are most effective in forming positive relationships with their stepchildren when they do not make early attempts at discipline or control (Hetherington, 1999; Hetherington & Clingempeel, 1992), it is likely that because of the social roles of women, stepmothers make attempts to become parental figures earlier than do stepfathers (Brand, Clingempeel, & Bowen-Woodward, 1988). This may account for higher ratings of closeness with stepmothers than with stepfathers (Sturgess, Dunn, & Davies, 2001). Mason, Harrison-Jay, Svare, and Wolfinger (2002) found that stepparents are very similar to parents in the frequency of private talks, help with homework, transporting children, and enforcement of rules. Not surprisingly, although both parents enforce the rules, the stepparent is rarely the chief rule maker or enforcer.

Because the communication issues of boundary management, conflict resolution, and role negotiation are central to blended family development (Goldsmith & Baxter, 1996), more scholars in communication are beginning to examine communication within stepfamilies. Baxter, Braithwaite, and Nicholson (1999), for instance, examined turning points and developmental trajectories of 53 blended families. Turning points are transformative events that alter a relationship in some important way (either positively or negatively), and trajectories are sequences of turning points into pathways. While they report 15 primary types of turning points in blended families, changes in household configuration, conflict, holidays/special events, quality time, and family crisis were the most frequently reported. In addition, over the first 4 years of the blended family, they report the five basic trajectories of blended family development as accelerated, prolonged, stagnating, declining, and high-amplitude turbulent.

Accelerated trajectories characterized 31% of the blended families studied. *Accelerated blended families* reflected a pattern of relatively rapid movement toward "feeling like a family." These families often entered the blended family with moderate levels of feeling like a family and progressed, with positive turning points outnumbering negative turning points by 3.65 to 1. *Prolonged blended families* (28% of families) entered the trajectory at lower levels of feeling like a family and progressed toward feeling like a family at a much slower rate, with positive turning points still outnumbering negative turning points at a ratio of 3 to 1. *Stagnating blended families* (14% of families) began their blended families with lower levels of feeling like a family (like prolongeds), but remained low through the 4 years. Positive turning points still outnumbered negative turning points but only at a ratio of 2 to 1. *Declining blended families* (6%) began their blended families with high levels of feeling like a family followed by a general decline over time. Negative turning points outnumbered positive turning points in declining families by about 2 to 1. Finally, *turbulent blended families* (22%) had rapid and successive positive and negative turning points followed by dramatic increases and decreases in feeling like a family. Although it is not surprising that accelerated and prolonged types of blended families reported feeling more like a family, the turbulent type also reports higher amounts of feeling like a family than declining and stagnating blended family types. The accelerated type was also differentiated from the declining type by the amount of conflict in that accelerated families reported less conflict than did declining families.

Braithwaite, Olson, Golish, Soukup, and Turman (2001) used the accelerated, prolonged, stagnating, declining, and turbulent trajectories to identify *boundary management*, *solidarity*, and *adaptation* as salient issues in blended families. Accelerated families developed rather traditional families, family roles, norms, boundaries, and expectations. Prolonged blended families were described as adaptable, flexible, and willing to negotiate family-specific roles, norms, boundaries, and expectations. Declining blended families were characterized by conflict, ambiguous and strained family roles, and divisive family boundaries. Stagnating blended families felt they had been "thrown together" and experienced awkwardness concerning familial roles and expectations. Although they sought a traditional family arrangement, the instability and unmet expectations led to consistent feelings of dissatisfaction and artificiality. Turbulent blended families were characterized as diverse, unstable, and unpredictable. Unrealistic expectations of forming an instant family were associated with discomfort and strain.

While the above scholars examined communication over time in developing blended families, Braithwaite, McBride, and Schrodt (2003) examined the day-to-day interactions of stepfamilies through examinations of diaries kept by parenting teams. Parents most often talked with coparents in the other household on the telephone. Most reported that these interactions were short, generally had to do with topics such as the children, and involved little conflict. In addition, adults were moderately satisfied with the interactions.

Extended Families

Extended families include families in which three generations are represented. Frequently, these include parents, grandparents, and children. Adult children are moving back into their parents' homes, and many of them are bringing their children with them. About 5.6 million children (or about 5.6% of adult children or adult children with their children) live in a household of their grandparents (U.S. Census Bureau, 1999; 2001). Of those, 1.4 million lived with their grandparent with neither parent co-residing in the home and 2.4 million (42%) of grandparents report responsibility for their grandchild's care (U.S. Census Bureau, 2000). About 22 million adult children live at home with their parents (Mitchell & Gee, 1996). In addition, the number of children living with grandparents in African American homes may reach 15% (Chase Goodman & Silverstein, 2001). The inclusion of adult children and, often, their children creates a unique dynamic whereby

Figure 2.7   This extended family crosses three generations, with Grandma, her two daughters, and her older daughter's three children.

the parent and the grandparent may both adopt parenting roles. One student in my family communication class personifies this situation; she reports that both her mother and her grandmother parented her, with her mother adopting the traditional masculine role of resource provider and her grandmother adopting the traditional role of nurturer/caregiver.

Summary

The overall panorama of family life has become an increasingly diverse picture of families living in the United States. A greater number of couples are now cohabiting, as either a substitute for, or precursor to, marriage. In addition, the traditional nuclear family, with a resource-providing father and nurturance-providing mother now makes up only 10% of all family forms (although this number increases to 24% if one includes resource-providing mothers as well). With the increasing prevalence of divorce (34% to 50%), many families transition through single-parent or cohabiting single-parent forms. Not surprisingly, with half of all marriages in the United States being remarriages each year, many families are blended, binuclear, or stepfamilies. These families experience a variety of challenges as various members attempt to struggle into their appropriate roles within this family form. To further round out this picture, some married couples have no children, whereas some gay couples live together as if they are married. In addition, a growing number of these gay couples are currently raising children. Finally, some children live in an extended family, living with both their parents and their grandparents.

Given this changing landscape, a greater number of political and religious organizations are expressing their views regarding the preference of one family form over another. Traditional nuclear families are held up as the standard by which all other family forms are judged. A variety of laws currently exist attempting to reinforce this notion. In addition, many religious leaders have attempted to sway political leaders regarding heated issues such as gay marriages and single-parent homes. In addition, social science research vilifies nonmaternal child care. In sum, according to rhetoric of the political and religious outcry regarding families, the only justifiable alternative is the traditional nuclear family where the father goes out to work and the mother stays at home and raises the children. Unfortunately, only 10% of us are fortunate enough to live in traditional nuclear families.

KEY TERMS

blended and binuclear families
cohabiting couples
conservative views of family decline
couples with no children
extended families
feminist views of the family decline

gay families
liberal views of the family decline
nuclear families
Personal Responsibility and Work
    Opportunity Reconciliation Act
single-parent families

QUESTIONS FOR APPLICATION

1. Describe your family form. What were the impacts of this form on your family communication?

2. The form of the family is changing in contemporary society. What type of family form surprised you the most in terms of its representation among the general population? Why were you surprised?

3. In what ways have the government, religion, and the media shaped your perceptions of the family and the appropriateness or superiority of certain family forms over others?

4. What are your perceptions of single-parent families? Gay families? Stepparents? Children who were raised by their grandparents? Where do your assumptions come from?

5. Did both of your parents work while you were growing up? What types of jobs did they hold? In what ways did your parents' jobs influence your family positively? In what ways did your parents' jobs influence your family negatively?

3 Theoretical Approaches to Understanding Communication in the Family

Introduction of Theory _____

At this point, we have a full understanding of the definitions of *family, communication,* and *family communication.* We also have more understanding of the complexities of families in the 21st century through our exploration in Chapter 2 of the various family forms and their potential impacts on family communication. To most fully understand the nature of families and the communication dynamics within them, however, we must fully understand the nature of **theory.** Before you turn off completely at the abstractness of this concept in the face of the concreteness of the types of families we have just discussed, let me try to persuade you that theories will be concretely useful to us in our application to families. By focusing on families, theories can be socially meaningful and applied.

Theories give us a mechanism for understanding phenomena, and families are one such phenomenon. Theories provide us with several functions that will be highly useful as we go about the business of understanding families. First, theories can **describe** phenomenon (Littlejohn & Foss, 2005). In other words, theories can answer the "what?" question. To be more specific, understanding *what* single-parent families, binuclear families, and gay families are is all the work of description. Description can also allow us to delineate the similarities and differences of families (and their accompanying definitions). Families are all the same because they all exhibit the characteristics of relatedness, nurturing, and control, as we described these concepts in Chapter 1. In addition, they are all different in that single-parent families have a single head of household, and binuclear families have a biological mother and stepfather in one home and a biological father and stepmother in another home. Gay families have parents who are homosexual and live in a committed relationship with their partner. This offers a nice understanding of the *types* of families that are out there, but it does little to help us understand the complex differences and outcomes associated with each family type. The second function of theories can help us on this front.

Second, theories can help **predict** concrete outcomes (Littlejohn & Foss, 2005), or in other words, they help enumerate *how* something will occur. This is especially important with families because governmental agencies, religious groups, and concerned parents are all interested in the potential effects of communication among family members. Specifically, governmental agencies and religious groups frequently form theories that allow them to predict that traditional nuclear families produce different outcomes than do single-parent homes in terms of better academic performance and less delinquency among the children in those homes (e.g., McLanahan & Sandefur, 1994). Alternatively, parents with teenagers may be interested in predicting the best form of communicating with their teens about risky sexual behavior and the potential outcomes associated with it. They might want to know, for instance, that parent-child closeness is associated with reduced adolescent pregnancy risk through teens remaining sexually abstinent, postponing intercourse, having fewer sexual partners, and using contraception more consistently (e.g., Miller, Benson, & Galbraith, 2001). Regardless of *why* these outcomes are occurring, simply knowing that closeness predicts these outcomes is good enough to encourage mothers and fathers to try to be closer to their adolescent children. However, theories can offer us much more than simply description and prediction.

Most important, theories can provide **explanations** for phenomenon (Littlejohn & Foss, 2005). In this way, theories can help us understand the "why?" question. In other words, theories can not only help us differentiate among various family forms and their predicted outcomes but can also help us understand *why* these differences exist. In other words, knowing that nuclear families are traditionally from higher-income and lower-risk situations can help explain why they provide kids with the stability and guidance necessary to perform well in school and perform socially acceptable behaviors. In addition, theories can help us understand why parents who are closer to their kids are probably more likely to talk to them about more "risky" topics such as safe sex and therefore provide much-needed information to help their children choose to perform less risky sexual behaviors (*explanation*). The outcomes associated with those risky behaviors (e.g., pregnancy, sexually transmitted diseases) are therefore less likely to accrue (*prediction*). As you can see, theories that provide explanations are stronger than theories that only predict in that they also provide predictions for outcomes. Therefore, understanding the *why* necessarily informs the *how*. Closeness with parents leading to more talk about sexually risky behavior and its consequence is the why, and less negative sexual outcomes is the how (i.e., more talk leads to less negative sexual outcomes).

Finally, theories can help us **control** the outcomes in question (Littlejohn & Foss, 2005). Knowing that kids who are closer to their parents are less likely to engage in risky sexual behavior, for instance, allows us to make policy recommendations. Theories allow us to draw socially meaningful implications with the strength to explain why. To be more specific, if parents are encouraged to be closer to their teens and, further, encouraged to talk more openly with their kids about sex and its potential risks, then it is possible that sexually risky outcomes among adolescents can be diminished. We see, then, that strong theories can *describe, predict, explain,* and *control* phenomena and the outcomes associated with them. Instead of providing esoteric and abstract conceptualizations with very little real-world meaning, theories can provide us with the very vehicles that make it possible to describe, predict, explain, and control socially meaningful outcomes with regard to families and the communication that occurs within them.

Family Communication Theories

Now that we understand why it is that we actually like theories (for their ability to help us describe, predict, explain, and control family communication), let's review three theories that you should find particularly useful in understanding your own families of origin. Although many additional theories will be introduced throughout this text, these three theories are highlighted in a separate chapter because of their enduring ability to describe, explain, and predict communication behavior within families across a wide variety of situations and forms. **Roles theory** helps us understand why various members of our family behave and communicate in the ways they do. Roles theory argues that you can predict a role holder's behavior by the roles he or she holds. Mothers are most likely to be the *nurturers*, for instance, whereas fathers are most likely to be the *resource providers*. These roles provide powerful prescriptions for behavior and expectations for how those behaviors should be carried out. **Family systems theory** allows us to understand the ways in which families operate not as individuals but as members of a collective group known as a family. This perspective assumes that the whole of the family is greater than the sum of the parts and that you can never fully understand a family and its communication by attempting to understand its individual constituents. Finally, **rules theory** helps us understand the complex nature of communication rules that occur within families. For instance, families often contain unwritten rules for who talks to whom about what. Specifically, it may be OK to talk to your big sister about the sensual nature of the encounter you had with your girlfriend or boyfriend last night, but there may be strict sanctions if the same conversation were carried out with your mother or father.

Roles Theory

Roles theory assumes that we all hold a variety of roles and that those roles dictate the behavior we will use to carry out those roles on the stage of life. Thus, mothers are simply playing at being moms, and fathers are similarly acting out the role of dads. To flesh this out a bit more, it would behoove us to visit Goffman's (1959) earliest delineation of roles (drama) theory. In it, he argues that there is no such thing as a stable "self" but that we are all really a composite of all the various roles we hold. While self is a topic worthy of its own course, the concepts most relevant to our discussion of families include *roles, role expectations, performances, front-stage behavior, back-stage behavior,* and *wings.* **Roles** can be thought of as the various positions we hold in relation to others. We can be mothers, fathers, daughters, boyfriends and girlfriends, wives, husbands, educators, friends, students, and so on. You get the picture. Each role has its own set of expectations associated with it as well as its own set of behaviors that best fulfill its function. **Role expectations** include anticipated behaviors associated with a particular role. Mothers, for instance, are expected to be available and devoted to their children. This would explain the intensely negative reactions that society has to substance-abusing mothers or mothers who abuse, neglect, or abandon their children. These behaviors are simply not part of the expectation of motherhood and in fact run counter to notions of what "good mothers" *should* do. In addition, "fathers should earn an income" is another example of a powerful role expectation. Stay-at-home dads often become the brunt of jokes regarding slothfulness, laziness, and the like—this at a time when the value of stay-at-home mothers' jobs is estimated at $131,471 per year (O'Brien, 2002). Nonetheless, violations of expectations for role behavior can have very powerful evaluations associated with them.

Performances include all behaviors associated with a particular role. Good daughters should obey their mothers, clean their rooms, never swear (in front of their mothers!), be respectful, and so on. Sisters should be loyal. Fathers should be strong, rational, industrious, and hard working. I'm confident that if pressed, you could delineate a whole set of behaviors associated with any familial role. According to Goffman (1959), these performances are carried out on a stage. The **front stage** is where you perform your role. For instance, mothers are expected to perform their role as "mother" in the home environment and whenever they are in the presence of their children. However, you would not expect this same woman to perform her role of mother in the boardroom with her colleagues. Her colleagues would find this highly offensive indeed because this situation would call for front-stage behavior as "professional/colleague/coworker." This same situation could be considered back stage for the mother role because the woman may feel freer to swear, be less likely to cook, and be less vigilant about the safety of her environment than she would be at home (she might not put safety covers over her office electrical outlets, for instance). In other words, the **back stage** is anywhere where you do not feel the pressure to perform one of your primary roles. You can thus "let down" on the behaviors that were important in the other role. Of course, according to Goffman, you are probably performing some other role there because we are either always performing when we are in the presence of others or carrying around a "generalized other" for whom one performs at all times. In other words, Goffman would argue that a woman who highly identifies with her mothering role will always behave in ways that are consistent with the performance of that role (almost as if her child could always see her).

Finally, if you have ever been on a stage, you will be aware that a stage has wings behind the curtains and off to the sides where actors prepare for their roles. Similarly then, Goffman (1959) argues that **wings** are those areas where mothers, fathers, sisters, brothers, and so on prepare for their roles. When I choose my clothing (costume), I'll choose apparel that is appropriate for my role. This makes some sense because I certainly did not wear silk blouses at home for my daughter to spit up on when she was an infant, and similarly, I don't wear my "painting" jeans around the office. In addition, we may have several **performance experts** in the wings who help us prepare for our roles. Not unlike other mothers I know, I frequently called good ol' big sis to get the scoop on the best techniques for getting my daughter to sleep on a schedule, which medicines work best on high fevers in the middle of the night, and when I could go back to work without upsetting the attachment balance. Like most performance experts, she was also not given any credit as I carried out my role, pretending that I had had the "intuitive mother wisdom" all along.

Family Roles

Family roles are important to the extent that they dictate behavior and affect the communication associated with those roles. Families are a high-task situation in that many jobs must be performed for groups to function as families. Roles within the family help us coordinate task completion. In my own family, for instance, I am in charge of educational development. Anything that comes under the heading "education" falls to me. When Huw (my oldest stepson) began the process of applying to college, I was well aware that I would be the one in charge of guiding him through this task. The boys' biological mother, however, is an emergency room nurse. She is therefore responsible for the maintenance of physical health, and all doctors' appointments and the like fall to her. When Huw dropped the motorcycle, badly scraping his knee, it was his mother who came over to our house to clean the wound with a toothbrush (no kidding!). As this illustration shows, roles help us organize who does what in families.

Nurturing Roles

Nurturing roles include many different subroles and accompanying tasks. Nurturing basically includes the provision of care, warmth, and an environment capable of encouraging the growth and development of family members. This can include the **provider,** who supplies the resources required to allow for the types of activities necessary to encourage growth and development. Nurturing roles also include a **nurturer** who provides care in all its various forms (e.g., feeding, bathing, cuddling, communicating). Overlapping with these roles is the **developer,** or the person who is in charge of ensuring growth and development as a human across physical, social, emotional, and intellectual realms. Finally, included in the nurturing roles is the **health care provider,** or the person who generally maintains family members' health through arranging for doctors' visits, applying bandages, dispensing medicine, and the like.

Provider(s). The family member in charge of provision of resources supplies the money, food, clothes, and other durable items that maintain the household. Historically, fathers' economic contributions to development have been more heavily valued than their contributions to child care and housework (Griswold, 1993). Although the changes in society cited earlier may make it seem less likely now than in the past, this still appears to be the case in the majority of households. In fact, reviews of the extensive literature on economic resources and marriage show consistently that greater economic resources are significantly associated with higher rates of marriage for men (e.g., Xie, Raymo, Goyett, & Thorton, 2003). This is especially the case for measures of earning potential (current earnings, earnings over the next 5 years, future earnings, past earnings, and lifetime earnings). These same measures of earning potential did not predict marriage for women. Furthermore, as women's earnings rise, they become more independent and report a decline in the desire for marriage (Oppenheimer, 1997). Finally, only 23% of women in dual-earner couples earned as much as, or more than, their husbands in 1997 (Brennan, Chait Barnett, & Gareis, 2001). This figure is consistent with a more recent analysis of U.S. Census 2000 data showing that 19% to 30% of wives in dual-career families earn more than their husbands (Winkler, McBride, & Andrews, 2005). However, this trend appears transitory in that only 60% of couples maintain this disparity for more than 3 years. Thus, there still exists a strong societal pressure in our society for the man to be the primary resource provider for the family. So much so that if he is deemed less likely to earn money or the woman makes more money, he is less desirable as a marriage partner.

Regardless of this pressure on the man to be the primary resource provider of the family, we are beginning to see a preponderance of mothers entering the workforce as well. As you may recall from Chapter 2, the number of married-couple families with wives in the labor force has increased from 31% in 1976 to 51% in 2000 (compared with 70% of women without an infant). This figure is even higher for educated women (64%) and black women (66%; Bachu & O'Connell, 2001). Remember also that the percentage of working mothers increases as their children grow, with working mothers with children under 6 increasing to 59% and those with children between 6 and 17 increasing to 74% (U.S. Census Bureau, 2003a). Thus, between half and three quarters of mothers work outside the home.

Certain factors enhance the likelihood that mothers will be resource providers. Mothers cite economic need as the most pressing consideration (Israelson, 1989). However, women who score higher on traditional male characteristics are also more likely to work (Krogh, 1985), whereas women who are traditionally more feminine are more likely to take on more feminine caregiving tasks (Burroughs, Turner, & Turner, 1984). Furthermore, a husband with more pro-feminist views is also more likely to have a wife in the workplace (Biaggio, Mohan, & Baldwin, 1985).

Nurturers. The provision of nurturance includes providing care, support, and warmth (including, but not limited to, child care and household tasks). Similar to resource providers, nurturers seem equally split along gender lines.

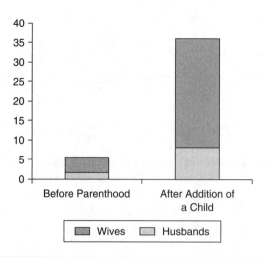

Figure 3.1   Number of Household Chores
SOURCE: Houston and Holmes (2004).

Whereas men are expected to be the primary resource providers, women are expected to be the nurturer-caregivers. This gender division is apparent both before and after children are added to the family. Before parenthood, wives complete 67% of the household chores (3.9 chores a day on average), and husbands complete the remaining 33% of chores (1.9 chores a day on average) (Huston & Vangilisti, 1995; MacDermid, Huston, & McHale, 1990). Following the addition of a child, there is a sixfold increase in the number of family-related activities performed, from 5.8 per day to 36.2 per day (see Figure 3.1). New mothers increase to 5.3 household tasks and 22.7 child care tasks. New fathers, in comparison, increase their household tasks to 2.4 per day while accruing an additional 5.9 child care tasks. Women in dual-earning couples report spending an average of 15 hours a week on household tasks compared with men's 6.8 hours (Stevens, Kiger, & Riley, 2001). As these numbers make obvious, women are completing more traditionally nurturing tasks than are men.

Although this disparity in task load is striking to the observer, women complete up to two thirds of household work before they feel that the division of labor is unfair (Lennon & Rosenfield, 1994). However, women who contribute highly to the family income are more likely to perceive an unequal division of household labor as unfair compared with women who earn less than their husbands (Stevens et al., 2001). Furthermore, the *perception* of relational and psychological shared parenting is more important in predicting marital satisfaction than the actual division of the child care tasks (Ehrenberg, Gearing-Small, Hunter, & Small, 2001). Men, alternatively, feel that the workload is unjustly divided when 36% of the tasks fall on them. Interestingly, men contribute more to the household and perceive greater fairness when both they and their wives perceive their contributions to be more competent (Grote, Naylor, & Clark, 2002).

Consistent with these findings, women who work outside the home still perceive that their primary role is as nurturer in the home (MacDermid et al., 1990), as do their husbands. Both spouses appear to be comfortable with this understanding (McHale & Huston, 1984). Even among women who work 30 hours or more, only 12% thought that men should be equally responsible for chores (Crouter, Perry-Jenkins, Huston, & McHale, 1987). Consistently, wives who became mothers reduce their involvement in work for pay and increase their involvement in household work (MacDermid et al., 1990). Thus, it appears that in at least two thirds of families, both men and women perceive that women should be (and are) the primary providers of nurturance in the family (Gilbert, 1994). One potential explanation for this gender role division is that women's self-esteem may be linked to the role of primary caregiver, particularly when the child is an infant (Josephs, Markus, & Tafarodi, 1992). Lest it be thought that all dual-working couples *must* split tasks along gender lines, Gilbert (1994) found that nearly one third of dual-career couples were "role sharing," in that both spouses were actively involved in household and parenting duties.

Development Expert (physical, social, emotional, and intellectual). Closely linked to the role of nurturer-caregiver is the role of physical, social, emotional, and intellectual development. Obviously, if women perform more of the child care tasks, they will be preparing the food, dressing the child, and so on to ensure the **physical growth and development** of the child. However, it is also obvious that the ability to provide food, clothing, and shelter depends on the resource provider's ability to furnish these necessities. Furthermore, fathers are frequently involved in the physical development of the child in terms of sports achievements and rough-and-tumble play (Huston & Holmes, 2004). More fathers are coaches, push the bike for the first ride, and are outside throwing the ball with their child. Physical development includes both growth and accomplishment. Further consideration of these contributions of parents is provided in Chapter 6 on socializing children.

Social development includes becoming a socioemotionally competent communicator. Although both parents contribute to this process through their many modeled interactions with their children, many children rely on their mothers for information about how to interact socially. Mothers of 3- to 5-year-olds were found to have a direct effect on their children's social competence through their coaching and their communication style with their children (Mize & Petit, 1997). Linking physical and social development, most adolescents acquire information regarding sex from their mothers, and their mothers are more effective at reducing risky sexual behavior and the outcomes associated with them (Jaccard, Dittus, & Gordon, 2000). Thus, mothers may be highly influential in socializing social competence.

Consistently, mothers may be more instrumental in encouraging **emotional development** as well; mothers have been known to encourage the expression of "strong emotions" (anger, frustration, pride) by their sons compared with the weaker emotions (sadness, fear) (e.g., Mulac, Studley, Wiemann, & Bradac, 1987; Shields, 1987). Finally, mothers are highly instrumental in encouraging **intellectual development.** In fact, parents seem to have almost intuitive abilities to stimulate their children's learning (Papousek, Papousek, & Haekel, 1987), and most caregiver behaviors provide teaching to their infants (Van Egeren & Barratt, 2004). Mothers are particularly adept at stimulating their infants; most frame their communication to infants as "motherese," or specialized speech addressed to infants (Yingling, 1995). Given that mothers most often adapt their work schedules to accommodate the needs of the children (Chait Barnett, Gareis, Boone James, & Steele, 2003), it is highly likely that mothers also provide the most focus with regard to academic achievements as they assist with homework and in other ways provide the groundwork for intellectual growth (e.g., reading to the child and otherwise communicating with the child in ways that encourage intellectual maturation; Laakso, Poikkeus, Eklund, & Lyytenin, 2004).

Health Care Provider. Health care provision is the last role that falls under nurturance. Not surprisingly, because women are doing a majority of the child care tasks, they are frequently relied on to nurse their babies through illnesses; arrange for doctors, dentists, and eye exams; and generally attempt to maintain the health of their offspring. It is frequently the case that they nurse their spouses as well. In addition, extended families can be included here in that children are now nursing their elderly parents in the home, and more positive outcomes are expected in mother-daughter than mother-son relationships (Cicirelli, 2003). Furthermore, more mothers are portrayed as fulfilling the caregiving role in magazine depictions, and these magazines (mostly aimed at mothers) include child's health issues as a major topic (Francis-Connolly, 2003). Only mothers were the focus of a research project examining the beliefs of mothers regarding potential injuries to their preschool children (Weatherman, 2003). It is fair to assume from this research that more women are expected to fulfill health care roles in the family.

Resource provision and nurturing roles across family forms. Based on this review of findings, it appears that both men and women play the resource provision and nurturing (nurturing, development, health care) roles now. Regardless of this verifiable fact, it still appears to be the case that the man is expected to be the *primary resource provider,* based on the fact that earning potential is a consistent predictor of marriage for men, and the woman is expected to be the *primary nurturer,* based on the fact that she will cut back on outside work-related activities and ungrudgingly complete a greater share of the household and child-rearing responsibilities. This proves especially problematic for single mothers raising children (84% of all single-parent homes), because the mother head of household is often expected to be the resource provider *and* the nurturer. This may account for the fact that up to one third of mother-headed households live below the poverty line (Connecticut Health Policy Project, 2003). Single mothers struggle to fulfill both the resource provision and nurturer roles simultaneously. As we have seen above, most women place greater role salience on their nurturing mother role and spend less time at work or leave work altogether when their children are small. Thus, single mothers experience a great deal of role strain as they attempt to balance out resource provision and nurturing roles. This strain should play itself out in communication in the family such that the mother who must work to support her children has less time to spend communicating in nurturing ways with her children (e.g., less time to help with homework, to have a leisurely cuddle in the morning before school, to chat over dinner) and may experience more role strain and stress, which may also play itself out in the *quality* of the communication when communication does occur.

Such role strain should also be apparent for single fathers, although there appear to be fewer single fathers living below the poverty line, which indicates that they may prefer their resource provision role over their nurturing role (as society dictates and as indicated by the research indicating that women do more of the child care tasks). Little research exists regarding the provision of resources or nurturing in the blended home, but the research reviewed in Chapter 2 indicating that stepmothers are more involved in the parenting role than are stepfathers indicates that the traditional roles of male resource provider and female nurturer continue to prevail in the blended home. Very little research exists regarding the breakdown of resource provider and nurturer roles in cohabiting, married with no children, gay, and gay couples with children families. It can still be expected, however, that one person is *primarily* responsible for each role within each household. For example, in the gay couple who adopted children in Florida (the Rosie O'Donnell example from Chapter 2), one of the partners quit his nursing job to stay home full-time with the children while the other partner went out to work. It should therefore be expected that the roles of resource provision and nurturers are in evidence in families regardless of their form. These roles, in turn, allow us to predict that the nurturer in these families communicates in more nurturing ways, while the resource provider may be the more distant communicator who is allowed more freedom to influence through his or her communication when it occurs.

Controlling Roles

Although providing a nurturing environment is essential for encouraging growth in the family, it is not the only element to ensure development. Control, or limiting behavioral options of other family members, is also central to ensuring goal attainment within the family. Certain members of the family will be more instrumental in providing guidelines and limitations for family members' behaviors. Controlling roles can be enacted through (a) **behavior control,** or setting guidelines and disciplining; (b) **decision making,** or choosing among options available to the family; (c) **boundary maintenance,** or deciding who is in or out of one's family circle; and (d) **financial-organization,** or managing the funds available to the family.

Behavior Control. As soon as children became active, it is imperative to set limits and provide guidance through discipline. The most striking illustration is the gate the mother erects to control access to unsafe areas of the house. Soon after a child is able to reason, however, rules for conduct are established and children are expected to behave within those (Baumrind, 1996). Although both parents can be active in the process of behavior control, usually one parent is the primary rule enforcer. Many children report that their father enforced the rules, but it was usually the mothers who made the rules and carried them out on a day-to-day basis. This makes sense in terms of the probability that the mother is in the home more often and provides the nurturing role, whereas the father is more often out of the home providing the resources to run the home. While the literature does not make clear who disciplines more, the preponderance of studies on discipline focus on mothers as the key socializing agent for children. However, we do know that fathers enact more stringent attempts at control; they are more likely to respond to children's noncompliance with punishment, and children, in turn, are more likely to obey their fathers (Grusec & Lytton, 1988). Consistently, children are more likely to obey their mothers in the presence of their fathers (Lytton, 1980). Mothers, alternatively, appear to use verbal admonishments, criticisms, and threats (Hetherington, Cox, & Cox, 1978). In a more authoritative vein, mothers may also attempt to reason with the child (Lytton, 1980). So although mothers may be the primary disciplinarians in the home, fathers may be more likely to use stronger threats of punishment.

Decision-Making, Family Boundary Maintenance, and Financial Organization. Similarly, usually one person is in charge of the decision making for the family. This person chooses among behavioral options for the family. These decisions can be as large as deciding where the annual vacation is going to be to as small as where the family buys most of its clothing. Regardless, this person carries a lot of power, in that his or her decisions affect the behavior and outcomes for the entire family. It is possible that mothers frequently carry out this role because of their greater involvement in house maintenance, but it is also possible that the father is the decision maker because of his role as resource provider. A certain amount of status and power is frequently accorded this role.

Family boundary maintenance. One further method of limiting behavioral options is through family boundary maintenance. Parents frequently attempt to control their child's environment to ensure what they deem to be the child's best behavior. Most of us remember that one friend who was not allowed to visit or with whom we were not allowed to associate. In this way, our parents decide who is and who is not acceptable for interacting with their children. The belief here is that children influence one another through their behavior. Family members are also limited in their interactions with other extended family members as well. Some children grow up without ever knowing their cousins, and sometimes their grandparents, because of existing family feuds. Perhaps not even in their conscious awareness, they are being limited to who is considered within or outside the family boundary. As a rather dramatic example, I grew up next to my uncle and aunt, but in a community of property lines and no fences, a fence was erected between our properties following a family feud concerning my grandparents' inheritance. I was allowed to play with Hope and Tom (my cousins), but it was clear that our parents would not speak. Such limitations are those of family boundary maintenance.

Tammy Afifi and Paul Schrodt (2003) argue that such family boundary maintenance may be especially relevant within families that include divorce. Parents move out, locks are often changed, and the exiting parent is often not permitted in the house, or when he or she is, they must obey new rules of entry such as knocking before coming in. As we have seen in Chapter 1, many government and social science agencies define families as "sharing a household." While problematic definitionally, this household includes geographic and material boundaries that distinguish who is in, and who is out, of one's family. Thus, the "leaving parent" or spouse may feel that he or she is no longer a part of the family because of being outside the boundary. This may become even more complicated when new spouses and stepparents and sometimes their children enter the family household and now nonbiologically related individuals are living together as one family. Physical boundaries are especially salient in divorced and stepfamilies.

Postdivorce and stepfamily situations also provide fertile ground for conflict over *rules/roles* and *privacy* boundaries (Afifi & Schrodt, 2003). Stepfamilies offer a potentially turbulent environment as children struggle with too many holders of the *same* role. The common refrain "you're not my mom/dad!" shouted at the top of one's lungs is a perfect example of a child telling a stepparent that he or she has overstepped the boundaries in trying to parent the child. In essence, the child is saying, "That's my mom's job; you are not my mom. My mom is part of my family and you are NOT." Consistently, postdivorce families and stepfamilies are rife with conflicts over privacy issues. Often, children protect the privacy of the parents in one household as a type of loyalty. I'll never forget the time Huw (my oldest stepson) said, "I know . . ." and both my husband and I looked at him expectantly, and he said ". . . *stuff.*" Eventually we learned that his mom and stepdad were soon to be married and surmised that this was the "stuff." He felt the strong need to protect the privacy of his mom even though the two families work hard together to have a conflict-free zone for the children's sake. Two years later, the boys maintained the privacy of their mom's pregnancy as well. Thus, children in stepfamilies and binuclear families have strong drives to protect the privacy, roles/rules, and physical boundaries across the families.

Financial organization. Finally, the financial organizer can be seen through the dictum, "He who holds the gold, rules." The person who manages the finances usually has a greater say in how finances are distributed and dictates how much is spent on which household or personal items. Some families manage to have two financial managers, but it is a rare couple that agrees on how to run the finances. Many couples find it easier to have one member in charge of this daunting task; disagreements over finances are always at the top of the list in terms of most frequent arguments (Newton & Burgoon, 1990). Therefore, usually one member of the household is responsible for organizing the finances.

The importance of the financial organizer is highlighted by the difference between dual-worker and dual-career couples. Whereas dual-career couples receive a salary (e.g., teachers, doctors, lawyers), dual-worker couples receive only an hourly wage. This produces strikingly different financial scenarios. Financial organizing is much more stressful for dual-worker couples who cannot expect exponential increases in salary at times that coincide with important life changes (e.g., adding a child, having a child start school or college). The financial organizer in the dual-worker couple has a greater challenge trying to manage the day-to-day finances while also planning for the future. The dual-worker couple is also more affected by financial stress in that they often cannot afford assistance with housework and child care that would allow them the luxury of more time to spend with their children. In this way, finances and the person who organizes them can have a profound effect on the quality of the communication in the family.

Organizing the finances can be particularly challenging in divorced families, where long, protracted legal battles can dictate the amount of finances devoted to each household. This can be particularly stressful in the step- or binuclear family because resources are now being devoted to biological and nonbiological children simultaneously. Communicationally, this can result in high levels of destructive conflict that may also include the children; parents have been known to ask children to ask the nonresidential parent for the child support. These types of loyalty tests can put much strain on relations between the children and both of their parents.

Dealing With Role Strain: Dual-Worker
and Dual-Career Families and Gender Roles

SOURCE: *Close To Home* © John McPherson. Reprinted with permission of Universal Press Syndicate. All rights reserved.

As we have seen previously, the roles of resource provider and nurturer are often highly gender biased, with the male expected to contribute most heavily to the economic side of the family and the female expected to contribute most heavily to the child care and household maintenance side of the family. Therefore, it is confusing and stressful for both members of the family dyad when the male and the female each contribute to the economic side of the family. However, this is often the case; 78% of workers are married to employed spouses, and in three quarters of these couples, spouses who are both employed full-time (Bond, Galinsky, & Swanberg, 1998). Some families adapt to this stressful situation by having the females adopt family-friendly jobs that allow them to work less and spend more time in the home (a *career-altering strategy*; Chait Barnett et al., 2003). This allows the woman the benefit of having roles that are not defined by the family and still having her family roles primarily dictate her sense of self. Others *work at home*, which blurs work and home boundaries and creates a stressful situation of its own. Some adopt a *family-altering strategy* of starting a family later (Helms-Erikson, 2001) or having fewer children (Chait Barnett et al.,

2003). Still others make the full commitment to work and pay the consequences of having less time and attention to devote to child care and household tasks. Regardless of the strategies adopted, maintaining both resource-providing and nurturing roles can have consequences in terms of interrole conflict and role strain.

A few concepts from roles theory are worth visiting here. The concepts of interrole conflict and role strain are particularly relevant to dual-worker (i.e., both workers are compensated hourly) or dual-career (i.e., both workers are paid a salary) heads of households (the most typical family form; Hayghe, 1990). **Interrole conflict** occurs whenever the performance of one role interferes with the performance of another role. Working mothers are well aware of interrole conflict because the expected behaviors associated with their jobs often prevent them from performing those expected behaviors associated with performance of the mother role. Being at the office, for instance, contradicts the need to be at home that many new mothers feel. Even now that my daughter is 2, I still feel the pressure to go into the house from the guest house where I'm working on this book where my nanny is attending to my daughter's nap instead of me. In terms of communication, constant attention to the whereabouts of an active toddler often takes away from the ability to focus singular attention on one's spouse who has a very important story to tell at the end of his or her stressful day. Both examples illustrate how behaviors associated with one role's performance can detract from the performance of another role held by the same role holder.

Figure 3.2   Time constraints are the biggest drawback that children of dual-career parents note, as exemplified by these parents hurrying to get themselves to work after getting the children off to school.

Although much literature emphasizes the fact that women have more interrole conflict than men (e.g., Almquist & Angrist, 1993; Arnold, 1993; Novack & Novack, 1996), evidence exists affirming that men are reporting that work and home are equal in terms of importance ("Study Finds," 2004). Furthermore, men report similar levels of work-home conflict as do women (Bond et al., 1998) and are now as likely as women to have made career sacrifices in favor of family responsibilities (Moen, 1999; Twenge, 1997). Interrole conflict is a tangible issue for both men and women in dual-career situations.

Work relationships can also interfere with marital relationships and cause interrole conflict in that way. This pattern has been explained by the work-family spillover model, which postulates that a marital partner's stress, emotions, or experiences at work or home spill over into the other domain (Larson & Almeida, 1999). Three processes by which work has been identified to interfere with home life include time interference, energy interference, and psychological interference (Small & Riley, 1990). *Time interference* represents time at work diminishing time at home. *Energy interference* refers to fatigue associated with work that diminishes the energy the spouse has to devote to the home and the spousal relationship. *Psychological interference* refers to absorption with work concerns that takes away from the mental energy available for the home relationship. In an attempt to study this model, Doumas, Margolin, and John (2003) found that in general, spouses reported more positive marital interactions on days when they worked less, were more energetic, ate more, and relaxed more. They also found that wives were more reactive to their husbands' work stress than vice versa. It is likely that this work-family spillover stress exists in all families that include dual earners.

Role strain typically occurs when one either feels uncomfortable with one's role or does not entirely know how to enact the behaviors associated with one's roles. This can result in a less than optimum performance associated with that role. New spouses and new parents often struggle to understand the complexities of all they are expected to accomplish under the role of wife/husband or mother/father. Consistently, new stepparents are especially prone to this role strain as they struggle to adapt to the role of stepparent. Although "stepparent" already implies that they are one step away from being a real parent, they are now trying to enact behaviors as if they *are* a parent. The enactment of communication and behaviors associated with this role is particularly difficult. Not only does the new stepparent not "feel" like a parent yet, but the children may actively resist this role as they try to maintain the previously established boundary of their old family (as discussed under boundary maintenance roles). As noted previously, self-perceived competency in one's role as father enhanced the degree of involvement fathers had with their children (Huston & Vangilisti, 1995). Role strain can be associated with diminished competencies and time devoted to that role. In other words, if parents and stepparents don't perceive themselves as competent in those roles, they are less likely to *communicate and behave* in ways that are consistent with that role.

One thing that can help alleviate these pressures is the relationship of role holders to other role holders. This may help explain why two-parent homes provide better outcomes for children. For instance, spouses who hold **complementary roles** feel less pressure to perform behaviors associated with potentially competing roles. Complementary role holders generally perform opposing behaviors that help facilitate the opposite role. More traditional nuclear families that have the woman as the primary nurturer for the children and the man as the primary resource provider will feel less interrole conflict, for instance, because they each perform behaviors that do not detract from, but rather add to, the performance of the other role. Nurturer and resource provider roles complement each other in that both members have clear guidelines for their behavior and know they can rely on the other for the fulfillment of the necessary opposing task. Nurturers can stay at home and take care of their children because the other parent is out earning the money to support the family. Resource providers can be absent from the home for the better part of the work week because they know that their partner is at home looking after the children. Both roles are necessary but are being fulfilled by a different role holder, and thus, the behaviors of the various roles do not contradict each other within the same person. In support of the greater ease of this complementary role relationship, the majority of couples support the view that the woman should be the nurturer and the husband should be the primary provider (MacDermid et al., 1990). A lack of complementary role holder can be at the heart of much role strain for single-parent head of families.

Reciprocal role holders may find a similar balance to complementary role holders in that reciprocal role holders alternate opposing tasks so that each is performing only one role at a time. A school teacher who works 9 months a year (resource provider) and has a stay-at-home spouse (nurturer) who then goes out to his or her house-painting job for the other 3 months (resource provider) while the school teacher stays at home (nurturer) is a great example of a family with reciprocal role holders. Both partners perform nurturing and resource provision, but while they are performing their role, the other partner performs the opposing task. Thus, no two partners are resource providers and nurturers simultaneously.

Families that find themselves in the increasingly common dual-worker or dual-career situation more typically assume **symmetrical roles**. When two members of the same family perform the same role, these roles are said to be symmetrical. When both parents are resource providers, they are symmetrical role holders. Generally, both members feel more pressure to also be symmetrical role holders with regard to nurturing, but it is unlikely that both will be truly symmetrical in this sense. Although men perform more household duties when their spouse works (Perry-Jenkins, Pierce, & Goldberg, 2004), it is still likely that women perform far more behaviors associated with child care and housework (Huston & Holmes, 2004). Huston and Holmes report that working mothers were employed an average of 30 hours a week while performing 26 household and child care tasks, whereas their husbands worked 34-hour weeks and performed about 5 household and child care tasks. Although both family members share resource provision, they do not share equally the nurturing responsibilities within the household. It is worthwhile remembering, however, that the *perception* of relational and psychological shared parenting is more important in predicting marital satisfaction than is the actual division of the child care tasks (Ehrenberg et al., 2001).

Finally, the effects of dual-career couples are not limited to interrole conflict and role strain. There are other potential effects for wives, husbands, and children as well. Working wives are physically and psychologically healthier (Holland Benin & Edwards, 1990), more physically active (Kessler & McRae, 1982), have higher self-esteem, and feel less social isolation (Burke & Weir, 1976). They also feel less economically dependent on their husbands and are less likely to garner their identities from their husbands and children. Furthermore, it has been found that wives who earn more than their husbands may potentially threaten their husbands' self-esteem (Menaghan, 1982). On the other hand, children from dual-earner homes rate their families as high in family strength, supportiveness, and concern (Greenstein, 1990), as well as in lessons of versatility and flexibility (Ford, 1983). Children's reports about the situation are not entirely rosy, however; they also note that that their families had many time constraints (Knaub, 1986). Thus, dual-earner families have unique challenges and strengths compared with single-earner families. It is likely that the effects of dual-earner households are consistent across nuclear, step- and binuclear families and families with gay heads of household.

Family Systems Theory

Whereas roles theory provides us with an individual-level explanation for why family members behave the way they do, family systems theory stresses that the whole of the family is more important relative to the individual contributions each family member provides. Family systems theory is derived from a more general systems theory that argues that systems (of which families are one example) can be understood only in their entirety. In this way, the concepts of wholeness, interdependence, and homeostasis are all central to understanding the mechanisms of family systems theory. The systems theory concept of **wholeness** emphasizes that "the sum of the whole is greater than the individual parts." Thus, families can be understood not through individual members' experiences (which can vary widely from one another—think "beloved sister" and "black sheep" here) but, rather, through the unique dynamics and overall climate achieved in a family; that is, families should be measured at the system level (e.g., size, rigidity, climate) rather than at the individual family level (e.g., perceptions of satisfaction, emotional experiences). A family systems theorist would argue that one can never fully know the inside mechanisms of a family unless one is fully enmeshed in that system.

The system's theory concept of **interdependence** stresses the intricate and necessary interrelationships of family members. Interdependence stresses that family members rely on one another to promote the functioning of the family. Borrowing from the concepts of roles theory, this becomes evident in two-parent households, where one parent is the resource provider and the other is the nurturer-caregiver. Both functions *must* be achieved for the family to function, so both parents rely on one another, and the children rely on both of the parents. In addition, the parents rely on the children to define their roles as caregiver and provider. In other words, they could not function as nurturers or providers without the children in the complementary roles.

The concept of homeostasis (balance) stresses the nature of families as goal-attaining systems. The primary assumption here is that families have *goals* (e.g., well-raised children, social and emotional well-being, family satisfaction) and set about to attain them. The concept of **homeostasis** emphasizes the balance that families attempt to achieve as they set about attaining these goals. The 15-year-old daughter who becomes pregnant and runs off to Las Vegas to marry the tattooed plumber who fixed the family bathroom last summer sets the family off balance in terms of attaining the educational goals that they perceive will provide their family members with greater physical and emotional well-being. Thus, family members will set about attempting to regain balance within the family system. In a situation where regaining balance is more attainable, a father may restrict a son who snuck out in the middle of the night and took the family car for a joy ride that ended in a police car in order to attempt to regain control over the son's future well-being. Discipline may be seen as an attempt to regain balance within the family and move individual family members toward attainment of socioemotional competence. Most important from a family communication standpoint, Broderick (1993) articulates several characteristics of a social system that make families unique compared with other nonsocial systems. First, families use *communication,* which functions to connect the self-aware, self-directed, independent identities within the families. Second, families must use *psychopolitical negotiation* to achieve joint decisions by members with individual needs and independent wills. Thus, families require a far more elaborate executive mechanism than is found in other types of systems. Third, *attributions* regarding families must be made at the social systems level. In other words, attributions about a system are different (e.g., size, rigidity, development) from those of individuals (e.g., marital satisfaction). Fourth, families use *social distance regulation* as they approach and avoid members within the family and across family boundaries.

Families as Self-Regulatory Goal-Attaining Systems

Broderick (1993) further outlines family systems theory with an emphasis on explaining goal attainment in the family through self-regulatory attempts. Family systems theory assumes that families seek goals and set about trying to attain them. Goals can be higher order, such as the health and well-being of family members, or lower order, such as having a nice home, taking a family vacation each year, or attaining good educations for the children. Thus, families set goals and self-regulate the family in pursuit of those goals. According to Broderick, several principles characterize families as goal-seeking systems: (a) families pursue goals, (b) families select goals and mobilize support, (c) someone must execute the movement toward these goals, and (d) progress must be monitored and corrections made for deviations from the goal destination. An illustration will make this more obvious. Consider my friend Candace's extended family. The Medefind family has the higher-order goal of health and well-being of all family members. To achieve this higher order-goal, the lower-order goal of family gatherings is encouraged. Traditionally, the adult daughters are mobilized to organize the events, but ultimately the eldest Mrs. Medefind executes the events through telephone calls and so on. In addition, all family members are relied on to provide the refreshments. My good friend, Candace, aware that the rule for such events was to bring a moderate portion of food with only sufficient amounts to divvy this food up equally among partygoers, made numerous attempts to get all family members to provide larger amounts of food so that the children were not limited to one cookie each, for example. This, however, was not seen as being in line with the lower-order goal of family gatherings, and the eldest Mrs. Medefind swooped in to correct this deviation from the goal. She mobilized both her eldest daughter and her eldest daughter-in-law to telephone this errant daughter-in-law (Candace) to attempt to get her back in line with the group by providing only the minimum amount of food required and accepting that the others would as well. Through this example, we can see the selected goal (family events with minimum amounts of food), the mobilization of support (the daughters organizing the events), the execution of the movement toward the goal (Mrs. Medefind), the monitoring of the progress toward the goal (Mrs. Medefind), and corrections for deviations from the goal (Mrs. Medefind via the eldest daughters). Even through mundane family examples such as this, family systems principles of goal attainment and self-regulation can be observed.

Broderick (1993) delineates six models regarding goal attainment within the family. These include the *normative model*, the *developmental task model*, the *psychopolitical model*, the *opportunity matrix model*, the *reflexive spiral model*, and the *unified transcybernetic model*. All these models enhance our understanding of how families go about the business of setting goals and self-regulating in the attainment of them. These models should generalize across various family forms and should thus be applicable to cohabiting couples, married couples with no children, gay couples and families, nuclear families, single-parent families, blended or binuclear families, and extended families.

The Normative Model. The normative model assumes that the mechanism of self-regulation within the family is the social norm that operates on three levels: (a) socialization/induction (*guilt*), (b) induction of social sanctions (*shame*), and (c) formal penalties (*fear*). Thus, family members are induced to behave in line with their family's goals because of norms of society inculcated in the individual, because of the results of deviations from the norm, and through coercion. Family members submit to the goals of the group because they will feel guilty if they don't, they will be shamed if they don't, or they will be punished if they don't. For example, a daughter can engage in less risky sexual behavior than she desires (to maintain the family goal of healthy well-educated family members) either through guilt (she'll feel miserable if she is riskier), shame (her parents make her feel miserable when they catch her in compromising positions with what's-his-name), or fear (she's afraid she'll get caught and won't be able to see her boyfriend for a year). Therefore, according to the normative model, the primary motivator for acting in line with family goals is following the norm.

The Developmental Task Model. Broderick (1993) asserts that norms are not the only mechanisms regulating family members' behavior but that developmental issues also come into play. According to the developmental task model, family goals grow out of the family's adjustments to the interaction of three forces: (a) evolving individual developmental needs of family members, (b) shifting normative prescriptions as families progress from one life cycle stage to another, and (c) changing challenges imposed by changing family structure and situations. Therefore, goal-directed behaviors change over time in families as individual members develop and as the developmental stage of the family changes. For example, individual family members may be influenced by the developmental stage they are experiencing. My husband, for instance, says that the process of raising a child at this stage of life (he's 47) is much different from the first time around when he was 29. At that point in his life, he felt much more pressure to be the resource provider than he does at this stage when his career is well developed and he knows he can count on his salary to continue to increase at critical junctures in our sons'/stepsons' and daughter's lives. Therefore, he spends more time in the nurturing role with our daughter than he was able to do early on with my stepsons because he doesn't have to expend so much time and effort worrying about being the primary resource provider. His individual-level developmental needs affect the overall lower-order goal of spending more leisure time together.

Furthermore, the developmental or life stage of the family also affects the goals that are operating at any given time. Couples with no children right after marriage have goals to maintain a positive living environment, but that goal may become much more important after they learn they are about to become parents. Again, resource provision may become more salient in that the father in particular may feel more pressure to earn more money to provide the type of shelter necessary for raising little "Sara." Money that previously would have been funneled into fun leisure time activities will now be spent on new houses or refurbishing rooms to prepare them for baby.

Alternatively, so-called empty nesters may sell their current abode (much to the consternation of their adult children) because they don't need the space they once had. Life stage of the family can similarly affect the goals a family enacts or emphasizes at any current time. The developmental task model focuses on the influences of individual-level and family life stage developmental issues and how they influence goal-seeking and attainment in the family.

The Psychopolitical Model. The psychopolitical model's primary difference from the normative and developmental task models is that it assumes that individuals within the same family may share the same overarching family goals, but their individual wills and desires are frequently a source of conflict and differences about the best ways to *achieve* those goals. This model recognizes the unique contributions of individual family members in that it assumes that (a) family members have quite independent needs, opinions, and agendas; (b) consensus can never be taken for granted and may be achieved only through conscious, purposeful negotiation among family members; (c) individual agendas, priorities, strategies, judgments, and political resources are the central factors involved in determining outcomes within the family; and (d) norms of the larger society (as well as constraints imposed by the family's present situation) enter the process only as they might be reflected in the individual member's priorities (Broderick, 1993).

Anyone who has ever lived in a family and tried to negotiate a family vacation can appreciate this model. Basically, families can have goals and the means to attain them and still find their individual members at great odds with one another regarding the methods with which to achieve these goals. In other words, a family and its constituents can all desire the emotional. well-being of its members and can see the benefit of achieving this goal through a family vacation. Discussions surrounding the venue for this vacation, however, can become quite heated and may seem to actually detract from emotional well-being in that one member may be very angry with the location, activities, or length of the family vacation. This again points toward the developmental task model, as well; my oldest stepson, for example, was very accommodating of family vacations *until* he had a girlfriend. Subsequently, wherever we went didn't matter as much as his accessibility to AIM (AOL instant messaging) and *any* length was too long! You may have experienced similarly heated debates over the age of your first date or the negotiations over your curfew. Parents and children most certainly both want to maintain the well-being of the children in a family, but over the years, they most undoubtedly will have disagreements over the methods that will allow them to achieve it. Adolescent development is necessarily a time when individual wills, agendas, and priorities become central to ensuing family goals. However, competing wills, needs, and political agendas can be operating in individual family members at any time in the family's or individual's development.

The Opportunity Matrix Model. The opportunity matrix model grew out of the observation that family actions are substantially shaped by the configuration of the immediate spatial, temporal, material, and social environment (Broderick, 1993). In other words, it's fine to *want* the best possible health care for your children, but if you don't have the resources, basically, it's not going to happen. Family form may be especially salient here; for example, single-parent households may not have the income or the insurance benefits allowing them the best health care. The underlying principle of the opportunity matrix model is that all human action may be thought of as occurring at the intersection of an intention *and* an opportunity. This opportunity structure is a function of four potential components:

1. *Spatial configuration* (i.e., characteristics of the accessible physical environment)

2. *Temporal patterning* (e.g., imposition of routines, schedules, calendars)

3. *Material milieu* (availability of material objects and utilities—food, furniture, fixtures, vehicles, weapons, tools, etc.)

4. *Social milieu* (presence or accessibility of particular social categories of individuals—e.g., parents, pastors, police officers) (Broderick, 1993)

In other words, if you want your children to be healthy (higher-order goal), and you see playing outside as part of achieving that health (lower-order goal), but you live in a high-rise tenement with no backyard and in a bad neighborhood, then this limitation in spatial configuration will make it less likely that you will be able to attain this family goal. Similarly, your family may see individual rooms as essential to the development of adolescent autonomy and esteem, but if the family has four children and only three bedrooms, this goal will again be limited by spatial opportunities.

Furthermore, you may be a father who is primarily responsible for resource provision—with all the attending pressures that entails. Your family may also have the goal of creating less traditionally sex-typed children, and thus, you may want to spend as much time with your children providing child care as does your wife who also works. However, given the pressures and demands of your job on your daily schedule as well as the pressures to travel for work that your high-paying professional career requires, you simply will not have the time necessary to care for your children to the same extent as your wife (à la the work-family spillover model). Your family goals are thus thwarted by time constraints.

Third, your family may not have the resources available to provide for the health care and educational well-being of your children. The fact remains that 39% of female-headed families with children live below the poverty line as do 7% of married couples with children. Therefore, many families may find themselves in the position that their financial means do not allow them to achieve their desired ends. There are children living in poorer areas, attending less challenging schools, who are simply less likely to go to college because their families did not have the money to move to a better neighborhood with a better school. Frankly put, some goals are simply not attainable without the funds to support them.

Finally, your family may not be able to attain its goals because it does not have the social networks necessary. A family, for instance, may want their children to have a close-knit extended family that lives nearby and provides physical, emotional, and psychological support to family. However, the realities of our ever-increasing mobility make it less likely that this familial social support will be there. Therefore, the social milieu is simply not available. Social restrictions also affect families who want to raise children with liberal values while living, for example, in the South. It *is* possible, but less likely than while living in alternative areas where more liberal values are endemic to the social environment. You can see, then, that one's spatial, temporal, material, and social resources can severely limit the type of familial goal attainment possible.

Reflexive Spiral Model. The reflexive spiral model assumes that families commonly and repetitively engage in patterns of interaction that lead toward outcomes that bear no obvious relationship to the values or goals of any family members—often seeming in opposition to family goals. This model features the unmediated, reflexive reactivity of family members to one another's inputs (Broderick, 1993). Therefore, family members' behavior may often be less affected by their personal goals and values than by their interpersonal reflexes. For example, although hostility of family members to each other may be in opposition to the attainment of the emotional well-being of the family members, it is quite likely that individual family members will be hostile toward each other from time to time. In the reflexive spiral model, hostility levels of various members are seen to be a function of the following:

1. *Escalation factors* (e.g., other family members' hostility and individual level reactivity)

2. *Dampening factors* (e.g., the costs of one's own level of hostility)

3. *Contingency factors* (e.g., historic grievances or positive experiences)

Depending on the various combinations of escalation, dampening, and contingency factors, stability, positive outcomes, or runaway escalations of hostility can result. More specifically, if a husband's *escalation factors* (his wife is relatively hostile today and he's had a really, really bad day at work and is feeling particularly reactive) are greater than his *dampening factors* (he knows his wife will dismiss his mood as having a bad day and not take it out on him later with her own harangue or withdrawal of sexual favors) and a *history of past grievances* is present (the garbage disposal has clogged for the

100th time in 2 years and no one has done anything about it—*again*), then, not all that surprisingly, the husband's expressions of hostility will erupt. All this is regardless of the husband's desires for a harmonious home with a stable happy family that does not include any expressions of negative emotions at all. This model is particularly insightful regarding familial goal attainment, because rational goal attainment is much easier to articulate than to achieve when those messy emotional reactions start getting in the way. This model reminds us that our familial goals and our actual behavior will not always be consistent with one another as we seek to achieve those goals.

Unified Transcybernetic Model. Finally, the unified transcybernetic model combines the best of all the above models into the most complete family systems theory explanatory calculus. Basically, this model incorporates norms, developmental task processes, psychopolitical negotiation, opportunity matrices, and reflexive spirals into one complete theoretical model explaining goal-seeking and self-regulatory behavior in families. The unified transcybernetic model postulates (a) that the cybernetic functions of goal selection, goal seeking, and self-regulating interact with a family's opportunity matrix such that family members interact with each other in patterned ways (both goal-directed behaviors and reflexive-vectored behaviors included) and (b) that the family executive function and status-mentoring functions are emergent by-products of the psychopolitical process (Broderick, 1993). Finally, this model assumes that individual-level needs, developmental factors, social pressures, and shifts in the family opportunity structure all affect family patterns. A family is goal-seeking and self-regulatory to the extent that norms, development, psychopolitical factors, opportunities, and reflexive patterns of behavior allow. For example, a family will achieve its goal of physical health and well-being, if, and only if, the following are true for that family:

1. The norms of the situation influence the family in a healthy lifestyle (e.g., gyms are us).

2. Developmentally, the family is at such a place that all members have the time, energy, and inclination to exercise and eat properly (e.g., typically *not* right after the birth of the first child),

3. Psychopolitically, family members have similar agendas, wills, needs, and wants (yeah, right!),

4. The family has the spatial, temporal, material, and social resources necessary (e.g., no one has cancer or some other life-threatening illness most likely out of their control).

5. No reflexively mediated processes are causing family members to behave in ways that are antithetical to the family goals (e.g., family members are not having bad days or in other ways responding negatively to past grievances that are rearing their ugly heads).

In sum, family systems theory provides us with a complete model capable of explaining, predicting, describing, and controlling family members' goal attainment and self-regulation. As a theory, it fulfills all the functions of theory and can help us most fully understand the goal-seeking behavior of families, regardless of their various forms.

Rules Theory

SOURCE: *Stone Soup* © 2001 Jane Eliot. Reprinted with permission of Universal Press Syndicate. All rights reserved.

Just as roles guide our behavior, rules of communication shape how we communicate with various family members. According to Shimanoff (1980), a **rule** is "a followable prescription that indicates what behavior is obligated, preferred, and prohibited" (p. 57). Applying this to families, rules inform us regarding the best way to verbally talk to, or nonverbally communicate with, other members of our family. In this way, rules help us know that we are *obligated* to tell our mothers what time we will be home and with whom we are going out. Rules also help us know that within families, it is *preferred* that we communicate in pleasant (as opposed to unpleasant and hostile) ways. Finally, rules help us know that swearing at our mothers or sharing the most intimate details regarding our sex lives is strictly *prohibited*. Rules theory has a long-standing tradition within communication (e.g., Cushman, 1977) and will be highly useful to consider in its application to family communication.

Verbal Rules of Communication

Rules regarding verbal communication within the family can prescribe appropriate behavior and prohibit others. These rules can be either explicit or implicit (Smith, 1982). *Explicit rules* are openly discussed and agreed on. In most families, there are well-stated rules about communicating whereabouts with adolescent children who are gaining independence. My two adolescent stepsons, for instance, know that they must communicate where they are going, who they are going with, and what time they can be expected home. After verbally communicating this information, they are also well aware that if any of these plans change, they are to inform one of their parents immediately. These explicit rules are clearly stated and well-understood. *Implicit rules*, however, are more subtle and are understood in unstated ways. For example, my husband and I never ever say anything remotely negative about their mother in front of the children. Nowhere is this rule explicitly communicated or documented. However, this rule is well understood; in fact, my eldest stepson complained to me about it as he was talking about the painful process of disentangling himself from his mother as he emotionally prepares to go to college in the fall. In turn, my stepchildren rarely talk about their mother or stepfather in derogatory terms in my house. This again was never stated explicitly; however, we all understand that loyalty among coparents and between parents and children prescribes such behavior.

Although verbal rules in families are extensive and cannot be covered in their entirety here, two examples bear mentioning. First, explicit and implicit rules are most highly apparent between adolescent children and their parents. As adolescents strive for autonomy from their parents, explicit rules regarding territorial markers become more evident, with many early teens resorting to hand-scrawled signs reading "Keep Out!" or "Enter at your own risk!" posted clearly on bedroom doors (Guerrero & Afifi, 1995). Implicit rules also abound with well-understood and unstated prescriptions regarding taboo topics with adults. For instance, although gender of parent and gender of child can have a significant influence, in general, adolescents avoid talking about sex and dangerous situations with their parents (Guerrero & Afifi, 1995). However, if adolescents do talk with their parents about sexual matters, they are more likely to do so with mothers than with fathers, and mothers are generally more effective at getting their kids to actually reduce their sexually risky behavior (e.g., Miller et al., 2001). Thus, while explicit and implicit rules abound throughout the developmental life span of the family, they are especially apparent during adolescence.

Nonverbal Rules of Communication

Nonverbal communication may be similarly dictated by explicit and implicit rules. Nonverbal communication includes **kinesics,** or overall use of the body, including gestures and posture. For instance, insulting hand gestures and slumping postures may be explicitly prohibited within a family, whereas animated facial expressions may be implicitly encouraged. **Vocalics,** or communication through the use of voice, can similarly be dictated by explicit or implicit rules of communication. How many times, for instance, have you heard a mother say explicitly to a loud child, "Indoor voice!" Still other mothers, however, try to communicate this message through the more subtle means of implicitly teaching the rule by using a lowered, quieter voice herself in hopes that the errant child will match her tone. **Proximity,** or communication through the use of space, is another type of nonverbal communication in the family that will be dictated by explicit and implicit rules. Standing too close, for instance, may be subtly discouraged through compensatory steps backward and not entering your parents' bedroom when the door is shut may be explicitly stated and understood. **Haptics,** or communication through the use of touch, may be similarly prescribed explicitly and implicitly. One parent may be highly affectionate, whereas the other is less affectionate. Over time, children implicitly learn which parent is more receptive to hugs and kisses. Alternatively, parents no doubt spend time explicitly teaching close-talking, highly intimately touching 3-year-olds not to touch there! Finally, parents can implicitly or explicitly communicate rules regarding **chronemics,** or communication through the use of time, and **artifacts,** or communication through the use of physical objects. In other words, parents may have explicit rules about time limitations on television or computer usage, but they may also have implicit rules about the extent to which sexually explicit depictions are allowed on the walls of their house.

Summary

Theories regarding family communication can be highly useful in terms of helping us describe, predict, explain, and control family communication and its outcomes. Although innumerable theories are useful in family communication research, three theories are highlighted here because they are particularly useful in helping us have the best understanding of family communication. *Roles theory* helps us understand the roles that various members hold as they aid the family's functioning through their communication behavior. Traditional gender role delineations help us further understand the tendency for men to adopt resource provider roles and for women to adopt nurturer-caregiver roles even when the family is a dual-earning household. The dual-earning household is a particularly challenging family situation, where members often experience interrole conflict and work-family spillover stress. Roles theory also helps us understand the complexity within single-parent homes when family members are expected to hold competing roles (e.g., resource provider *and* nurturer) simultaneously. Furthermore, roles theory helps us better understand boundary regulation in families—a concept that holds special relevance for step- and binuclear families. *Family systems theory* helps us understand families as goal seeking and self-regulating. This theory also helps us understand the many factors (e.g., norms, psychopolitical processes, opportunities, developmental processes, reflexive behavioral spirals) that influence how families achieve their overarching goals (e.g., health, well-being). These theories help us understand family functioning regardless of the form of the family. Finally, *rules theory* helps us understand the explicit and implicit rules that prescribe, obligate, and prohibit us in the ways we communicate with various family members. These explicit and implicit rules are evident at both verbal and nonverbal levels and operate within all family forms.

KEY TERMS

back stage

complementary roles

control

description

developmental task model

dual-earner couples

explanation

explicit rules

family systems theory

front stage

gender-linked roles

implicit rules

interrole conflict

nonverbal communication

normative model

opportunity matrix model

performance

prediction

psychopolitical model

reciprocal roles

reflexive spiral model

role expectations

role strain

roles

roles theory

rules theory

stress

symmetrical roles

theory

unified transcybernetic

verbal communication

wings

work-family spillover

QUESTIONS FOR APPLICATION

1. Using the concepts from roles theory, analyze your family of origin. Who were the primary nurturers, resource providers, and so on? Did your family have symmetrical, complementary, or reciprocal role holders?

2. Analyze the gender role specialization in your family. Who was the primary nurturer-caregiver? Who was the primary resource provider? Did both of your parents work? If so, who worked the most? Who nurtured the most?

3. Depict your family members as a mobile. Analyze your family according to family systems theory using the concepts of wholeness, interdependence, and homeostasis. How did the behavior of one member of this highly connected system affect the behavior of the other members? How did your family seek goals and self-regulate in pursuit of those goals?

4. Differentiate between normative, developmental task, psychopolitical, opportunity matrix, reflexive spiral, and unified transcybernetic models of self-regulating goal seeking in families. Using the concepts from these models, which factors most influenced how your own family of origin sought goals?

5. What rules were operating in your family of origin as you grew up? What were some examples of explicit rules? Implicit rules? Are there also examples of verbal and nonverbal explicit and implicit rules you can provide? Were these rules particularly evident during your adolescent years?

4

Forming the New Family Pairing: Two Become One

No doubt, many of you will be thinking of developing your own family either now or at some point in the future. If you are a traditional student, you are probably dating or seriously dating and thinking about the future possibilities of family development that your current opportunities might afford. Doubtless, you are interested in how people use communication to enter relationships (i.e., relationship developmental processes) and maintain relationships with greater and greater levels of commitment. Processes of communication in the development of new relationships are no longer limited to the young 20-somethings, however. As more and more families dissolve through divorce (between 34% and 50%; Kreider & Fields, 2001) and with up to half of marriages every year in the United States being remarriages (46%; National Center for Health Statistics, 1995), it becomes obvious that the processes of communication endemic to relational development leading to marriage are of interest to individuals with a broader age range and more diverse prior relational experiences than previously. Therefore, you *and* your parents may be interested in cohabiting relationships (and their effects on subsequent marriage), engagement, and eventually marriage. It is assumed throughout this chapter that the processes that guide first marriages are similar to those processes that guide subsequent marriages and communication processes. Patterns of courtship for remarriage, however, often involve more long-term implications for child adjustment in remarriages where children are involved (Montgomery, Anderson, Hetherington, & Clingempeel, 1992). The general stages and processes the developing remarriage couple goes through, however, are quite similar to the processes that developing first marriage relationships go through. Throughout this relationship development process, you can see how the communication processes of nurturing and controlling the other come into play in the newly developing family. As couples develop communicationally over time, they begin to relate through *nurturing* behavior (i.e., providing caregiving for each other much in the same way a parent nurtures a child), and as the relationship develops, processes of relational *control* become apparent as the two people attempt to coordinate their (and sometimes their children's in the case of remarriages) unified lives together.

This chapter reviews development of the new family form via social-psychological, psychoanalytic and communication perspectives. *Social-psychological processes* of relationship development include consideration of factors relevant to subsequent relationship development and communication. *Psychoanalytic perspectives* consider how our early attachment experiences with caregivers translate into our tendencies to communicationally approach or avoid romantic relationships. This approach considers our attachment to our parents and how that translates into our choices in romantic relationships. Finally, *communication perspectives* establish theories of relational development (i.e., uncertainty reduction, social exchange theory, and social penetration model) and relational stages. The chapter ends with a consideration of the early marital union (prior to the addition of children) and factors related to marital and communication satisfaction.

_____ Social-Psychological Bases of Attraction

Factors Relevant to Relationship
Initiation, Communication, and Development

For those of you who are currently "between relationships," you may be interested in the process of how those dreadful-wonderful initial communication interactions come into being. In other words, what factors promote initial communicative interactions? For those of you who are currently "hanging out" with or beginning to see someone exclusively, you may wonder how people move through relationship development using communication to attain greater levels of closeness and greater levels of commitment. This section of the chapter presents several factors related to promoting initial communicative interactions and several factors related to predicting the desire for developing future relationships through the use of communication.

Establishing Initial Communicative Interactions

Many of the factors related to initial face-to-face communicative interactions are nonverbal as newly attracted partners signal their attraction to one another. One of the earliest models of courtship cues (or initiation rituals) frames these early communication interactions within nurturing behavior as partners signal to each other that it is safe to approach. These early courtship communication cues include (a) attention-gaining cues, (b) recognition or courtship readiness, (c) positioning, and (d) resolution (Scheflen, 1965). **Attention-gaining cues** indicate hesitancy and ambivalence as potential communicators decide whether to approach or avoid each other (Burgoon, Buller, & Woodall, 1996). As nurturing behaviors, these communicative cues often include submissive-appearing cues and parent-child-like interactions. Many attention-gaining cues are similar to those used to initiate a conversation in that they include making eye contact. What is unique about this use of eye contact is that it is often fleeting, accompanied by glancing downward when caught in the act of gazing. These behaviors often mimic childlike behaviors in that they are coy, often accompanied by head down stances and glances upward.

Recognition or courtship readiness indicates the communicator's interest and availability (Scheflen, 1965). Nonverbal indicators of readiness include eyebrow raises and other indicators of nonverbal immediacy (e.g., gaze, more direct body orientation, smiling), again nurturing the other to feel safe enough to approach. Some research also shows that cues may vary with sexually oriented individuals; men who are more sexually oriented are more likely to smile, laugh, and use flirtatious glances, and women who are more sexually oriented are more likely to lean forward more and tilt their heads (Simpson, Gangestad, & Biek, 1993). Burgoon et al. (1996) also report that *improved muscle tone* (e.g., better posture, tightened stomachs and buttocks) and a *seemingly alert appearance* (e.g., brighter eyes, rosier skin) may accompany courtship readiness as does *self-preening behavior* (e.g., smoothing hair, straightening clothing, checking makeup). Burgoon et al. (1996) emphasize that this stage is still characterized by submissive behaviors—again indicating a type of nurturing of the other.

Positioning for courtship includes direct facing, which facilitates direct and personal conversation and also functions to shut other people out (Burgoon et al., 1996; Scheflen, 1965). Again, many of the cues that indicate nonverbal immediacy are evident here in that communicators signal to each other that they are listening attentively and are fully immersed in the conversation—so much so that they give the impression that they are ignoring all others. Many nonverbal communication cues accompany this position, but heightened and prolonged eye contact, direct body and facial orientation, and chairs turned inward toward one another can all signal this positioning for courtship (Burgoon et al., 1996). Conversations also appear highly animated now as communicators exaggerate behaviors through emphatic gestures and loud laughter. Communicative responsiveness is also evidenced through head nodding, postural mirroring, and some synchronized movements. Parent-child-like interactions continue, as well, as partners begin to nurture each other through touch and grooming behavior. However, sexually provocative behaviors, including pelvis and chest positioning, also accompany this stage. Consistently, submissive nurturing seems to be the overarching pattern here.

Resolution, or the final stage of courtship, includes sexual contact and copulation (Burgoon et al., 1996; Scheflen, 1965). This stage differentiates courtship from quasi-courtship, which may include many of the flirtatious behaviors described above but does not result in sexual consummation of the relationship. Obviously, there may be some time delay between positioning and resolution. However, the earlier behaviors of courtship seem to be determined in order to reach this final stage of sexual interaction. Although this perspective may seem dated, these rituals are not variant over time in that they are apparent once physical contact comes into play. Initial contacts are not made just through face-to-face means, however. In this age of technological advances, many couples now rely on the less personal methods of initial contacts available through the Internet.

In this day and age of Internet access, the role of computer access and the Internet cannot be ignored in terms of the communication functions of establishing initial interactions, maintaining early (and subsequent) contacts, providing outlets for disclosures relevant to relationship development and maintenance, and disentangling from relationships. In terms of establishing initial interactions, online dating services can simply no longer be overlooked. An online search on Google brought up 5,930,000 hits for "dating service"—nearly 6 million sites! These include (but are certainly not limited to) match.com, matchmaker.com, bookofmatches.com, lovecompass.com, and a few sponsored links that include eHarmony.com, true.com, and perfectmatch.com. Today's busy singles are eschewing the bar or church youth group scene and turning more and more to Internet services to find their match. In fact, in 1999, match.com (the proclaimed global leader in online dating) claimed to have been the basis for 700,000 marriages and currently boasts millions of members. eHarmony.com claims to base their matches on scientific research that matches singles' compatibilities on 29 dimensions that include the overarching dimension of character and constitution, personality, emotional makeup and skills, and family and values. The site also claims to be the fastest growing and boasts numerous personal accounts of successful matches. More and more people are not only meeting each other over the Internet, they are also making connections with long-term commitments associated with them.

In terms of maintaining early contacts and attractions, many of these communication services rely on relatively anonymous e-mail connections (filtered through their sites) that can lead to subsequent use of actual e-mail accounts, telephone contacts, and initial face-to-face contacts. E-mail is used as a method of relationship development (the topic of our next session). In addition, burgeoning "blogging" sites such as "livejournal.com," "myspace.com," and "blogspot.com" are becoming more and more popular. I was quite surprised (and more than a little intrigued) when my eldest stepson's (Huw's) ex-girlfriend (Nicole) revealed to me that they had gotten back together after a short respite because she had shown him several "livejournals" that revealed to him just how hurt she was by the current situation. I was amazed that intimate (and what used to be private) journals could now be made public (either with limited or full access to the public) so that one could actually communicate with one's friends and lovers one's deepest darkest secrets in a non-face-to-face environment. Then to add to my growing enthusiasm about the uses of the Internet for relationship maintenance through communication, I learned that my stepson's current girlfriend (Roxanne) used livejournal.com to delineate her painful process of breaking up with him so he could be with girlfriend #1, encouraged her friends to read it, and voilà!, they're back together still to this day! Thus, the Internet is currently being used not only as an e-mail and instant messaging service but as a method of communication for initiating, developing, and maintaining romantic relationships.

Factors Related to Mate Selection, Communication, and Relationship Development

Now that you know how the process of courtship can be initiated through communication behaviors, you might want to know how people go about selecting the mate they want to initiate courtship with. Several factors have been found to predict getting past that first communication encounter to actually developing a relationship with the person who has caught your eye and sparked your interest. The phrasing of the last sentence might tip you off—one thing that brings people to desire continuing to communicate with another person is **attraction**. Obvious *physical attraction* can initially gain your interest, but social and task attraction have also come into play. Do you want to communicate and hang out with this person because you find him or her funny, pleasant, and intelligent (i.e., *social attraction*)? And could you do the requisite tasks of life and, potentially, of family with this person (i.e., *task attraction*)? Thus, **competence** is also a strong predictor of relationship development. Will he be a good father? Is he or she a competent cook? Can that person deal with mechanical issues?

With regard to physical attraction, a now famous study by Berscheid and Walster (1974) showed that although females and males desire physically attractive dates, females consider other communication relevant characteristics; they desire intelligent, considerate, and outgoing dates as well. This finding is consistent across a variety of studies (e.g., Berscheid, Dion, Walster, & Walster, 1971; Berscheid & Walster, 1972, 1974, 1978). In terms of predicting the most successful dates, however, Berscheid and Walster (1974) found that matching on physical attractiveness was the most important. Not only did more attractive individuals desire more attractive dates, they also had a better time with more attractive dates. Similarly, less attractive daters desired less attractive dates and had a better time with them. It would appear that *matching* on attractiveness is more important to the future success of the relationship than is the *actual level* of physical attractiveness.

This **similarity hypothesis** holds true not just for physical attractiveness, however. Individuals have a strong desire to communicate with and be with other individuals whom they see as similar. This similarity seeking begins with **racial and ethnic endogamy**, or the tendency to marry within a group (Surra, Gray, Cottle, & Boettcher, 2004). This tendency has been used, in fact, to try to explain the lower rates of marriage among African American females. African American females are thought to be experiencing a "marriage squeeze" because of a shortage of marriageable men (Bulcroft & Bulcroft, 1993; Crowder & Tolnay, 2000; Fossett & Keicolt, 1991; South & Lloyd, 1992). Reinforcing the notion that males should be the primary resource providers in terms of family roles, African American men are thought to be less marriageable because of lower economic opportunities (e.g., South & Lloyd, 1992) and greater institutionalization rates (e.g., Fossett & Kiecolt, 1991). Contrary to the hypothesis that individuals marry within their racial and ethnic groups, however, African American men are entering interracial marriages more than are African American women (Crowder & Tolnay, 2000).

Economic potential is another factor found to be associated with desire for continued communication and relational development leading to marriage. As discussed in Chapter 3, roles complementarity in marriage facilitates smoother family functioning. Thus, not surprisingly, and again confirming our earlier claims that men are expected to be the resource providers and women are expected to be the nurturer-caregivers, men's labor force participation has a positive effect on women's marriage behavior (Cooney & Hogan, 1991; Fossett & Kiecolt, 1991; South & Lloyd, 1992).

In other words, men are more likely to marry women who see them as having the potential to be a resource provider in the family. Furthermore, although women's economic potential was initially hypothesized to predict a decline in women's rates of marriages (because of the lack of need for a resource provider), their economic potential also positively affects their tendency to marry (e.g., Goldstein & Kenney, 2001; Sassler & Schoen, 1999; South & Lloyd, 1992). Both men and women are attracted to marriage partners whom they see as potential earners in the family. It may be that men are still expected to be the *primary resource providers*, but both men's and women's tendencies to marry are predicted by their economic potential.

Education similarly has a positive influence on marriage for both men and women (e.g., Goldstein & Kenney, 2001). The growth in importance in educational attainment predicting marriage is seen as an outgrowth of the need for greater education to attain greater economic success (Surra et al., 2004) and is seen to contribute to the tendency for educated individuals to marry other educated individuals (Mare, 1991). Finally, people who live in geographic **proximity** (a nonverbal communication variable) are also more likely to date and eventually marry (Fossett & Keicolt, 1991). Thus, simply living nearer to someone increases the chances that you will date that person and eventually marry him or her. Finally, two theoretical approaches exist that predict the communicative process of mate selection: evolutionary approaches and social exchange approaches to mate selection.

Evolutionary Approaches to Mate Selection

According to **evolutionary psychology**, individuals are assumed to select partners who will enable their reproductive success and promote survival of their offspring (Kenrick, Groth, Trost, & Sadalla, 1993; Singh, 1993). According to this perspective, then, potential mates not only nurture each other but also predict the level of nurturing the other can provide to their children. Because men and women are differentially involved in the rearing of offspring, men and women are expected to seek different qualities in their mates (Simpson & Gangestad, 2001). According to this perspective, women depend on men to provide for their offspring and therefore value their partners' economic status much more than men do (Ben Hamida, Mineka, & Bailey, 1998), providing yet another explanation for men as resource providers. In addition, women prefer men who will be able to protect their offspring and thus show a preference for men who nonverbally appear physically large, strong, and physically attractive (Ben Hamida et al., 1998; Kenrick et al., 1993). Alternatively, men, in an attempt to increase their ability to reproduce, exhibit greater permissiveness and sexual availability in short-term mating relationships (Schmitt & Buss, 1996; Simpson & Gangestad, 2001). Also, men prefer women who are fertile and possess good genetic health and therefore prefer health, beauty, and youth of partners (Ben Hamida et al., 1998; Kenrick et al., 1993). Innate biological drives to procreate successfully (including the successful nurturing of children) may be at the heart of mate selection.

Social Exchange Theories

Alternatively, social exchange theory offers a more cognitive and less biological explanation for mate selection and relationship development through communication. **Social exchange theory** argues that when considering whether to develop or maintain a relationship, individuals consider the potential rewards of the relationship relative to its potential costs (Thibaut & Kelley, 1969). Rewards are the tangible potential positive outcomes of the relationship. These can be *endogenous*, or internal to the relationship, or *exogenous*, or external to the relationship. Rewards can include economic security and potential competent parenting (endogenous rewards) or a supportive extended family or living in a great neighborhood (exogenous rewards). Costs, on the other hand, are the tangible losses associated with any potential relationship. A relationship can be costly in terms of time and energy expended (endogenous costs) or in terms of unpleasant interactions with one's in-laws (exogenous costs). According to social exchange theory, an individual decides to develop or maintain a relationship as long as the *comparison level* is high or, in other words, as long as the rewards outweigh the costs. If the comparison level drops below the *comparison level of alternatives* (the person's repertoire of alternative possible relationships), then the person will choose to dissolve that union in favor of a more rewarding alternative.

Research in support of Rusbult's investment model of commitment (a social exchange theory; Rusbult, 1980, 1983) supports the relationship between rewards and costs and satisfaction, commitment, and stability over time (Surra et al., 2004). Specifically, rewards derived in dating relationships strongly predicted increases in satisfaction over time (Sprecher, 2001). However, men were more satisfied to the extent that they believed that their partners benefited more from the relationship than they did. Alternatively, a partner's own investments and potential alternatives were the best predictors of commitment (Sprecher, 2001). Finally, those with greater need dependence (as opposed to need satisfaction) were the most likely to stay in the current relationship (Drigotas & Rusbult, 1992). Thus, the concepts of rewards, costs, comparison levels, and comparison level of alternatives can all be useful in predicting satisfaction with, commitment to, and maintenance of relationships.

Communication Theories and Models of Relationship Development

Because most of you will move toward marriage (9 of 10 of you will eventually marry; Goldstein & Kenney, 2001; Sassler & Schoen, 1999), albeit at later ages in your life than in previous times (26.8 years for men and 25.1

years for women; U.S. Census Bureau, 2001), it is useful to consider that the transition to first marriage occurs within marriage markets (Lichter, LeClere, & McLaughlin, 1991). As discussed earlier under relational development, transition to marriage is often based on *propinquity*, or individuals' proximity in space and time (Fossett & Kiecolt, 1991). In addition, individuals assess the economic and interpersonal assets of a potential partner. Mate selection is predicted to occur in three stages. The first stage of mate selection is seeking information about potential partners (through communication). The second stage is determining the quality of the match with any potential partner. The third stage is communicating more with a potential partner to decide whether to develop or reject a relationship (Sassler & Schoen, 1999). Several theories flesh out these processes in more detail.

Uncertainty Reduction Theory

Uncertainty reduction theory predicts that the uncertainty associated with early stages of a relationship prompts increases in information gathering (Berger & Calabrese, 1975; Berger & Kellermann, 1994). These increases in information are also assumed to negatively predict uncertainty. Thus, early relational processes are thought to be predicted by the desire to reduce uncertainty through gathering more and more information about the other. Uncertainty reduction theory assumes that individuals interested in developing relationships use several strategies—passive, active, and interactive—to gain information regarding their potential mates. *Passive strategies* include observations of the other either in structured tasks or in situations where they might be more relaxed and themselves. If you see an attractive person in the classroom and observe him or her giving a presentation in class or chatting with friends in the quad, you are using passive strategies to get to know that person. *Active strategies* include asking others for information about the potential mate. If your interest remains high, you may begin to approach his or her friends regarding information of that person's availability for pursuing, for instance. Finally, *interactive strategies* include communicating directly with the person and may even include interrogation. Arranging activities so that you "accidentally" bump into the other person daily or setting up a date would fall under interactive strategies. All these strategies are intended to reduce uncertainty regarding the other and facilitate the decision to continue in the pursuit of a relationship.

Social Penetration Theory

Social penetration theory (Altman & Taylor, 1973) is a theory of disclosure in communication that argues that individuals in relationship development go through various communication phases, or stages, in their movement toward greater relationship stability. The first phase, *orientation*, is when the relationship partners explore a great breadth of topics in the interest of ascertaining potential compatibilities. Here, much demographic information is shared. Not much depth is achieved during these initial stages because the relationship partners share information that is value neutral in their attempts to gain greater knowledge about the attitudes and beliefs of the other person before sharing potentially risky evaluative information. The second phase, or the *exploratory affective stage*, is attained when individuals have assessed the other as a potential mate, and more risky information about attitudes, emotions, and feelings are shared. This is an attempt to ascertain whether the other partner will continue to be accepting even when a person shares in greater depth with regard to potentially riskier social information. Assuming that all goes well here, individuals are assumed to advance to the *affective exchange* phase, where individuals share in much greater depths their fears, loves, wants, and desires. More trust is developed here because the assumption is that the other partner will not leave the relationship. Much evidence supports the relationship between intimacy and greater sharing of evaluations, direct criticisms, and open conflict (Benoit & Benoit, 1987; Christopher & Cate, 1985; Fitzpatrick & Winke, 1979; Knapp, Stafford, & Daly, 1986; Lloyd & Cate, 1985). Finally, *stability* is assumed to result because individuals now possess a full range of breadth and depth on topics, and information is perhaps less self-disclosive because individuals already possess high quantities of depth and breadth of information on the other.

Dialectic Models

Given that this theory has been criticized for assuming that partners move only toward greater and greater closeness over the course of the relationship, Altman, Vinsel, and Brown (1981) developed a **dialectic model** to explain how partners vacillate through periods of closeness and distance in relationships. This approach is more sophisticated in that it recognizes the typical waxing and waning that all relationships experience in terms of their trajectories of closeness. Dialectic approaches help us understand how relationships change over time (Baxter, 1988; Baxter & Ebert, 1999; Baxter & Montgomery, 1996) and assume that relationships are constantly in a state of flux as a result of opposing forces such as autonomy-connectedness and openness-closedness. These opposing forces are better predictors of relationship turning points. This perspective is considered with greater depth in the chapter on balancing autonomy needs with intimacy development (Chapter 7).

Following from social penetration theory, Knapp (1984) defines stages of relationship development as *initiating* (meeting), *experimenting* (small talk), *intensifying* (greater disclosure), *integrating* (living as couple), and *bonding* (public commitment) stages. The strength of this stage model is that it also delineates the stages of deterioration as *differentiating* (begin disengaging), *circumscribing* (constricted communication), *stagnating* (inactivity), *avoiding* (physically unavailable), and *terminating* (death of the relationship). Although all these models are social-psychological in terms of describing the communication processes we go through for relational development, they fail to consider potential underlying psychodynamic processes of attraction that may be at work (or play).

Psychoanalytic Bases of Attraction

If I asked you to think about what attracted you to your current or last romantic partner, very few of you would probably say, "He reminded me of dear old Dad," or "She was just like my mom." However, the psycho-dynamic approach of attachment theory would argue that, subconsciously, you might indeed be more likely to be attracted to, communicate with, and approach someone who is like your parents in an effort to attach with that person. The argument is that you learned how to love, how to approach or avoid communicationally, and how to be attached to someone during your earliest dependent interactions with your parents, and thus, when you want to attach to a romantic partner in the future, you attempt to model or mimic these same approach or avoidance communicative processes by attaching to someone very similar to your parents. In fact, you may have noticed this tendency in yourself after a relationship broke up—when you were more likely to see what you didn't like about your partner. Or more likely, you may have a good friend who constantly gets into relationships with guys who have exactly the same kind of controlling disposition. In your all-powerful position of observer, you may ask yourself, "Why does she always end up with these *loooosers*?!?" After reading the next section of the chapter, you may ask yourself if she might be reenacting her relation-ship attachment with her father. This section explores early childhood attachments and their subsequent effects on later romantic attachments.

Attachment Theory: The Effect of Early Parental Attachment on Romantic Relationships

Bowlby (1973, 1980, 1982) argues that infants are biologically primed to form attachments to caregivers to form a bond that ensures the safety and development of the infant. The infant thus uses the caregiver as a "secure base," and the parent gives the infant a sense of security. As the infant explores the world, he or she seeks comfort and safety from the caregiver in times of crisis, need, or fear. This comfort and safety is at the heart of the nur-turing that the mother provides to the infant. The type of attachment formed with the caregiver depends on the level of parental communication sensitivity (i.e., the parent's communicative responsiveness to the infant's care-seeking behaviors). Infants whose parents are consistently and appropriately respon-sive to their signals are more likely to develop **secure attachments**. Caregiver-nurturers of secure infants are reliable and caring, and thus secure infants learn to be trusting of others and that they are worthy of attention. If primary caregiver-nurturers are inconsistent in their communicative responsiveness, infants likely develop an insecure attachment style. One such insecure attachment style is the **anxious-ambivalent attachment**. These infants become carefully attuned to their caregiver's actions and whereabouts because they are uncertain if the caregivers will be communicatively responsive in times of need. In other words, these infants become anxious about the availability of their caregivers. Because their caregivers were inconsistent, these infants learn that others are untrustworthy and that they, themselves, may not be worthy of attention. Finally, if primary caregivers are generally communicatively unresponsive and cold, infants likely develop **avoidant attachments**. These infants, because they have learned that their caregiver-nurturer's communicative responsiveness is unreliable, do not seek comfort in times of need; instead, they learn to care for, and depend on, themselves.

Bowlby (1982) posits that the responsiveness of the parent shapes infants' **working models** (i.e., schemas about the world). Working models help individuals predict the behavior of others and also influence the interpretations of others' behavior (Bretherton, 1992; Collins & Read, 1990). Bowlby's concept of *inner working models* has been incorporated into the work of Bartholomew and Horowitz (1991). They indicate a four-category model of attachment styles in adults. These prototypes, or working models, were based on *self-image* and *images of others*. In other words, they suggest that attachment styles during infancy influence an individual's specific notions of *self-worth* and *trust in others*. Thus, infants who develop secure attachments likely have high self-worth and high trust in others. Through their caregivers' actions, they have learned that they are worthy of being loved and that others can be trusted. Infants who develop **anxious-avoidant attachments** likely have low self-worth and high trust in others. Because they have had to be attentive to their parents' communicative actions to determine when they will be available and responsive, these infants have learned that their value lies within other individuals; they depend on others' impressions of them to determine their worth as a person. In adulthood, this attachment style is known as **preoccupied** because this person is preoccupied with others to determine his or her own sense of self-worth. In contrast, infants who develop **avoidant** attachments likely have high self-worth but low trust in others. These infants learned that others cannot be trusted and therefore they must rely solely on themselves. Consequently, they have also learned that they are not worthy of love and attention. Bartholomew and Horowitz also suggest a fourth category, labeled **fearfuls**, who have low self-worth and low trust in others. Although this category is rare, these individuals are characterized as avoiding relationships because they do not trust others and do not believe they are worthy of love.

Much work has extended Bowlby's (e.g., 1980) and Ainsworth's (1991) initial work on early childhood attachment to later romantic attachments arguing that individuals reenact their parental attachment style and ensuing

Figure 4.1 The earliest days of attachment include many childlike communication displays of submissiveness.

communication with their current romantic partners. Subsequent research has been supportive of this delineation: Secures strive for communicative interdependence with their partners, preoccupieds are communicatively overinvolved and dependent, and avoidants are communicatively underinvolved and autonomous (Collins & Read, 1990; Feeney & Noller, 1991; Hazan & Shaver, 1987). In support of this general pattern of communication, extensive research has shown innumerable relationships between attachment style and the communication behaviors of self-disclosure (e.g., Mikulincer & Nachshon, 1991), emotional regulation (e.g., Mikulincer, Shaver, & Pereg, 2003), excessive reassurance seeking (e.g., Shaver, Schachner, & Mikulincer, 2005), nonverbal involvement (e.g., Guerrero, 1996; Guerrero & Burgoon, 1996), and communication of respect in relationships (e.g., Frei & Shaver, 2002). Although a complete review is not possible here, there is no doubt that romantic attachment style affects communication behavior within romantic relationships.

Because parental attachment only inconsistently and weakly predicts subsequent romantic attachment, my colleagues and I (Le Poire et al., 1997; Le Poire, Shepard, & Duggan, 1999) suggest that while attachments are affected by early infant communicative experiences, it is also likely that experiences throughout one's childhood can also influence attachment and ensuing communication behaviors. In other words, although attachments during infancy might have been quite positive, the effect of a father's affair and abandonment of the family when one is 7, or worse, when one is 13, could have a strong effect on one's likelihood of approaching relationships fearfully or fearlessly in the future. Consistently, having a parent die or having a parent develop a serious illness might create a situation where the child is expected to be the caregiver for a parent, and thus the attachment style might change again. Therefore, we argue that *securely attached adults* most likely had parents who were available and consistently loving throughout their childhood. Secure Stans and Sarahs are the individuals you know who walk up to and communicate confidently with others, trust that they won't be left, and know that they are lovable.

Preoccupieds, alternatively, were likely abandoned at some point *throughout* their childhood (Le Poire et al., 1997; Le Poire et al., 1999). Thus, preoccupation with one's romantic partner may be the result of inconsistent parenting *or* the loss of one parent physically or emotionally at some point during one's development. A preoccupied may have had a parent who was absent in some way or another. Children who lose a parent in the home through divorce, physical abandonment, or death may experience some level of preoccupation with their romantic partners because they may always harbor the fear that their partners will unexpectedly leave them. Children whose parents traveled frequently for their jobs may experience similar fears, as might children whose parents were emotionally unavailable through escape behaviors, such as substance abuse or workaholism. Finally, children with parents with some serious physical or mental debilitation (e.g., narcissism, depression) may be similarly abandoned in that their parents were not available to care for them. Preoccupied Pauls or Paulas are the people you know who are obsessed with their partners. They love everything about their partner, fantasize and talk constantly about their partner, feel in emotionally consistent ways with how their partner is feeling about them currently, and monitor the whereabouts of their partner constantly for fear that if they fail to watch their partner, their partner might simply disappear.

Unlike earlier forms of attachment theory, this extended attachment theory argues that children who were **role reversed** (or expected to give care to their caregivers) are most likely to become avoidants (either dismissive-avoidants or fearfuls as identified by Bartholomew and Horowitz, 1991) because they developed their identities through being caregivers for their inconsistently available and unhealthy parents (Le Poire et al., 1997; Le Poire et al., 1999). This can happen in a variety of ways. Children may be expected to take care of an immature or overly self-absorbed caregiver. Alternatively, they may have to physically take care of a parent who had a debilitating accident. Furthermore, they may have needed to nurse a parent through hangovers or similar residual effects of substance abuse (e.g., running the house, keeping the younger siblings out of their parent's way, calling the job to make excuses for absences, etc.). Finally, they may have taken care of their parents by taking care of a sibling with a mental or physical handicap. Regardless of how it occurred, this child was *role reversed* in that he or she was expected to be a caregiver for his or her parent while the

Table 4.1   Parental Attachment Style, Likely Childhood Experiences, and Resulting Romantic
                   Attachment Style

Parental Attachment	*Likely Childhood Experiences*	*Romantic Attachment*
Secure	Consistently responsive caregivers ⟶	Secure
Anxious-ambivalents	Abandonment (Physical or emotional) ⟶	Preoccupied
Avoidants (dismissive or fearfuls)	Role reversal (caregiving the caregiver) ⟶	Dismissive avoidant

parent failed to be a caregiver for the child. This child was simultaneously role reversed *and* abandoned in that the parent failed to meet the child's needs. Because role-reversed children learn that close intimate relationships result in loss of self and total absorption in the needs of the other, avoidants generally attempt to control the degree of closeness they experience with others. Thus, they often seem to avoid relationships altogether (fearfuls) or avoid too much communication of intimacy (dismissives). In general, relationship partners generally find avoidants warm and giving initially (as they form the early bonds of a relationship) and then cool or avoidant as they recede or retreat to protect their easily lost sense of self. These are the dating partners who suddenly become very busy, have highly active lives outside their primary relationships, or don't want to become overly "serious."

Consistent with Bartholomew and Horowitz (1991), we argue that children who attach differently to their parents are likely to experience varying fears as they approach subsequent relationships (Le Poire et al., 1997; Le Poire et al., 1999). Two fears that are particularly relevant to forming subsequent relationships are abandonment and intimacy fears. **Abandonment fear** is the level of anxiety one experiences about potentially being left by one's relationship partner. **Intimacy fear** is the anxiety level one experiences regarding being smothered by one's relational partner's demands for closeness. Specifically, we argue that secures should have low fears of intimacy and low fears of abandonment because they should have fairly positive working models of self and other as argued by Bartholomew and Horowitz (1991). Secures are that lucky bunch of relationship partners who approach relationships fearlessly. Contrast this with preoccupieds (i.e., grown-up anxious-ambivalents), who have a high fear of abandonment (due to their childhood abandonment) with an underlying moderate fear of intimacy (because being close to someone means they are likely to be left). Preoccupieds are those individuals who are obsessed with, or hypervigilant over, their partners. These are the folks who *love* new technology and the security that constant contact can offer.

Table 4.2   Romantic Attachment Style

Type of Relationship Fears	Secures	Preoccupieds	Avoidants
Intimacy	Low	Moderate	High
Abandonment	Low	High	Moderate

Cell phones, pagers, AIM (AOL instant messaging), e-mail, and the like are constant companions for the preoccupieds, who like to monitor the whereabouts of their partners at all times. Finally, avoidants have a high fear of intimacy (fearing a loss of self), with an underlying moderate fear of abandonment because they were simultaneously enmeshed and emotionally abandoned. They fear being overly close in relationships because it means that they may lose their sense of self as they take care of others. Alternatively, they are fairly attractive partners in that they really know how to see to the heart of the matter and are the best of caregivers. In other words, these are the dismissive Dans and Danas who initially appeared to be the most caring and warm caregiver you had ever met. They were initially *very* attractive as partners because they seem to be so accepting of all aspects of the individual—including the needy parts. Unfortunately, the same vulnerabilities that made them so attracted to you in the first place (i.e., reliving those early childhood attachments) also made them fear that they might be smothered by your neediness. Thus, dismissive Dan or Dana may back off rather quickly when they learn just how needy you, in fact, are.

The Influence of Partner's Attachment Style on the Communication of Involvement

Some of you may be concerned (for your friends and loved ones—or maybe even for yourself) that one's attachment style might doom one to a life of attachment misery and despair in communicatively approaching romantic relationships. Fear not, dear reader, because in my own research, we argue that the final form of the attachment style is actually a function of the interaction between how one attached to one's parents and how one's partner is attached to him or her (Le Poire et al., 1997). In other words, how your romantic partner attaches to you can actually modify the types of fears you entered the romantic relationship with, and thus make you more (or less) securely attached.

This idea is not uncontroversial, however, because many argue that attachment style is stable across situations and throughout life (Dontas, Maratos, Fafoutis, & Karangelis, 1985; Erickson, Sroufe, & Egeland, 1985; Main, Kaplan, & Cassidy, 1985; Waters, Wippman, & Sroufe, 1979). However, there is some counterevidence supporting the claim that a relationship partner can actually have an effect on the final form of the attachment (Hazen & Hutt, 1990; Quinton, Pickles, Maughan, & Rutter, 1993; Rutter & Quinton, 1984). Furthermore, many attachment theorists argue that the difference between general and specific models may have more to do with the situational dynamics of a particular relationship than with an adult attachment style in general (Bartholomew & Horowitz, 1991; Bowlby, 1973, 1982; Read & Miller, 1989).

Secures

The idea that one's partner can modify one's attachment style is predicated on the notion that your relationship partner can actually modify your fears in the specific relationship, and therefore, differential combinations of partners should lead to varying experiences of attachment (Le Poire et al., 1997; Le Poire et al., 1999). For instance, someone entering a relationship with a secure attachment from childhood and paired with a romantic partner who is also securely attached should maintain low levels of both intimacy and abandonment fears and therefore continue to approach fearlessly (this is the most common situation, by the way; see Table 4.3). Alternatively, this same securely disposed individual will have altered fears when paired with a preoccupied or a dismissive-avoidant partner. The preoccupied partner's demandingly high level of emotional needs may increase the secure's originally low intimacy fears, and the secure partner may begin to exhibit some characteristics of the dismissively avoidant and exhibit compensation for the high levels of involvement expressed by the preoccupied. On the other hand, although the secure entered the relationship with a low fear of abandonment, the dismissive-avoidant partner's lower levels of involvement may intensify the secure's abandonment fears, and he or she may begin to compensate for this lowered involvement level through higher expressions of involvement. Thus, the approach or avoidance communication of one's romantic partner may enhance or dampen fears and cause behavior that appears to be different from the predisposition with which one entered the relationship. Although the secure can become less secure in relationships with partners who have other attachment styles, it is also possible that being paired with a secure partner can make a preoccupied or dismissive-avoidant even *more* secure.

Preoccupieds

Consider the situation in which preoccupieds interact with romantic partners who are securely attached to them. Preoccupieds interacting with secures may have their abandonment fears lessened after the repeated exhibition of trustworthy behavior on the part of the secure partner and thus may begin to exhibit a greater degree of secure-appearing behavior. Alternatively, preoccupieds in relationships with dismissive-avoidants are faced with very low levels of involvement. The dismissive-avoidant exacerbates the preoccupied's

Table 4.3   The Interaction Between Parental and Partner Attachment Styles on Intimacy and
Abandonment Fears and Reciprocity and Compensation of Involvement

Partner Style			
Parental Style	*Secure*	*Preoccupied*	*Avoidant*
Secure	Low intimacy fears	Moderate intimacy fears	Low intimacy fears
	Low abandonment fears	Low abandonment fears	Moderate abandonment fears
	Reciprocity of involvement	Compensation of involvement	Compensation of involvement
Anxious-ambivalent	Moderate intimacy fears	Moderate intimacy fears	Moderate intimacy fears
	Moderate abandonment fears	Lowered abandonment fears	Increased abandonment fears
	Reciprocity of involvement	Reciprocity of involvement	Compensation of involvement
Role reversed	Moderate intimacy fears	Increased intimacy fears	Lowered intimacy fears
	Lowered abandonment fears	Lowered abandonment fears	Increased abandonment fears
	Reciprocity of involvement	Compensation of involvement	Reciprocity of involvement

abandonment fears, and this combination can lead to the greatest exhibition
of compensation in the form of high nonverbal expressions of involvement,
expressiveness, and pleasantness. Finally, preoccupieds in relationships
with other preoccupieds may have their intimacy fears increased because
they are met with the demands of the other preoccupied, but they may ultimately achieve a decrease in abandonment fears as the preoccupieds cling
to one another, and this co-preoccupation makes them feel more secure (as
evidenced in Le Poire et al., 1997; Le Poire et al., 1999). It is expected that
preoccupieds paired with other preoccupieds will exhibit more security and
therefore will exhibit involvement more like secures.

Dismissive-Avoidants

Finally, consider the person who had a role-reversed parental attachment
style in combination with the various styles. Dismissive-avoidants paired with
secure partners should have their fear of intimacy decreased because the secure
partner is less demanding but, as we argue (Le Poire et al., 1997; Le Poire
et al., 1999), should still exhibit some avoidant tendencies because of their
own inability to protect their boundaries with regard to the normal needs of

the secure partner. Thus, they should be expected to exhibit moderate levels of compensation to expressions of involvement through low levels of non-verbal involvement, expressiveness, and pleasantness. Alternatively, dismissive-avoidants with preoccupied romantic partners should produce the most compensation in the form of the lowest exhibition of nonverbal involvement, expressiveness, and pleasantness because this person tries to avoid too much intimacy. Finally, dismissive-avoidants paired with dismissive-avoidants might actually decrease each other's fear of intimacy, because they seek stimulation in activities outside the relationship. Similar to the preoccupied-preoccupied combination, it is likely that this will create more feelings of security and thus the dismissive-avoidant will be more comfortable expressing low to moderate levels of involvement (see Table 4.3).

With regard to the research findings for nonverbal involvement behavior in romantic couples, we found (Le Poire et al., 1997) evidence that partners influence attachment styles in that parental and partner attachments both influenced the final form of romantic attachment, with partner attachment appearing to have more influence than parental attachment. We (Le Poire et al., 1999) also found support for the contention that parental and partner attachment are both important in predicting approach and avoidance communication behavior in that *role-reversed females paired with avoidant partners* were less kinesically and vocally involved and were less kinesically pleasant. Furthermore, females with *preoccupied partners* reciprocated levels of involvement, in that they exhibited greater kinesic involvement, expressiveness, and pleasantness when interacting with their romantic partners. *Role-reversed females with more secure partners* exhibit greater vocal expressiveness. Finally, and most consistent with current theorizing, *role-reversed males paired with preoccupied partners* exhibited less kinesic involvement and pleasantness. Thus, both the parental and the partner attachment style were important in predicting nonverbal communication patterns of approach and avoidance. So for those of us with insecure attachments, the good news is that our partner can actually elicit more secure-appearing behavior from us.

Now that we know what attracts us to others both sociopyschologically and psychodynamically, you might be interested in knowing how couples transition to greater depth and intimacy in relationships. The next section considers the important relational turning points of *casual dating, serious dating, commitment,* and *engagement.*

Relational Stages of Development

Communication During Casual Dating, Serious Dating, Commitment, and Engagement

Dating—now there is an old-fashioned term for you. In fact, you probably don't even call it "dating" anymore, do you? Countless other phrases and names are more appropriate at the moment, all of which indicate the various levels of commitment the winsome twosome are experiencing. The terms you use to describe your relationship might communicate the wrong impression to your intended other. You might be "hooking up," which usually indicates a highly transitory, physical, and potentially short-lived relationship. You might be "hanging out," which indicates that you are willing to spend time with the person to experiment to see if you might like to "hang out" further. You might be hanging out with groups of friends each evening and ending up with the same person every night (my undergraduates tell me that this is the current norm at UCSB—"nobody *dates* anymore!— pshhhaw!"). You might be "seeing someone," which indicates a longer dating relationship with perhaps some level of exclusivity. And perhaps, eventually, you might even have a "boyfriend," "girlfriend," or "significant other." Those of you who have been through the paces understand just how harrowing the correct use of the terms can be! God forbid you look like you are moving along the relationship too quickly. Or worse, what if you appear desperate—or vulnerable—or needy? Yikes! Suffice it to say, transitioning from one relational stage to the next is tricky business. Here are some tips on how you know when you have moved from casual dating to serious dating. Such transitions are usually accompanied by "relational turning points" that indicate a shift in the nature of the relationship.

Although many of you may associate the transition from casual dating (i.e., seeing someone for fun with the potential to casually date numerous individuals) to more serious dating (i.e., associated with greater commitment and often with monogamy) with joy and jubilation, research evidences that this transition to greater commitment is a particularly difficult stage of relational development (Solomon, 1997), which may present many *communication difficulties*. Generally, transitioning to serious dating is characterized by greater conflict and more intense negative emotions (e.g., Aune, Aune, & Buller, 1994; Billingham & Sack, 1987; Christopher & Cate, 1985). In addition, Braiker and Kelley (1979) found that open conflict increased from casual to serious dating. However, they also found that open conflict decreased again once the relationship transitioned to a level of intimacy commensurate with serious daters. Consistently, Billingham and Sack (1987) found that verbally aggressive behavior increased from casual dating to serious dating (i.e., where marriage was desired but engagement had not been discussed) but then diminished again when couples committed to engagement.

What causes this level of communication difficulty in more serious relationships? Hocker and Wilmot (2000) offer that this increased level of irritation, conflict, and expression of hostility may be due to increasing interdependence and opportunities for goal interference. This explanation is consistent with communication researchers Denise Solomon and Leanne Knobloch (2001, 2004), who suggest that moderate levels of communication intimacy associated with the transition from casual to serious involvement may correspond with increased uncertainty about the relationship and greater interference from partners in everyday activities. In other words, as intimacy develops and lives become more intertwined, participants in relationship development may begin to have more of their typical behavioral routines interrupted. In early going, relational partners may often choose not to express irritations with their partners (Cloven & Roloff, 1994). In fact, Roloff and Cloven (1990) found that individuals withhold, or fail to communicate, an average of 40% of their irritations with their dating partners. However, as intimacy increases, partners apparently feel more permission to communicate negative emotions as they begin to express more dissatisfaction with their partners (Cloven & Roloff, 1994).

Not only may partners begin to interfere with each other's behavioral sequences, but they may also begin to experience greater levels of uncertainty at moderate levels of intimacy (Knobloch & Solomon, 2002). These greater levels of uncertainty may have to do with critical relationship communication events, such as the "first big fight" (Siegert & Stamp, 1994), expectation violations (Afifi & Metts, 1998), and problematic events (Samp & Solomon, 1998). Furthermore, these experiences of relational uncertainty may be associated with cognitive jealousy, whereas greater intimacy is tied with emotional jealousy (Knobloch, Solomon, & Cruz, 2001). Cognitive jealousy involves thoughts (worry) or doubts about a partner's infidelity, whereas emotional jealousy is an affective reaction to a perceived (real or imagined) threat to the relationship. Thus, transitioning to serious dating may be rife with communication difficulties because of increasing interdependence, opportunities for goal interference, increased relational uncertainty, and greater interference from partners in everyday activities.

One final clue as to the intimacy of the dating relationship is the communicative explicitness used to request dates. As daters become more intimate, they are less explicit when requesting future dates except in the highest conditions of intimacy where explicitness is increased (Solomon, 1997). This may indicate that in early days, daters want to be explicit about the nature of the request to indicate clear romantic intent. As the relationship heats up and daters see more and more of each other, the requests may become less and less explicit as the daters begin to experience all types of activities together. Finally, as daters transition to greater levels of intimacy, they may need to be explicit about their requests as *dating* requests because they engage in so many activities together that the boundaries of dating become unclear. Thus, explicitness seems greatest at low and high intimacy and lowest at moderate levels of intimacy.

From the above review, we might garner some information about what happens communicationally when a relationship transitions to greater stability and engagement. At this stage, as intimacy increases and the couple's lives become more seamlessly integrated, there are lower levels of conflict, fewer expressions of aggression, and greater explicitness in dating requests. It seems that in engagement, couples have made it over the bumps, grinds, and uncertainties of the moderate intimacy phase (i.e., serious daters) and move toward greater stability. However, Kelly, Huston, and Cate (1987) indicate that the high positive correlations between love and problem solving that existed during casual and serious dating diminish when partners reached the commitment to marry. In other words, the relationship between love and problem solving were not as evidenced during the engagement phase. This indicates that this period may be filled with the confidence that partners are committed to such an extent that they may feel less need to work on the relationship and the communication.

Cohabitation

In this day and age, a book on family communication would be remiss to skip cohabitation as an important relational turning point, either as an end point or as leading to marriage. As you might remember from Chapter 2, in recognition of the greater number of heterosexual couples choosing to cohabit instead of getting married, the relationship category "unmarried partner of the opposite sex" was added to the 1990 U.S. Census Bureau questionnaire (Kalish, 1994). The numbers of unmarried-couple households increased from 1.3 million in 1978 to 3.0 million in 1998 (Zinn & Eitzen, 2002) to 5.5 million (4.9 million reported opposite-sex partners) in 2000 (Simmons & O'Connell, 2003). More than half of today's marriages are preceded by cohabitation, and a majority of adults under 40 have experienced one cohabiting union (Bumpass & Sweet, 1989, 1995). Cohabitation is arguably a family status (Brown, 2000), with 40% to 43% of cohabiting couples having residing children (Bumpass, Sweet, & Cherlin, 1991; Simmons & O'Connell, 2003) and 2.2 million children living with a cohabitating parent (Manning & Lichter, 1996). Thus, cohabitation deserves attention as a potential family form that may have communication patterns very similar to married couples.

In terms of attempting to understand the similarity between cohabitation and marriage, Surra et al. (2004) maintain that three perspectives predominate. First and foremost is the perspective that *cohabitation is marriage*. This perspective is supported by several researchers who found that cohabitation is similar to marriage in terms of ages at entry (Bumpass et al., 1991), qualitative similarity (assuming marriage is the intended endpoint) and frequency of disagreements (Brown & Booth, 1996), racial homogamy (Schoen & Weinick, 1993), contraceptive use and sexuality of female partners (Seltzer, 2000), and individual partner's levels of depression (Horwitz & White, 1998). Much research exists, however, showing the inferiority of cohabitation in relation to marriage (e.g., lower relationship quality, lower satisfaction, higher conflict, higher physical aggression), as well as the superiority of cohabitation to marriage (e.g., higher rates of interaction, more equal division of household labor; Surra et al., 2004). The second perspective is that *cohabitation is a stage of courtship* that logically leads to the progression of marriage. The argument here is that cohabitation acts as a testing ground of sorts for subsequent marital compatibility. This perspective is supported by the fact that 77% of individuals indicate that cohabitation is acceptable for those wanting to ensure that their marriage will last (Hall & Zhao, 1995), as well as that 50% to 60% of recently marrieds cohabited first (Bumpass et al., 1991; Bumpass & Lu, 1998). The third perspective is that *cohabitation is the same as being single* and does not constitute a family form at all. This perspective is supported by research that indicates that singles were more similar to cohabitants in terms of fertility plans, mental health, financial matters, per capita income, and home ownership (see Surra et al., 2004, for review). Regardless of whether cohabitation is marriage, cohabitation is a stage of courtship, or cohabitation is the same as being single, cohabitation is a significant turning point in relationship development that can, as we have seen, lead to marriage.

Marriage

As the old song goes, next comes marriage. Obviously, the transition from casual dating to serious dating is fraught with communication difficulties that include conflict, increases in uncertainty, goal interruption, interference with daily behavioral routines, and increased communication of irritations and verbal aggressiveness. Luckily for those of us in transition to the greater commitment associated with engagement, these same problems seemed to diminish as our relationship increased in intimacy and we began to settle down. This section explores the next relational turning point from engagement to marriage.

Marriage and Health

Why marry? According to Barbara Defoe Whitehead (author of the book, *The Divorce Culture*), in testimony before the Senate Subcommittee on Children and Families, people who are married are quite simply better off than those who are not married. She goes on to articulate that

> on average, they are happier, healthier, wealthier, enjoy longer lives, and report greater sexual satisfaction than single, divorced or cohabiting individuals (Waite & Gallagher, 2000). Married people are less likely to take moral or mortal risks, and are even less inclined to risk-taking when they have children. They have better health habits and receive more regular health care. They are less likely to attempt or to commit suicide. They are also more likely to enjoy close and supportive relationships with their close relatives and to have a wider social support network. They are better equipped to cope with major life crises, such as severe illness, job loss, and extraordinary care needs of sick children or aging parents. (*Testimony of Barbara Defoe Whitehead*, 2004)

Although a plethora of findings support the claim that married individuals report significantly better health than nonmarrieds (e.g., Stack & Eshleman, 1998), the relationship between marriage and better physical and mental health seems to be moderated by marital satisfaction for women (Gallo, Troxel, Matthews, & Kuller, 2003). Specifically, women in highly satisfying marriages had lower levels of biological, lifestyle, and psychosocial risk factors when compared with married women in unsatisfying relationships, cohabiting women, and single women (single, divorced, or widowed). Marriage does benefit a woman's health—but only if she is satisfied. This interaction between satisfaction and marriage holds true for mental health as well. Although married individuals reported the best overall mental health, if their marriages were classified as unhappy, they actually had poorer mental health than never-married, divorced, or widowed individuals (Gove, Hughes, & Briggs Style, 1983). Janice Kiecolt-Glaser, from the department of psychiatry at the Ohio State University, claims that better health outcomes may be linked to communication. She argues that the resources associated with close personal relationships diminish negative emotions and enhance health in part through their positive impact on immune and endocrine regulation (e.g., Kiecolt-Glaser, McGuire, Robles, & Glaser, 2002b). She actually argues that the negative emotions may stimulate immune dysregulation, which may be one of the core mechanisms underlying conditions such as cardiovascular disease, osteoporosis, arthritis, Type 2 diabetes, and certain cancers (Kiecolt-Glaser et al., 2002b). Conversely, then, unhappy marriages may be rife with negative emotions and may thus explain the poorer mental and physical health of unhappily married individuals. Thus, the satisfaction of the marriage is important to take into account when considering the effects of marriage on physical and mental health.

Marriage and Communication Satisfaction

The research on marriage and health benefits begs the question, What makes some marriages happy and others unhappy? And what is the role of communication in ensuring marital satisfaction? Despite the high levels of intimacy and commitment that couples experience during courtship, most couples fail to retain these levels of satisfaction in marriage (Vangelisti & Huston, 1994). In fact, some research exists that claims that married individuals most typically experience a linear decline in their marital satisfaction over time so that the longer they are married, the more dissatisfied they become (e.g., Blood & Wolfe, 1960; Lewis & Spanier, 1979). This hypothesis is borne out in the work of Huston, McHale, and Crouter (1986) who found that on average spouses experience a decline in both marital satisfaction and their love for one another. This finding held constant for married couples with and without children (MacDermid, Huston, & McHale, 1990).

Vangelisti and Huston (1994) examine the possibility that marital satisfaction may be multidimensional. They thus assessed interactional (communication), macro-behavioral organization, and contextual factors of marital satisfaction. Interactional marital satisfaction included satisfaction with communication, influence, and sex. Macro-behavioral organization included satisfaction with individual leisure time activities, the amount of time couples spend together, and the division of household labor. Finally, contextual factors included the time spent with members of their social network and the partner's financial situation. Their results showed that decline in marital satisfaction occurred across all domains except financial situation. This held constant for couples who added children and those who did not. However, mothers who had infants within 1 year of marriage showed the sharpest decline in satisfaction with the division of the household tasks and loss of leisure time activities. Mothers who had children between 1 and 2 years after marriage were less dissatisfied with the transition. However, fathers were more dissatisfied with the division of household labor task when their children were born within this time frame.

Even though marital satisfaction declines over time in marriages, not all marriages are unhappy ones (Fincham, 2004). In other words, many of the declines are from satisfied to slightly less satisfied rather than from satisfied to *un*satisfied. However, much literature attempts to differentiate between *distressed* and *nondistressed* couples. Distressed couples are seriously dissatisfied, whereas nondistressed couples are generally satisfied. In terms of communication, distressed couples interrupt each other more (Schaap, 1984), criticize and complain more (e.g., Fichten & Wright, 1983), offer more negative solutions (Weiss & Tolman, 1990), and disclose less (e.g., Birchler, Clopton, & Adams, 1984). In general, then, distressed couples communicate in more negative ways with one another. On the positive side, satisfied couples agree more often (Schaap, Buunk, & Kerkstra, 1988), reciprocate negative affect less often (Gottman, 1979; Levenson & Gottman, 1985), and more accurately decode each other's nonverbal behaviors (Noller, 1984). Furthermore, more satisfied couples make more positive attributions for partner behavior (Bagarozzi & Giddings, 1983; Holtzworth-Monroe & Jacobson, 1988; Jacobson, 1984; Weiss, 1980) and engage in more positive communication (Gottman, 1994; Gottman, Coan, Carrere, & Swanson, 1998; Markman & Kraft, 1989; Newton, Kiecolt-Glaser, & Malarkey, 1995; Weiss & Heyman, 1990). In terms of tangible things that couples can do to increase their communication satisfaction, the time couples spend "debriefing" about what happened during their day is positively related to their relational satisfaction (Vangelisti & Banski, 1993). Therefore, increasing debriefing time at the end of the day could significantly improve relational satisfaction.

The fact that marital satisfaction declines over time supports the claim that marriages go through three stages (Pearson, 1993). The first phase, or *the happy honeymoon phase,* begins immediately following the wedding. This period is filled with optimism and the continuation of romantic love. The second stage includes *disillusions and regrets.* At this point in the marriage, one or both members of the marital union fear they have made a mistake by getting married, as the reality of the work of marriage collides with the dreams of the earlier honeymoon stage. The final stage includes *accommodation*, where marital partners come to some sort of rectification of their highest hopes and worst fears. At this stage, marital partners are expected to experience conjugal love in addition to, or as a replacement for, romantic love. The declines in marital satisfaction over time can be explained by the tendency for marital couples to go through these stages.

One final quality that could affect the marital satisfaction of the couple is the **marital type** of the couple. In a now famous study in communication, Mary Anne Fitzpatrick (1988) delineated three primary marital types based on an extensive content analysis of the literature on marriages. *Traditionals* hold conventional values, value stability over spontaneity, and are highly interdependent. They show a high degree of sharing and companionship during marriage. In addition, they are generally not conflict avoiders. *Independents* hold unconventional values, including that marriage should not constrain individual freedoms. Finally, *separates* hold both the viewpoint of the traditional and the independent couples in that they have conventional values and value stability over spontaneity, but they do not believe in a high degree of interdependence among the couple. They maintain psychological distance and also avoid conflict. While 60% of couples agree on their marital type, the remaining couples were either unclassifiable or perhaps fall within mixed categorizations.

In terms of *communication outcomes* associated with the various marital types, self-disclosure and conflict are related to marital type (Fitzpatrick, 1988). Independents disclose the most, followed by traditionals, with separates disclosing the least. In addition, separates are confrontational, whereas traditionals display more conciliatory messages. Furthermore, independents show significantly more negative affect during conflict. Surprisingly, given their more confrontational nature, separates also exhibit the most compliance during communication. It is possible, then, that marital satisfaction is related to couple type. In addition, it is also highly likely that mismatches among the marital types may manifest themselves in less satisfying relationships, with one couple member attempting to be traditional and the other attempting to be separate or independent.

Summary

Developmentally, families begin through courtship and mating rituals in which communication processes are fundamental. This is true regardless of whether individuals are moving toward first marriages or commitments or remarriage and potential stepfamilies. This chapter explored how all individuals use communication to develop relationships that have the potential for resulting in long-term mate selection and marriage. To that end, *factors related to initial interactions* were considered. Early courtship communication cues signaling readiness for courtship include (a) attention-gaining cues,

(b) recognition or courtship readiness, (c) positioning, and (d) resolution. *Motivations for relationship maintenance*—including attraction, economic potential, similarity, and education—were considered. Furthermore, *evolutionary psychology* theory argues that motivations for relationship maintenance include the viability of the mate for bearing and rearing children, whereas *social exchange theory* argues that relationships will be maintained and developed if the potential rewards of the relationship outweigh the potential costs. On the psychodynamic side, parental and romantic *attachments* were explored for their potential to underlie romantic attachment and ensuing communication processes. In other words, the early experiences we have in attaching to caregivers lay the foundation for subsequent relationship attachments and our communication tendencies within them. Those of us who attached securely to our caregivers are likely to approach relationships fearlessly, whereas those of us who were abandoned are more likely to have fears of abandonment as we approach relationships, and those of us who were role reversed as children are likely to be fearful of intimacy as we approach relationships. Fortunately, our partner's romantic attachment style can moderate those fears in that securely attached partners are likely to dampen existing fears of intimacy and abandonment, whereas preoccupied partners are likely to enhance existing fears of intimacy and dismissively avoidant partners are likely to heighten existing fears of abandonment. In terms of *relationship stages*, the communication approaches of *uncertainty reduction theory*, *social penetration model*, *dialectic models,* and *Knapp's relational stages* were considered. Uncertainty reduction theory argues that we use communication to reduce our initial uncertainty about potential romantic partners. Social penetration theory argues that we use communication to move through various stages of relationships, and dialectic models theorize about the ways in which communication is used to establish and maintain certain levels of intimacy and autonomy within our romantic relationships. Finally, turning points in relationships were considered to the extent that they affect the communication in relationships as relational partners transition from *casual dating* to *serious dating* to *engagement*, potentially to *cohabitation*, and finally to *marriage (or marriage-like commitments)*. Transitioning from casual dating to serious dating is marked by increasing difficulties in communication, whereas transitioning to engagement seems to be accompanied by increases of smoothness in communication. Cohabitation seems to be a process very similar to marriage in that many of the communication processes appear to mirror each other. While marital satisfaction tends to decline over time in most marriages, marital satisfaction can be greatly influenced by communication satisfaction, such that more satisfied marital partners tend to reciprocate more positive communication interactions and reciprocate fewer negative communication interactions. This marital communication satisfaction can have long-term effects on the physical and mental health of the married couple in that greater communication of negative affect (in distressed couples) has been related to poor immunological functioning and greater tendencies for long-term health consequences such as poor cardio functioning and some forms of cancer. These satisfaction and health outcomes may also be related to the communication behaviors, which have been associated with the various marital types of traditionals, independents, and separates.

KEY TERMS

anxious ambivalents
attachment theory
attraction
casual daters
dismissive-avoidants
economic potential
education
engagement
evolutionary approaches to mate
   selection
marital stages
marital types
marriage
marriage and health

marriage and satisfaction
propinquity
role reversal
romantic attachment
secures
serious daters
similarity
social exchange theories
social penetration model
stages of courtship
stages of relationship development
uncertainty reduction theory
working models

QUESTIONS FOR APPLICATION

1. What factors first attracted you to your most recent dating partner? Were they social psychological or psychodynamic in nature?

2. Analyze your most recent dating relationship in terms of your own attachment style. How did you attach to your parents? What significant events came into play? How do you attach in your current or recently past dating relationships? Have you evidenced different attachment styles with different partners? (If you haven't had many romantic relationships at this point, you can consider your friendship attachments).

3. Did evolutionary or social exchange principles come into play in your most recent choices for dating partners? Why or why not?

4. How did uncertainty reduction, social penetration, and dialectic processes come into play as you developed your longest romantic relationship?

5. In your and your friends' experiences, has transitioning from casual dating to serious dating been associated with communication difficulties as outlined in the text? Did you notice these difficulties abating at any point in your relationship?

6. Describe your parents' marital satisfaction. What types of things tipped you off that your parents were happy/unhappy? How was marital satisfaction affected by their communication behavior? In other words, in what ways did they communicate that offered information about their marital satisfaction?

5 Communication in the Newly Formed Family: Adding Children

Figure 5.1   New parents often struggle with balancing the children and their careers.

As you begin to imagine the development of your family, many of you will be dreaming of the successful integration of children into your family unit. In fact, so strong is the societal pressure to have families organize child-producing activities, that before you are even married, and perhaps before you are even of the age to become engaged, curious and well-meaning grandparents, uncles, and parents will begin to query your potential interest in rearing children. This is especially the case once you have become engaged. This public level of commitment is associated with freedom for many interested parties to question your intent to raise children. This is only the beginning, however, of the communication changes that accompany adding children to any family unit (single-parent homes, nuclear families, blended families, extended families, adoptive families, and families choosing surrogacy). Referring back to roles theory in Chapter 3, adding children places an added saliency on the new role of parent that causes a whole host of behaviors to change as the family becomes reoriented around the child. Many of these changes are communicative: (a) communication surrounding the pregnancy, (b) communication with the new infant/child, (c) communication surrounding the burgeoning workload associated with adding children, (d) changes in communication between the parents (and accompanying decreases in marital satisfaction), and (e) changes in communication with the children as they develop into preschoolers and school-age children. Changes in communication between the parents and between the parents and children are not the only ways adding children affects the family. Adding children often adds sibling relationships with their own unique communicative dimensions. Furthermore, adding stepchildren is another way that families can develop, and the addition of stepparent and stepchildren roles brings ensuing communication and other problems into focus. The addition of the stepparent may also bring additional children into the family, and with them, new stepsibling and sometimes half-sibling relationships are developed. These unique types of sibling relationships bring their own host of unique communication problems as well. Such is the focus of the current chapter.

The Effects of Pregnancy on Communication

Although not all families add children through pregnancy (e.g., adoptive families, families using surrogacy, stepfamilies, extended families, foster homes), a majority of families are developed through pregnancy. Expectant parents experience many physical, cognitive, and emotional changes when they are expecting a baby—all of which can translate into changes in communication patterns between the parents. Parents may express concerns, discuss many practical issues (e.g., childbirth, child care, genetic testing), discuss role expectations after birth (e.g., who will get up with the baby in the night), and experience increases in intimacy and potential decreases in sexual activity. Although these changes seem numerous, they are likely to pale in comparison to the communication changes within the couple unit immediately following the child's birth.

Communication within the family can also be affected by, and associated with, the many fears women experience associated with pregnancy and childbirth (Melender, 2002). Specifically, 78% of expecting mothers reported fears relating to pregnancy, childbirth, or both. These fears concern childbirth, the child's and mother's well-being, health care staff, family life, and cesarean section. Expectant mothers are more likely to communicate their fears if they are in a negative mood. In addition, many expectant mothers are approached by well-meaning friends, families, and even strangers with negative stories of their own birthing and child care experiences, and these negative stories were related to greater expression of fears. Furthermore, expectant mothers' fears are greater after hearing alarming information or receiving information regarding diseases and child-related problems. Thus, communication from others regarding pregnancy and childbirth can be a significant predictor of the fears women experience during pregnancy. In addition, women may experience insecurity about their physical appearance and anxiety about their expertise as "mother" (Ruble et al., 1990). These fears and experiences are not limited to mothers however. Expectant fathers may experience greater ambivalence and anxiety as well (e.g., Gerzi & Berman, 1981). All these concerns may be associated with changes in communication in the family.

The communication between expectant parents is likely to change as well. Specifically, expectant mothers have evidenced a greater sensitivity to the meaning of verbal and nonverbal communication (Rubin, 1975). This change in sensitivity may be associated with more problematic communication within the family. Other communication surrounding the impending birth of the child may include discussions about birthing plans, birthing classes, tests for potential genetic abnormalities, and plans for child care. These communication topics may be of particular relevance to expecting parents in single-parent, nuclear, blended, and extended-family situations. All these discussions may prove fruitful for relationships, however, in that pregnancy can create greater closeness in couples (Feeney, Hohaus, Noller, & Alexander, 2001) because a woman may feel a greater sense of caring from her husband (in the nuclear or blended-family situation). This sense of closeness may vary by couple type, however. Pregnant wives in traditional marriages felt they received more nurturance than wives in independent marriages (Fitzpatrick, Vangelisti, & Firman, 1994).

Another communication change accompanying pregnancy may be increased use of Internet sources of information. As the parenting role becomes more salient, both expectant parents may begin to "surf the Web" for information regarding the stage of pregnancy and concerns with regard to which of the thousands of baby paraphernalia are actually necessary as opposed to superfluous. Many sites will e-mail expectant mothers weekly updates on their pregnancy, newsletters, opportunities for chat room communication with other parents, and of course, opportunities for buying necessary baby items (e.g., babycenter.com, americanbaby.com).

The need to buy necessary apparatus points to another concern expectant parents may have—money for the birth and all the essentials. Having babies is expensive business. A hospital birth alone can run up a bill upward of $20,000. Those without insurance may feel especially burdened here. Then the costs of the first necessary equipment combined with long-term considerations of child care and higher education costs can send prospective parents into a tailspin with regard to financial concerns. Thus, finances may be a topic for consideration and an added source of stress during pregnancy as well.

Addition of a Child and Changes in Communication

Having a baby biologically is not the only way children are added to families. Adoption represents about 4% of the children added to households. In addition, as adoptions become increasingly difficult to achieve, transracial adoptions are becoming more common (Shanley, 2003), especially for older couples or couples who already have biological children. My sister and her husband, for instance, adopted my niece after several failed attempts at pregnancy and one miscarriage. They had three boys biologically but desperately wanted a girl. Karen is Korean, and they were able to adopt her through Holt, a Christian organization that organizes international adoptions from several different countries. Similarly, a colleague of mine in Illinois adopted two daughters from China, where laws against multiple births and the high premium on boy babies make adopting girls from China easier. Most recently, another colleague of mine in Texas legally adopted a 5-year-old girl from Russia. These adoptions are unique in that the differences in physical features make it obvious to others that the children are not biologically related to their parents. In addition, many of these children are considered "special needs" in that they often have physical challenges. Regardless of whether babies are born into or adopted by families, the dramatic changes in the family's life and their satisfaction and communication are consistent (O'Brien & Zamostny, 2003). Both this study and one on adding children through surrogacy (e.g., MacCallum, Lycett, Murray, Jadva, & Golombok, 2003) indicate that the stigma once associated with adoption and surrogacy arrangements is diminishing; 100% of the surrogacy couples studied had told their family and friends about the surrogacy and were planning to tell the child as well. In addition, communication scholars Erin Shank Krusiewicz and Julia Wood (2001) indicate that the storytelling themes of adoption entry (i.e., dialectic tensions, destiny, compelling connection, rescue, and legitimacy) affirm adopted children and adoption as a valid way of currently adding children to the family.

Although adoption from birth and surrogacy are the closest in family forms to adding children through pregnancy, children can be added to families in other ways as well. Stepfamilies are created through the high remarriage rates that now place up to 15% of children in blended or binuclear homes. Many new parents, then, are parents through marriage instead of birth. In addition, 5% of children are being raised in extended families where they are being raised by their grandparents alone or their grandparents and their biological parent(s). In many of these homes, grandparents fulfill a majority of the child-rearing roles. Thus, children can be added to families through pregnancy, adoption, surrogacy, remarriage or marriage with preexisting children, or extended families. The next section detailing the communication changes in a family adding an infant to the household is primarily related to families that add children through pregnancy, adoption of infants, surrogacy, and extended-family situations where the pregnant mother resides. Adding older children (in stepfamily and older children adoptions) is considered in the latter portion of this chapter.

Increases in Workload and Changes in Communication

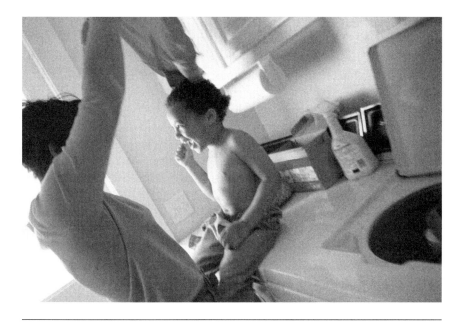

Figure 5.2   New parents' household and childcare tasks increase sixfold after the birth of a child.

Most of the research on the effects of adding children chronicles two changes in the family unit—both of which are likely to result in dramatic changes in family communication. First, there is an exponential *increase in the child care and household tasks*. Second, the parenting couple seems to experience an appreciable *decline in marital satisfaction*. These things seem to go hand in hand. Following the initial experiences of exhilaration and awe at the birth of one's child, the workload begins to become evident and has considerable consequences on the nature of family life and the communication within it. Ted Huston and Erin K. Holmes (2004) report that in two-parent families prior to the birth of an infant, wives or nurturer-caregivers complete approximately 67% of the household responsibilities (about 5.4 household tasks per day), and husbands complete the other 33% (or 2.3 household tasks per day). These findings are fairly consistent throughout the literature (Belsky & Kelly, 1994). After the birth of the child, however, there is a well-documented sixfold increase in the number of family-related household tasks per day, with tasks increasing from 5.8 per day to 36.2 per day (Huston & Holmes). This striking contrast is felt by both parents, although the gender division of tasks begins to define the roles and communication behavior of the various household members. Specifically, new mothers increase their household task load from 5.3 to 28 tasks per day. New fathers, in contrast, increase their household task load from 2.4 to 8.3 tasks per day. Thus, mothers assume more of the traditional *nurturer* tasks, while fathers assist in the process. This change in workload may not only result in dramatically less time for communication between the new parents but may also change the nature of communication that does exist such that more communication is focused on the child and the organization and fulfillment of child care tasks.

What exactly is the nature of the increased household tasks, and what is the role of communication in their completion? Huston and Holmes (2004) asked parents to keep diaries of the child care-related tasks they completed each day. From most-frequent to least-frequent tasks that the mothers report, mothers change diapers, feed the child, soothe the child, dress the child, play quietly with the child, pick up after the child, put the child to sleep, read to the child, set rules and handle misbehavior, play rough-and-tumble with the child, help the child to learn skills, bathe the child, plan the child's activities, and get up at night with the child. In other words, they complete the routine nurturing and care of the child. While at least 50% of these reported nurturing tasks *require* communication for their fulfillment (soothing the child, playing quietly with the child, putting the child to sleep, reading to the child, setting rules and handling misbehavior, playing rough and tumble with the child, helping the child to learn skills), it is likely that communication with the infant accompanies the fulfillment of *every* task (i.e., changing diapers, feeding the child, dressing the child, bathing the child, and getting up at night with the child are all likely to include communication). In other words, almost all the routine nurturing caregiving tasks rely on communicative behavior for their successful execution.

We already know that mothers do the lion's share of these routine nurturing and communicative tasks, but what percentage of each of these routine tasks does she complete? Huston and Holmes (2004) report that mothers change diapers, feed the child, soothe the child, bathe the child, help the child learn skills, and put the child to sleep nearly 80% of the time. Given the nature of these tasks, mothers assume the major components of child care and communication with the child. To further round out this picture, you might wonder just who gets up with the child in the middle of the night (infants wake up to feed in the night every 1.5 to 2 hours for the first 6 weeks, at which point they begin to spread out the feedings to 3 to 4 hours per night up to 8 to 12 weeks, depending on the weight of the child). Once again, mothers earn the weariness prize by getting up with the child at night around 72% of the time. Not only do mothers nurture and communicate more with the child, they perform these child care responsibilities with a considerable sleep debt. This sleep debt has also been associated with diminished functioning and increased problems with emotions and communication.

What do fathers do? Less is known about the transition to fatherhood experienced by dads (Strauss & Goldberg, 1999). We do know, however, from Huston and Holmes's (2004) data that the largest percentage of rough-and-tumble play is assumed by dads—up to 55%. Fathers also set rules and play quietly with the child up to 35% of the time. In addition, Cowan (1988) reports that fathers experience a more dramatic transition to parenthood after the infant is 6 months old. It is unlikely a coincidence that infants are much more communicative and interactive when they reach 6 months old. This greater communicativeness may be the impetus for the father's greater involvement in child care. It appears that the transition to fatherhood is more gradual than it is for mothers who land quite squarely among the nurturing and communication changes to their day-to-day routine from the time the infant is born. Given this slower transition, it is likely that fathers experience more stress associated with parenthood after the initial excitement of being a new parent wears off (Berman & Pederson, 1987).

In terms of a father's involvement in child care, the more competent he perceives himself to be at child care and the more he thinks his wife views him as competent, the more a husband contributes to both housework and child care (Huston & Holmes, 2004). Specifically, fathers who perceive themselves as more skilled at child care perform more child care activities than those who don't (Bonney, Kelley, & Levant, 1999; Feldman, Nash, & Aschenbrenner, 1983). In addition, mothers' perceptions that their husbands are good at family work actually predict the amount of housework and child care the husband reports doing (Huston & Holmes, 2004). In other words, a wife's belief in her husband's competency at child care is related to his contributed household labor. Communication plays a role here; mothers who perceive their husbands as more competent are more likely to communicate this perception to their spouses in a variety of ways (e.g., praise, nonverbal signs of encouragement and approval). In addition, fathers who are more maritally satisfied before the birth of a child feel more competent as parents (Bonney et al., 1999; Cowan & Cowan, 1987). This is consistent with other research showing that the closeness marriage partners feel before parenthood is related to the degree of competence fathers feel with their infants up to 6 months of age (Cox, Owen, Lewis, & Henderson, 1989). Finally, women with less traditional views of gender ideology are more likely to have husbands who are more involved with their children (Arendell, 1996; Barnett & Baruch, 1987), as are wives who prefer their husbands to be involved in child care (McHale & Huston, 1984). Thus, (a) wives, (b) the quality of the marital relationship, and (c) wives' communication behavior clearly affect the level of involvement between fathers and their children.

Although the solution seems simple—wives, have better relationships with your husbands and communicatively praise your husband's child care efforts more if you want him to be more involved with the children—this may be difficult in light of the fact that more expectant mothers believe that they are more skilled at child care than are their partners (McHale & Huston, 1984). In fact, both parents confirm this belief after the child is born. Thus, it seems best to curb messages of incompetence from mothers to fathers. And yet, an example from my own life points up how difficult this can be in light of protecting the infant. Like most mothers, I'm a growling bear when anything untoward approaches my cub—and unfortunately and ashamedly, this includes my husband. After a lengthy walk in the yard so that I could get ready for the day, my husband and daughter walked into the kitchen, and the first words out of my mouth were "What's Rachel eating?" It was dirt, of course! But the time for "thank you for letting Rachel learn so much about nature and letting her explore the world in ways I dare not" was gone because her health and safety came first. Making your spouse feel you believe in his or her competency as a parent might require that you not *always* put your child's safety first, if in fact it really isn't threatened. Let's face it; a little dirt in the digestive tract rarely hurt anyone.

More controversially, some have actually argued that mothers act as "gatekeepers" to fathers' relationships with their children and may actually limit fathers' involvement through their communication behavior (Allen & Hawkins, 1999; Belsky & Volling, 1987; DeLuccie, 1995). Allen and Hawkins suggest that women have a hard time sharing child care with fathers due to high expectations and a desire to manage household and family tasks. They also suggest that this is especially true for mothers who have an identity based around their children and their house, who have high standards for housework and child care, and who hold more traditional attitudes about womanhood. These mothers communicate these beliefs to their husbands, who in turn respond by being less involved with their children.

You might remember from Chapter 3 that regardless of the inequity in workloads between wives and husbands on domestic labor, less than one third of women report that the allocation of tasks is unfair (Blair & Johnson, 1992; Demo & Acock, 1993; Hawkins, Marshall, & Allen, 1998;

Thompson, 1991). However, performing traditional "female" tasks of domestic labor is associated with greater depression in women and sometimes even in men (Barnett & Shen, 1997; Glass & Fujimoto, 1994; Golding, 1990). This is an especially double-edged sword, because women often ask their husbands to do more of these tasks (Benin & Agostinelli, 1988; Blair & Johnson, 1992; Dempsey, 1997). This bears itself out in the findings regarding men who are pressed to contribute more to child care by their working wives (Crouter, Perry-Jenkins, Huston, McHale, 1987). When fathers do assist their wives, they are obviously reluctant and show signs that they feel they are being exploited. In fact, the more fathers with working wives are involved in child care, the more they complain, criticize, and show general dissatisfaction with their wives (Crouter et al., 1987). To fully round out this picture, fathers who feel the division of labor is unfair also report being more negative toward their wives and less in love with them. Thus, some of the decreases in marital satisfaction associated with having a child that we will see below may be more related to overall life changes and overall division of household labor satisfaction than to a decline in marital satisfaction, in particular. In other words, dissatisfaction with the division of child care tasks may result in more negative communication between spouses (i.e., greater negativity, more complaining, criticizing) and reductions in marital satisfaction overall.

Changes in Marital Communication and Satisfaction

Given the relative work demands associated with a new infant, it comes as no surprise that this intense focus on the child takes time away from nurturing the mother-father relationship. A well-documented decline in marital satisfaction is reported accompanying the birth of a baby (Feeney, Hohaus, Noller, & Alexander, 2001). Most famously, LeMasters (1957) declared the birth of a baby a "crisis" in the life of a family that overwhelms classically unprepared parents. Since this famous study (and somewhat in reaction to it), however, other researchers have documented that parenthood may actually increase satisfaction in certain marriages, decrease satisfaction in some marriages, and cause no change in others (Belsky & Kelly, 1994; Cowan & Cowan, 2000; Feeney et al., 2001).

In an attempt to explain the evidenced declines in marital satisfaction, Huston and Holmes (2004) offer three potential alternative explanations for the findings of cross-sectional studies (studies that occur at one point in time only and do not truly investigate marital satisfaction *before* and marital satisfaction *after* the birth of the child). First, Huston and Holmes suggest that these studies cannot rule out the possibility that lower satisfaction existed in these couples prior to the birth of a child. Second, it is also possible that unhappy couples may stay together because they believe their child will be better off in an unhappy intact home than in a divorced family. Thus, it is possible that parents, as a group, include less satisfied couples than would a group of marrieds who are not parents (Shapiro, Gottman, & Carrere, 2000;

Waite & Lillard, 1991; White, Booth, & Edwards, 1986); that is, it's possible that they were unhappy before and stay together for the sake of the child's upbringing. Finally, other factors may account for the differences in marital satisfaction such as that any parent group studied is likely to be younger and married less time than the comparable nonparent group (Huston & Vangelisti, 1995; Moore & Waite, 1981). Although these studies provide evidence that married couples with children are less satisfied than married couples without children, it is likely that other factors besides parenting contribute to this finding. Like the findings regarding single-parent home impacts on children (you might remember that the negative impacts of single-parent homes are more likely accounted for by poverty and depression), even though it is still the case that parental decreases in marital satisfaction are well documented, it is just as likely that other factors—besides the birth of the child—account for the differences. This claim is well supported by the longitudinal studies that include a nonparental control group. In general, these studies show that marital satisfaction declines over time regardless of whether or not a couple become parents (e.g., Cowan & Cowan, 1988; Karney & Bradbury, 1997; Kurdek, 1993; MacDermid, Huston, & McHale, 1990; McHale & Huston, 1985).

Findings regarding parental satisfaction are not limited to cross-sectional studies, however. In other words, many longitudinal studies document changes in marital satisfaction over time—measuring marital satisfaction both before and after the birth of a child (e.g., Belsky, Lang, & Rovine, 1985; Ruble, Fleming, Hackel, & Stangor, 1988; Tomlinson, 1987). Huston and Holmes (2004) maintain that these studies are limited, as well. First, it is possible that expectant parents experience increases in marital satisfaction as they anticipate the birth of their first child and that the changes in marital satisfaction following the birth are actually regressions back to the mean levels of satisfaction that existed prior to the pregnancy. Second, it is possible that all marital couples experience a decline in marital satisfaction, especially during the early years of marriage during which most births are likely to occur (e.g., Glenn, 1998; Vaillant & Vaillant, 1993). Finally, they suggest that participants may be tipped off to the nature of the study because of the before and after birth measures and may conform to what they know is the common wisdom regarding marital satisfaction and childbirth and may confirm the expected findings unwittingly.

It is also important to recognize that the *timing* of childbirth can play an important role in marital satisfaction. It seems that the old adage that you should wait to have children until you have had time to enjoy your spouse for awhile is borne out by the research. Specifically, Helms-Erikson (2001) found that couples who became parents just shortly before or shortly after marriage are less satisfied than parents who become parents later in their marital life (i.e., "on-time," or "delayed"). In addition, Vangelisti and Huston (1994) found that mothers who had infants within 1 year of marriage show the sharpest decline in satisfaction with the division of the household tasks and loss of leisure time activities. Mothers who had children between 1 and 2 years after marriage are less dissatisfied with the transition. However, fathers are more dissatisfied with the division of household labor tasks when their children were born within this time frame.

It is also possible that some of the declines in marital satisfaction reported above are due to the changes in the amount of time that couples are able to spend alone doing leisure-related activities. Specifically, whereas couples spend 44% of their time in activities together prior to the birth of the child, they spend only 22% of time together following the birth of the baby (Crawford & Huston, 1993). In addition, the types of leisure activities change for new mothers and fathers. New mothers do more leisure activities that they enjoy, whereas men experience a greater restriction on the types of activities they enjoy (Crawford & Huston, 1993).

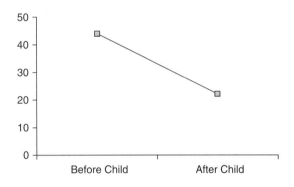

Figure 5.3   Shared Leisure Activities (in % of total time)
SOURCE: Crawford & Huston, 1993.

Time for communication between couples may change as well. New parents are not able to spend as much time talking as before (McHale & Huston, 1985). However, physical expressions of affection do not appear to be affected by parenthood, nor do verbal expressions of affection, attempts to make each other laugh, sharing feelings, and attempts to "do something nice for each other" (MacDermid et al., 1990). In fact, some husbands actually appear to compensate for the reduction in verbal talking time by increasing their affection after the birth of the child (McHale & Huston, 1985). In terms of sexual activity, new parents do not appear to exhibit more of a decline than nonparents (except at the end of pregnancy and immediately following the birth; Huston & Holmes, 2004). New parents may become very efficient in their use of communication. In particular, new parents communicated more effectively and problem solved more efficiently than nonparents (Cowan & Cowan, 1988).

Infant-Caregiver Communication

Figure 5.4   Mothers' communication with infants provides the earliest foundation
for language acquisition and intellectual development.

The decreased time that new parents have to spend communicating may
be the result of increased time communicating with the new addition to the
family. This communication is seen as essential to the healthy development
of the child. The earliest interactions between parents and infants profoundly affect the emotional, cognitive, and social development of the infant
(Van Egeren & Barratt, 2004). In this way, the earliest infant-caregiver
interactions lay the foundations for the child's ability to communicate
effectively. Regardless of the theoretical or methodological perspective
taken in examining infant-caregiver interactions, adult responsiveness to
infant cues (i.e., contingency and sensitivity) is identified as core to the
process of optimal child development (Van Egeren & Barratt, 2004).

Infants are born with well-equipped visual and auditory abilities that allow
them to tune in to their parents' communication (Van Egeren & Barrett,
2004). Visually, infants appear to be particularly attracted to characteristics
that resemble the human species (Mondloch et al., 1999; Valenza, Simion,
Cassia, & Umilta, 1996). In addition, infants see best at 12 to 24 inches,
which is primarily the distance their caregivers' faces are from them when

they are being held (Haynes, White, & Held, 1965). Furthermore, babies seem to be attracted to the contrasts that the human faces exhibit (Slater & Johnson, 1998). In fact, infants soon begin to show a preference for their mother's face (Barrile, Armstrong, & Bower, 1999).

Vocally, infants are attracted to speech sounds as well (Jusczyk & Bertoncini, 1988). Because fetuses can sense auditory stimuli long before they are born, they are able to discriminate low-frequency sounds when they are newborn (Spence & Freeman, 1996). They are thus quickly able to discriminate between male and female voices (Miller, 1983), as well as between parents' voices and strangers' voices (Ockleford, Vince, Layton, & Reader, 1988). In fact, they actually prefer their mother's voice to that of a female stranger (DeCasper & Fifer, 1980). These sensitivities to vocalics also appear to be rooted in the need for security in that infants perceive up-and-down glides in pitch that provide important information about affect and security (Papousek, Bornstein, Nuzzo, Papousek, & Symmes, 1990).

Soon thereafter, infants begin to encode their own vocalic communication (what researchers refer to as nondistressed vocalizations; Van Egeren & Barratt, 2004). By 6 to 8 weeks, infants can begin to approximate vowel sounds (Lieberman, 1984). By 8 to 12 weeks, they can coo, and by around 6 months, infants can babble (Oller, 1986). These vocalizations seem to be specifically aimed at communication, in that infants actually vocalize more when their parents are around than when they are alone (Masataka, 1993), and when parents respond to these vocalizations, infants engage in even more vocalizations (Legerstee, 1991).

Distress vocalizations occur in the first 4 to 5 months (Stark, Rose, & McLagen, 1975) and are highly potent and arousing signals for caregivers (Van Egeren & Barrett, 2004). In fact, distress cries may be the most adaptive form of communication that infants possess. Mothers, fathers, women, men, parents, and nonparents can all correctly interpret the earliest distress cries (Papousek, 1989). However, mothers are better at distinguishing distress cries for food as opposed to those of discomfort (Stallings, Fleming, Corter, Worthman, & Steiner, 2001).

In general, all parents, regardless of culture, respond to distress cries by holding, rocking/bouncing, singing, or talking in melodic rhythms (Keller et al., 1996; Papousek & Papousek, 1991). If the child is momentarily out of the parent's reach, the parent begins rapid-fire, high-pitched verbalizations with a pitch that falls by the end (Papousek, Papousek, & Bornstein, 1985). Parents generally find this crying so aversive and arousing that they actually try to anticipate their infants' distress crying and try to prevent it before it occurs (Papousek & Papousek, 1990). Because infants often avoid eye contact when they are distressed, mothers of distressed infants attempt to reestablish eye contact through increased touch, smiling, and social play (Beebe & Stern, 1977).

Besides vocalizations, infants rely on other forms of nonverbal communication as well. Increased gaze between mothers and infants is related to greater vocalizations by both, but especially for mothers (Stevenson,

Ver Hoeve, Roach, & Leavitt, 1986). In addition, infants who use gestures more frequently may actually acquire language more quickly (Van Egeren & Barratt, 2004). Children who point relatively early (some as early as 3 months) use more gestures overall and have better speech comprehension (Butterworth & Morissette, 1996).

Communicating With Preschool and School-Aged Children

Parents of preschoolers are transitioning from purely nurturing roles to more disciplinarian and authoritative roles (Galinsky, 1981). Preschoolers acquire language skills at enormous rates of speed and are also able to run, skip, and jump—a combination that leaves parents wondering why they were so happy when their baby learned to toddle! All this newfound knowledge leaves the preschooler ready to test the boundaries of behavior on many levels. Parents tire of the word *no*!—especially when they hear it repeated back to them over and over again! In this way, toddlerhood is often seen as similar to adolescence in that the toddler is trying to establish independence from the caregivers. This increased exploration is often met with behavioral limitations designed to protect their children from dangers.

Parents also find themselves faced with decisions regarding whether or not to send their advanced toddler to preschool. Advances in the ways parents communicate with children, tendencies to send toddlers to preschool, and advances in the types of television programming children are exposed to all create more competitive environments for children entering elementary school. In fact, some have actually claimed that these advances have led teachers to include traditionally first-grade material in their kindergarten classes to keep up with the advanced nature of the typical kindergartener's knowledge. Most of us are familiar with the advertising campaign encouraging parents and caregivers to read to their children. Shared reading with children is related to preschoolers' listening comprehension when parents use nondirective reasoning with their children, but not when parents use physical punishment (Gest, Freeman, Domitrovich, & Welsh, 2004).

Preschool is not only a place for children to acquire academic readiness but is also seen as a socializing agent for authority figures (i.e., teachers) and establishing and maintaining relationships with peers (e.g., Van den Oord, Rispens, Goudena, & Vermande, 2000). In other words, not only are preschoolers learning numbers, letters, shapes, and colors, but they are also learning not to hit little Tammy over the head with the red triangle! Speaking of problematic behavior on the playground, mothers' relations with children are especially important because mothers' insightfulness regarding their children's behavior is related to more prosocial behavior with peers (Oppenheim, Goldsmith, & Koren-Karie, 2004).

Following the birth and socialization of children in the home and in child care environments, traditionally, parents send their children to elementary school when they are about 5 years of age. This stage of parenthood is seen as *interpretative* in that the child expects the parents to interpret the broader world around them (Galinsky, 1981). School is another socializing agent for children. Again, children learn that there are other authority figures besides Mommy and Daddy. Children begin to become more independent as they establish relationships with other caregiver/adults and other children. Furthermore, children begin to be stimulated in the learning environment to take advantage of their spongelike brains and facilitate academic learning across a variety of traditional disciplines (reading, writing, and arithmetic). Finally, children in school learn to socialize with others and learn important lessons about communication, conflict resolution, playing fair, and gender roles—lessons that may or may not have been emphasized in the home previously.

Parent-child communication can change during this time, with parents and children having less time to spend in communication with one another. However, it may be that the *quality* of the interactions is more important to the nature of the relationship than the quantity of communication. Specifically, Dixson (1995) found that the quality of everyday interactions between mothers and their elementary-age sons predicted relationship satisfaction more than did the amount of time mothers communicated with their sons. Mothers who felt that their sons understood them, listened to them, and had less conflict with them were more satisfied.

Now more than previously, communication about chores may also be a significant part of the communication landscape between parents and their school-aged children. About 13% of weekly household chores are performed by school-aged children (Blair, 1992). As children mature, they tend to take on more tasks (Antill, Goodnow, Russell, & Cotton, 1996; Goodnow, Bowes, Warton, Dawes, & Taylor, 1991), and these tasks become more defined by traditional gender lines (e.g., McHale, Bartko, Crouter, & Perry-Jenkins, 1990). While parents may dole out these tasks for socialization purposes or for need (Coltrane, 2000), children's satisfaction with completion of these tasks may vary based on family form. For instance, boys from dual-earner families who complete more household tasks report greater satisfaction, less stress, and better relationships with parents (Crouter, McHale, & Bartko, 1993). However, these same researchers found that boys from single-parent homes who complete more household tasks report less satisfaction, greater stress, and lower-quality relationships with their parents. In addition, how parents communicate may affect the extent to which children participate in household chores. Specifically, Coltrane (2000) reports that parents and stepparents who encourage their children more have sons who complete more of the housework. Finally, high allocations of responsibility for household tasks have been associated with better overall competence among primary school children (Amato, 1989).

Communication in Sibling Relationships

SOURCE: Adam @ Home © 1998 by Universal Press Syndicate. Reprinted with permission. All rights reserved.

The addition of children to a family does not mark the transition in changes in communication only between parents and children, however. One of the most important and under-studied relationships in the family may be those between siblings (Floyd & Morman, 2005b). The sibling relationship plays an important role in the emotional, cognitive, and behavioral development of children (e.g., Bank & Kahn, 1982; Boer & Dunn, 1992). Sibling relationships may be especially challenging for children because when this relationship is conflictual or distressing, terminating the relationship is not an option (e.g., Hetherington, Henderson, & Reiss, 1999). Although sibling relationships can be as rewarding as more voluntary friendships (through affection and other positive communication interactions), they can also provide more costs than friendships in the form of greater communication of negativity and conflict (e.g., Buhrmester, 1992). Not only do siblings understand the best ways to console one another, but they also understand the most effective mechanisms of annoying one another (e.g., Dunn & Kendrick, 1982). So great is this tendency to annoy that siblings have been observed to have conflict as much as seven times in 1 hour (e.g., Perlman & Ross, 1997). Not surprisingly, adolescent and young adult siblings increasingly disengage communicatively as they become more involved in nonfamilial relationships (e.g., Anderson & Rice, 1992).

What is it that makes sibling relationships such a fertile ground for conflictual communication? One explanation is that siblings see each other as competitors for a fixed amount of resources that exist in the family. The **naive theory of affection** holds that siblings perceive the affection that parents have as a finite resource (Robey, Cohen, & Epstein, 1988). Communication researchers Kory Floyd and Mark Morman (2005a) tested this theory on adult sons and fathers. Adult sons' recollections of their fathers' affection were negatively related to the number of siblings they had. In other words, the more siblings they had, the less affection they perceived from their fathers. Fathers' recollections were not affected by number of siblings. Siblings perceive the amount of affection to be fixed and shared out among siblings, whereas parents do not.

Siblings not only see each other as competition for parental affection, but they also display affection with each other differently than they do in other family relationships. Floyd and Morr (2003) examined nonverbal affection within three different family relationships and found that family members display the most affection within their marriages, less affection within their sibling relationships, and the least affection within their sibling-in-law relationships. These findings are not all that surprising in light of the earlier-reviewed study that adolescent and young adult siblings increasingly disengage communicatively as they become more involved in nonfamilial relationships (e.g., Anderson & Rice, 1992).

This competition for scarce resources may not simply affect the communication of *affection* in parent-child and sibling relationships. Siblings may compete for *attention* from parents, which they may also see as a scarce communication commodity. My two stepsons provide the perfect example of this competition for my husband's attention at the dinner table. Regardless of the topic, if Huw is holding his dad's attention on any topic, Jake invariably attempts to redirect the conversation to a topic that has more relevance to him so that he can wrest the conversational floor away from Huw. So consistent is that pattern of interruptive behavior that it has become a running joke at the dinner table, with both siblings interrupting each other repetitively mere seconds after the other. This sibling competition may be seen in stepfamily situations as well.

Adding Children Through Remarriage: Communication in the Stepparent-Stepchild Relationship

As mentioned in the introduction, pregnancy, adoption, and surrogacy are not the only way to add children to the family. This next section explores what happens to a family in which children are added through remarriage: Or put another way, a family in which a new parent is added to the children in a preexisting family. These relationships and the resulting communication may be especially problematic when the new stepparent brings his or her own children because new stepsibling relationships and communication will also result. New stepsibling and half-sibling communication are considered here as well.

Figure 5.5   This Caucasian father and Chinese baby illustrate that children are
added through adoption (4% of kids) as well as through childbirth;
transracial adoptions are helping to recognize that the earlier stigmas
of adoption are beginning to fade.

Stepparent-Stepchild Communication

Stepparent-stepchild communication may be especially problematic
because although stepparents chose their new family, stepchildren are often
brought into the relationship involuntarily. Communicationally, stepmothers and stepfathers have both been known to attempt to ingratiate themselves to their new stepchildren (e.g., Bray & Berger, 1993; Hetherington,
1999), often under the auspices of unrealistic expectations for instant
reciprocal love (Visher & Visher, 1988). When met with consistent resistance and aversive behavior from stepchildren (especially stepdaughters),
stepparents may become more distant and disengaged and as a result
may communicate less warmth, control, and monitoring than parents in
intact families do (e.g., Hetherington & Clingempeel, 1992; Hetherington
& Jodl, 1994). Stepfathers, in particular, have been found to be less
involved, critical, and concerned about minor issues such as homework,
manners, dress, and so on (Hetherington, 1993). In terms of communication outcomes, most studies report greater levels of conflict and communication of negativity between stepparents and children, especially when
adolescent stepdaughters are present (e.g., Hetherington & Clingempeel,
1992; Hetherington & Jodl, 1994).

Stepparent-stepchildren communication may be especially problematic as it relates to disciplinary encounters. Stepparents have been found to be more effective when they initially establish warm supportive roles with their stepchildren and support the role of the biological parent with regard to discipline (Hetherington, 1999). When a stepparent must discipline, however, discipline is more effective when the biological parent and the stepparent agree on child-rearing practices and communication, and the biological parent supports the stepparent's efforts without abdicating responsibility (Clingempeel, Brand, & Segal, 1987). Stepmothers have more communication problems with stepchildren than do stepfathers (e.g., Clingempeel, Brand, & Ievoli, 1984), which may be due in part to the expectation of remarried fathers that the stepmother will assume the primary role of caretaker and disciplinarian (e.g., Fine, Voydanoff, & Donnelly, 1993). These communication problems may be further exacerbated by more competitive relationships with noncustodial biological mothers (Hetherington & Jodl, 1994) who tend to stay more actively involved with their children and may invoke more loyalty conflicts for children (e.g., Hetherington & Jodl, 1994).

Stepsibling Communication

Children in remarried family situations may have to communicate with a diverse and complex array of full siblings, half-siblings, and stepsiblings (e.g., Ganong & Coleman, 1994; Ihinger-Tallman, 1987). This array of relationships may have communicative consequences even for fully biologically related children. Specifically, fully related brothers brought from a mother's previous marriage into families with stepfathers communicate less positively and exhibit more rivalry with and disengagement from one another than fully related brothers in intact families (e.g., Hetherington, 1989; Hetherington & Clingempeel, 1992; Hetherington & Jodl, 1994). Some closeness is created in the potential face of adversity, however, in that fully related sisters in stepfamilies are closer and more protective toward one another; however, brothers rarely receive this type of communication of support from either sisters or brothers (Hetherington, 1989; Hetherington & Clingempeel, 1992). The communication of disengagement from adolescent and young adult siblings becoming more involved in nonfamilial relationships discussed earlier is more pronounced in full-sibling relationships in stepfamilies (e.g., Hetherington & Clingempeel, 1992) and is even more pronounced in young adulthood for nonbiologically related stepsiblings (e.g., Hetherington, 1999).

Communication between stepsiblings may vary from that between full siblings in important ways. They may be especially sensitive to differential parenting by the residential biological parent (Hetherington, 1999). Despite this potential sensitivity, many residential stepsiblings provide both support and companionship for one another through communication behavior (Ihinger-Tallman, 1987). In addition, studies of stepsibling conflict do not evidence patterns in excess of full-sibling relationships (e.g., Ganong & Coleman, 1987). Studies of continued communication into adulthood produce conflictual findings, however, in that substantial contact (White & Reidmann, 1992) and greater distance have been reported for stepsiblings compared with biological siblings in intact homes (Hetherington, 1999; Hetherington & Jodl, 1994).

New sibling relationships and communication patterns are also established within step- or blended families through new half-siblings. Up to one third of children in stepfamilies will have a new half-sibling in 4 years (Bumpass, 1984), and half-siblings who share residence regard themselves as siblings (e.g., Ganong &Coleman, 1987) with all the ensuing benefits compared with stepsiblings (Bernstein, 1989). Differential treatment of half-siblings in blended families may include less sibling rivalry because differential treatment may be attributed to biological relatedness (Hetherington, 1999). Communication between residential half-siblings may not differ substantially from that between full siblings.

Summary

The addition of children to a family unit is marked by significant changes in the nature and quality of family life and family communication. Infants may be added to several family forms (e.g., cohabiting couples, nuclear families, single-parent families, blended families, extended families) through pregnancy, adoption, and surrogacy. *Adding infant children* to cohabiting couple and nuclear families has been likened to a "family crisis" and is accompanied by dramatic *changes in the domestic workload* and surrounding communication and decreases in reports of *marital satisfaction*. In addition, communication within marriages and cohabiting relationships may be affected by the new demands for communication with the growing child. Communication during *infancy* is marked by *vocalic and visual readiness* for communication in children and an amazing matching by parents in terms of *receptivity* and *responsiveness* to an infant's cues. The *preschool years* are marked by *increasing independence* by the child and *increasing disciplinary attempts* by the parent as they redefine themselves as nurturer-disciplinarians. *School-age children* similarly increase their independence as they are socialized in school by their teachers and their peers, and their communication with their parents may change during this time in both quality and quantity as the parents become *interpreters* for the child. Adding children to preexisting families may also result in the development of new *sibling relationships*. These sibling relationships may be marked by increasing competition for the scarce communicative resources that exist in families. Siblings engage in a high level of conflict as they compete for the communication of attention and affection from their parents.

Older children may also be added in stepfamily, extended family, and adoptive family situations and may bring unique communication challenges. *Stepparent-stepchild* communication may be particularly problematic as stepparents attempt to fulfill similar roles as preexisting parents. This parental role-holding communication may result in conflict between step-parents and resistant stepchildren (especially adolescent girls). Stepmothers may also attempt to fulfill more disciplinary communication roles in the family and may be met with more resistance. Stepfamilies may also include the addition of children from the stepparent's earlier relationships and thus new *stepsibling relationships* may be formed. Even full-sibling relationships change when added to stepfamilies, but stepsibling relationships may promote similar forms of conflict, competition, and support as in full-sibling relationships. Furthermore, many blended families emerge through the addition of *half-siblings* for all the stepsiblings. Half-siblings provide a new dimension to blended families in that stepchildren appear to compete less with half-siblings than they do with full or stepsiblings.

KEY TERMS

changes in communication	pregnancy
changes in domestic workload	preschool years
changes in marital satisfaction	school-aged children
discipline	sibling relationships and communication
half-sibling communication	socialization by teachers and peers
independence	stepparent-stepchild communication
infancy	stepsibling communication
parental responsiveness	vocalic and visual preparedness

QUESTIONS FOR APPLICATION

1. Your siblings or others you know may be adding children to their families presently. In your experiences, what communication changes accompany pregnancy and the addition of infant children to the family? In what way do the experiences these new parents have mirror those found in the literature? Did they experience changes in domestic workload, communication, and marital satisfaction?

2. Think of someone you know who is adopted. Did their experiences differ significantly from others you know who were added to families through birth?

3. Think of your own sibling relationships (or those of others you know). What unique communication existed in this relationship in terms of competition for scarce resources in the family as well as through support? How much did you fight compared with your other family relationships?

4. Think of your own stepfamily situation (or that of someone you know well). How was the communication between the stepparents and stepchildren affected by the transition to this new family form? How does this mirror the findings regarding the unique nature of communication in this difficult relationship?

5. Think of your own blended or stepfamily situation (or that of someone you know well). How did the presence of stepsiblings and half-siblings change the nature of the communication in the family? In what ways were the stepsibling relationships similar to other sibling relationships? In what ways were the half-sibling relationships similar to or different from other sibling relationships?

6 Nurturing and Controlling Communication: Raising Socioemotionally and Intellectually Competent Children

Regardless of the ways in which your family of origin added children (through birth, adoption, surrogacy, stepfamilies, extended families), it is likely that the parental figures in the family concerned themselves greatly with your well-being. Parents, stepparents, and grandparents all want the children in the family to grow up healthy. This overarching concern for health and well-being translates into communication styles and practices designed to influence several domains of development. To ensure their children's health and safety, parents and caregivers communicate in ways designed to help children develop *intellectually, physically, emotionally,* and *socially* in ways that promote their best health and well-being. To ensure their children's success in life, they also communicate in ways that help children develop intellectually and *academically* in line with their peers. To ensure that their children thrive and survive, parents attempt to communicate in ways that help their children develop *physically* in ways that enhance their health, well-being, and safety. Parents and other caregivers might also communicate in ways that ensure that their children mature emotionally in line with the current cultural trends for boys and girls: Will sons be strong? Will daughters be happy? Furthermore, and not unrelatedly, parents almost certainly communicate in ways that ensure their children's development of friendships and other social relationships. To help us understand how parents facilitate these academic, physical, emotional, and social developmental milestones in their children, parental communication strategies of both *nurturing* and *control* are examined here. What communicative strategies of control and discipline do parents, stepparents, and residential grandparents use to ensure these outcomes? Furthermore, to what extent does parental communication of warmth and affection promote intellectual, physical, emotional, and social competencies? Such developmental milestones and the ways in which parents can affect them through their communication is the focus of this chapter.

Control: Providing Discipline and Guidance Through Communication

Parenting Styles: Communication Strategies

Much work has examined the ways in which parents discipline their children and the various effects those **parenting styles** have on outcomes relevant to the socialization of children. Consistent with the perspective of this textbook, parents frequently vary their communication with their children along the dimensions of *responsiveness* (warmth/nurturing) and *demandingness* (control) in their attempts to guide their children's behavior. Parents who are *responsive* invoke **parenting practices** and communication that are warm and that provide reciprocal responses to their children's communicative behavior, clear communication and person-centered discourse, and the atmosphere for secure attachments with their children (Baumrind, 1996). Parents who are nonresponsive are at the opposite ends of these continua. *Highly demanding* parents use the parenting practices and communication strategies of confrontation, monitoring, and consistent and contingent discipline. Less demanding parents do not attempt to exercise much impulse control over their children's behavior. The examination of the effects of parenting styles and their communication can be facilitated by an examination of the responsiveness (nurturing and warmth) dimension and demandingness (controlling) dimension (Baumrind, 1996; Maccoby & Martin, 1983).

Authoritarian Parenting: The Communication of High Demandingness and Low Responsiveness

Baumrind (1966) delineates three types of parental control: *authoritarian, permissive,* and *authoritative.* The **authoritarian parent** is positioned at the intersection of *high demandingness* and *low responsiveness* (Maccoby & Martin, 1983). This parent overtly attempts to shape, control, and evaluate the behavior of the child in accordance with an absolute standard of conduct from some higher authority (e.g., religion). An authoritarian parent arbitrarily enforces restrictive directives (Baumrind, 1996). This parent seeks obedience from a child and uses punitive and forceful measures and communication to curb self-willed behavior. The authoritarian parent keeps the child in a subordinate nonautonomous role and does not encourage communicative give and take (Baumrind, 1978). Because this parent is most concerned with impulse control of the child at the expense of a loving and accepting environment, he or she is less concerned with warmth than with control. A student from my family communication class provided an example of an authoritarian parent. During her self-proclaimed willful stage, she was sent to live with her father. Following a particularly willful night out on the town, he provided her with a firm beating and forbade her from leaving the house for 3 months (other than to go to school or church). Not surprisingly, this response was met with greater obedience but also a lesser sense of affection toward her father.

The developmental outcomes associated with authoritarian parenting (communication of high demandingness and low responsiveness) have been less than optimal. In terms of communication outcomes, preschoolers with authoritarian parents were more discontent, withdrawn, and distrustful, as well as more insecure and apprehensive, less affiliative toward peers, and more likely to become hostile or regressive under stress (Baumrind, 1967). Furthermore, children with authoritarian parents report greater school-related conflict with parents because of demandingly high levels of expectations (Eskilson, Wiley, Muehlbauer, & Dodder, 1986). This continues into adolescence; adolescents with authoritarian parents report greater discord with parents (Baumrind, 1967, 1971). Academically, these same adolescents exhibit poorer grades, lower academic adjustment, and lower self-esteem (Lamborn, Mounts, Steinberg, & Dornbusch, 1991). Consistently, students designated as underachievers tend to provide descriptions of parents as overly strict, punitive, and highly demanding (i.e., authoritarian; see, e.g., Dornbusch, Ritter, Mont-Reynaud, & Chen, 1990).

Given these communicative and academic outcomes, it comes as no surprise that authoritarian parents have children with lower self-esteem (Buri, Louiselle, Misukanis, & Mueller, 1988). For instance, parents who are overprotective and use external or negative punishment and deprivation of privileges (i.e., authoritarian parenting) have children with markedly lower self-esteem (Halpin, Halpin, & Whiddon, 1980). Children also reported lower self-esteem if their parents used psychological control, demanded submissiveness, and suppressed autonomy (i.e., authoritarian parenting; Amanat & Butler, 1984). Authoritarian parenting is clearly associated with poorer communication, greater conflict, poorer academic performance, and lower self-esteem.

Permissive Parenting: The Communication of Low Demandingness and High Responsiveness

Figure 6.1   Permissive parents allow their children to explore and set very few limits on the behavior of the child.

In contrast, a **permissive parent** is positioned at the intersection of *high responsiveness/warmth* and *low demandingness/control* (Maccoby & Martin, 1983). This parent attempts to behave in nonpunitive, accepting, and affirmative ways toward his or her child's actions, impulses, and desires. This parent allows the child to regulate his or her own behavior and avoids extrinsic motivators and externally imposed rules and structure (Baumrind, 1996). To this end, the permissive parent uses reason and manipulation to affect the child's behavior and can be seen as highly nurturing and less controlling. Another student told of her single mom who attempted to be her friend and hang out with her friends. Although she enjoyed the greater degree of autonomy this less controlling environment provided her with, she often found herself wondering about the true concern her mother had for her when she showed up at 4 in the morning to no parent waiting tearfully by the phone and no punishment. She actually wished her parent would exercise *more* control. Thus, a permissive parent might communicate acceptance at the expense of communicating a concern for the well-being of the child.

Outcomes associated with permissive parenting (communication of low demandingness and low responsiveness) have also been less than optimal. For instance, preschoolers with permissive parents lacked self-control and self-reliance (Baumrind, 1967). Communicationally, children with permissive parents report higher school-related conflict due to exceedingly low expectations (Eskilson et al., 1986). Furthermore, students designated as underachievers tended to provide descriptions of parents as lax in their disciplinary techniques (i.e., permissive; e.g., Dornbusch et al., 1990). Academically, adolescent children with permissive parents have poorer grades, lower academic adjustment, and lower self-esteem (Lamborn et al., 1991). Consistent with children of authoritarian parents, children of permissive parents exhibit higher conflict, poorer academic adjustment, and lower self-esteem.

Authoritative Parenting: The Communication of High Demandingness and High Responsiveness

Authoritative parents attempt to be both nurturing and warm (*responsive)* and highly controlling *(demanding)* of their children's behavior (Maccoby & Martin, 1983). These parents direct their child's activities in a rational, issue-oriented manner. In contrast with the authoritarian parent's reliance on rules and regulations as the standard, the authoritative parent encourages verbal give and take, explicitly delineates the reasoning behind a particular rule, and solicits a child's objections to a rule. The authoritative parent values both the development of autonomous self-will and disciplined conformity (Baumrind, 1966). This parent is able to provide an accepting environment as well as a highly structured one. Authoritative parents, then, explain the logic behind a restriction on a car's use as being related to the lack of the child's ability to actually financially support the use of such a car (i.e., logical consequences). These parents also listen carefully to their child's tearful explanation regarding losing a job and the need for a car for school-related activities. In the end of the day, however, the child is driven to school and other activities but also knows that his or her point of view was taken seriously and that if the child alters the logically linked behavior (i.e., gets a job), he or she will regain car privileges.

The authoritative parenting style has been associated with the most positive socialization and communication outcomes. Communicationally, preschool children with authoritative parents were the most socially responsible and independent, self-controlled, affiliative, self-reliant, explorative, and self-assertive. They were also realistic, competent, and content. This finding of authoritative parents having more socially responsible and independent children was constant across studies (Baumrind, 1971) in that authoritative parental behavior was associated with independent, purposive behavior for girls. Authoritative parenting was also associated with more social responsibility in boys and greater achievement in girls.

Academically, authoritative parenting has also been associated with better competence among primary school children. Specifically, high parental support and high parental control were associated with better competence outcomes for primary school children (Amato, 1986). Interestingly, higher competence was also associated with higher allocations of household responsibility and low levels of parental punishment. Authoritative parents who are responsive and demanding both in terms of support and control, but who are not overly punishing and provide children with clear expectations for performance on household tasks, have children with the highest competence.

Authoritative parenting has also been associated with better academic outcomes in adolescents. Authoritative parents affect an adolescent's self-efficacy and self-esteem and enhance scholastic performance by creating situations in which their child can be effective and by sending positive messages about their child's qualities and competencies (Steinberg, Elmen, & Mounts, 1989). Also, the ways in which authoritative parents assist their children in managing their homework creates greater perseverance, time management, self-reliance, and planfulness, as well as self-regulatory skills (Strage, 1998). In particular, authoritative parents tend to use scaffolding (i.e., modeling the desired learning strategy or task followed by shifting the responsibility to the child) as they supervise homework, and this scaffolding has been associated positively with their child's performance on math achievement tests and gains in academic achievement (Pratt, Green, MacVicar, & Bountrogianni, 1993). Furthermore, children of authoritative parents were the most cognitively motivated, competent, and achievement oriented (Baumrind, 1991) and were the most intrinsically motivated (Ginsburg & Bronstein, 1993). They also attained the highest math and verbal achievement (Baumrind, 1991). This is consistent with the finding that adolescents with authoritative parents earn better grades than adolescents with authoritarian or permissive parents (e.g., Dornbusch, Ritter, Leiderman, Roberts, & Fraleigh, 1987) and demonstrate greater levels of academic adjustment and competence (Lamborn et al., 1991).

Although the authoritative style of parenting has been firmly associated with student's academic achievement, it is the child's self-esteem that predicts social, personal-emotional, goal commitment, institutional, academic, and overall adjustment of college freshmen (Hickman, Bartholomae, & McKenry, 2000). Furthermore, a child's self-esteem has been associated with social adjustment, academic achievement, and vocational aspirations (Rice, 1992). Parents with authoritative styles of parenting have children with higher self-esteem (Buri et al., 1988) and self-actualization (Dominguez & Carton, 1997). Consistently, parents with positive and functional child-rearing techniques and relations during adolescence had children with higher self-esteem (e.g., Bell, Allen, Hauser, & O'Connor, 1996; Kashubeck & Christensen, 1995). Parents who reported stronger companionship with their children and used nurturing, rewards, and positive punishment with their children (i.e., authoritative parenting) had children with higher self-esteem (Halpin et al., 1980). In addition, African American parents who were more supportive toward their children and African American and Euro-American parents with higher behavioral control had children with higher self-esteem and academic achievement (Bean, Bush, McKenry, & Wilson, 2003).

It is likely that differing parenting styles communicate differential beliefs in children's abilities and promote mastery orientations or learned helplessness. For instance, it is likely that authoritative parents who are highly demanding through the use of confrontation, monitoring, and consistent and contingent discipline (Baumrind, 1996) are more likely to have children with a higher sense of mastery orientation. Such children should internalize goals, such as academic ones, and begin to experience some measure of competence over them. In addition, because authoritative parents communicate higher expectations for their children, these children should set higher expectations for themselves. In fact, the research in this area supports the relationship between authoritative parenting and mastery orientations toward academic life. College students with parents with authoritative styles of parenting (i.e., more autonomy, demands, and supports provided to children) had greater mastery orientations toward their academic work compared with students whose parents were authoritarian or permissive (Strage & Brandt, 1999). Specifically, students with authoritative parents were more confident, persistent, and positively oriented toward their teachers.

Parenting Practices: Using Communication to Enact Discipline

Parenting practices associated with each parenting style are invoked through communication behavior. Highly demanding parents (e.g., authoritarian and authoritative) use the parenting practices of (a) monitoring (e.g., awareness of and communication about children's whereabouts), (b) control (e.g., communication about rules and expectations for behavior), and (c) restrictions (e.g., communication about limitations on certain activities) (Hartos, Eitel, Haynie, & Simons-Morton, 2000). Less demanding parents are

Table 6.1   Parenting Styles and Practices and Socialization Outcomes

	Authoritarian	*Permissive*	*Authoritative*
Demandingness/ control	High	Low	High
Responsiveness/ nurturing	Low	High	High
Socialization Outcomes for Children			
Communication	Less affiliative with peers, hostile, regressive, greater parent-child conflict	Greater school-related conflict with parents	Affiliative with peers, more independent, self-controlled and self-assertive, less conflict with parents
Academic	Underachievers, lower academic adjustment, poorer grades	Underachievers, lower academic adjustment, poorer grades	Higher achievement tests, more competent, better grades, higher academic adjustment
Self-esteem	Low	Low	High
Mastery orientation	Low	Low	High

lower on these dimensions. Highly responsive parents use the parenting practices of (a) the communication of warmth, (b) reciprocal responses to children's communicative behavior, (c) clear communication and person-centered discourse, and (d) the provision of the atmosphere for secure attachments with their children (Baumrind, 1996). Less responsive parents are lower on these dimensions. The use of communication to enact discipline through parenting practices may receive further insights from the consideration of the (a) development of mastery orientations through the communication of expectations and the (b) use of reinforcement and punishment to alter behavior.

Developing Mastery Orientation Through the Communication of Expectations

As we saw under the section on parenting styles, children can vary to the extent that they experience a mastery orientation or a learned helplessness orientation with regard to tasks. Children with *mastery orientations* learn that they can achieve and that persistence pays off, whereas children with *learned helplessness* orientations learn that they are incompetent and give up quickly. Mastery orientation and learned helplessness have been studied with regard to academic outcomes. Students with mastery orientations prefer challenging tasks that promise to enhance their competence (Strage & Brandt, 1999).

In addition, students with mastery orientations are more confident, persistent, and focused in the face of unexpected difficulties and failure and are less likely to be deterred by critical feedback (e.g., Cain & Dweck, 1995; Deiner & Dweck, 1978; Henderson & Dweck, 1990; Jagacinski, 1992; Strage & Brandt, 1999) compared with their learned helplessness peers.

Inputs. Because high expectations are part and parcel of more demanding parents, it is likely that parents communicate their high expectations to their children. According to Rosenthal (1973, 1981), who studied the communication of interpersonal expectations in a variety of contexts, parents should communicate their high expectations to their children in four ways. First, parents' expectations are communicated to their children through the **inputs** they provide to their children. Inputs include the quantity and the difficulty level of the information a child is expected to understand. A parent who expects his or her child to master academic content communicates with the child in more challenging ways than does a parent who expects that his or her child will not be able to achieve. My husband is a good example of a parent who provides challenging inputs to his children. When explaining a biological process for my children at the dinner table (I kid you not!), my husband maintains the difficulty of language at a level commensurate with those individuals he works with who all have a bachelor's of science degree at minimum. He then expects that the boys will either understand at that level or will ask questions until they understand fully the processes he's describing in elaborate detail. And amazingly, they generally understand the processes.

Outputs. Second, parents' expectations are communicated through the **outputs** the parents require. Outputs include the number and level of sophistication of the products completed by the child. My youngest stepson Jake and I generally go 'round and 'round regarding essays and the like. He attempts to write the bare minimum number of words in the "Jake scrawl," and I generally insist that he flesh out his paragraphs, make complete arguments, use complete sentences, and rewrite or type so that his teacher can actually understand what he's trying to communicate. Besides potentially thinking I'm overly demanding, at the end of the day, he understands that I know and expect that he can do it better.

Climate. Third, parents' expectations are communicated through the **climate** that they provide for their children. Although parents who expect their children to achieve provide a demanding environment, in general, people who expect others to do well are more pleasant and warmer toward them in supportive ways as well. This combination of demandingness and warmth approximates the authoritative style of parenting. This authoritative style of parenting has been associated with many better academic outcomes, including greater intrinsic motivation for success (Ginsburg & Bronstein, 1993). Warm supportive demandingness may be highly effective in terms of communicating high expectations to one's children and ultimately assisting children to attain a mastery orientation toward challenging tasks, whether the tasks are academic or otherwise.

Feedback. Finally, parents' expectations can be communicated to their children through the types of **feedback** they give their children in response to their successes and their failures. Attribution theory is highly useful here in terms of understanding how children might internalize responses to their successes and failures. Children who do well at a task and are responded to with internal dispositional attributions are more likely to achieve a mastery orientation. In other words, saying, "You are really smart" to a child who has done well helps the child to internalize the belief that he or she is smart and has the ability to achieve. Alternatively, making a situational or external attribution for the same stellar performance promotes learned helplessness in the child. For example, a parent who says, "That must have been an easy test," promotes the belief in the child that he or she does not possess the ability to achieve in that arena. On the other hand, situational attributions for *negative* performances promote mastery orientations, whereas dispositional attributions for negative performances promote learned helplessness. For example, if a child performs badly on an examination, interpreting the performance as being due to inadequate studying promotes a mastery orientation, whereas interpreting the performance as being due to a lack of skill or knowledge leads to a learned helplessness orientation. In other words, attributing a failure to not studying adequately promotes the belief that the child possesses the internal dispositional tendency to do well in a particular area, but because of the situation, he or she did not prepare adequately. Therefore, adequate preparation in the future will lead to greater success. Alternatively, attributing the failure to the child's innate inabilities creates the belief that he or she can't perform well and that no amount of studying or preparation will rectify his or her lack of ability. In sum, mastery orientation can be instilled through dispositional attributions for successful performances and situational attributions for failures. Alternatively, learned helplessness can be instilled through dispositional attributions for failures and situational attributions for successful performances.

The Communication of Reinforcement
and Punishment: Social Learning Theory Principles

Much of the work on disciplinary styles and parenting practices is based in learning theory (Darling & Steinberg, 1993). For instance, remember that Baumrind (1996) argues that authoritative parents who are highly demanding use the communication strategies of confrontation, monitoring, and consistent and contingent discipline. This notion of consistent and contingent discipline is derived from learning theory. Learning theory (Skinner, 1974) postulates that behavioral tendencies are strengthened or weakened by the contingent responses to them. Communicative responses can be *reinforcing*, in that they strengthen the behavior they follow, or *punishing*, in that they serve to extinguish the behavior they follow. Communication reinforcements can be positive or negative. *Positive reinforcement* immediately follows a behavior (contingent response) and strengthens that behavioral tendency through some sort of reward or positive outcome. For instance, if my daughter Rachel uses the potty, she gets several positive communication reinforcers, including excitement of those around, getting to be called a "big girl," and getting to wear "a big girl diaper" (Huggies Pooh Pull-ups). This contingent and positive response is performed under the auspices of strengthening the tendency to use the potty (hey, she's up to three or four times a day; it seems to be working). *Negative reinforcement*, on the other hand, immediately follows the behavior (contingent response) and is the removal of an aversive stimulus. In other words, negative reinforcement works like aspirin, in that taking an aspirin takes away the pain and strengthens the tendency to take the aspirin again in the future. My parents were big on negative reinforcement. If I got good grades or the like, my "reward" was that they told me I didn't have to do the dishes. I *hated* doing the dishes, so this worked quite nicely.

Punishment is the presentation of aversive stimuli in contingent response to behaviors a parent wishes to eliminate. Studies have shown that mothers and fathers use punishment differentially. Fathers, for instance, are more likely to respond to children's noncompliance with punishment, and children, in turn, are more likely to obey their fathers (Grusec & Lytton, 1988). Consistently, children are more likely to obey their mothers in the presence of their fathers (Lytton, 1980). Mothers, alternatively, appear to communicate aversive stimuli in the form of verbal admonishments, criticisms, and threats (Hetherington, Cox, & Cox, 1978). In a more authoritative vein, mothers may also attempt to reason with the child (Lytton, 1980). When my eldest stepson Huw had his car taken away until he got a job to pay for the over-haul to his engine, which was necessary because of his not filling the oil, he was being punished for his negligent behavior. This is also an example of natural and logical consequences, in that Huw's car blowing up on the free-way was the natural consequence of his failure to attend to his car mainte-nance, and his having to pay us back for the repairs was the logical consequence of his failure to attend to his car maintenance. The following section elaborates these concepts more.

In terms of the uses of reinforcement and punishment in parenting, many parenting advocates are now espousing *natural and logical consequences* (see Healthy Parenting Initiative, 2004). Natural and logical consequences serve as reinforcements and punishments, but they are naturally or logically related to the behavior in question. **Natural consequences** are the direct and contin-gent effects of the behavior. For instance, if a child leaves his or her skate-board outside in the rain, the wheels **will** rust. The natural consequence is the outcome (i.e., rusted wheels), which is a direct result of the behavior (i.e., leaving the skateboard in the rain). Natural consequences are assumed to be the best in terms of disciplinary outcomes because children learn that their behavior has consequences irrespective of parents' reaction to it. **Logical consequences** are closely related to outcomes associated with the behavior

"What do I think is an appropriate punishment? I think an appropriate
punishment would be to make me live with my guilt."

SOURCE: Copyright © The New Yorker Collection 2000 Barbara Smaller from cartoonbank
.com. All rights reserved.

but are not naturally occurring. Logical consequences are usually put into
place when the natural consequences would put the child in harm's way.
Children who play with matches would naturally be burned, but wise parents
intercede prior to this unfortunate consequence and dole out the logical consequence of restricting the child's access to matches (see parenting practices
above). Logical consequences are typically enacted at all age levels but seem
particularly useful with adolescents who are well able to use reason and logic.
Naturally, an adolescent who stays out late drinking and then drives may be
met with the natural consequence of a near-fatal car accident (the stuff
that parental nightmares are made of). Because parents wish to avoid this in
the future, the logical consequence for drinking and driving would be the
revocation of driving privileges and limitations on friendship activities. Both
natural and logical consequences have the advantage of being directly or
indirectly related to the behavior in question. It removes the "parent as
dictator" role, because the child's behavior is directly or indirectly related to
the pursuant outcomes. Logical consequences require more parental intervention and thus put more burden on the parent to fulfill the authority role.

Control and Discipline Through Communication in Adolescent-Parent Relationships

To help ease his homesickness, college freshman Wayne Diltz had recorded some key conversations with his parents.

SOURCE: *Close to Home* © 2003 John McPherson. Reprinted with permission of Universal Press Syndicate. All rights reserved.

Although controlling and disciplining communication is important throughout the developmental life span of the child, it may be especially problematic during adolescence because of adolescents' growing desire to exert control over more and more domains of their own lives. In general, adolescence is a period of development that parents anticipate with fear, awe, and dread. Most new parents begin to fret about the impending conflicts even as they celebrate the current relationship they have with their infants and toddlers. My husband, for example, is fast to point out to friends that our relationships with our 14- and 18-year-old boys are relatively conflict free and close and that we are very lucky. He then quickly asks any parents with teenage daughters what to expect when our toddler "becomes of age." They frequently point up difficulties in mother-daughter relationships and less in father-daughter and father-son relationships. He loves to torture me with his new "findings" already. In fact, and not surprisingly, these types of gender effects are borne out in the literature; mother-adolescent daughter conflict is more frequent and accompanied by greater negative affect than conflict in other parent-child relationships (Laursen & Collins, 1994).

What causes potential increases in conflict and decreases in closeness between adolescents and their parents? Many argue that the main impetus for change in the relationship between adolescents and their parents is the adolescent's *striving for autonomy and independence.* But what causes this striving for autonomy in adolescents? Many individual-level approaches argue that the physical, cognitive, and social changes brought about by puberty cause adolescents to desire greater independence from their parents. Unfortunately, these physical, cognitive, and social changes also cause many parents to want to exercise greater control over their adolescents as concerns about sexuality and sexual exploration and experimentation torment parents, who are generally concerned about the health and well-being of their children. The very processes that encourage adolescents to want to explore are the same that make the parents want to curtail the exploration. In fact, a student in my family communication class recently reported that when she began menstruating, her mother responded by getting angry with her! Such are the confusing emotions and responses that surround the adolescent development within the family.

How, then, do the adolescents' strivings for greater independence coexist with parents' temporary attempts to regain control over their developing adolescent? Many have argued that adolescence, as a stage in family development, has often been considered the source of great conflict for parent-adolescent relationships. According to Brett Laursen and Andrew Collins (2004), the impetus for this conflict varies by perspective. Current *psychoanalytic approaches* emphasize autonomy seeking and ego identity development based in pubertal changes. *Evolutionary approaches* emphasize that adolescence is a time to experience adult feelings of sexuality meant to lead the developing child-adult into newly formed relationships that will move the adolescent away from their childhood home. Finally, *cognitive approaches* argue that adolescents' advanced cognitive and reasoning abilities allow them to understand their relationships with parents in ways similar to peer relationships and that any ensuing conflict is from the inability of the parent to adjust quickly enough to these changes. In general, then, adolescents and parents have differing timetables for the impending autonomy of the adolescents in the family, and these differing timetables may be the source of parent-child communication difficulties (Collins & Luebker, 1994).

What exactly are parents of adolescents concerned about? In general, they fear *reduced closeness, decreased perceptions of authoritativeness,* and *increased conflict* with their adolescents as they strive for greater and greater autonomy from parental control attempts. In fact, this struggle for control over behavioral domains can be evidenced in adolescents' manifestations of competencies. To be specific, whereas high levels of parental warmth and parental control were associated with primary school children's competencies, high levels of parental warmth and *low* levels of parental control were related to adolescents' competencies (Amato, 1986). This may indicate that high levels of control are more appropriate to elicit competencies among younger children, but not in adolescents, who are beginning to assert a greater and greater degree of control over multiple behavioral domains (Smetana, 1995). This may be reinforced through the common parenting practices of allowing adolescents more negotiated unsupervised time (e.g., Borawski, Ievers-Landis, Lovegreen, & Trapl, 2003). According to Smetana (1995), adolescents and parents struggle over moral (e.g., questions of right and wrong), conventional (e.g., swearing), personal (e.g., clothes choices), multifaceted (e.g., lip rings), prudential (e.g., smoking), and friendship (e.g., regulating relationships) domains.

Desire for greater control over one's life may be associated with decreases in the communication of closeness between parents and adolescents. With regard to the communication of *closeness*, adolescents feel less close and are less interdependent with their parents as they increase in age (Laursen & Williams, 1997). This is accompanied by similar declines in the time that adolescents spend with parents (Larson, Richards, Moneta, Holmbeck, & Duckett, 1996). Given the changes in amount of time spent together and subjective feelings of closeness, it is not that surprising that adolescents report less companionship and intimacy with parents (Buhrmester & Furman, 1987). Also consistent with these decreases in intimacy is an accompanying decrease in physical affection. Specifically, less cuddling is evidenced as adolescents mature, but compensations are made in the form of greater information sharing and expressions of feelings (Hartup & Laursen, 1991). The unfortunate part about the increases in sharing feelings is that they probably are not all positive. More specifically, both parents and adolescents report more frequent negative expressions of emotion and less frequent expressions of positive emotions compared with parents of preadolescent children (Steinberg & Silk, 2002).

Consistent with these decreasing reports of closeness, adolescents also report more "taboo topics," or topics they avoid discussing with their parents (Guerrero & Afifi, 1995). These taboo topics are also an attempt of the adolescent to assert greater control over their lives. Not surprisingly, communication regarding sexual experiences was the most often avoided topic. This was especially true between daughters and fathers and between sons and mothers. However, adolescents also avoided talking about dangerous behaviors, friendships, and negative experiences with their parents as well. Many domains of personal conversation require less closeness between parents and adolescents as adolescents avoid talking about them with their parents. Consistent with the research on adolescent-parent communication with mothers versus fathers, adolescents avoided fewer topics with their mothers than with their fathers.

Given the increased importance of communicating with one's peers as opposed to parents during adolescence, adolescents generally perceive communication with their parents less positively than their parents do. Mothers, for instance, often report greater warmth and affection among family members than do adolescent children (Noller & Callan, 1988; Silverberg &

Steinberg, 1990). Furthermore, mothers tend to underestimate the degree of conflict in the parent-adolescent relationship and overestimate its severity (Steinberg, 2001) and the extent of conflict's negative repercussions (Silverberg & Steinberg, 1990). In addition, adolescents report that they spend less time talking with their parents than their parents do (White, 1996).

Perceptions of communication between adolescents and parents may also vary by gender of parent. Specifically, adolescents report talking more with their mothers than with their fathers (Steinberg & Silk, 2002; Youniss & Smoller, 1985). In addition, all adolescents, but especially girls, perceived their mothers as more understanding and accepting than their fathers (Youniss & Smoller, 1985) and were more apt to share feelings with their mothers (Steinberg & Silk, 2002). Fathers, alternatively, were perceived as the imposers of authority and judgments (Youniss & Smoller, 1985) who were primarily sources of information and materials (Steinberg & Silk, 2002). In addition, fathers were perceived as less willing to discuss personal or emotional issues (Youniss & Smoller, 1985). This may be due in part to fathers' greater tendency to interrupt children during a disagreement—especially during the height of puberty (Hill, 1988; Steinberg, 1981). Regardless of this adolescent tendency to view fathers as authority figures, fathers who were more involved with their children earlier in life were closer to their adolescents later in life (Flouri & Buchanan, 2002). This was especially the case for daughter-father relationships.

These differential perceptions of closeness with mothers and fathers may be due in part to the nature of conflict resolutions evidenced in the various relationships. Specifically, adolescents are more likely to compromise with their mothers than with their fathers, and sons are more likely to disengage during conflict than are daughters (Smetana, Yau, & Hanson, 1991; Vuchinich, 1987). As part of an overall climate of warmth and support, mothers may be more willing to compromise in an attempt to be conciliatory.

Regardless of these differences in perceptions of the adolescent-parent relationship, parents should rest assured that their communication with their adolescents is important. Specifically, parent-adolescent relationships are the most influential in important adolescent decisions (Collins, Maccoby, Steinberg, Hetherington, & Bornstein, 2000). In addition, positive communication between parents and adolescents can also be related to outcomes for the adolescents. Specifically, adolescents who view their communication with their parents as positive report greater positive feelings of self-worth, enhanced well-being, and better coping behaviors (Buri, Kirchner, & Walsh, 1987; Jackson, Bijstra, Oostra, & Bosma, 1998; Lanz, Iafrate, Rosnati, & Scabini, 1999). In addition, supportive as opposed to discouraging remarks, combined with challenging communication, have been associated with adolescents' self-representations (Hauser, Powers, & Noam, 1991). Finally, more effective communication in the form of effective and limit-setting communication to adolescents helped ameliorate the negative effects of parental marital separation in the form of fewer behavioral problems and more positive adjustment (Linker, Stolberg, & Green, 1999).

_____ Nurturing: Providing Support and Love

As seen in the previous sections, nurturing or warmth provides a necessary component alongside control to create parenting styles and practices and the best possible socialization outcomes for children. In an attempt to delineate the ways in which nurturing facilitates the healthy development of the child, a review of **roles theory** is instrumental here. In other words, some parent or other assumed the role of nurturer-caregiver (most likely your mother, as we have seen from previous research). Within this role, several types of development may be central to the nurturing process. Specifically, parents who assume the developmental role concern themselves with the physical, emotional, academic, and social development of the child. **Systems theory** is also useful here, in that the attainment of physical, emotional, academic and social development is likely to be part of the family system's overarching goal to enhance the overall well-being of the children within the system. Below, we discuss the ways in which parents help children develop competencies and attain well-being across these physical, emotional, academic, and social realms.

Enhancing Physical Development Through Communication

Figure 6.2   Parents assist their children's physical development through the types of activities they engage in with them.

Parents concerned with the physical development of their children may nurture them in attempts to maintain their physical health. They may be involved in activities surrounding health maintenance (e.g., eating right) and health care (e.g., doctor's visits and vaccination administration). This physical developer may also be interested in maintaining the health of the child through encouraging physical activities that ensure the health, safety, and well-being of the child. Finally, a physical development role holder may also nurture the sexual development of the child through interactions regarding physical development throughout adolescence and sexual issues and health maintenance. This section explores the nurturance of the physical development of the child.

Encouraging Physical Activity Through Communication

While mothers are typically the health care providers, encouraging the physical activity of children often falls to fathers. Even immediately after the birth of the infant, fathers are generally more involved in the rough-and-tumble play with their infants. Huston and Holmes (2004) found that fathers completed roughly 55% of the rough-and-tumble play with their children. In addition, many fathers become more involved with their children as they move into the toddler years—where rough-and-tumble play is more acceptable. Fathers also encourage greater physical development in the form of freedom to explore, encouraging independence (Parke & Brott, 1999), and playing more physically with children than do mothers (Dickson, Walker, & Fogel, 1997; Parke, 1981; Parke & Brott, 1999). Not surprisingly, fathers spend more time in play with their children than they do completing caregiver tasks (MacDonald & Parke, 1986)—reinforcing the notion of fathers as playmates. Some have even called fathers the "primary playmate" in juxtaposition to mothers' "primary caregiver" role (Roggman, Boyce, & Cook, 2001). Based on the type of play fathers engage in with their children, fathers often become not only the primary, but the preferred, playmates (Clarke-Stewart, 1978; Lamb, 1997; Yogman, 1994).

Maintaining Physical Health Through Communication

Consistent with the maintenance of the health and well-being of the child, one parent or the other is usually responsible for the child's well visits (scheduled check-ups that are preventive), intermittent doctor and dentist appointments, nursing through illnesses, and generally cuddling and nurturing a child following minor scrapes and falls or during periods of sickness. Because maintaining physical health generally involves nurturing behavior, this responsibility often falls to mothers. Whereas concern about physical ailments dominates the early years of development when children experience the normal gamut of colds, the flu, and, potentially, chicken pox (although children are vaccinated for this nowadays), the adolescent years are filled with concerns about protecting the child from the potential effects of risky sexual behavior. Communication about the potential health effects of risky sexual behavior is well housed within the health maintenance role within the family.

Sexual Development and Adolescence

One physical domain over which parents would like to exert some control is the sexual activity of their adolescent (Smetana, 1995). This domain most accurately falls within the health maintainer role; sexual activity relates to greater health risks for the adolescent, so this concern for health and well-being naturally results in parents' desire to control their adolescents' sexual activity. Because of the rapid changes in the physiological development of the adolescent combined with the desire for increased autonomy from parents, adolescents experiment with sex and sexual intercourse in an attempt to rush adulthood. In fact, one recent study found that 60% of high school children report having sexual intercourse with at least one partner during high school (Ponsford, 2004). To further round out this picture, more than 30% of teens report losing their virginity by the age of 15 (Meschke, Bartholomae, & Zentall, 2002). Regardless of these findings and their associated health risks, many parents neglect to address directly sexual issues with their adolescent children. In fact, only about 50% of adolescents report that their parents talked about sex with them (Jaccard, Dittus, & Gordon, 2000), and this estimate is based on the average of widely disparate reports. Not only are adolescents reporting that sex is a taboo topic with parents (Guerrero & Afifi, 1995), but apparently parents are uncomfortable with the topic as well. Regardless of this apparent discomfort, adolescents report that they want more information about HIV and AIDS (Kaiser Family Foundation, 2001) and the consequences of sexually transmitted diseases (STDs) (Kaiser Family Foundation, 2000). Indicative of children's earlier awareness of sex in our society, even children as young as 10 want more information about how to know when they are ready to have sex, how to handle peer pressure, and how to obtain and use birth control (Kaiser Family Foundation, 1998). Regarding the source of this sexual risk information, over 85% of adolescents reported that they desired more communication with their parents (Hutchinson & Cooney, 1998).

When one examines the nature of adolescents' knowledge regarding risky sexual behavior, it is not that surprising that adolescents desire more information. The typical adolescent is frightfully unaware of the consequences of, and risks associated with, sexual activity. For example, among sexually active 15- to 17-year-olds and young adults, most do not consider themselves to be at risk of contracting a sexually transmitted disease (68%) or HIV (87%; Office of National AIDS Policy, 2003). Consistently, three of four (75%) 15- to 17-year-olds underestimated the incidence of STDs among their age group, and nearly one in four (22%) inaccurately believed that birth control pills are at least "somewhat effective" at preventing STDs (Kaiser Family Foundation, 1998).

To further illustrate the sexual risks to adolescents, consider that of sexually active teens, slightly less than half report consistently using birth control (48%; Kaiser Family Foundation, 1996). Not surprisingly, nearly one in five (19%) sexually active adolescent girls become pregnant each year (Alan Guttmacher Institute, 1999). In addition, one in four (25%) sexually active adolescents contracts an STD (Kaiser Family Foundation, 1996), and adolescents and young adults (between 13 and 24) contract HIV at a rate of two per hour (Office of National AIDS Policy, 2003). Strikingly, even though England, France, Sweden, and the Netherlands all report similar or slightly higher levels of adolescent sexual activity, their rates of teenage pregnancy are less than half that in the United States (Warren, 1992). Rates of pregnancy for teenagers under 15 are five times greater in the United States than in these similar European communities (Warren, 1992). Thus, while it is unclear whether these differences are due to the educational system or due to parent-child communication about sex, it seems that reevaluation of the sexual education system in terms of reducing sexually risky outcomes is necessary.

As parents everywhere shudder at the thought of these rates of pregnancy, STDs, and rates of HIV transmission, it is likely that they still find it challenging to discuss sexual topics and risky sexual outcomes with their children. In fact, most parents who do talk with their children about sex convey good old-fashioned biological information to their children (e.g., menstruation, body differences, puberty, and "the sperm inseminates the egg and pregnancy occurs" physiological mechanics; DiIorio, Kelley, & Hockenberry-Eaton, 1999; Downie & Coates, 1999; Kaiser Family Foundation, 2001; Young Pistella & Bonati, 1998) instead of the more desired information about social pressure and relationship development (Kaiser Family Foundation, 1998). Other topics parents may fail to provide information about include foreplay, sex roles, abortion, and intimate relationships (Downie & Coates, 1999). Interestingly, parents may avoid talking with their children about contraception and family-planning facilities even when they know that their children are sexually active (Young Pistella & Bonati, 1998).

The good news, however, is that regardless of the content of the sexual communication parents have with their children, this communication has been related to adolescent awareness of the risks and responsibilities associated with sexual behavior (Hutchinson, 1999) and has been linked to fewer episodes of sex, less sexual risk-taking (Hutchinson, 2002; Hutchinson, Jemmott, Jemmott, Braverman, & Fong, 2003; Luster & Small, 1994; Meschke et al., 2002), and abstinence (Miller, Benson, & Galbraith, 2001). Several studies, however, find no association between parent-adolescent communication and sexually risky outcomes (for review, see Miller et al., 2001). It is likely that in these cases, parenting style may be interacting with the content of the communication about sex (see below).

Furthermore, more frequent communication with parents about sexual issues also makes adolescents less likely to seek sexual information from their peers (Whitaker & Miller, 2000), who, as we know, are likely to have inaccurate information. This finding extends to closeness with parents in that adolescents who are less close to their parents are more influenced by peers with regard to sexual activity (Whitbeck, Conger, & Kao, 1993). In addition, daughters who believe their parents disapprove of contraception are more likely to seek help from female friends to acquire contraception methods (Nathanson & Becker, 1986). In sum, parents who are closer to their adolescents, communicate more with them about sex, and condone the use of contraception are more likely to have children who seek sexual information from them instead of their peers.

Because up to half of all parents are not likely to talk directly with their children about sex, it may be a relief to know that parenting style has also been associated with frequency of sexually risky behavior. A summary of more than 20 studies indicates that parent-child closeness is associated with reduced adolescent pregnancy risk through sexual abstinence, postponement of intercourse, having fewer sexual partners, and using contraception consistently (Miller et al., 2001). Consistent with the authoritative style of parenting, this review also found that parental supervision or regulation of children's activities was also associated with decreased risk of pregnancy (measured not only through reports of pregnancies but also by age of first intercourse, contraception use during first intercourse, and consistent use of contraception). Authoritative parents seem to provide the right mix of warmth and parental control necessary to provide their children with the tools necessary to reduce their risk of pregnancy—regardless of whether or not they are talking directly with their adolescent children about sex and the potential outcomes of risky sex.

Given that many parents probably fear talking with their children about sexual activity and that sexual risk protection might communicate values indicative of acceptance of premarital and adolescent sexuality, a consistent finding in the literature also indicates that parents' values against teen intercourse (or unprotected intercourse) decrease the risk of adolescent pregnancy (Miller et al., 2001). In addition to biological information, many parents provide moral information with regard to desired abstinence to prevent undesired pregnancies (DiIorio et al., 1999; Raffaelli & Green, 2003) and may frequently avoid discussing birth control, sexually transmitted infections, and condom use, which may suggest the condoning of premarital sexual activity (Hutchinson & Cooney, 1998; Raffaelli & Green, 2003), but these issues may be of more interest to adolescents, as reported previously. Parents' values are clearly communicated and instilled in their children and result in less risky sexual behavior. Other factors not related directly to parenting style also predict increased risky sexual behavior. For instance, lower income, dangerous neighborhoods, being raised by a single parent, having sexually active or currently parenting siblings, and being a victim of sexual abuse all relate to greater risk of adolescent pregnancy (Miller et al., 2001).

Once again, mothers are the nurturer and health maintenance role holders in that mothers are more likely to discuss sexual topics with their adolescents than are fathers (DiIorio et al., 1999; Downie & Coates 1999; Hutchinson, 2002; Hutchinson & Cooney, 1998; Raffaelli & Green, 2003). Fathers are more likely to communicate with their sons about sexual issues and avoid discussions with their daughters (Downie & Coates, 1999). Not only do fathers make themselves less available for these discussions, but fathers also report feeling uncomfortable broaching the subject of sex with their children (Nolin & Petersen, 1992). Thus, mothers appear to be more central to providing sexual education for their children. Although it might seem unfair that the bulk of the sexual communication burden falls to the mother, the evidence also indicates that the mother's communication is more successful in decreasing sexually risky behavior than the father's communication and that this is especially true for daughters compared with sons (Miller et al., 2001).

Enhancing Socioemotional Development Through Communication

Besides physical development, as a parent, you will undoubtedly be concerned about your child's competent socioemotional development. Many researchers have concerned themselves with this socioemotional competence. Although the definitions of social competence vary considerably (Stafford, 2004), most researchers examine the childhood competencies that naturally emerge through development or those that might be facilitated through child-parent interaction. Similar to Stafford (2004), this text assumes that a child has social competence to the extent that his or her behavior facilitates culturally desirable outcomes.

Encouraging Friendships

Figure 6.3   Parents use communication to encourage the social development of friendships at early ages.

With regard to social development, many parents are concerned that their children are popular and accepted by their friends. This is, in fact, consistent with many definitions of social competence (Rose-Krasnor, 1997). Furthermore, the parent-child relationship has been associated with a child's social status with his or her peers (e.g., Peery, Jensen, & Adams, 1985; Putallaz & Heflin, 1990) and in the development of a child's prosocial disposition (Radke-Yarrow, Zahn-Waxler, & Chapman, 1983). Finally, children with parents with responsive and democratic parents (i.e., authoritative parents) were more popular, whereas children with less responsive and more restrictive parents (i.e., authoritarian parents) were more likely to be rejected by their peers (Dekovic & Janssens, 1992).

Mothers of 3- to 5-year-olds were found to have a direct effect on their children's social competence through their communicative coaching and their communication style with their children. Specifically, coaching in the form of resilient framing of negative peer events (i.e., guidance in and support of cooperative, nonconfrontational behavior) and endorsement of prosocial strategies were associated with lower aggression, greater social skills, and higher peer acceptance (Mize & Petit, 1997). Communicationally, mothers' synchronous behavior (i.e., behavior that matches and is timed in response to the child's behavior) was a better predictor of children's social competence than was maternal warmth. In fact, in the second study of 3- to 6-year-olds, children who were more synchronous with their mothers were better liked by peers and rated as less aggressive by teachers. This is consistent with mothers' coaching, in that children with mothers who elaborated more in their discussions are rated as both more socially skilled and less aggressive. Thus, mothers with more synchronous communication styles with their children who simultaneously coach their children in elaborated ways have children who are more socially skilled.

Interestingly, having strong peer relationships also facilitates further developments in social competence (Burleson, Delia, & Applegate, 1995) in that friends provide much needed support, information, affection, and self-validation, among many other important skills, such as conflict resolution (Rose-Krasnor, 1997).

Enhancing Sex Role
Development Through Communication

One other area of socialization for children concerns their development of sex role expectations. Although considerable debate exists regarding the impetus for these sex-typed behaviors, Harrington Cleveland, Udry, and Chantala (2001) indicate that 25% of males' sex-typed behavior and 38% of females' sex-typed behavior is biologically or genetically linked, and the remaining 75% and 62% of sex-linked behaviors are environmentally determined. A significant part of this environmental determination is enacted through the communication behavior of our parents. How do we

Figure 6.4   Parents often encourage sex role behavior through the types of tasks
                 they assign to their variously gendered children.

teach the girls to be girls and the boys to be boys? Initially, when children
are very young, we dress them differently. Girl babies are typically seen with
bows on their heads even before they have hair. A perusal of any store shows
a plethora of pink clothes for girls and blue clothes for boys. Why do parents
want their children identified accurately as girls or boys at such an early age?
The answer is simple: Parents want their girls to be treated like girls and their
boys to be treated like boys.

But this sex-role socialization does not stop with the display of promi-
nently gender-colored clothing. We also buy sex-typed toys for our children.
In other words, boys get guns and trucks and girls get dolls and Easy-Bake
Ovens. We don't stop there, however. We also give boys and girls differential tasks either for socialization purposes or for need (Coltrane, 2000). Boys
do more traditionally male jobs (e.g., taking out the trash, working in the
yard), and girls do more traditionally female jobs (e.g., setting the table,
doing the dishes, vacuuming; Lott, 1987; McHale, Bartko, Crouter, &
Perry-Jenkins, 1990). Finally, the research also shows that we communicate
differently with our boys than with our girls. Specifically, parents interact
more with their daughters (Doyle & Paludi, 1991), whom they expect to be
weaker and more delicate (Lott, 1987), and play more actively with sons
(Doyle & Paludi, 1991), with whom parents emphasize strength and aggressiveness (Lott, 1987).

Encouraging Emotional Adjustment Through Communication

Social competence is often linked to the ability of the child to be emotionally competent as well. The way that parents communicate with their children can be associated with the child's ability to both express and be responsive to emotions in others. Both expression of and responsiveness to emotions are related to social skills.

Whereas some studies link parenting style to academic success and adjustment (e.g., Brooks, 1996), others argue that emotional intelligence, as measured through social adjustment, may be as important as other more cognitive factors (Hickman et al., 2000; Mohr, Eiche, & Sedlacek, 1998). Emotional intelligence refers to the ability to guide one's actions through understanding, monitoring, and regulating feelings and emotions (one's own and others; Mayer & Salovey, 1997). So important is this emotional intelligence that some have claimed it may be more important than IQ in determining the ability to learn tacitly (e.g., Gibbs, 1995; Goleman, 1995), the ability to persevere to succeed in college life (Hickman et al., 2000), and the ability to be promoted (Gibbs, 1995).

If emotional intelligence is as important as intellectual abilities in predicting life's successes, what factors promote this emotional intelligence? Some have argued that parenting styles of discipline and warmth are actually rooted in the emotions that parents display to their children (Darling & Steinberg, 1993). More specifically, Darling and Steinberg argue that parenting styles are composed of a whole host of attitudes communicated to the child through an *emotional* climate.

Encouraging Sex Differences in the Expression of Emotion

Besides providing an emotional climate for our children through our overall disciplinary style of responsiveness and demandingness, it is also likely that we socialize our children differently with regard to emotional expressions and emotional responsivity. Females, for instance, are more expected to display positive emotions and are more likely to smile (a major component of pleasant emotional expression) compared with males (Hall & Briton, 1993). In addition, we also teach our females to be more emotionally expressive than males (e.g., Wagner, Buck, & Winterbotham, 1993), and this emotional expressiveness is more acceptable from women than it is from men. Although very young children express emotions similarly regardless of gender, girls become both more expressive and more accurate at expressing emotions than boys (Buck, 1975). Boys, in contrast, are taught that it is more acceptable for them to display stronger emotions (e.g., anger, frustration, and disgust) than weaker ones (e.g., sadness, fear, surprise) or to be unemotional (e.g., Mulac, Studley, Weimann, & Bradac, 1987; Shields, 1987). In fact, gender differences are greatest in the expression of fear and sadness (Allen & Haccoun, 1976). Consequently, men may be evaluated more harshly when they display such emotions, whereas women tend to express both strong and weak (or positive and negative) emotions without restraint or fear of negative evaluations (Hess & Kirouac, 2000). These differences in emotional expressiveness and responsivity may be part and parcel of the sex role socialization of children discussed earlier.

Encouraging Academic
Development Through Communication

Figure 6.5   Parents continue to encourage educational development through early reading, which has been linked to better academic outcomes later in life.

Besides physical and socioemotional development, a parent may be similarly concerned that their child masters the skills required of them in schools. The majority of us attended public schools, although a growing trend toward home schooling currently exists with up to 1.5% of all children (around 1.5 million) home schooled each year (Houston & Toma, 2003). Within these settings, parents want to ensure that their children excel intellectually to develop their reading, writing, and arithmetic skills to be in line with their peers (at a minimum). To this end, education has historically been considered the responsibility of the family (Stafford, 2004). In fact, children entering school with the basic learning capabilities already mastered have better peer relations and do better in school on measures of retention and graduation rates (Kagan & Cohen, 1995). It would seem that academic and social development go hand in hand. This is borne out by the literature showing that children who do better in school have fewer behavioral and social problems and get along better with their friends (Kagan & Cohen, 1995). Other outcomes are associated with better academic performance as well in that children who do better in school also tend to use fewer illegal substances, have better psychological well-being, and have lower rates of delinquency compared with kids who do more poorly in school. Children with poorer academic performances tend to act out, become delinquent, use drugs, get along poorly with friends, have greater rates of pregnancy, and have increased dropout rates (Durlak, 2001).

Given the relationship between poor academic performance and social outcomes, it is not surprising that parents devote much time to ensuring that their children do well in school. In fact, parents seem to have almost intuitive abilities to stimulate their children's learning (Papousek, Papousek, & Haekel, 1987), and most caregiver behaviors provide teaching to their infants (Van Egeren & Barratt, 2004). For instance, most caregivers frame their communication to infants in "infant-directed speech," or speech that is carefully constructed to attract the attention of the infant (Van Egeren & Barratt, 2004); they also use "motherese," which is specialized speech addressed to infants (Yingling, 1995). Characteristics of infant-directed speech include higher pitch, short emphatic words, exclamations, and gasps (e.g., Cooper & Aslin, 1989), as well as musicality and rhythm (Ochs & Schieffelin, 1984) and appear to be cross-cultural (Papousek, Papousek, & Symmes, 1991). Regardless of culture, parents appear to be intuitively aware of the needs of their infants as they attempt to stimulate and facilitate their child's future language acquisition through their own communication.

Furthermore, parents' communicative involvement with their children has been related to achievement in school. Specifically, parents who are more involved in their child's day-to-day lives have children with a greater internal locus of control in academic domains (Grolnick & Ryan, 1989). In addition, children's perceptions of their parents' expectations (Patrikako, 1997), aspirations, and support (Marjoribanks, 1997) were related to their own educational and career aspirations. This is consistent with all the earlier literature indicating that parental responsiveness and demandingness (i.e., *authoritative parenting*) relate to greater academic achievement.

Summary

Parents and caregivers, regardless of family form (single parents, nuclear families, adoptive families, gay families, extended families), socialize their children in physical, socioemotional, and academic ways. Central to all these outcomes is the process of *nurturing* and *control*. *Parenting styles* illustrate the centrality of nurturing and control; *authoritarian* parents are low on nurturing (*responsiveness*) and high on control (*demandingness*), *permissive* parents are high on nurturing (responsiveness) and low on control (demandingness), and *authoritative* parents are high on nurturing (responsiveness) and high on control (demandingness). All these parenting styles include *parenting practices*, which are communicative behaviors specifically aimed at guiding children's development. These parenting practices and communication have been associated with various physical, socioemotional, and academic outcomes for children. In general, authoritative parenting is associated with the best communicative (e.g., development of prosocial behavior), academic (e.g., GPA, mastery orientations), emotional (e.g., self-esteem and self-actualization), and mastery orientation outcomes for children. Considering parenting practices and communication specifically leads to consideration of the *communication of expectations* from parents to children and the ensuing *mastery orientation* that may result. Understanding the communication of disciplinary practices is also enhanced through consideration of *learning theory concepts* (e.g., reinforcement and punishment) and *natural and logical consequences*. Disciplinary communication and parenting practices may be especially difficult in adolescent-parent relationships because adolescents attempt to exert more control over their own lives. Regardless of parenting styles, parents also communicate in ways to encourage their children's development *physically* (in terms of sexual communication between adolescents and children), *socially* (in terms of modeling and coaching social relationships and in terms of sex role socialization), *emotionally* (in terms of emotional intelligence and emotional expressiveness), and *academically* (in terms of stimulating their children for ultimate intellectual growth).

KEY TERMS

academic development	negative reinforcement
authoritarian parents	parenting practices
authoritative parents	parenting styles
emotional development	permissive parents
emotional intelligence	physical development
learned helplessness	positive reinforcement
logical consequences	punishment
mastery orientation	sex role socialization
natural consequences	social development

QUESTIONS FOR APPLICATION

1. Differentiate between authoritative, authoritarian, and permissive styles of parenting based on the two dimensions of *responsiveness* (i.e., nurturing and warmth) and *demandingness* (i.e., control). What style did your parents adopt?

What parenting practices and communication did they use to enact these styles?

2. In what ways are physical, social, emotional, and academic outcomes associated with authoritative, authoritarian, and permissive parenting and practices for preschoolers and adolescents? In what ways were your own physical, social, emotional, and academic outcomes affected by your parents' parenting styles and practices?

3. Differentiate between mastery orientation and learned helplessness. How does the communication of expectations facilitate mastery orientation in children? In what ways did your own parents facilitate your own mastery orientation or learned helplessness?

4. Differentiate between reinforcement and punishment and natural and logical consequences in terms of socialization outcomes for children. How did your parents use communication behavior to reinforce and punish your behavior while you were living with them? How did your parents use communication to convey natural and logical consequences for your behavior?

5. In what ways can parents' communication help promote less risky sexual behavior in their children? How did your own parents communicate about sexual behavior with you? What impact did this have on the level of riskiness of your own sexual behavior?

6. In what ways does parents' communication facilitate sex role socialization in children? How did your parents communicate sex role expectations to you? In what communicative ways did they facilitate your own identification with your own gender?

7 Nurturing Communication in Marital Relationships: Encouraging Closeness, Stability, and Satisfaction Through Communication

"Im sorry, dear. I wasn't listening. Could you repeat
what you've said since we've been married?"

SOURCE: Copyright © The New Yorker Collection 2000 Robert Mankoff from cartoonbank.com.
All rights reserved.

Given the demands of family life on time and energy (as seen in Chapter 5 on the addition of children to the family), it is not that surprising that self-help books abound regarding the importance of communication to maintain romantic love, reclaim the spark that fizzled, and keep your husband (or wife) happy in the sack. The early days of wine and roses, long leisurely walks on the beach, gazing longingly and lovingly into your partner's eyes, and staying in bed until noon are replaced with 6 a.m. morning wake-up calls of infants cooing, children watching cartoons, computers revving up in whatever multiplayer game is the flavor of the month, shuttling children to and from practices and games, preparing meals, cleaning up, fitting in the chores that piled up during the week, and other generally frenetic behaviors necessary to maintain the household in some semblance of working order. If you and your partner have time for a quick snog (i.e., kiss) and a tweak of the backside during all this, you feel like the day has gotten off on the right track.

Whereas the last chapter focused on the parent-child relationship across all family forms and the use of nurturing and controlling communication to raise socioemotionally competent children, this chapter focuses on marital relationships and the use of nurturing communication to promote marital stability and satisfaction. Not all families include marital relationships (e.g., single-parent households, extended family), but remember that 110 million adults (56%) are married in the United States (U.S. Census Bureau, 2003a) and it is likely that up to 92% of us will be in marriages or in marriage-like commitments throughout the span of our lifetimes (Kreider & Fields, 2001). In addition, while many of us will divorce, up to half of all marriages are remarriages (46%; National Center for Health Statistics, 1995). Thus, processes of *nurturing communication, satisfaction,* and *stability* in marriages will be highly relevant to most of us at some point in our lifetimes. Because it is unlikely that any of us enter marriage with the desire to eventually divorce, it is timely to consider communication and related processes that contribute to the stability of the marriage. In addition, although it is possible to be highly committed to an unhappy marriage, it is likely that most of us would also prefer to be in stable *and* satisfying relationships. This chapter considers communicative and related processes that contribute to both stable and satisfying marital relationships. While these processes are also important to the maintenance of stable and satisfying familial relationships, in general, processes of the communication of closeness between parents and children (especially with adolescents) were considered in Chapter 6.

Communication is central to encouraging closeness in marital relationships, and the maintenance of this closeness may relate to both marital satisfaction and marital stability. In fact, so important is communication in establishing marital satisfaction that up to half of women's satisfaction with marriage has been accounted for by communication behavior (Richmond, McCroskey, & Roach, 1997). Communication behavior is important to predict marital satisfaction and stability. Gottman and Levenson (1992) argue, based on numerous behavioral investigations, that successful marriages have a 5:1 ratio in terms of positive to negative communication behaviors. They found that couples who displayed more positivity than negativity when they spoke to each other were more satisfied, less likely to have thoughts about divorce, less likely to have actually separated, and less likely to have divorced. This is especially important to marriages in which one or both partners are distressed (i.e., less satisfied). Consistent with this line of research, individuals in distressed relationships tend to display more negative affect, less positive affect, and more reciprocity of negative affect (i.e., matching of negativity of emotional expressions) (e.g., Noller, 1984). In fact, negative behaviors are the most predictive of marital satisfaction (e.g., Gottman & Levenson, 1986; Huston & Vangelisti, 1991), with negative communication behaviors being more predictive of marital satisfaction than positive behaviors (e.g., Broderick & O'Leary, 1986). This is the case despite the fact that happier partners display more positive communication behaviors than unhappy partners (e.g., Cutrona, 1996).

Given this emphasis on positive over negative communication behavior in satisfied marriages, it is also highly likely that the maintenance of marital satisfaction and stability is related specifically to the positive communication behaviors of nurturing and closeness within marital relationships. The ability to maintain communicative closeness, however, may be thwarted by an individual's need for autonomy, or self-directed behavior. The *dialectic tensions* created by our simultaneous desires to be close and autonomous are considered here as well, as are our individual and marital needs to maintain privacy. Several communicative processes have been related to the maintenance of closeness: (a) self-disclosure, (b) expressions of affection, (c) communication of support, (d) emotional regulation and expression, and (e) sexual intimacy and communication. These communicative processes and their relationship to marital satisfaction and stability are the focus of this chapter.

Maintaining Closeness in Marital Relationships

There are many reasons for researchers' conclusion that marriages with greater communication of closeness tend to be more satisfying. One piece of evidence comes from examining the connection between self-disclosure (how much personal information a person shares with someone else) and marital satisfaction. People who disclose more intimate information with their spouse are generally more satisfied with their marriage (Hendrick, 1981; Hendrick, Hendrick, & Adler, 1988). Furthermore, when both people prefer the same level of intimacy as their partners, they tend to be happier (Sanderson & Cantor, 2001). This is true not only for married couples but also for dating couples (Sanderson & Evans, 2001). Not surprisingly, the opposite is also true. Partners who want different levels of intimacy are typically less satisfied than couples who want the same level of intimacy. People who want more intimacy than their spouse are often frustrated by their partner's lack of comfort with intimacy and their partner's lack of self-disclosure (Miller, 1990; Miller & Read, 1991).

Assuming that marital satisfaction is related to the communication of closeness in the marital relationship, it is useful to differentiate between **stable marriages** (i.e., marriages that endure and do not end in divorce) and **satisfying marriages** (i.e., marriages that partners evaluate positively). Many marriages may not have closeness and high marital satisfaction, but they are stable and enduring. Specifically, one landmark study revealed that stable marriages differ from the ideal happy marriage (Cuber & Haroff, 1965). Their research revealed five types of enduring (stable) marriages—only two of which included high levels of marital closeness and marital satisfaction. *Vital marriages* represent the ideal marriage in that spouses share true intimacy and find their greatest satisfaction in life with each other. *Total marriages* are similar to vital marriages in that the spouses share true intimacy and find their greatest satisfaction with each other, but they are also highly involved in each other's activities (including outside work). The final three types of enduring marriages do not include closeness or marital satisfaction. *Conflict habituated marriages* center on tensions and disagreements that manifest in the communicative behaviors of nagging, quarrelling, sarcasm, condescension, and, potentially, physical violence. *Devitalized marriages* center on duty and maintenance of the relationship despite the loss of romantic love. Finally, *passive congenial marriages* provide stability for the couple whose members do not expect love but use the marriage base to direct their energies elsewhere (e.g., toward work or relationships external to the marriage). This research reveals that closeness is related to marital satisfaction in that the two couple types that share closeness are satisfied. This research also illustrates, however, that marriages can survive without closeness. In other words, marriages do not need to include the communication of closeness to avoid divorce. However, marriages that do include the communication of closeness can be *both* satisfying and stable. Therefore, the communication of closeness is essential to have the winning combination of marital stability *and* marital satisfaction.

Offering even more support for the relationship between closeness and marital satisfaction and marital stability, the circumplex model describes family functioning in terms of family cohesion and family adaptability (Olsen, Russell, & Sprenkle, 1989). This model posits that families are well functioning to the extent that they are cohesive (i.e., have emotional bonding) and adaptable (are responsive to situational and developmental demands with changes in power structures, roles, and rules). The authors argue that evidence exists supporting a linear relationship between cohesion and marital stability and satisfaction and between adaptability and stability and satisfaction (Olsen & Tiesel, 1991). Therefore, cohesiveness (i.e., closeness) and adaptability are both key to the long-term functioning of the family unit as a whole.

Dialectic Models of Relationship Maintenance: The Autonomy-Closeness Dialectic

Once individuals have established their primary relationship, entered marriage, and started to have children, many are concerned with how to balance their own and their partner's needs for *closeness* and *autonomy* in the family. These needs for closeness and autonomy create a dialectic tension in any relationship whereby one person's need for the communication of closeness can be in direct opposition to their partner's needs for self-directed behavior. The demands of **closeness** (e.g., intimate conversations, cuddling, sexual activity) often come head-to-head with time constraints imposed by the household and child care tasks inherent in the family (e.g., organizing the house, preparing the meals, and overseeing homework, the demands of children, and their activities) and the needs of both partners to maintain **autonomy** (e.g., having independent senses of self, directing their own behavior, controlling their own activities). For instance, you may want to spend long moments in delicious and well-deserved adult conversation with your partner when he or she gets home from work, but the toddler's demands for attention combined with your partner's need to drive the 10-year-old to soccer practice may make this impossible. Consistently, you desire the sexual activity that you were promised three times a week (just like all the books said), but you're so tired from managing the children and coping with little 18-month-old Johnny's demands for cuddling all day through his 17th cold that you feel like any more demands for touching are out of the question. Thus, your needs for intimate conversation (i.e., self-disclosure), physical affection, and sexual intimacy take a backseat to the time constraints of family life with all the tasks required. In addition, by the time you get to have the time for closeness, you or your partner may have lost the desire for intimacy and want that precious 15 minutes at the end of the day before bedtime to unwind, chill out, and basically be on your own for awhile. Therein lies the tension between closeness and autonomy needs in the family.

In these ways, the demands of daily family life interfere with marital closeness and make it difficult to maintain. Assuming that marital closeness is directly related to marital satisfaction, it is not that surprising then that marital satisfaction declines over the first 10 years of marriage (e.g., Cowan & Cowan, 1988; Glenn, 1998; Karney & Bradbury, 1997; Kurdek, 1993; MacDermid, Huston, & McHale, 1990; McHale & Huston, 1985). As we observed in Chapter 5, this is especially the case for married couples who add children, where marital satisfaction is highest in the preparental and postparental stages (Benin & Robinson, 1997). Thus, the age-old advice and wisdom suggesting that couples wait to have children appears to be supported once again in that the primary couple has time to devote to their relationship and its success *before* jumping on the wild ride of activity that is family life. However, because nearly half of all marriages in the United States are remarriages, many marital couples jump into the intimacies of married life with children already to hand. These families may not experience a preparental stage and thus may have their intimacy affected by the influence of children early on. You might remember that my husband came with a full complement of children as a free added benefit of marriage. I moved from a one-bedroom condo in sunny Santa Barbara's downtown district (complete with a yard attended to by the communal gardener) to a five-bedroom house in the suburbs (with a fair commute to work and a large piece of land) complete with a husband, two kids, and a dog. The demands of household and child care came as quite a shock and immediately had an impact on when and how my husband and I could express closeness.

Every relationship has dialectic tensions between competing needs, and marital relationships are no exception. Marital couples need expressions of closeness and nurturing, but the individual members also need autonomy to have time alone and the ability to engage in self-directed behavior. The need for autonomy, or self-directed behavior, interferes with the ability to be close. Conversely, the need for closeness and intimacy takes away an individual's ability to be self-directed and autonomous. In other words, engaging in individual goal-directed behavior (e.g., working out in the yard) takes away the ability to use that time to cuddle, nurture your partner through a crisis, or whisper sweet nothings in your partner's ear. At the same time, the demands to be close through conversations (e.g., self-disclosure and debriefing), physical affection, and sexual intimacy take time away from an individual's ability to be self-directed and independent in his or her activities (e.g., run to the mall, play sports, go out with the guys). In this way, the needs for autonomy and closeness compete with each other. This section of the chapter explores the dialectic tensions between autonomy and intimacy in the marital relationship and its effect on marital satisfaction and marital stability.

Although several dialectic models exist, communication researcher Leslie Baxter's (1990; Baxter & Montgomery, 1996) dialectic approach to relationship maintenance is highlighted here because it emphasizes the ongoing tensions between contradictory impulses that exist in already developed *family* and *marital* relationships. Central to the notion of dialectics in relationships is the idea of contradiction. A **contradiction** refers to the unity of opposites in that two concepts are wed together at the same time that they compete with, or diminish, one another (Baxter & West, 2003). The qualities of relationships that compete with one another form the anchors for the same idea, where, for instance, total closeness—that is, no autonomy can exist—is at one end of a continuum and total autonomy—where it is impossible for closeness to exist—is at the opposite end of the continuum. Although autonomy and closeness are opposing concepts, they are both necessary within relationships. Therein lies the dialectic tension between autonomy and closeness. Ideally, marital couples provide at the same time a safe haven in which nurturing and closeness can occur (e.g., cuddling, self-disclosing, comforting, emoting) and a secure base from which the individual members of the couple can emerge and act independently in their day-to-day activities (i.e., autonomy). Thus, in their purest forms, closeness exists to allow autonomy, but closeness and autonomy rarely exist simultaneously.

Autonomy and closeness are not the only dialectic contradictions in marital relationships, however. Many communicative dialectic tensions have been delineated, but the four that are the most relevant to discussions of marital satisfaction, marital stability, and family life in general are these:

1. Autonomy and closeness (connectedness)

2. Openness and protection (closedness)

3. Novelty and predictability

4. Positivity and negativity (Baxter, 1990)

In support of a greater attention to autonomy and closeness needs, autonomy-connectedness and openness-closedness are both given the greatest importance in terms of predicting relational turning points (Baxter & Ebert, 1999). As discussed previously, *autonomy* refers to desires to be independent from our families, whereas *intimacy* refers to our desire to be close to our families. As we have seen above, much research exists linking goals for intimacy and matching of intimacy between partners and marital satisfaction. *Openness* refers to our desire to be emotionally vulnerable while revealing personal information to our families, whereas *protection* (or closedness) refers to our strategic attempts to protect ourselves from our families by not revealing potentially risky information to them. Protection is especially apparent to the extent that marital partners desire privacy or maintain secrets from one another, other family members, or from nonfamily members. This will become more apparent through our review of communication privacy management (CPM) theory below. *Novelty* refers to our desire for excitement and change, whereas *predictability* refers to the comfort of stability. Below, we will refer to research showing that those with highly idealized notions of what it means to be, and have, a partner in early courtship exhibit greater disillusionment following marriage. Part of the disillusionment can be explained through the distinction between the early and *novel* first months of relating compared with the boring but *stable* days of patterned marriage and stability. *Positivity* refers to our desire for evaluating our family members in positive ways, whereas *negativity* refers to the inevitability of our evaluating some things about our family members negatively. The dialectic tension between positivity and negativity is especially relevant to marital satisfaction in that, as we have seen previously, positive and negative communication patterns in marriage affect both marital satisfaction and stability. Thus, *closeness-autonomy, openness-protection, novelty-predictability*, and *positivity-negativity* are particularly relevant communication dimensions in the maintenance of marital and family stability and satisfaction.

Protectedness in Marriage: Communication Privacy Management (CPM) Theory

The openness-protection communication dialectic provides an especially rich forum for considering the relationship between privacy and secrets and closeness between marital partners. Communication privacy management (CPM) theory argues that individuals desire to control private information because they have ownership over it and because revealing the private information might make them vulnerable (see Caughlin & Petronio, 2004, for a review). Control over private information is achieved through rules about regulation of (a) *boundary permeability* (i.e., the degree of access given to private information), (b) *linkages* (i.e., connections formed through allowing others inside of a privacy boundary), and (c) *ownership* (i.e., individuals with access to the private information). Intuitively, it would seem that privacy in marital relationships might detract from the overall closeness of the couple. This is in fact the case in marital relationships where marital partners maintain privacy and secrets *from* the other marital partner. In this case, one marital partner is surrounded by the boundary, has no linkage to the partner, and has sole ownership over the information, and decreased closeness should result. This might be the case if one partner hides a drinking or gambling problem from the other partner. However, it is also possible that privacy and secrets may be held by the marital couple as a unit. In this situation, privacy and secrets may enhance the bonding between the marital couple. Collective boundaries are constructed through the linkages created through the sharing of the personal information between the marital couple. Marital partners are surrounded by the boundary, partners are linked to one another, and the couple "co-owns" the private information. They become comrades in adversity, as it were, both working to protect the secret information from exposure. This co-ownership can create greater bonds and closeness between the couple. This might be the case, for instance, if marital partners try to keep one partner's drinking and gambling from other family members and from outside family members. Thus, privacy maintenance may actually enhance closeness for a marital couple. Although this model is considered here with regard to marital couples and ensuing closeness, it is possible that the CPM has implications for sibling relationships and whole family secrets as well (see Vangelisti, 1994a; Vangelisti, Caughlin, & Timmerman, 2001). This model may be especially useful for families that include gay heads of households while maintaining privacy and for other families who maintain privacy surrounding drinking behavior or other secrets within the family. Regardless, privacy may enhance or detract from the communication of marital closeness and may affect marital satisfaction and stability.

The Communication of
_____ Closeness in the Marital Relationship

What exactly is closeness and how is it related to marital satisfaction and marital stability? **Closeness** refers to psychological distance in the relationship, with couples experiencing closeness feeling less psychologically distant from one another and couples not experiencing closeness feeling greater psychological distance from their partners. Marital partners can communicate this diminished sense of psychological distance (closeness) through a variety of means. For instance, Sanderson and Cantor (2001) indicate that couples with greater intimacy goals (a) engaged in more activities together, (b) gave each other more social support, and (c) had greater influence on each other's thoughts, values, and future goals. Intimacy, then, is equated with frequency of joint activities, degree of social support, and greater mutual influence. Is this the extent of closeness, however? Closeness is multifaceted in that many components come together to form the overall intimacy of the couple. All the factors enhancing closeness discussed here are communicative in nature; that is, they create a decreased sense of distance between the spouses through specific types of communicative behavior. For instance, the amount of information individuals share with each other on a daily basis (e.g., *self-disclosure*) creates a greater feeling of closeness or reduced distance in the relationship. This may be complemented by the amount of *physical affection* (e.g., hugging, kissing, touching, physical proximity) the couple shares during the course of the day. Furthermore, couples may be closer to each other to the extent they provide *social support* to each other (e.g., comfort each other, rally to each other's causes). Married couples may increase their closeness to their partner through the degree of emotional sharing they exhibit or by the extent to which they are vulnerable to each other's moods and feelings (e.g., *emotional regulation*). Finally, couples can express or create closeness through the amount and types of *sexual intimacy* they share. This portion of the chapter explores intimacy to the extent that married partners self-disclose, express affection, show social support, are responsive to each other's emotional regulation and expression, and express sexual intimacy.

Self-Disclosure

Remember from Chapter 4 on developing relationships, self-disclosure is central to individuals' getting to know a large amount of information about each other. Self-disclosure, however, remains an important part of relationships throughout the trajectory of relationships as individuals attempt to remain close throughout their married life. Self-disclosure, then, as sharing information about self, is related to remaining close in marital relationships and marital satisfaction and stability. Although gender is purported to account for a small degree of the variance (Dindia & Allen, 1992), men and women appear to disclose to varying degrees, and it bears mentioning because these degrees can be related to marital satisfaction. In general, women are more likely to disclose than men, and men tend to be more inexpressive than women (e.g., Dosser, Balswick, & Halverson, 1986). However, men have been found to disclose as much factual, descriptive information as do females (e.g., Rubin, Hill, Peplau, & Dunkel-Schetter, 1980). In addition, perhaps because men are less disclosive in general, husbands' expressiveness seems to affect both husbands' and wives' marital satisfaction more than wives' expressiveness (e.g., Huston & Vangelisti, 1995). Furthermore, discrepancies between the level of disclosure by husbands and wives have been associated with less marital adjustment (e.g., Davidson, Balswick, & Halverson, 1983). Finally, the positivity or the negativity of the disclosure may interact with the degree of self-disclosure; higher marital satisfaction was associated with greater disclosures that conveyed positive feeling toward the spouse (Schumm, Barnes, Bollman, Jurich, & Bugaighis, 1986). Negative disclosures were not related to marital satisfaction.

Remember from Chapter 4 that according to social penetration theory, developing relationships are assumed to increase in self-disclosures of depth and breadth. This breadth and depth may predict future relationship success in terms of marital stability and marital satisfaction. In fact, relationship development breadth predicted the greatest satisfaction early in relationships, whereas the lack of relationship development breadth predicted both lowest satisfaction and discontinued relationships later in the trajectories of couples (Flora & Segrin, 2003). Having a broad range of knowledge of one's partner through self-disclosure is necessary to both marital stability and marital satisfaction.

Although not traditionally thought of as self-disclosure, much of what used to be considered mundane conversation has recently become the focus of emotion researchers. **Emotional bids,** or a marital partner's direct or indirect request for attention, interest, conversation, or emotional support, are at the heart of marital satisfaction (Gottman, 2001). The claim here is that mundane attempts at conversation—for example, "Wow! It's a nice day today"—are actually requests for attention from one's spouse and that the response can determine marital stability. *Turning toward* is when the partner acknowledges the request or evidences a connection (i.e., "Prettiest day I can remember"), whereas *turning away* is ignoring the request for connection (i.e., continuing to read the newspaper). *Turning against* is the most destructive because the partner responds in a hostile manner that overtly rejects the bid for connection (i.e., "Yeah, right" or "I'm trying to read here"). These ideas are very similar to notions of confirmation and disconfirmation in the interpersonal communication research arena (e.g., Buber, 1965; Laing, 1961; Watzlawick, Beavin, & Jackson, 1967). A wife's use of turning away and a husband's use of both turning away and turning against were related to later destructive conflict patterns of attack-defend (one spouse attacks while the other defends himself or herself) or suppression-withdrawal (one spouse suppresses the conflict and the other withdraws from the conflict). Attack-defend patterns were related to early divorce, and suppression-withdrawal patterns were related to later divorce. Spouses' communicative responses to emotional bids during mundane conversations can actually predict marital stability.

This work on emotional bidding is similar to the work of Vangelisti and Banski (1993) on debriefing conversations at the end of the day. These conversations inform marital partners about the events, thoughts, and emotions the other experienced while they were separated for the day. The amount of time partners spent in debriefing conversations at the end of the day did not affect the marital satisfaction of the partners, but the partner's rating of the importance of these conversations predicted marital satisfaction for both men and women. In addition, there was a stronger association between the discrepancy in talk time between the two partners and marital satisfaction for wives than for husbands. Thus, mundane conversations (such as debriefing ones) appear to be an important mechanism for partners in terms of maintaining closeness and marital satisfaction in the relationship.

Expressions of Affection

Figure 7.1   Expressions of physical affection are one way of communicating
closeness in marriage and family life.

Remember those early days when you couldn't keep your hands to yourself around your romantic partner? Communication researcher, Kory Floyd
(1997) argues that this affectionate communication is critical for relational
definition. Not surprisingly, however, time, children, and household tasks
teach you to keep those hands to yourself. How does physical affection
change over time in marital relationships? Many couples who were very positive and affectionate prior to marriage may begin to settle into more stable
behavioral patterns after marriage (MacDermid et al., 1990; Vangelisti,
2002). These stable patterns may include reduced frequency of affectionate
behavior soon after marriage (Huston, Robins, Atkinson, & McHale, 1987).
While it is likely that all married couples will decrease touch following marriage, it is also the case that more satisfied couples use closer distances for
conversation than do less satisfied couples (Guerrero, 1994). Recent studies
have also shown that marriages marked with disillusionment or an abate-
ment of love, a decline in overt affection, perceptions of a spouse's declining
responsiveness, and an increase in ambivalence are more likely headed for

divorce than are couples without such markers (Huston, Caughlin, Houts, Smith, & George, 2001). Also consistent with the disillusionment model, newlyweds' initially high levels of affection followed by declines in affection over the first 2 years of marriage was predicted by shorter courtship length, men's younger age at marriage, men's lower premarital ambivalence, higher levels of premarital maintenance behavior by both partners, rapid rates of falling in love, and both partner's deeper feelings of love during courtship (Niehuis, 2001). Consistently, when recently divorced individuals were asked to describe reasons for the dissolution of their relationship, they cited loss of interest in the relationship, diminished love, and loss of affection (Buehlman, Gottman, & Katz, 1992). Not surprisingly, negative affectivity can affect physical displays of affection as well; for example, marriages that include a depressed wife report less affection than couples without a depressed partner (Coyne, Thompson, & Palmer, 2002). Affection communicates a sense of closeness, and greater declines in affection following marriage are related to less satisfaction and less stability in marriages.

Communication of Support

Self-disclosure and expressions of affection are not the only means of establishing closeness in marital relationships, however. Given the number of situational and developmental stressors that families experience, individuals within families often rely on one another to receive social support in times of crisis. Disclosing about these stressors and potential traumatic events can have mental and physical health benefits (Kelly, 2002; Smyth & Pennebaker, 2001). The extent to which marital partners are seen to be supportive has also been related to marital satisfaction, and social support can be related to feelings of closeness in a couple (Barbee & Cunningham, 1995; Sprecher, Metts, Burleson, Hatfield, & Thompson, 1995). This is especially the case among married individuals who are experiencing health care. Specifically, unsupportive behavior of one's spouse was related to distress in kidney transplant patients only to the extent that they were dissatisfied with the relationship with their spouse (Frazier, Tix, & Barnett, 2003). Marital satisfaction also related to greater distress overall. Not only are married couples more likely to view each other positively when they are more satisfied, but they may also overlook less supportive behavior. Further illustrating the strength of perceptions, the *perception* that a marital partner was supportive was more important than the actual degree of support provided in terms of predicting marital satisfaction (Dunkel-Schetter & Bennett, 1990).

Supportive behavior within couples is also important during pregnancy and infertility treatment. Wives in traditional, separate/traditional, and separate/independent marriages felt they received significantly more nurturance since pregnancy than did wives in independent marriages (Fitzpatrick, Vangelisti, & Firman, 1994). Studies have also shown that although having a baby is generally more important to a female's self-esteem, having a husband who saw having children as important, was invested in trying to have a baby, or wanted to talk with his wife about wanting to have a baby all predicted (a) greater positivity while communicating about infertility and (b) greater perceptions of closeness by the wife (Pasch, Dunkel-Schetter, & Christensen, 2002).

Supportive communication can have dramatic effects on physical health as well (Cunningham & Barbee, 2000; Sarason, Sarason, & Gurung, 1997). For instance, mothers who received more social support (including from their spouse) had babies with higher birth weights than mothers who received less social support (e.g., Feldman, Dunkel-Schetter, Sandman, & Wadhwa, 2000). Supportive communication can not only influence marital satisfaction but can actually influence physical health outcomes as well. You might remember from Chapter 4 on the health benefits of marriage that better health outcomes may be linked to communication (Kiecolt-Glaser, McGuire, Robles, & Glaser, 2002a). Supportive communication may be one of the resources associated with close personal relationships that diminish negative emotions and enhance health in part through their positive impact on immune and endocrine regulation (e.g., Kiecolt-Glaser, McGuire, Robles, & Glaser, 2002b). On the flip side, if unsupportive spouses evoke greater amounts of negative emotions, these negative emotions may stimulate immune dysregulation, which may be one of the core mechanisms underlying conditions such as cardiovascular disease, osteoporosis, arthritis, Type 2 diabetes, and certain cancers (Kiecolt-Glaser et al., 2002b). Unhappy marriages, then, may be rife with negative emotions, which explain the poorer mental and physical health of unhappily married individuals. Supportive communication may facilitate greater physical health through its ability to ameliorate negative emotions. Alternatively, less supportive communication and the resulting negative emotions may actually be a detriment to physical health.

Given that supportive communication has been linked to marital satisfaction and that partners who provide undesired responses can produce undesirable outcomes (e.g., Albrecht, Burleson, & Goldsmith, 1994), you might be curious about what types of communicative behaviors are seen as appropriately supportive. According to Burleson and Mortenson (2003), a growing body of evidence suggests that *solve strategies* (i.e., approach-based, problem-focused responses where the supporter tries to solve the supportee's problem) and especially *solace strategies* (i.e., approach-based, emotion-focused responses where the supporter attempts to be a source of comfort à la Cunningham & Barbee, 2000) and highly *person-centered strategies* (i.e., responses that explicitly acknowledge, elaborate, legitimize, and contextualize the feelings of the distressed, à la Burleson, 1994) are the most sensitive and effective in terms of providing support. On the other hand, messages that are *dismissive* (i.e., responses that minimize the existence of a problem) or *escapist* (i.e., responses that avoid the problem altogether) are not effective (Cunningham & Barbee, 2000). This is consistent with extensive research by Burleson and his colleagues (see Burleson & Mortenson, 2003) showing that messages that are low in person centeredness (i.e., that deny the other's feelings, criticize the other's feelings, challenge the legitimacy of the feelings, or tell the other how he or she should act or feel) are the least effective in terms of supportiveness. This may be consonant with Gottman's (2001) ideas of turning toward, turning away, and turning against during mundane conversations and the interpersonal concepts of confirmation and disconfirmation. Goldsmith, McDermott, and Alexander (2000) found that responses to requests for support were seen as supportive if they where helpful, supportive, or sensitive. *Helpful* responses were utilitarian in terms of problem solving. *Supportive* responses were relationally reassuring, and *sensitive* responses were emotionally aware. Therefore, responses that are highly problem oriented, solace providing, and high in person centeredness are more effective in terms of providing support in marital relationships and should be associated with greater closeness and higher marital satisfaction and potential increases in physical health to the extent that they help regulate negative emotions (the topic of the next section).

Emotional Regulation and Expression

Not unlike supportive communication, much of the work in close intimate relationships revolves around the communicative expression of emotions and emotional management. This "emotion work" has been seen as underrepresented and underappreciated in terms of computation of household and child care workload. However, much of this emotion work falls to the female nurturer-caregivers in the family (Strazdins & Broom, 2004). Specifically, one reason cited for men experiencing greater health benefits from marriage than women (Waite & Gallagher, 2000) is that they receive more social support in commitment and caring from their wives than vice versa (Zinn & Eitzen, 2002). Emotions are a particularly rich area of study in family and marital relationships because of the irrationality associated with family life and all that it entails (Vangelisti, 1993).

Experiencing various emotions in relationships has also been related to marital satisfaction and stability. Specifically, feeling sad or hurt in the relationship was associated with positive relationship functioning (high satisfaction, low conflict, and low avoidance), and feeling angry was associated with negative relationship functioning (low satisfaction, high conflict, and high avoidance; Sanford & Rowatt, 2004). It is possible that allowing one's self to experience sadness and hurt in a relationship implies a certain degree of trust and vulnerability in the relationship, whereas greater expressions of anger may be associated with self-protection and low trust. Allowing oneself to be more vulnerable implies a higher degree of closeness in the relationship. In contrast, feeling anxious or threatened was positively associated with relationship anxiety. This anxiety may similarly be associated with trust and closeness in the relationships. It would appear that expressions of weaker emotions, indicating emotional vulnerability in the relationship, suggest the potentiality of greater closeness and are associated with more positive marital satisfaction and less conflict. Anger and anxiety, however, may indicate less closeness and trust and actually work against this functioning in that they are associated with negative outcomes for marital satisfaction and conflict.

Consistent with this notion of greater trust, being able to be emotionally vulnerable to one's spouse is another way that emotions affect relationships. Relationship partners may be affected by their partner's moods. Have you ever thought, "Oh dang, my boyfriend Rocco's in a foul mood—what did *I* do *now*?" Chances are you are among those of us with low self-esteem who tend to interpret our significant other's negative and ambiguous mood as being our fault (Bellavia & Murray, 2003). In addition, those with low self-esteem are also more likely to feel rejected and more hostile toward their bad-mood partners than are those with high self-esteem.

Furthermore, a partner's general level of affectivity can affect marital processes as well. Partners with more general negative affectivity exhibited a tendency to make more maladaptive attributions regarding their spouse (Karney, Bradbury, Fincham, & Sullivan, 1994). In other words, marital partners who are more negative in general tend to be more negative about their spouse and affect the marital quality in that way. In fact, premarital assessments of negativity predict satisfaction in marriage (e.g., Kelly, Huston, & Cate, 1985) as well as declines in relational satisfaction over time (Gottman & Krokoff, 1989; Levenson & Gottman, 1985). This negative affectivity is similar to the effect of depression in marriages and is explored more fully in Chapter 9.

This negative affectivity appears related to gender as well. Whereas wives are more expressive overall (expressing both more positivity and negativity) compared with husbands (Noller, 1984; Notarius & Johnson, 1982), women are more critical when interacting with their partners compared with men (Hahlweg, Revenstorf, & Schindler, 1984). This is consistent with the research on distressed couples showing that distressed wives communicate more negatively toward their husbands than do distressed husbands (e.g., Gottman & Krokoff, 1989; Noller, 1985; Notarius, Benson, Sloane, Vanzetti, & Hornyak, 1989) and that wives are also more likely to recip-rocate (i.e., match) the negative behavior of their spouses (Notarius & Pellegrini, 1987). Thus, wives are less able to "break out of the cycle" of negative behavior because they are less likely than husbands to be able to respond to negative behavior with positive behavior (Notarius et al., 1989). One might naturally assume that this greater negativity of wives would result in declines in marital satisfaction for both husbands and wives, but it is actually the husband's negativity that has been the most related to declines in marital satisfaction (Gottman & Krokoff, 1989), especially for wives (Huston & Vangelisti, 1991). In other words, husbands' negativity predicts lower marital satisfaction in wives, but wives' negativity does not equally predict lower marital satisfaction in husbands.

Sexual Intimacy and Communication

Closeness in marriage can also be enhanced through *sexual intimacy* and associated communication (e.g. Greeff, 2000). Although the early stages of romantic life included high levels of eroticism and a high frequency of sexual relations, the same household and behavioral routines that interfere with other types of intimacy also interfere with sexual activity as well. Prepare yourselves, because many of my students find this section of the course highly disappointing. I consider it to be a valuable service in terms of having what Pearson (1992) calls *lowered and realistic expectations*. Many of you will be in the earliest throes of the most exciting romance (i.e., high levels of novelty), but remember that family life and all it entails in terms of household labor and children's demands interferes with intimacy at all levels (i.e., high levels of stability). In what is considered the most scientific study to date of sexual activity in America, Laumann, Gagnon, Michael, and Michaels (1994) completed 3,500 face-to-face interviews with a random sample of men and women between 18 and 59. Surprisingly, married individuals have more sex than nonmarrieds; nearly 40% of marrieds have sex at least twice a week compared with 25% of singles. To break this down a bit more, for the married people sampled, a small percentage of both men

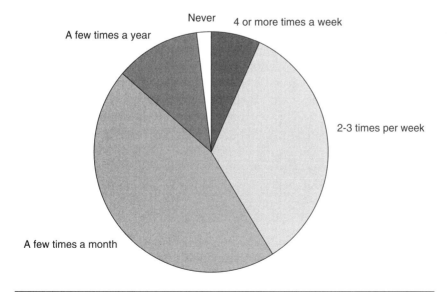

Figure 7.2   Frequency of Sex in Married Couples' Lives

SOURCE: Laumann, Gagnon, Michael, and Michaels (1994).

and women reported having sex four or more times a week (7%), about a third reported having sex two to three times a week (32% of women and 36% of men), the greatest majority reported having sex a few times a month (47% of women and 43% of men), another small percentage reported having sex a few times a year (12% of women and 13% of men), and a small minority reported never having sex (3% of women and 1% of men).

Thus, the most frequently occurring amount of sexual activity among married couples is at least twice a week. On the positive side, the researchers also found that compared with singles (who are rumored to have the most interesting and varied sex lives—can you say *Sex in the City*?), married individuals had the most sex and the most orgasms, and 40% of both married men and women describe their sex lives as extremely satisfying both emotionally and physically. So although you thought you might be having sex more than twice a week when you were married, the good news is that you will be having more sex than if you were single *and* it will be more satisfying.

If the largest number of married couples are having sex twice a week (40%) *and* the same number of married individuals are highly satisfied with their sex lives (40%), you might be wondering about the nature of their sexual activity. Laumann et al. (1994) found that men and women are fairly traditional in their sexual behavior in that nearly everyone reported that vaginal intercourse was their preferred and most common sexual activity. Not surprisingly, men think more about sex every day (54%) than women (19%), and more men have orgasms every time they have sex (75%) than women (29%). Men also find receiving (50%) and giving (37%) oral sex more appealing than women (33%; 19%; Mackay, 2000). Males also request sex more frequently than females and are the initiators of sexual activity in marriages. Wives most often accommodate their husbands' preferences.

Both interpersonal communication and sexual communication can enhance sexual satisfaction. Specifically, the better a man understands his partner's sexual preferences and the more the partners' preferences match, the more sexually satisfied both married partners are (Purnine & Carey, 1997). Thus, communicating about preferences and reaching an understanding about those preferences seems essential to increasing sexual satisfaction for both partners. In addition, sexual communication satisfaction mediated the role of sexual attitude similarity in terms of predicting sexual satisfaction (Cupach & Metts, 1995). Once again, sexual communication seems highly related to sexual satisfaction. Lawrance and Byers (1995) also found that social exchange principles (from Chapter 4) can predict sexual satisfaction in that when relationship rewards exceed costs, relative reward levels exceed relative cost levels and perceived equality of rewards and costs exist across relationship partners, sexual partners are more sexually satisfied. Relationship satisfaction also added to the model.

Compared with many nonscientific reports of extramarital affairs reporting higher figures, the Laumann et al. (1994) study found that only 25% of men and 15% of women reported extramarital affairs. This is consistent with the attitudes of those surveyed; the researchers found three patterns of beliefs about sexuality inside and outside of marriage. About half of the sample was described as *relational* in that they believed that sex should be part of a loving relationship but that it does not necessarily need to be in a marriage. They were also highly disapproving of extramarital sex. About one third of the sample was described as *traditionals*. Traditionals disapproved of premarital sex, teenage sex, extramarital sex, and homosexuality. Traditionals also reported that their sexual behavior is guided by their religion. Finally, about one quarter of the sample were described as *recreational* in that they believed that sex need not have anything to do with love.

In general, then, most people believe sex should be within marriage, and most married couples report having sex twice a week. This form of closeness and the communication surrounding it can add to the marital satisfaction and stability of the couple.

Factors Related to Marital Satisfaction That May Influence Marital Communication

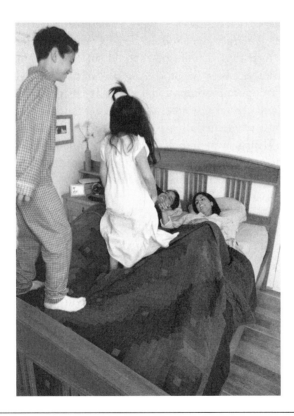

Figure 7.3　　The addition of children often interferes with the ability of married couples to be intimate and may be one of the reasons so many research studies evidence a decline in marital satisfaction after adding children.

The above research and theorizing illustrates the relationship between the communication of closeness in marriage and marital satisfaction. However, this text would be remiss not to recognize the whole host of sociological and psychological factors related to marital satisfaction that may affect communication outcomes as well. Given that most of us enter marriage with the intent of having a satisfying as well as successful (e.g., enduring) marriage, it is useful to delineate the demographic factors associated with marital satisfaction. Not unlike what the previous research between the communication of closeness and marital satisfaction reveals, it is likely that many of these demographic characteristics influence the communication of closeness in the marital relationship and influence marital satisfaction and stability in that way.

Demographic Characteristics and Potential Communication Outcomes

Although the extent of the studies on marital satisfaction and demographic characteristics is vast, we will focus our attentions here on a summary provided by Zinn and Eitzen (2002) in their work on diversity in families. First and foremost, marital satisfaction has been related to *homogamy on social characteristics*. Specifically, spouses who are similar in terms of socioeconomic status, religion, race, age, and intelligence tend to have more satisfying marriages. In short, these similarities should make the communication of closeness in marriages easier. Second, *economic and personal resources,* such as income, education, and occupational status are related to greater marital satisfaction. Again, greater resources should allow the marital couple greater luxuries in regard to greater time together for shared activities, including communication. Third, even though *dual-earner couples* experience more difficulties in terms of role demands, they tend to be more satisfied. Related to the discussion under greater resources, dual-earner couples should have greater resources, which allow them greater time for establishing closeness through communication. Fourth, *division of household labor* has been related to marital satisfaction, but remember that women take on many more tasks than men (even when they are working) before they feel the division of labor is unfair. It is likely that communication plays a role here as spouses coordinate their household labor tasks. Fifth, *role fit,* or the level of agreement between spouses on decision making, division of household responsibilities, financial issues, and child care, also predicts marital satisfaction. Again, role fit implies a comfort with role-associated communication, which should also enhance marital satisfaction. Sixth, *social class* also predicts marital satisfaction in that working-class couples are more likely to accept traditional gender roles in marriage. Such traditional gender roles are likely to predict communication behavior and comfort with this gender-associated communication, which should be related to greater marital satisfaction. Seventh (and as indicated previously), the *presence of children* relates to decreases in marital satisfaction. Because children are associated with increases in task load and decreases in the marital communication of closeness, it is not surprising that the addition of children should be associated with less marital satisfaction. This simultaneously aids our understanding of the fact that *life stage* relates to marital satisfaction in that marital satisfaction appears highest both before having kids and when the children are adults.

The Role of Cognition in Marital Satisfaction and Potential Communication Outcomes

In addition to these demographic factors associated with marital satisfaction, cognitive or psychological factors have been associated with marital satisfaction as well. In other words, the ways in which our marital partners perceive us can affect the ways in which they communicate with us and can ultimately affect our marital satisfaction. Uniquely blending a study of stability with a study of satisfaction, Pearson (1992) studied couples who had endured in marriage for 40 to 70 years. She identified eight factors associated with satisfied couples. These factors included *lowered expectations, unconditional acceptance, positive distortion, becoming one, remaining two, sexual satisfaction, coping with conflict,* and *persistence.* In other words, couples who had survived marriage *and* reported that they were happy to tell the tale had realistic and lowered expectations regarding what their spouse or the relationship could do for them. Somewhat in juxtaposition to this, they also accepted each other's foibles while wearing rose-colored glasses to interpret their spouse's behavior and characteristics in the most positive light. In terms of closeness and autonomy, these successful long-time married individuals also blended being close and having a shared identity with autonomy and independence. Furthermore, they were satisfied with both the quantity and quality of their sex lives, and they coped well with conflict, or goal interruptions, in their relationships. Finally, and of no small importance, these couples report tenacity and stick-to-itiveness.

Consistent with Pearson's (1992) notion of accepting each other's foibles and wearing rose-colored glasses, Neff and Karney (2003) found that married couples who were more globally satisfied had both positive *and* negative perceptions of their spouse but were more likely to *weight the positive perceptions as more important than the negative perceptions.* This is also consistent with Pearson's (1992) idea of positive distortion. Thus, focusing on the positive over the negative appears to be a theme among couples who report greater marital satisfaction. Consistently, partners were more maritally satisfied when their partners perceived them positively as opposed to negatively—regardless of how they saw themselves (Sacco & Phares, 2001). The authors interpret this finding to mean that *self-enhancement* (i.e., your partner sees you as better than you see yourself) is more important in marriage than *self-verification* (i.e., your partner's perception of you is similar to the ways in which you perceive yourself). Consistently, married couples were more satisfied and had more stable marriages when their partners held *idealized notions* of them (Murray,

Holmes, & Griffin, 1996a, 1996b). This positive distortion and idealized notion of marital spouses is likely to translate into communication behavior. In other words, it is likely that marital partners communicate their expectations of positive idealized behavior to their spouse and that their spouse, in turn, confirms these expectations by communicating in more positive ways, which ultimately should result in increases in marital satisfaction. Idealized notions of spouse can therefore create a self-fulfilling prophecy of sorts.

This idealized-notion-of-spouses research is supported by research on marital satisfaction and the attribution process and related communication behavior (e.g. Bradbury & Fincham, 1992). Marital couples who were asked to explain marital difficulties provided explanations for their partner's behavior. Marital partners who were in distressed marriages (i.e., less satisfied) showed a tendency to accentuate the negative events in their marriages and de-emphasize the positive. In other words, unhappy married partners were more likely to attribute the problems in their marriage to negative behavior on the part of their spouse. Positive behaviors were more likely to be discounted or weighted less heavily. Thus, while more satisfied couples tend to overestimate the positive, less satisfied or distressed couples tend to overestimate the negative in their relational partners. This translated into communicative behaviors as well, in that these maladaptive attributions were related to less effective problem-solving behaviors and greater reciprocation of negativity from one's spouse.

Consistent with the idea that spouses may communicate their expectations to their spouses, the *expectations* that spouses bring into the relationship also interact with their communication skills to predict marital satisfaction. In other words, spouses with positive expectations for marriage who communicated positively had the most stable marital satisfaction (McNulty & Karney, 2004). Alternatively, those with positive expectations for marriages who communicated negatively evidenced the steepest declines in marital satisfaction. Thus, violations of expectations appear to exert a powerful influence in that those who expected positive communication but experienced negative communication were the least satisfied.

Summary

In sum, it is likely that most of us will be in marriages or marriage-like commitments at some point in our lifetime. This chapter focused on the communication of closeness in marital relationships and the extent to which it enhances both marital satisfaction and marital stability. Marital relationships can be challenging in that the demands of day-to-day life require focusing on a multitude of activities, which may detract from the communication of closeness. Dialectic models of relationship maintenance help us understand this tension in terms of a *closeness-autonomy dialectic* whereby individuals within families and marital relationships attempt to balance their desires for closeness with their needs for independence. Although several dialectics are relevant to the communication of closeness in marital couples, the openness-protectedness dialectic can best be understood through the communication privacy management theory, which considers the effects in terms of closeness of one marital partner or both marital partners maintaining a secret.

The communication of closeness has been linked to marital satisfaction and also aids in our understanding of the differences between *marital satisfaction* (marriages that are emotionally gratifying) and *marital stability* (marriages that are enduring). Closeness can be seen at the heart of marital satisfaction and can be defined as reduced psychological distance within the relationship. Closeness in marital relationships may be strengthened through several communication mechanisms: *self-disclosure, expressions of affection, emotional regulation, communication of support,* and *sexual intimacy.* In addition to these clearly communication behaviors, it is also likely that sociological and psychological factors may be related to communication behavior and predict marital satisfaction and stability in that way. Thus, *demographic* and *cognitive* factors are considered to the extent that they may influence the communication of closeness within the marital couple. In general, more satisfied married couples tend to view each other more positively (both perceptually and attributionally) and communicate with each other in more positive ways.

KEY TERMS

attributions

autonomy

closeness

closeness-autonomy

communication

communication privacy management

demographic factors

dialectic models

emotional regulation

expressions of affection

marital satisfaction

marital stability

novelty-predictability

openness-protection
(closedness)

perceptions

positive distortion

positivity-negativity

self-disclosure

sexual intimacy

support

QUESTIONS FOR APPLICATION

1. Describe the tensions inherent between closeness and autonomy in your family of origin. How did your parents cope with the competing needs of various family members? If your parents were not married, how did the closeness-autonomy dialectic manifest itself in other important relationships in your family?

2. Differentiate between marital satisfaction and marital stability. Is it possible to have marital stability without marital satisfaction? How would you describe

your own family in terms of marital satisfaction and marital stability? What is the relationship between closeness and marital satisfaction and marital stability? How did your parents' level of closeness affect their marital satisfaction and marital stability?

3. How was closeness expressed through self-disclosure, expressions of physical affection and positive regard, emotional regulation, support, and sexual behavior in your parents' relationship? How did this relate to the degree of closeness you observed in your parents' relationship?

4. What demographic factors predict marital satisfaction? What is the relationship between marital satisfaction and closeness? How did each of these demographic characteristics play themselves out in your family of origin?

5. What cognitive and communicative factors predict marital satisfaction? To what extent did your parents positively distort their perceptions of each other? How did this distortion relate to their communication with each other and ultimately to their level of marital satisfaction and stability?

8

Control in Marital Relationships and the Family: Conflict, Constructive and Destructive Conflict, and Violence

Frustration-Aggression Hypothesis
Catalyst Hypothesis
Skills Deficiency Approach

Summary

Key Terms

Questions for Application

Although intimacy and closeness within the family can create a secure base for individuals as they go about their business in the world, intimacy and closeness can also create a fertile ground for conflict and, potentially, constructive or destructive communication patterns. In the last chapter, we discussed how the dialectic tension between creating closeness and intimacy in marital relationships could clash with individual family members' needs for autonomy. Such a tension can be expressed as a conflict, because individual members are experiencing a struggle as a result of the perception of incompatible goals, scarce rewards, and goal interference (Hocker & Wilmot, 2000). For example, at the end of the day, I might need "a little good loving" from my husband (i.e., to feel close and act affectionately). However, if Graham feels overwhelmed by the demands of his employees at work and the children at home, the last thing he wants from me are more "demands" for physical affection. Therefore, his needs for autonomy and separateness conflict with my needs for connection. Such is the stuff that conflict is made of; my goal of intimacy is incompatible with his goal of autonomy, and he has interfered with my ability to attain the scarce resource of affection.

Conflicts exist in families over all sorts of issues, not all of which are dialectical tensions. Marital couples have been known to have conflict concerning finances, child rearing, leisure activities, expression of affection, criticism of one another's lifestyle, the irritability of one partner, and the number of activities they take part in together (e.g., Cupach, 2000; Sillars, 1986). How couples manage these conflicts has been studied extensively, and therefore, the majority of the studies reviewed in this chapter focus on marital couples. However, many of the conflict models presented are more general in that they may be applied to parent-child conflict, sibling conflict, and extended-family conflict across all the family forms (cohabiting couples, married couples with no children, single-parent families, nuclear families, families with gay heads of household, blended families, and extended families). Although the literature primarily deals with marital conflict, the implications for all types of family conflicts are considered along the way.

None of us "likes" conflict, but the ways in which we manage the conflict can result in more or less positive outcomes in the family relationship. In other words, although all of us might feel slightly bruised by conflictual communicative interactions, it is possible that the conflict, if resolved well, can create greater closeness and greater understanding in the family relationship and can lead to positive outcomes. If resolved poorly, however, the conflict can lead to destructive outcomes in the form of hurtful communication, intense emotionality, and irrational behavior (e.g., Vangelisti, 2001; Vangelisti & Young, 2000). There appears to be a precipice right between getting closer and falling apart. This chapter highlights work on constructive and destructive communication patterns during conflict. Also, this work on conflict can be seen as fulfilling the *control* function in family relationships in that individuals in conflict often try to persuade or influence their partners to move to their point of view. Therefore, work on interpersonal influence processes during conflict is also emphasized. Finally, the escalation of irrationality, intense emotionality, and hurtful behavior in families can lead to verbal aggressiveness and violence in relationships. Although not all conflicts result in violent outcomes, this chapter also explores characteristics of the battered and the batterers as well as some potentially explanatory models for why violence occurs in families.

The Nature of Conflict

As alluded to in the introduction, **conflict** can be defined as "an expressed struggle between at least two interdependent parties who perceive incompatible goals, scarce rewards, and interference from the other parties in achieving their goals" (Hocker & Wilmot, 2000, p. 9). This definition can help us understand why marital satisfaction is higher for couples who have greater similarity in terms of ethnic homogamy, educational similarity, religious similarity, and so forth. Because they come into the relationship already agreeing on fundamental goals such as whether or not to have children and how to raise them, couples who are more similar initially may be more satisfied in family and marital relationships because they may have a tendency to have less conflict. For example, couples who are more traditional (i.e., the wife fulfills the nurturer role while the husband primarily fulfills the resource provider role) may have less conflict because they have agree *beforehand* that the wife will fulfill most of the household responsibilities and the husband will fulfill the provider role. This may help explain the seeming inequities in these roles and why traditional women accept more inequities in household responsibilities compared with traditional husbands. They have already agreed that the family would function in this way, and conflicts are less likely to accrue because goal interference is less likely to happen or be perceived. Thus, greater similarity may enhance smoother family functioning in that conflict, or goal interruptions, is less likely to result because the goals of the couple are more likely to be similar.

In our society, most individuals are conflict aversive; that is, most of us report that we dislike conflict and even fear its potential destructive outcomes. Regardless, the nature of intimacy and closeness is such that it makes it more likely that goal interference and ensuing conflicts will occur. More specifically, high levels of investment in a relationship or family (i.e., more loving, caring, and concern) actually make it *more* likely that conflicts will occur (e.g., Braiker & Kelley, 1979; Shantz & Hobart, 1989). Having closer relationships increases the frequency of interaction and our level of concern, which ultimately enhances the likelihood that members of close familial relationships will interfere with each other's goals (Sillars, Canary, & Tafoya, 2004). This is the heart of the paradox of conflict; we don't want to hurt the ones we love, yet these same loving familial relationships provide a rich forum in which conflict is more likely to occur.

The answer seems straightforward: If conflict is inevitable in close relationships characterized by high levels of concern for others, engage in conflicts that create positive outcomes and then conflict seems consistent with loving relationships. Unfortunately, not all of us have the communication skills necessary to engage in **constructive conflict,** or conflict that builds on the strengths of the relationship (i.e., enhances closeness, increases understanding, results in a net gain in positive feelings). Even those of us with the best communication skills can engage in **destructive conflict,** or conflict that is damaging to the relationship (e.g., results in hurt, reduces closeness, damages trust). Thus, the nature of the conflict can be drastically different depending on whether the processes and outcomes are constructive or destructive. This chapter attempts to delineate the differences between destructive and constructive conflict and the individual and interpersonal factors that make it more or less likely that destructive or constructive conflict occurs within families.

Given the assumption that family life provides a rich forum for goal interference, it might be useful to investigate how often conflict occurs in families (for a review see Sillars et al., 2004). Sillars et al. report that 80% of married couples say that they have conflict once a month, while 6% report disagreements once per week (McGonagle, Kessler, & Schilling, 1992). This is fairly consistent with another study, which reports disagreements between married individuals two to three times per month (Kirchler, Rodler, Hölzl, & Meier, 2001). Parents and adolescents report more conflict than in marital relationships—about two conflicts per week (Montemayor, 1986), which is consistent with Laursen's (1993) report that adolescents report 7.4 conflicts per day across a variety of relationships. Finally, sibling relationships are the most conflictual, with siblings observed or estimated to have conflict six (Lollis, Ross, & Leroux, 1996) or seven times (Perlman & Ross, 1997) *per hour.* (My youngest stepson, Jake, assures me that this number is accurate). Given this review, it is apparent that family life is rife with conflict in that conflictual episodes in families occur hourly for siblings, weekly for parents and adolescents, and at least monthly for marital couples.

Although these estimates are useful at painting an overall picture of family life, it may be that conflict frequency is higher in families who are experiencing greater developmental stress or distress (i.e., less satisfaction and stability). Specifically, newlyweds and those adjusting to marriage

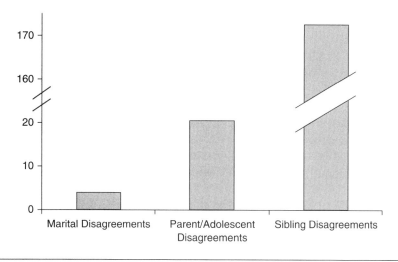

Figure 8.1   Family Disagreements (number per month)

Figure 8.2   Siblings have conflict as many as six or seven times an hour, and parents are often called on to intervene.

SOURCE: Photo courtesy of Jennifer and Chad Gibson.

typically have more conflict (e.g., Crohan, 1986); couples who are married longer report fewer disagreements (e.g., McGonagle et al., 1992). Thus, conflict is higher in couples who are adjusting to marriage and adding children. In addition, distressed couples (couples low in marital satisfaction) spend more time in conflict, have more frequent conflicts, and spend more time avoiding conflicts than nondistressed couples (e.g., Schaap, Buunk, &

Kerkstra, 1988). What is unclear from these types of studies is whether conflict predicts marital distress or marital distress predicts greater conflict. In other words, do unhappy couples fight more or does fighting make previously happy couples unhappy? The research on developmental stressors and conflict suggests that stressors *lead* to conflict. It is also possible that distressed couples have more conflicts that are *perpetual* (repetitive conflicts with no apparent resolution), as opposed to typical and minor conflicts, and may be more destructive than constructive. The following section presents models of conflict that help us understand destructive as opposed to constructive outcomes of conflict.

Models of Conflict

Models or theories of conflict are useful to the extent that they help us understand the predictive factors leading to conflict, the conflictual episode itself, and the potential constructive or destructive outcomes of conflict. In this way, *the explanatory model of interpersonal conflict* helps us understand both constructive and destructive conflict. The second model, *the four horsemen of the apocalypse* model, helps us understand the actual conflict processes that operate destructively in relationships. In other words, it identifies methods of communicating that damage both satisfaction and stability in marital relationships. The third model, *the social structural model of demand-withdraw*, examines the general tendencies of one spouse to demand changes in the other, followed by the other spouse's tendency to withdraw.

Explanatory Model of Interpersonal Conflict

The unique feature of the explanatory model of interpersonal conflict is that it attempts to explain the entire process of the conflict from beginning to end. It helps us understand far distant (e.g., historical context) and more immediate factors (e.g., precipitating events) that lead up to the conflict, the actual conflict episode itself, and the immediate (e.g., hurt feelings) and distant consequences (e.g., entrenched resentment) of the conflict. The factors relevant to this process include the *distal context, proximal context, conflict interaction, proximal outcomes*, and *distal outcomes* (Cupach & Canary, 1997). The distal and proximal contexts provide the background information necessary to understand the conflict. The conflict interaction includes the actual conflict episode and communication behaviors. Finally, the proximal and distal outcomes are the short-term and long-term consequences of the conflict.

To be more specific, the **distal context** refers to the more historical factors that predict conflict. These historical factors include the background and personalities of the individuals involved in the conflict. These factors are especially relevant in families where they endure over time. In other words, prior grievances are likely to wreak havoc and provide the emotional intensity that strong familial conflicts are made of. In addition, certain individuals may be more or less hostile or aggressive, and this could increase their chances for conflict as well. The **proximal context** refers to the more immediate factors preceding the conflict episode and includes the goals, rules, emotions, and attributions that individuals make immediately prior to the conflict. In other words, the eliciting event and how individuals think about that eliciting event are inherent in the proximal context. **Conflict interaction** refers to the inter-personal influence strategies, tactics, and communication patterns that indi-viduals use during the conflict itself. These are discussed more fully below in the discussion of interpersonal influence strategies. The **proximal outcomes** refer to the immediate consequences or results of the conflict. These outcomes often include cognitive processes (e.g., perceptions and attributions), emo-tional reactions (hurt feelings, anger, frustration), and behavioral tendencies (e.g., withdrawal). The **distal outcomes** refer to the long-term consequences of the conflict that are either removed from the actual conflict episode or delayed. These outcomes are generally longer-term and again include cogni-tive processes (e.g., marital satisfaction), emotional reactions (e.g., long-term feelings of hurt or anger), and behavioral tendencies (e.g., more negative communication behavior and marital instability).

An example would prove useful here. My sister, Barbara, and her husband, Robert, have four kids. Prior to adopting their fourth child Karen (from Korea), you can imagine the conflict that must have occurred. In terms of *dis-tal factors*, my brother-in-law Robert never intended to have children—none, nada, zilch, zero. They already had three, and while he was happy about that *now*, it had never been a part of his projected life goals. Now also consider that Robert is from New York (Long Island), and like a lot of New Yorkers, he can be quite expressive (i.e., direct and loud) regarding his wants and desires. My sister, Barbara, on the other hand, has always wanted a large brood—she was born to have children, loves children, and is very nurturing. She is less likely to address conflict directly, in general, but has also had a 14-year history with Robert and has learned to fend quite well for herself. In terms of the *proximal factors*, after having two boys, Barbara and Robert thought their third baby was going to be a girl. They had already bought loads of pink frilly outfits and my sister had "bonded" with the idea of finally having a girl in the house. When Kevin was born, my sister became wed to the idea of attempting to have another baby so that she could finally have her girl. After many failed attempts at pregnancy (she was now close to 40) and a miscarriage of twins that left her emotionally devastated, Robert and Barbara decided to consider adoption. The *conflict episode* itself included many lengthy and emotional discussions about the meaning of life, the need to procreate versus adopt, Barbara and Robert's individual and joint identity needs, the potential responses of the other children to an adopted sibling, and so on. The *proximal outcomes* included feelings of not being heard, being misunderstood, attributions of malintent on each other's parts, and general feelings of hurt and disappointment. Finally, the *distal outcomes* included greater understanding, adoption of Karen, greater involvement in the religious community (the adoption agency was Christian), and greater marital satisfaction and stability (they've been married 24 years now). As this example illustrates, the explanatory model of interpersonal conflict facilitates a greater understanding of the factors that precede, are immediate to, and follow the conflict episode.

The explanatory model of interpersonal conflict is further useful because it helps us understand destructive and constructive communication outcomes. The processes of destructive and constructive conflict can be understood best by identifying the factors that result from the conflict episode (i.e., proximal and distal outcomes). Conflicts are defined as destructive or constructive only by the conflict interaction itself and the outcomes that result. In other words, conflicts that result in negative outcomes (e.g., hurt, marital dissatisfaction, and marital instability) are considered destructive, whereas conflicts that result in positive outcomes (e.g., increased closeness, increased understanding, greater marital satisfaction and stability) are considered constructive. According to the explanatory model of interpersonal conflict, these outcomes of conflict are considered either proximal, in that they are the short-term consequences of the conflict, or distal, in that they are the long-term consequences of the conflict. Thus, constructive conflict can result in positive proximal outcomes (e.g., feeling closer to one's spouse) or positive distal outcomes (e.g., having greater marital satisfaction and stability). Destructive conflict can result in negative proximal (e.g., maladaptive attributions, increases in expressions of negativity) and distal outcomes (e.g., decreases in marital satisfaction and stability). A conflict can be considered constructive if the actual communication episode and the outcomes are positive or destructive if the actual communication episode and the outcomes are negative.

Four Horsemen of the Apocalypse Model

The four horsemen of the apocalypse model (also known as the *behavioral cascade model of marital dissolution*) describes and explains destructive patterns of conflict in marriage. According to John Gottman (1994), who spent a long time studying married couples and attempting to determine which communication behaviors predicted divorce, four types of conflict behavior tend to mark distressed couples, or couples who evidence low levels of marital satisfaction and high levels of marital instability. He consistently found that couples in distress display greater expressions of *criticism, contempt, defensiveness,* and *stonewalling*. In his popular-press book on why marriages succeed or fail, he calls these four behaviors the "four horsemen of the apocalypse," because he argues that these indicators portend the death of a marriage when they are disproportionate to other more positive communication behaviors. In other words, a greater percentage of these behaviors compared with more positive communication behaviors indicates a problematic marriage relationship. **Criticism** includes negative evaluations and attacks on the partner's behavior and personality. Gottman argues that although all marriages include complaints that are specific, criticisms are highly accusatory and usually involve attacking the other on a more global level. Criticisms can include passing judgment, laundry lists of complaints, and accusations of betrayal or untrustworthiness.

Contempt includes expressions of extremely negative affect toward a partner and can often include psychological abuse and intentional insults. Indicators of contempt include name-calling, eye rolling, facial expressions of disgust, sneers, mockery, and hostile humor. It is likely that the intentional use of insults within conflict in marital relationships results in hurt because hurtful messages from romantic partners and other family members elicit greater feelings of hurt than those from other people (Vangelisti & Crumley, 1998). Such hurt as part of a larger pattern of negative communication can be destructive to family relationships in that negative communication (e.g., attacking the other, defensiveness, crying, ignoring the message), greater distancing behavior, and lower relationship satisfaction can result (e.g., Vangelisti, 1994b, 2001; Vangelisti & Crumley, 1998; Vangelisti & Young, 2000). Vangelisti and Young (2000) found that individuals who perceive a message to be intentionally hurtful reported that the hurtful message had more of a distancing effect on the relationship than those who perceived that the hurtful message was unintentional. Furthermore, and in line with previous research on expressions of contempt, or intentionally harmful messages, general patterns of hurtful communication were associated with greater relational distancing. Expressions of contempt can therefore be harmful to family relationships.

Not surprisingly, the use of criticism and contempt often leads to defensiveness. **Defensiveness** includes self-justification in an attempt to maintain one's sense of self (usually presented in the face of criticism or attack). Defensiveness includes denying responsibility, making excuses, cross-complaining, and whining. **Stonewalling** includes responding to an onslaught of negative affect with withdrawal and flat facial affect. Stonewalling implies that the issue is not worth addressing or worthy of an emotional response. Gottman (Gottman & Levenson, 1988) notes that men are more likely to respond by stonewalling because they tend to be more physiologically responsive during conflict, which can result in greater discomfort with prolonged conflict and may cause men to feel more intense pressure to withdraw from conflict situations. Stonewalling is one such mechanism used to withdraw. Gottman's research is supported by other research indicating that individuals in distressed marriages use more criticism, complaints, disagreement, and sarcasm during conflict than do individuals in nondistressed marriages (e.g., Revenstrof, Vogel, Wegner, Hahlweg, & Schindler, 1980; Schaap et al., 1988; Ting-Toomey, 1983).

It is important to note that although criticism, contempt, defensiveness, and stonewalling are all destructive forms of conflict that can result in less marital satisfaction and more marital instability, not all marriages that evidence these communication behaviors are unsatisfactory or unstable. Most marriages, regardless of level of satisfaction and stability, evidence these communication behaviors from time to time. What is important to recognize is that these communication behaviors become problematic for marital relationships when they become more commonplace. Remember from Chapter 7 that Gottman's most cited finding is that successful marriages have a 5:1 ratio in terms of positive to negative communication behaviors (Gottman & Levenson, 1992). Couples who display more positivity than negativity *during* conflict episodes are more satisfied, less likely to have thought about divorce, less likely to have actually separated, and less likely to have divorced. It is therefore not the presence of these four behaviors in combination (criticism, contempt, defensiveness, stonewalling) that predict divorce but, rather, the ratio of these negative behaviors to positive behaviors that is more predictive. In other words, the presence of these communicative behaviors from time to time during marital conflict does not portend the end of the relationship. It is, rather, the existence of high levels of these negative communication behaviors that elicits a *behavioral cascade*, or reciprocity of this negativity, which results in the most destructive outcomes in terms of marital satisfaction and marital stability.

Social-Structural Model of Demand-Withdraw

Consistent with Gottman's (1994) idea of stonewalling is research on demand-withdraw patterns during marital conflict (e.g., Caughlin, 2002; Caughlin & Vangelisti, 1999). A large body of research illustrates that when wives want changes in a relationship, they are likely to make demands that are followed by their husband's tendency to withdraw (e.g., Baucom, Notarius, Burnett, & Haefner, 1990; Christensen & Shenk, 1991; Gottman & Levenson, 1988). This pattern of conflict is destructive in that dissatisfied marriages often evidence the demand-withdraw pattern of conflict, and these same marriages frequently end in divorce (e.g., Heavey, Christensen, & Malamuth, 1995; Noller, Feeney, Bonnell, & Callan, 1994; Schaap et al., 1988). One of the reasons these marriages may end in divorce is that this particular destructive conflict pattern is not easily alterable (e.g., Jacobson, Follette, & Pagel, 1986). Although the relationship between demand-withdraw and current marital satisfaction is repeatedly evidenced, the relationship between demand-withdraw and *changes* in marital satisfaction over time is less clear. Communication researcher, John Caughlin (2002) found that patterns of demand-withdraw were associated with concurrent marital dissatisfaction but that patterns of demand-withdraw predict *increases over time* in wives' marital satisfaction. The relationship between demand-withdraw and marital satisfaction is less clear than originally thought.

The social structural model of demand-withdraw attempts to explain this pattern of wife demand followed by husband withdraw. This model argues that wives are relatively powerless in marriages, which leads wives to be more dissatisfied with their marriages than are husbands (e.g., Heavey, Layne, & Christensen, 1993; Jacobson, 1990; Klein & Johnson, 1997). If one defines power through earning power, you might remember research here indicating that wives typically earn less than their husbands (in about 80% of marriages) and that women typically compensate for these lower wages by doing the more subservient roles of household chores and child care. Because women are generally less satisfied in marriages than are husbands (see, for instance, Vangelisti & Daly, 1997), they are more likely to desire change in their relationships than are husbands, who are generally satisfied with their more powerful role in the relationship. This greater desire for change on the part of wives is then assumed to result in a greater number of criticisms, complaints, and demands from wives compared with husbands. In turn, because men are expected to desire maintenance of the status quo (in anticipation of maintaining their powerful position), it is assumed that they are more likely to withdraw, or avoid their wives' demands. Although much research supports this pattern of wife demand and husband withdraw, husbands were found to be more demanding than wives when their desire for change was high; thus, high demanding behavior is predicted by desire for change in the partner regardless of gender (Caughlin & Vangelisti, 1999). Inconsistent with the earlier literature reviewed, this pattern of *husband* demand-*wife* withdraw has been associated with increases in the marital satisfaction of wives (e.g., Heavey et al., 1995; Heavey et al., 1993). Similar patterns of demand-withdraw have recently been found in parent-adolescent dyads (Caughlin & Ramey, in press), with demand-withdraw patterns occurring most often from parents to adolescents.

Conflict Styles

To best understand constructive and deconstructive conflict within families, it is useful to identify *conflict styles* as well as *conflict strategies*. This section of the chapter explores general tendencies toward coping with conflict and the *styles* of conflict resolution that individuals bring into the relationship (i.e., distal factors predicting conflict). Subsequent sections examine specific *conflict strategies*, or the actual communication behavior used during conflictual episodes. Such conflict strategies result in more or less effectiveness in the form of persuasive effectiveness and the tendency to elicit certain types of communication behavior in response.

There appear to be several conflict styles that benefit the stability of marriage, regardless of satisfaction, and that can be constructive in that way. Along with the majority of work on conflict that characterizes conflict styles as *direct-indirect* and *competitive-cooperative* (Sillars et al., 2004), the styles that appear to be more constructive can be characterized along these dimensions as well. It appears that conflict can be constructive if partners match on their approaches to the conflict, even if the approaches, at first glance, appear to be dysfunctional. Remember that Gottman (1993, 1994) studied factors that predicted the marriages that were stable compared with marriages headed for divorce. Among the couples he studied, he identified three types of conflicting couple types that he defines as stable. In other words, these conflict styles are constructive to the extent that they aid the enduring nature of marriage. It is important to recognize again, however, that these matched styles are successful because the conflicting couple types evidence a ratio of 5:1 positive to negative communication behaviors during their conflict. It is not just their *style* of coping with conflict, but it is also their tendency to use positive behaviors such as humor and soothing along with more negative communication strategies and behaviors that function to promote greater marital stability. The balance between the conflict style and fun and harmonious interactions makes these couple types function well.

Avoiders

Avoider couples appear to avoid or minimize conflict. They are *indirect* and *cooperative* in their conflict style. Very little gets resolved in the conflicts that do get expressed, and frequently, these couples "agree to disagree." These couples display little negative affect, little positive affect, and have a high level of neutral interactions. Although age-old wisdom would indicate that avoiding conflict might lead to a hydraulic effect (or a "jacking up" of subsequent conflict episodes where old issues rear their ugly heads), Gottman (1993, 1994) finds that couples who successfully avoid, dodge, or minimize conflict episodes actually enhance the stability of their marriages. My brother, Rob, and his wife, Debbie, are a perfect example of a couple who avoids conflict. They are both very low key, and while they might seem to have low-level underlying hostility, they rarely express themselves in conflictual ways. As Gottman predicts, their marriage has been stable for 30 years (including through the development of their children, both of whom are now in college). Thus, avoiding conflict can actually be constructive in terms of stabilizing marriages and helping them function effectively.

Volatiles

By contrast, *volatile* couples appear to engage in conflict with a vengeance. Volatile couples can be characterized as *direct* and *competitive* in their conflict styles. These couples display high levels of negative affect, *very* high levels of positive affect, and very little neutral interaction (Gottman, 1993, 1994). Volatile couples are the couples you know who always seem to be in some battle or other over something seemingly trivial, and they tend to battle loudly and vehemently—so loudly, in fact, that others around them may question why they bother to stay together at all. My Aunt Hazel and Uncle Bert bickered so intensely that they were almost uncomfortable to be around. Volatiles rarely attempt to validate the other's perspective (or hear it at all), because persuasion of the other is the key element of their interactions. Although highly competitive styles of conflict are generally associated with destructive conflict outcomes (see Sillars et al., 2004), it appears that these intense periods of interaction are actually functional for these couple types in that it tends to fuse them together. This may be because they make up loudly as well; they often spend more time laughing and loving intensely. These couples tend to vacillate between intense negative interactions and even more intense positive interactions. It's almost as if this volatility and vacillation provides them with the uncertainty inherent in the earliest romances of most couples. Thus, volatiles function well together in that they love and fight intensely. My husband's brother Ian and his wife Tracy are a great example of a couple who argue loudly and intensely and also laugh and love intensely as well. Their intense conflict styles are actually constructive in that they facilitate the long-term stability of the couple. Ian and Tracy exemplify this; they have been married for 27 years.

Validators

Finally, *validator* couples validate the other's perspective during conflict. Validator couples can be characterized as *direct* and *cooperative* in their conflict styles. These couples have an ability to listen to and understand each other's points of view and emotions. These couples display moderate levels of both negative and positive affect and high levels of neutral interactions (Gottman, 1993, 1994). Although this matches what most consider the ideal conflict style, validators are able to support the other's viewpoint without necessarily giving in on the issue. In other words, validators can say, "Yeah, I can see how it would be really upsetting to not know where I was. It's too bad my cell phone battery died," and not feel guilty, horrible, or defensive because their partner felt bad. These partners seem to be able to see each other's perspective, support each other's perspectives and emotions, and not get defensive about their own role in the process. *Validation* is a term that comes up again in the conflict strategies section as an effective way to encourage constructive conflict episodes. Two validators can work well together to create more constructive, or positive, conflict outcomes. In fact, the marriage-like committed gay couple, Jon and Angus, whose ceremony photo and commitment certification letter were highlighted in Chapter 2, are an example of a couple who have been together 13 years (across two continents and various situation imposed separations) and whose conflict style evidences validation of each other's point of view. They do not avoid conflict but, rather, enjoy engaging the other's perspective to gain greater understanding of each other and their relationship. Conflict does not detract from, but rather enhances, their relationship.

Conflict Strategies (Interpersonal Influence) _____

Besides having various types of conflict styles, married couples in conflict can enact various conflict strategies in an attempt to influence their marriage partners to their points of view. Remember that conflict is defined as goal interference. To study what strategies marital couples use during conflict, Newton and Burgoon (1990) reviewed the three most typical goals that people have when interacting with each other. Based on an extensive review of the interpersonal influence and relational literature, they identified six strategies that fulfill three interpersonal goals during communication interactions. The three interpersonal goals they identify include instrumental, relational, and identity goals. *Instrumental goals* include the desire to attain something useful from one's partner. *Relationship goals* include the desire to maintain the relationship at a positive level. Finally, *identity goals* include the desire to maintain one's sense of self and promote that same sense of self in others (e.g., impression management). Within each of these three goals, Newton and Burgoon outline the types of strategies that marital partners use in an attempt to attain these goals.

Instrumental Goals

The first two types of strategies that Newton and Burgoon (1990) identify—content validation and content invalidation—fulfill the instrumental objective of goal attainment. **Content validation** basically accepts the arguments put forth by the other. As such, it is a positive strategy because it validates the perspective of the other. Content validation includes tactics such as (a) agreement on the issue, (b) description of the issue, (c) explanation of the issue, (d) summarizing the issue, (e) problem solving, and (f) positive information seeking. **Content invalidation** basically rejects the arguments put forth by the other. As such, it is a negative strategy to set about proving the other wrong. Content invalidation includes tactics such as (a) disagreement on the issue, (b) correcting the other, (c) exaggeration, (d) pseudo-accommodation, and (e) abstraction. Suppose that my stepson Huw and his girlfriend Roxanne are having an interpersonal conflict over whether or not she should ditch her biology class to go to a concert with him (OK, this really happened, but I don't know how the actual conversation went). Remember that they live in separate towns now because he is currently at UC–Riverside and she is back at home in the local college. He begins the argument with, "It'll be a blast. You don't need to go to your class anyway—it's just the lab." She *validates* the content of the first statement by saying, "It would definitely be fun. I love Evergreen Terrace," but she *invalidates* the content of the second statement by saying, "I can *not* miss another class since I've already missed two labs this semester." In sum, content validation supports the other's position, whereas content invalidation denies the other's position.

Relationship Goals

The second two strategies—other support and other accusations—operate to manage the relationship (Newton & Burgoon, 1990). **Other support** validates and confirms the other through acknowledgment, recognition, and endorsement and includes tactics such as (a) reinforcement of the other, (b) support of the other or the relationship, (c) emphasis of commonalities, (d) accepting responsibility, (e) concessions to the other, and (f) compliments. Other support is thus a positive strategy because it confirms or affirms the other person. **Other accusations** invalidate and disconfirm the other through attempts to negate the other and include (a) accusations/blaming, (b) implied accusations, (c) criticism of the other, (d) superiority over the other, (e) poking fun at the other, (f) giving advice, (g) threats, and (h) negative information seeking. Other accusations are a negative strategy because they try to deny the other person, the relationship, or both. Consider the above concert-ditching class episode anew. Now suppose that in response to Huw's, "It'll be a blast. You don't need to go to your class anyway—it's just a lab," Roxanne says, "Baby, you know I *always* want to be with *you*." This is a picture-perfect example of *other support*. She has reinforced Huw and their relationship simultaneously. However, she might also say, "If you had planned ahead, then you would have realized I had a class that night and scheduled it another night." Because Huw is *not* a planner and this statement carries lots of history, this is a picture-perfect example of *other accusations* (blaming and criticism) in that she is implying that it is his fault that they are having this conflict in the first place. In sum, other support validates the relationship partner and the relationship, whereas other accusations negate the relationship partner or the relationship.

Identity Goals

Finally, the last two types of strategies—self-assertions and self-defense—operate to maintain desired identities (Newton & Burgoon, 1990). **Self-assertions** involve strategies validating or promoting the self and include tactics such as (a) assertions, (b) self-promotion, (c) exemplification, (d) stubbornness, (e) disclosure, (f) wish statements, and (g) wants/needs statements. **Self-defense** involves strategies to excuse or justify one's behavior and includes (a) justifications, (b) excuses, (c) denials, and (d) self-inquiry. Let's take the concert-going, class-ditching example to the next conversational turn. Suppose that Huw now responds (somewhat in jest) to Roxanne's "Baby, you know I *always* want to be with *you*," with "Yeah, 'cause I'm the maaaaan—baby; you're never gonna find a boyfriend that treats you better than I do," then this would be a good example of *self-assertion;* Huw is shamelessly promoting himself. In anticipation of our next section on the results of the use of certain types of strategies, it is interesting to note that Huw responded to Roxanne's other support (a positive strategy) with self-assertions (another positive strategy). Suppose now, however, that Huw had decided to respond to the second half of what Roxanne said, "If you had planned ahead, then you would have realized that I had a class that night and scheduled it another night," by saying, "I *am* a planner—I got the tickets ahead of time, didn't I?" then he would be exemplifying *self-defense* strategies during which he denies her claim about him and provides alternative evidence in the form of a self-inquiry. Again note that Roxanne's use of a negative strategy (other accusation) was met with another negative strategy (self-defense).

Persuasive Outcomes and Reciprocity of Conflict Strategies

The interpersonal conflict strategies that marital partners use promote differential rates of success in influencing their partners (Newton & Burgoon, 1990). Specifically, husbands are seen as most persuasive when they use content validation and other support. Alternatively, husbands are the least persuasive when they use content invalidation. Wives are also more persuasive when they avoid the negative strategies. In other words, wives are seen as most persuasive when they use *less* content invalidation and *fewer* other accusations. To sum this all up then, the more positive strategies are perceived as being more persuasive by both husbands and wives.

In general, Newton and Burgoon's (1990) research supports the golden rule of conflict. In other words, reciprocity of conflict strategies was evidenced in that marital partners using more **positive strategies** (e.g., content validation, other support, and self-assertions) were generally met with other positive strategies, whereas marital partners using more **negative strategies** (content invalidation, other accusations, and self-defense) were generally met with other negative strategies. If marital partners were more positive, so were their partners. If marital partners were more negative, their partners were negative as well. The results were analyzed for husbands and wives separately. See Table 8.1 for matching and reciprocity of positive (+) or negative (–) communication behavior.

In terms of being constructive, then, positive conflict strategies beget more positive communication behavior and are seen as more persuasively effective. On the destructive side, negative conflict strategies elicit more negative conflict strategies (an escalation effect) and promote lesser perceptions of persuasive effectiveness. On a prescriptive note, then, it seems that adopting more positive strategies during interpersonal conflict (content validation, other support, and self-defense) produces more constructive conflict episodes in that less hurtful behavior is likely to accrue and perceptions of persuasive effectiveness are high.

Table 8.1   Patterns of Conflict Strategies: Reciprocity of Positivity and Negativity

Females who use	Met with males' use of
• Content validation (+) and self-assertions (+) • Content invalidation (−) • Self-assertions (+) and other support (+) • Self-defense, content invalidation, and other accusations (−) • Less self-defense (+) • Other accusations (−) and other support (+)	• Content validation (+) • Content invalidation • Other support (+) • Other accusations (−) • Self assertions (+) • Self defense (−)
Males who use	Met with females' use of
• Content validation (+) • Content invalidation (−) and other accusations (−) • Other accusations (−) and content validation (+) • Self-defense (−) and less content validation (−) • Other support (+) • Other accusations (−)	• Content validation (+) • Content invalidation (−) • Other support (+) • Other accusations (−) • Self assertions (+) • Self defense (−)

The Nature of Violence

Although not all conflict results in destructive behavior, it is nevertheless the case that some conflicts can become so destructive as to include violence. The inclusion of conflict and violence in the same chapter should not imply that all conflicts have the potential to be violent; rather, *some* conflicts can lead to violence (or situational couple violence). Alternatively, and in line with the general concept of control guiding this text, some relationships have general patterns of control in the relationship that make them more prone to larger patterns of violence, regardless of conflict levels or potential (i.e. intimate or patriarchal terrorism). The nature of family relationships (i.e., their enduring nature, the high level of emotionality, power inequities in the relationships, and long histories of grievances) make them more likely to include violence than other types of relationships (e.g., Anderson, Umberson, & Elliott, 2004). Despite the enforcement of stricter laws regarding family violence, domestic violence still exists in up to 30% of all marriages in America (American Psychological Association, 1996; Pagelow, 1992; Straus & Gelles, 1986), and 30% of females who are killed are murdered by an intimate (Greenfield et al., 1998; Rennison & Welchans, 2000). These statistics may seem extreme, but it is also the case that domestic violence is the leading cause of injuries to women between the ages of 15 and 44 (Novello, Rosenberg, Saltzman, & Shosky, 1992).[1]

To add to the complexity of these family situations, about 40% of women who report intimate partner violence live with children under 12 in the household (Rennison & Welchans, 2000). Many children are the victims of physical abuse and neglect as well. One thousand to 1,200 children die from abuse and neglect each year (Zinn & Eitzen, 2002); up to 90% are reported to be under the age of 5, and 40% are infants under the age of 1. Out of 3 million reports of abuse against children, an estimated 896,000 children were determined to have been abused or mistreated in 2002 (U.S. Department of Health and Human Services, 2004). Of these cases, over 60% were considered neglect, 20% included physical abuse, 10% were sexual abuse, and 7% were emotional maltreatment.

In addition to being the victim of physical violence, many children are likely to witness domestic violence. A recent review of 29 empirical studies on the effects of witnessing domestic violence indicates a relationship between witnessing violence and impaired development (Kolbo, Blakely, & Engleman, 1996). Their review indicates that children who witness domestic violence are at risk for maladaptation along behavioral, emotional, social, cognitive, and physical domains. *Behaviorally,* studies have indicated that children witnessing violence are more aggressive, disruptive, and prone to conduct disorders. *Emotionally,* children witnessing violence exhibit personality disorders, temper tantrums, inadequacy, and immaturity. In addition, they exhibit deficits in empathic responses. *Socially,* children witnessing domestic violence have been described as withdrawn and anxious, and alternatively aggressive and prone to fighting with their peers (similar to the conflict pattern evidenced by violent males). *Cognitively,* children witnessing violence have been described as underachievers and evidence lower verbal, cognitive, and motor abilities than children not witnessing violence. Finally, *physically,* children witnessing domestic violence present what have been termed psychosomatic bouts of eczema, epileptic fits, and failure to thrive. Thus, witnessing domestic violence can have serious detrimental consequences for the development of children in terms of behavioral, social, emotional, cognitive, and physical outcomes. This chapter, however, focuses most on spousal violence and the communication processes of control inherent in this relationship.

Is violence gendered? One of the *myths* surrounding violence is that *males are the batterers and females are the victims.* You probably thought this yourself and, to be honest, it makes sense that you would assume this. First, the violence of males against females produces the most devastating results. Second, males who are victims of violence are less likely to report this violence because of the fear of potential emasculation. Research shows, however, that similar levels of female-to-male and male-to-female aggression exist (e.g., Brush, 1993), with 12.8% of husbands and 11.7% of women using violence toward their respective spouses (Straus, Gelles, & Steinmetz, 1980). With regard to the use of specific types of violence, researchers also found no significant difference between wives' and husbands' reports of hitting, shoving, or throwing things (e.g., Brush, 1993; Straus & Gelles, 1986). Although many popularized versions of domestic violence (think Sunday night made-for-TV movies) depict burly abusive husbands and meek and mild victimized wives, it is likely the case that many family relationships include mutually battering spouses. Nearly half (49%) of couples reporting violence included couples in which both partners were violent (Straus et al., 1980).

What accounts for the disparity between your beliefs about violence being a gendered event and the reports above? Michael Johnson and Jenel Leone (2005) argue that there is a distinct difference between *common couple violence* (more currently known as *situational couple violence*) and *patriarchal* or *intimate terrorism*—a distinction that highlights the importance of the communication of control in this relationship. The examples showing equality of violence from both genders most probably represent situational couple violence, and the more dramatic examples showing that males are more often the batterers are more likely to exemplify intimate terrorism. Intimate terrorism is embedded in a general overall pattern of *controlling* communication behaviors indicative of the perpetrator's desire for control and domination over his or her partner. Johnson and Leone suggest that this pattern of controlling behavior is what is most often being referred to by the terms *domestic violence, wife beating,* and *spousal abuse.* Situational couple violence, alternatively, is not connected to a general pattern of control but, rather, includes specific conflicts that escalate to the use of violence. It is therefore likely that the matched amounts on hitting, shoving, and throwing things are examples of situational couple violence, whereas the more dramatic uses of violence for control discussed below are more likely the result of patriarchal or intimate terrorism. Most of the findings reported here refer to the latter type of domestic violence, during which males who desire a high level of control over their wives' lives are in fact the most likely perpetrators.

In support of your belief that intimate terrorism violence is a particularly male phenomenon, the Bureau of Justice Statistics reports that women are the victims in 95% of all domestic violence in 1994 (Maricopa Association of Governments, nd) and 85% in 1998 (Rennison & Welchans, 2000). In addition, the Bureau of Justice Statistics also reports that three of four victims of murder by an intimate are female (Rennison & Welchans, 2000). This same report indicates that about 900,000 reports of violence against women by an intimate were reported in 1998 compared with 160,000 reports of violence against men by an intimate. In addition, of all the violent crimes committed against women in 1998, 22% were committed by an intimate partner, compared with 3% of all violent crimes committed against men. Furthermore, 33% of female murder victims were killed by an intimate partner compared with 4% of males. Women report 5 times more violence at the hands of an intimate than do men, and 75% of murders by intimates are committed by males. These reports still indicate that males are more violent toward their partners and with more serious consequences. It is likely that these patterns of violence are related to general overarching patterns of controlling communication behavior in this relationship.

A *second myth* surrounding violence is that *violence is frequently a one-time occurrence in families.* This myth again is likely perpetuated by the differences between situational couple violence and intimate terrorism. Whereas situational couple violence *can* occur once (almost by definition), intimate terrorism is part of a general pattern of control. Most intimate terrorism abuse is repetitive and represents a relatively stable pattern of behavior (e.g., Infante, Chandler, & Rudd, 1989; Pence & Paymar, 1993). For example, 90% of women killed by a husband or boyfriend had reported at least one prior incident of abuse (Berry, 1998). Regardless that violence tends to be repeated, many choose to stay in violent relationships. Of female victims of dating violence, 40% continued their relationships (Henton, Cate, Koval, Lloyd, & Christopher, 1983), and a striking 60% of married violent couples were still together 2 years later (Jacobson, Gottman, Gortner, Berns, & Shortt, 1996).

Why do violent couples stay together? Or more to the point, why do many abused women stay with the abuser? The National Coalition Against Domestic Violence estimates that a victim returns to her abuser six times before finding the resources necessary to disentangle herself from the abusive relationship. The MAG (Maricopa Association of Governments) Regional Domestic Violence Council (nd) describes the very real and pragmatic reasons that victims of violent relationships stay with their partners. Quite pragmatically, women stay in abusive relationships because of the *fear of physical harm following separation*. Frequently, violent men of the intimate terrorism variety become more violent or even attempt to murder their spouses when they believe they are either reporting abuse or leaving the relationship (Dutton, 1998). For instance, 23% of one sample of women who filed protective orders reported reabuse once the injunction was in place (Carlson, Harris, & Holden, 1999). According to a U.S. Department of Justice report, women who are separated are 25 times as likely to be the victim of violent attacks by their intimate partner as are women who are married (Bachman & Saltzman, 1996). This fear of reprisal also prevents reporting of the violent incidents to the police (Rennison & Welchans, 2000).

In addition, the victim of spousal abuse may lack the financial resources to leave the relationship; abusive spouses frequently control the family resources and access to transportation. This is again consistent with the notion of intimate terrorism. Along with this larger pattern of control, the physically abusive partner may also limit her access to outside family and friends in an attempt to socially isolate the victim so that the abuser is her only source of support (Grisso et al., 1999). In line with intimate terrorism, growing research supports the notion that violent men monitor the activities of their children and intimates and regulate their friendships (e.g., Dobash & Dobash, 1998; Kirkwood, 1993). Furthermore, the frequency and severity of the violence may be sporadic and the batterer may promise that the last bout of violence was the last. The victim's own *cultural beliefs* about the religious and cultural sanctity of the family and keeping the family together may promote her continuance of the relationship. Finally, it is also likely that she may expect that abuse is normal, because she likely has a prior history of abuse and accompanying low self-esteem.

Several avenues of research attempt to explain why women stay in violent relationships, beyond the very real factors of fear of separation violence, lack of financial resources, social isolation, cultural beliefs encouraging family maintenance, history of abuse, and low self-esteem. The **battered woman's syndrome** focuses on the **learned helplessness** of the victims of violence. Remember from Chapter 6 on raising children that learned helplessness refers to the tendency to feel incompetent and nonefficacious. In other words, these theorists argue that women in violent relationships feel that they are responsible for the abuse and that they are unable to do anything about the abuse. Specifically, Walker (1979) suggests that once women fall into a pattern of abuse, they may lose sight of long-range planning and voice unrealistic expectations about their abusive partner's recovery. In line with the nature of the concept of learned helplessness, perceptions of alternatives may also be restricted or seem too dangerous to pursue. In contrast, **learned hopefulness** theory argues that women may stay in violent relationships because they are hopeful that their partner will change his violent behavior eventually. Barnett and LaViolette (1993) hypothesize that battered women learn to endure abuse largely because society creates a sense of female responsibility for the maintenance of the family.

Profile of the Battered

What type of woman is most likely to experience violence in intimate terrorism relationships? Research shows that women who are controlled by their partners through violence differ based on ethnicity, age, socioeconomic status, place of residence, and substance abuse tendencies. In addition, and in support of the theory of learned hopefulness, women who experience greater violence (in terms of frequency and severity) and stay in the relationship tend to frame their spouse's abusive behavior in ways that excuse the behavior and that are more accepting of the use of violence in relationships. Such framing may translate into communication behavior with the batterer.

Demographic Characteristics

Often, women differ in the level of violence that they may be at risk for or experience due to demographic characteristics. For instance, *black* women experience higher rates of abuse than do Caucasian and Hispanic women (Rennison & Welchans, 2000). Black women are more likely than white women to be murdered by an intimate (although since 1976, the number of never-married white women ages 20–44 murdered by an intimate nearly doubled). For every 1,000 women in a national sample, 12 black women, 8 Caucasian women, and 7 Hispanic women experience violence by an intimate (Greenfield et al., 1998). In addition, women between the *ages of 16 and 24* are the most likely to report violent victimization (murder, rape, sexual assault, robbery, and aggravated and simple assaults) from an intimate other. In addition, women who live in *low-income households* and rental properties experience more nonlethal violence than do women in houses with larger incomes (Rennison & Welchans, 2000). Also, women who live in an *urban area* experience more nonlethal victimization than women living in suburban or rural areas (Greenfield et al., 1998). Three quarters of the incidents of nonlethal violence against women by an intimate occur at or near her home.

Substance Abuse

A woman's use of substances may also be related to her tendency to be abused. Specifically, Miller, Downs, and Gondoli (1989) found that alcoholic women experienced more forms of violence from their spouses than did non-alcoholic women. They concluded that women's alcoholism is linked to spousal violence. Consistently, Gerson (1978) found that in 43% of alcohol-related acts of violence against marital partners, both the spouses had been drinking. In another 43%, only the offender had been drinking, and in 13% of the cases, only the victim was intoxicated. According to Sandmaier (1980), alcoholic women are also seen as more "sexually loose," which may provoke violence from males. In a kinder interpretation, Johnson and Leone (2005) argue that women in intimate terrorism situations are more likely to use substances as a coping mechanism.

Beliefs and History of Battered Women

Battered women also tend to hold different sets of beliefs and have different backgrounds than nonbattered women. These beliefs and backgrounds may result in differential communication behavior with the abuser. Follingstad, Laughlin, Polek, Rutledge, and Hause (1991) identified five types of battered women based on their experiences and beliefs. Supporting the controversial idea that violence is transmitted intergenerationally, women experiencing the highest frequency and severity of abuse in a long-term abusive relationship were most likely to have been *abused as a child*. With regard to relational framing, you might remember that individuals in the most stable relationships tended to *distort their perceptions of their partner in positive ways* (Chapter 7). Consistently, women in highly abusive relationships offered the most excuses for their batterer, attributed external reasons to the man's abuse, minimized the man's responsibility, felt that no negative effects occurred from the abuse, and accepted the idea that physical force would occur in relationships. With regard to why these women stayed in abusive relationships, these women were reasonably satisfied in the relationship and had several reasons for maintaining the relationship.

Profile of the Batterer

Similar to the victim of family or intimate violence, certain characteristics differentiate violent men from nonviolent men; again, these men are more likely to represent intimate terrorism than situational couple violence. In general, factors associated with the use of violence in men include traditional sex role expectations, communication deficits, poor impulse control, low self-esteem, alcohol/drug problems, abusive childhood, and denial (Gondolf, 1988). Consistent with the notion of patriarchal or intimate terrorism, men with *traditional sex role expectations* tend to view the domination and control of women as their right and privilege. For instance, Kantor and Straus (1987, 1989) found that there was a much greater likelihood of abuse when the male approved of violence and had blue-collar status. In fact, it was found that an alcoholic blue-collar man who approved of violence was 7.8 times more likely to abuse his wife than a man without these characteristics.

Batterers are also found to have *communication deficits*, including *low impulse control,* which may be fueled by their *low self-esteem* (Gondolf, 1988). These communication deficits are considered in more detail in the section on the communication skills deficiency model of violence. Furthermore, many batterers have been found to *abuse substances*—especially alcohol (Gondolf, 1988). Substances are seen to act as a catalyst for excessive aggression or violent behavior. For instance, Bushman (1993) determined that there was a causal relation between drugs and aggression. He found that low doses of depressants (including alcohol and barbiturates) lead to violence. Consistently, alcoholics as a group exhibit a greater degree of violent behavior than do nonalcoholics (Berglund & Tunving, 1985). In fact, 72% of abused women admitted to a shelter reported that their spouse not only had a drinking problem but also became extremely abusive when drinking (Lehmann & Krupp, 1984), and 86% of assailants arrested reported using alcohol on the day of the assault (Brookoff, O'Brien, Cook, Thompson, & Williams, 1997). Victims and family members also reported that 45% of these men used alcohol or drugs to the point of intoxication on a daily basis for the past month.

Similar to victims of violence, many violent men had an *abusive childhood* where they experienced or witnessed childhood violence (Gondolf, 1988). Jaffe, Babor, and Fishbein (1987), for instance, found that alcohol consumption *in combination* with childhood antecedents contribute to violent behavior. In other words, neither child abuse nor witnessing spousal abuse as a child is sufficient to cause physical abuse in males. If it were, then most men who were abused as children would grow up to be abusive. The literature shows that this is clearly not the case. Finally, violent men *deny* that violence is a problem and refuse to accept responsibility for the abusive behavior. Many of these common characteristics of the batterer have been included in the explanatory calculi of alternative models of violence in the family.

Models of Violence in the Family

Many attempts to understand violence in the spousal relationships focus on the communication behavior of the couple. Specifically, the *demand-withdraw* pattern of conflict is evidenced in violent relationships, with husband demand-wife withdraw as prevalent as wife demand-husband withdraw patterns. Second, the *frustration-aggression hypothesis* argues that violence results from goal interruption and the ensuing frustration that is experienced. Third, the *catalyst hypothesis* asserts that wives' coercive communication can sometimes act as a catalyst for husbands' use of violence. Finally, the *skills deficiency approach* argues that violent men's lack of effective problem-solving skills results in the use of violence in response to conflict.

Demand-Withdraw

Similar to the destructive pattern of family conflict discussed above where the wife demands and the husband withdraws, violent couples also exhibit this destructive pattern of conflict (Holtzworth-Monroe, Smutzler, & Stuart, 1988). However, in violent couples (as opposed to conflictual couples), the man frequently evidences the demand and the wife evidences the withdrawal (Babcock, Waltz, Jacobson, & Gottman, 1993; Berns, Jacobsen, & Gottman, 1999). This appears to be the case *except* when the violent man feels powerless in the relationship. Specifically, when the man felt the wife had more power than he did, more violence ensued following the wife demand-husband withdraw scenarios (Sagrestano, Heavey, & Christenson, 1999). Thus, it appears that controlling men in violent relationships may present more demands, whereas violent men who perceive themselves as powerless in the relationship respond to their wives' demands with violence.

Frustration-Aggression Hypothesis

DeTurck (1979) developed the frustration-aggression hypothesis, which argues that when personal goals are blocked (similar to the concept of conflict), frustration is experienced, which results in higher levels of aggression, threatening behavior, and violence. Similar to distressed couples who are more likely to interpret their partner's behavior negatively (Bradbury & Fincham, 1992), domestically violent men, compared with nonviolent men, are more likely to perceive their partner's behavior as threatening (Dugan, Umberson, & Anderson, 2001; Holtzworth-Monroe & Hutchinson, 1993). This perception of greater threat is irrespective of the actual objective content of the words and actions and is often followed by withdrawal from interaction and emotional disengagement (Umberson, Williams, & Anderson, 2002). Anderson et al. (2004) postulate that violent men experience a disconnect between their interactions and their emotional reactions to them. Umberson et al. (2002) argue that this repression of emotional experiences leads to further exacerbation of frustration, which can eventually lead to physical aggression.

Catalyst Hypothesis

The catalyst hypothesis offers an explanation of violence as resulting from partner challenge and coercive communication (Roloff, 1996); it suggests that verbal aggression from the abused may lead to physical aggression by the abuser. For this provocation from verbal aggression to physical aggression to occur, Roloff (1996) argues that violent males must have perceived face loss, and have a high desire to control, a high violence potential, and anger. *Face loss* refers to the batterer's perceived loss of esteem in the eyes of the marital partner. In other words, if the violent male perceives that his wife's verbally aggressive attacks of his self-image (i.e., face) are "illegitimate, unmitigated, central to the victims' self-concept, public" (p. 23) and cause a feeling of lack of control in the violent male, then the verbally aggressive face attacks may act as a catalyst for aggressive behavior. In this case, violence is used to correct the slight perceived by the violent male. As we have seen previously, physically abusive males tend to have a high need to control their partners. Roloff argues that this high need for control may be particularly activated by challenges from the partner and that violence may result in order to overcome increased resistance from the partner. This is consistent with earlier work indicating that wife demand provokes violence in relationships in which the husband feels powerless in comparison to the wife.

Roloff (1996) does not argue that this violent reaction exists in all men, however. He argues that a man must have a *violence potential* (i.e., a high perceived level of bodily harm that may be inflicted on another) in order for challenges, or coercive communication, to act as a catalyst. Finally, Roloff argues that *anger*, in the form of prolonged and uncontrolled arousal, is dysfunctional and can ultimately lead to violence. In sum, coercive communication (i.e., verbal face attacks) may serve to provoke physical retaliation in situations in which the male has a high need for control, a violence potential, and has problematic anger. If so, the partner plays a role in evoking different behaviors from her mate.

This approach has been criticized for blaming the victim of violence. In fact, other research shows that regardless of the type of response the wife of a violent man performs, the husband was still violent. Specifically, violent husbands continued to be violent when wives were violent themselves, used verbal defense, or withdrew (Jacobson, Gottman, Waltz, Rushe, & Holtzworth-Monroe, 1994). These researchers conclude that there is no response that wives could have provided that would have stopped the violence; the violence continued in response to either violent or nonviolent responses from wives.

Skills Deficiency Approach

As alluded to earlier, violence within families has been hypothesized to be the result of deficits in family members' communication skills (Infante et al., 1989). For instance, members of violent relationships lack both problem-solving and negotiation skills (e.g., Bird, Stith, & Schladale, 1991; Sabourin, Infante, & Rudd, 1993) and are less argumentative and more verbally aggressive (Feldman & Ridley, 2000; Infante et al., 1989). In addition, similar to other forms of destructive communication discussed earlier under the four horsemen of the apocalypse model, partners in violent relationships are more blaming, interrupting, invalidating, and withdrawing (Murphy & O'Farrell, 1997). Thus, partners in violent relationships tend to be less skilled communicationally with regard to problem-solving than are nonviolent relationship members.

The skills deficit model is also supported by research showing that batterers often have communication deficits that include lack of assertiveness and alternating between passiveness and aggressiveness (Gondolf, 1988). Further supporting this model, a batterer's most common response to problems and emotions is violence. With specific regard to communication, batterers are unable to label their emotions, are less disposed to possess or express their emotions, and are less aware of their affective states than are nonviolent men (Yelsma, 1996). Batterers also tend to have poor impulse control and evidence higher levels of hostility than nonbatters. This is attributed to the fact that every emotion they experience gets interpreted (or "reduced") to anger, which gets expressed through violence. This poor impulse control has been observed in physically abusive parents as well (e.g., Pianta, Egeland, & Erikson, 1989). Low-self esteem is often at the heart of violent behavior, in that batterers often feel insufficient as males and overcompensate through communicative shows of violence. They also feel very threatened by the degree of emotional dependence they feel on their partners, and this results in a strong fear of abandonment, which results in the communication of jealousy and possessiveness. Thus, violence in intimate terrorism situations may be partially due to a lack of communication skills.

Communication Skills Deficits in Parent-Child Abusive Interactions. While countless explanations for child physical abuse exist, disciplinary interactions between parents and children are frequently the immediate impetus for child physical abuse (Wilson, 2002; Wilson & Morgan, 2004). Thus, communication skills deficits during parent-child abusive interactions may support the skills deficit model of marital violence. Wilson and Morgan (2004) report that abusive mothers react differently than nonabusive mothers when their child does not comply with requests. Whereas nonabusive mothers consistently praised their child following compliance, abusive mothers were equally likely to criticize or complain immediately following compliance (Oldershaw, Walters, & Hall, 1986). Consistently, abusive mothers fail to reinforce positive child behavior (Cerezo, D'Ocon, & Dolz, 1996) and are equally likely to reward or punish compliant behavior. In addition, abusive mothers were more likely to continue to request compliance *after* the child complied (Oldershaw et al., 1986). In addition, abusive parents appear to "wind themselves up" by engaging in longer episodes of requesting compliance from a noncompliant child with increasing levels of punishing behavior (e.g., Reid, 1986). Abusive mothers appear not to perceive their child's behavior as being compliant even when it is.

In line with this perceptual bias, Wilson and Morgan (2004) also review research indicating that physically abusive parents attribute their child's frustrating behavior to internal, stable characteristics of the child (Larrance & Twentyman, 1983) or to view their child's behavior as an intentional attempt to upset them (Bauer & Twentyman, 1985) more than do nonabusive parents. This is consistent with the research reviewed above regarding violent men's tendency to perceive their wife's behavior in hostile or negative ways even when it was objectively not such. Once again, attributional biases appear to be operating in physical child abusive situations. So far in this text, these maladaptive attributional processes have been evidenced across distressed couples, couples who are violent toward one another, and parent-child physically abusive relationships.

Summary

Family relationships, because of increased closeness and frequency of interaction, are especially fertile ground for conflicts. *Conflicts,* or *goal interferences,* are prevalent across marital, parent-adolescent, and sibling relationships. However, marital conflict and violence were the focus here. Conflicts that promote positive outcomes (e.g., greater closeness, understanding, marital satisfaction, and marital stability) are considered *constructive,* whereas conflicts that promote negative outcomes (e.g., decreased closeness, misunderstandings, low marital satisfaction, and marital instability) are considered *destructive.* The *explanatory model of interpersonal conflict* is useful to the extent that it helps provide an explanation of the factors and outcomes (*distal factors, proximal factors, conflict interaction, proximal outcomes, distal outcomes*) associated with constructive and destructive conflict. Conflicts can be more or less constructive or destructive based on the conflict styles or conflict strategies that family members use. Conflict styles that vary on *directness-indirectness* and *competitiveness-cooperativeness* can be more or less constructive during conflict. *Avoiders* (couples whose members are indirect and cooperative) minimize conflict and produce constructive conflict in that way. *Volatiles* (couples whose members are direct and competitive) engage in conflict intensely but appear to compensate through even greater involvement in positive behavior and are constructive in their conflict styles as well. *Validators* (couples whose members are direct and cooperative) recognize each other's perspectives, maintain independent senses of perspective, and are constructive in their conflict styles. All these couples evidence a balance of more positive communication behaviors during conflict than negative ones.

On the flip side are couples who display destructive conflict patterns that are negative and highly reciprocal. Destructive behaviors associated with conflict are part of the *four horsemen of the apocalypse model* and include *criticism, contempt, defensiveness,* and *stonewalling.* Stonewalling is also evidenced during another destructive conflict pattern called *demand-withdraw,* during which wives typically demand changes in the relationship and husbands avoid or withdraw from the conflict. Specific *conflict strategies* (interpersonal influence tactics) can also be more or less destructive or constructive in that married couples tend to reciprocate negative strategies (e.g., content invalidation, other accusations, and self-defense) with other negative strategies and positive strategies (e.g., content validation, other support, and self-assertions) with other positive strategies.

Destructive conflict can sometimes escalate to violent proportions within families. *Situational couple violence* is likely when a specific runaway conflict leads to the use of violence when this is not the general pattern. *Intimate terrorism* is more often the case when one considers the general overall desire of the male partner to control the wife. In this way, *control* is central to the nature of spousal abuse. Certain types of wives are more likely to be the victims of violence (e.g., history of child abuse, demographic factors, beliefs about violence, and interpretation of spouse's behavior), and certain types of husbands are more likely to perpetuate intimate terrorism violence (e.g., history of child abuse, traditional sex role expectations, low communication skills, poor impulse control, alcohol abuse, low self-esteem). In addition, there are several reasons that physically abused wives might maintain the relationship with the abuser (i.e., fear of separation violence, lack of financial resources, social isolation, cultural beliefs encouraging family maintenance, history of abuse, and low self-esteem), including *learned helplessness* and *learned hopefulness.* Finally, several communication-based approaches help explain violence in families. These approaches include *demand-withdraw,* the *frustration-aggression hypothesis,* the *catalyst hypothesis,* the *skills deficits* model, and the *communication explanation for child abuse.* Specifically, the demand-withdraw pattern of conflict is evidenced in violent relationships, with husband demand-wife withdraw as prevalent as wife demand-husband withdraw patterns. Second, the frustration-aggression hypothesis argues that violence results from goal interruption and the ensuing frustration that is experienced. Third, the catalyst hypothesis asserts that wives' coercive communication can sometimes act as a catalyst for husbands' use of violence. Fourth, the skills deficiency approach argues that violent men's lack of effective problem-solving skills results in the use of violence in response to conflict. Finally, the communication explanation for child abuse argues that physical abuse against children may result from a lack of communication skills during disciplinary encounters between parents and children.

KEY TERMS

avoiders
catalyst hypothesis
competitive-cooperative strategies
conflict
constructive conflict
contempt
content invalidation
content validation
criticism
defensiveness
demand-withdraw
destructive conflict
four horsemen of the apocalypse
frustration-aggression hypothesis
indirect-direct strategies

interpersonal influence strategies
intimate terrorism
learned hopefulness
learned helplessness
other accusations
other support
profile of battered
profile of batterer
self-assertions
self-defense
situational couple violence
skills deficit approach
stonewalling
validators
volatiles

QUESTIONS FOR APPLICATION

1. Think of a recent conflict (e.g., goal interruption) interaction that you were involved in with a family member. Using the *explanatory model of interpersonal conflict*, describe distal and proximal factors that led up to the conflict. Describe the actual conflict episode and discuss the proximal and distal outcomes of the conflict. Was the conflict *constructive* or *destructive*? Defend your answer.

2. Using the same conflict as above, describe the actual conflict interaction in terms of *the interpersonal influence strategies* used during the conflict (e.g., content-validation, content invalidation, other support, other accusations, self-assertions, self-defense). Were your strategies more positive (e.g. content validation, other support, self-assertions) or negative (e.g., content invalidation, other accusations, self-defense)? How did your partner react? In what ways were reciprocity of interpersonal influence strategies apparent?

3. According to Gottman's *four horsemen of the apocalypse model*, what are the four destructive behaviors evidenced during conflict in couples who are more distressed? Did your parents evidence any of these in their communication behavior? Alternatively, do you and your last romantic partner display any of these behaviors? Does this mean your relationship is headed for disaster? Why or why not (be sure to include discussion of ratios of positive to negative communication behavior in your relationship and conflict episodes)?

4. Discuss the *three types of constructive conflict styles* according to Gottman (*avoiders, volatiles, validators*). How do these styles vary along the typical conflict dimensions of *indirectness-directness* and *competitiveness-cooperativeness*? What styles best represent your parents' styles of conflict? How were your parents' conflict styles related to their own level of marital stability and marital satisfaction (regardless of whether they are currently married)?

5. Discuss the *social structure of demand-withdraw* pattern of conflict. In what ways is this pattern destructive to relationships? How does this pattern manifest itself during conflict? How does this pattern differ in couples where violence is used? Have you ever observed this pattern of conflict in any of the married people you know? How did this pattern relate to overall patterns of marital satisfaction and marital stability?

6. Differentiate between *situational couple violence* and *intimate terrorism*. How is the communication concept of control related to intimate terrorism? How do these ideas relate to the myths that violence is gendered and that violence is a one-time occurrence? Are you aware of violence in any of the relationships you have come into contact with (these could be real or in the media)? Which concepts regarding the batterer and battered and the communication theories regarding the existence of violence work best to explain the violence in the relationship you are aware of?

Endnote

1. My doctoral student Carolyn Shepard completed one of her qualifying exams on violence in romantic relationships. She and I also coauthored a chapter that included violent relationships as a topic. She is responsible for providing a great amount of research for the section of the chapter on the nature of violence and the characteristics of the battered.

9 Nurturing and Controlling Communication Surrounding Undesirable Behavior in the Family

All this focus on closeness and conflict within families makes it obvious that all families, regardless of form (e.g., single-parent, nuclear, gay families with children, blended families, extended families), go through struggles. In fact, most families experience some sort of stressful event at some point. Let's face it; it's a rough world out there, and while families do the best they can to buffer their family members from problems, there is some tough stuff out there waiting for families and children to deal with. Some families experience substance abuse in one of the parents in the household. In still other families, adolescent children fall prey to substance abuse and all the negative effects associated with it. Alternatively, some families have children with eating disorders who starve themselves (i.e., anorexics) or exercise excessively and purge themselves (i.e., bulimics). Furthermore, some families have family members with serious mental health issues such as depression that cause them to communicate in aversive ways with other family members. The pain, betrayal, and fear that these family members experience cannot be overestimated. The day-to-day consequences of these psychological problems and behavioral manifestations can be devastating for family members.

This chapter focuses less on normal developmental stressors that all families face and more on interpersonal sources of nondevelopmental stress within the family. What makes the stressful examples offered in this chapter unique is that all these examples (e.g., substance abuse, eating disorders, depression) are stressful family events actually *caused by an internal member of the family*. Sometimes family members behave in such a way that their behavior is highly stressful to other family members. It is likely then that this person's stress-inducing behavior becomes the focus of communicative control attempts by other family members. This chapter explores the effect of undesirable behavior (i.e., substance abuse, eating disorders, depression) in the family. The chapter also examines the effects that family members' nurturing and controlling communication can have in diminishing undesirable behavior in one family member through family systems theory, coercion theory, and inconsistent nurturing as control theory.

Undesirable Behavior in the Family

Although not all families include undesirable behavior, many families do. Undesirable behavior may range from gambling addictions to sexual addictions, but it is likely that the communication behavior in the family is affected by the presence of this behavior. This chapter reviews three particularly problematic behavioral compulsions known to be present in and affect families: (a) substance abuse, (b) eating disorders, and (c) depression. While there are certainly more problematic behavioral compulsions in families, these three types of problems have been shown to affect, and be affected by, communication behavior in the family.

Substance Abuse and Communication in the Family

Most of you have witnessed the effect of substance abuse in families at some point in your life, and you are not surprised that substance abuse exists in families. The 2002 National Survey of Drug Use and Health reports that of the 69 million parents living with children in the home, 5 million parents (or 7%) were alcohol abusive or alcohol dependent (Substance Abuse and Mental Health Services Administration [SAMHSA], 2004a). In addition, 6 million children (10%) reportedly live in homes where substance abuse is an issue for parents (e.g., SAMHSA, 2003). This national report also indicates that fathers are more likely to be substance abusive than mothers. A recently released DASIS (Drug and Alcohol Services Information System) report indicates that while admissions to substance abuse treatment have increased by 23% among adults (in 2002), the percentage of adolescents admitted for treatment has risen 65% since 1992 (SAMHSA, 2004b). In addition, although alcohol was the primary substance of choice among adolescents in 1992 (56%), it is now a clear second (20%) to marijuana (64%, up from 23%). It is clear, then, that many families are affected by substance abuse either through parental substance abuse or adolescent substance abuse.

What is the nature of the effects of substance abuse in the home? First, the relationship and the communication between the substance abuser and his or her spouse is negatively affected. Second, children of substance abusers generally suffer from low self-esteem, anxiety, and substance abuse imitation—all of which might affect their subsequent communication behavior. Third, parents of substance-abusing and non-substance-abusing adolescents alike may worry about how best to communicate with their children about the potential health risks associated with substance abuse. Finally, siblings may adversely affect each other's substance use and abuse by either modeling the tendency to use or abuse substances or by sabotaging each other's attempts to deter future substance use.

Relational and Communication Effects

The relational effects of substance abuse on couples are well established (e.g., for a review see Le Poire & Daley, 2005). Research has shown that substance abuse is related to more *communication problems among partners* (Fals-Stewart & Birchler, 1998; Kelly, Halford, & Young, 2002) and *increased detachment and less desire for intimacy* (Carroll, Robinson, & Flowers, 2002). Thus, substance abuse causes communication problems and decreased closeness in couples. Substance abuse also affects conflict in that *increased partner verbal aggressiveness* (Straus & Sweet, 1992) and *physical abuse or violence* have also been evidenced in couples where one member abuses substances (Quigley & Leonard, 2000; Rodriguez, Lasch, Chandra, & Lee, 2001; Testa, Quigley, & Leonard, 2003; Wekerle & Wall, 2002). It is clear that alcohol and substance abuse are clearly related to both intimacy

Box 9.1   Differentiating between Substance Use, Abuse, and Dependence

So far, we have been using the terms *substance use* and *substance abuse* almost interchangeably. It would be a mistake to equate use and abuse, however, so let's take a moment to make the distinction clearer. Many of you may be going through an experimental phase where you temporarily abuse substances during your time at college. This is usually a phase, but this phase is definitely different from when you simply used substances.

The American Psychological Association defines substance use, substance abuse, and substance dependence in the following ways (Chemical Use, Abuse, and Dependency [CUAD] Scale; McGovern & Morris, 1992). *Substance use* refers to the use of alcohol and substances on either a regular or irregular basis. In general, a substance user partakes of substances, but such use does not result in getting into dangerous situations (e.g., becoming a danger to self or others) or diminished participation in other activities and relationships, such as having trouble with the law or hurting your relationships at work, school, or home (e.g., with coworkers, schoolmates, and family members). However, *substance abuse* refers to the use of alcohol, for example, to such an extent that you put yourself in danger (e.g., driving under the influence) or decrease your involvement in other activities (e.g., miss work due to a hangover or decrease involvement in physical activities like baseball) because of the substance.

Alternatively, *substance dependence* indicates a degree of physical reliance on the substance such that you need increasing amounts of the substance to get the same feelings you used to get when you used less (i.e., increased tolerance) and you feel physically ill when you don't get enough of the substance (i.e., physical dependence). Although substance abuse is dangerous, substance dependence is closer to the use of the term *addiction* (which has a very precise physiological definition); it implies that the dependent is reliant on the substance for daily living. Substance dependence includes the characteristics of substance abuse (e.g., getting into dangerous situations, getting into trouble with the law, harming relationships, and decreasing participation in activities) as well as physical reliance on the substance.

and conflict behavior within marital couples, even if it is not clear which came first. Furthermore, spouses of substance abusers are frequently affected in terms of both physical and mental health (e.g., Hurcom, Copello, & Orford, 2000). Spouses of substance abusers are known to be both more anxious and depressed, which can have long-term consequences on physical health. In sum, substance abuse in families adversely affects marital relationships as well as the physical and mental well-being of the marital partners in such a relationship.

Offspring Effects

At this point, you are probably wondering about the children in these families. If decreases in intimacy and increases in negative conflict behavior exist for parents, how are kids in substance-abusive homes faring? The detrimental effects of being raised by a substance-abusing parent are also well-known (e.g., Mothersead, Kivlighan, & Wynkoop, 1998). Kids raised in families that include substance abuse suffer from *increased maltreatment* (e.g., Sheridan, 1995; Shuntich, Loh, & Katz, 1998) and *increased probability of foster care* (Dore, Doris, & Wright, 1995). In addition, mothers recovering from an addiction are more likely to report greater parenting stress and greater use of problematic parenting behaviors (Harmer, Sanderson, & Mertin, 1999).

Given these dramatic effects of substance abuse on child-rearing practices, it is not that surprising that children from homes that include substance abuse evidence *increased maladjustment* (Rubio-Stipec, Bird, Canino, & Bravo, 1991) and a *higher incidence of anxiety disorders, conduct disorders*, and *depression* (Lachner & Wittchen, 1995; Merikangas, Dierker, & Szamari, 1998). These behavioral problems and mental health deficits manifest themselves psychologically, communicationally, and socially in that an adult sample of children of alcoholics were distinguished from children of nonalcoholics by *low self-esteem, anxiousness*, and *lack of emotional expression* (Lachner & Wittchen, 1995). Thus, children in substance-abusive families are more likely to be mistreated, act out in socially unacceptable ways, and evidence low self-esteem, anxiety, and depression.

Although the effects of parental substance abuse on anxiety and low self-esteem are quite well documented, other studies have not shown such an effect (Tweed & Ryff, 1991; Werner & Broida, 1991). Some have argued that there may be an interaction between the presence of substance-abusing parents and supportive relationships with nonabusing parents and siblings. In other words, if appropriate levels of parenting occur with the non-substance-abusing parent, it is possible that the child of an alcoholic might have high self-esteem and adaptive capabilities (Walker & Lee, 1998). It should be pointed out that there are contradictions in the literature here, in that the studies of the protective effects of sober parents found very little evidence of the *buffering hypothesis* (Curran & Chassin, 1996).

Besides problems with self-esteem and behavioral problems, many other studies explore the link between substance-abusive behavior in the family and the child's likelihood of abusing substances themselves. For instance, children from homes in which one or both parents are labeled problem drinkers have *evidenced alcohol disorders themselves* (e.g., Cloninger, 1987; Goodwin, 1985; Pihl, Peterson, & Finn, 1990; Sher, 1991; Tarter, Laird, & Moss, 1990; Windle & Searles, 1990). In addition, children from families that include a substance-abusive parent also evidence earlier onset of illicit substance use, higher rates of lifetime marijuana and cocaine use, and more frequent adolescent antisocial behavior (Windle, 1996). Consistent with the buffering argument presented earlier, some work has found that highly organized families and behavioral coping efforts may deter substance use initiation (Hussong & Chassin, 1997). Still other studies find no relationship between children of alcoholics' status and either the likelihood or severity of problem drinking (e.g., Havey & Dodd,

1993). Thus, while intuitively it seems likely that substance abuse may be intergenerational, the results of studies are inconclusive.

The Effects of Parent-Child Communication on Adolescent Substance Use and Abuse

Regardless of the existence of parental substance abuse in the home, adolescent children experiment with substance use and abuse, and parenting practices and communication may be related to the degree of riskiness associated with this experimentation. The 2003 National Survey on Drug Use and Health of nearly 70,000 individuals indicated that *children who report using alcohol under the age of 15 are more than 5 times as likely to report problems with substance abuse and dependence* than those who did not begin drinking until age 21 (SAMHSA, 2004c). Therefore, parents may be concerned that they create effective messages aimed at diminishing alcohol or other substance abuse at an early age. The news is good here in that parental influence is more profound than peer influence in accounting for substance use and that viable relationships with parents promote less involvement in drugs (Coombs, Paulson, & Richardson, 1991). On the flip side, communication problems between parents and children and inadequate discipline within the family predict adolescent substance use (Garcia-Pindado, 1992). How parents communicate with children, then, can have a strong influence on children's tendency to use or abuse substances.

Similar to the parenting styles research presented in Chapter 6, many studies of parent-adolescent relations and substance abuse support the use of both the communication of nurturing and control by parents in their attempts to curtail substance use and abuse in adolescents. Consistent with the earlier literature presented regarding parenting styles, *authoritative parents,* or parents who use a combination of warmth and control, are the most successful at attaining lower substance use among their adolescents. For instance, adolescents' substance use was associated with both family affection and parental control (Hall, Henggeler, Ferreira, & East, 1992). Consistently, perceived authoritative parenting was associated with lower levels of substance use for both boys and girls, whereas perceived parental disciplinary consequences of engaging in substance use was also important for girls (Fletcher & Jeffries, 1999). Finally, moderate amounts of parental control and parental support were more clearly related to decreased illicit drug use, while higher amounts of control and support were both predictive of decreased alcohol use (Stice, Barrera, & Chassin, 1993). This supports the contention that authoritative parenting styles are associated with less substance use among adolescents.

Also consistent with the earlier literature reviewed regarding parenting styles and outcomes, *authoritarian parenting* (e.g., high levels of control combined with low levels of responsivity) is positively associated with substance use and abuse. For instance, higher adolescent substance abuse was associated with higher levels of perceived parental control and lower perceived parental love (Pandina & Schuele, 1983). Consistently, frequency of adolescent substance use increased with high parental expectations and bad social climate in the family (Hurrelmann, 1990), and problematic drinking behavior was associated with low levels of family social support and with dysfunctional coping strategies (Schor, 1996). Thus, authoritarian parenting (low responsiveness combined with high levels of control) is associated with greater substance use and problematic drinking behavior among adolescents.

Besides parents' substance abuse affecting children and their spouses, and parents' discipline style affecting childrens' substance use, siblings can have powerful effects on one another's substance use as well. In fact, in some cases, sibling relations (especially sibling conflict) accounted for significantly more variance in substance use than did other family relations (Hall et al., 1992). Although parents play an important role in adolescent substance abuse, older-brother–younger-brother relationships also have a significant impact on younger-brother substance abuse (Brook, Brook, & Whiteman, 1999; Brook, Whiteman, Gordon, & Brook, 1990), as do sibling substance abuse (Handelsman et al., 1993; Lloyd, 1998; Merinkangas, Rounsaville, & Prusoff, 1992; Vakalahi, 1999) and sibling completion of substance abuse treatment programs (Feigelman, 1987). It has also been postulated that siblings may attempt to sabotage substance abuse recovery attempts (Huberty & Huberty, 1986). This is especially likely to manifest in older sibling relationships (Brook et al., 1999; Brook et al., 1990), where the effects of modeling have been shown to be stronger from older to younger siblings and older siblings' rivalry with younger siblings may result in greater attempts to sabotage the "good" recovering behavior of the substance abuser so that the older sibling may shine by comparison.

Children With Eating Disorders and Communication in the Family

Having a family member with an eating disorder in the family home presents a problem similar to that of having a substance abuser. The American Psychiatric Association Work Group on Eating Disorders (APA, 2000) estimates that the prevalence of eating disorders in the United States is between 0.5% and 4% of the general population. In essence, eating disorders affect about 5 to 10 million American women and 1 million American men (Crowther, Lilly, Crawford, & Shepard, 1992). In addition, the number of adolescents experiencing an eating disorder has increased over the last 50 years (Steiner & Lock, 1998). Quite strikingly, the mortality rate for anorexia nervosa is higher than for any other psychological disturbance with 5% to 10% dying within the first 10 years, 18% to 20% dying within the first 20 years, and only 50% ever reporting being cured (National Association of Anorexia Nervosa and Associated Disorders, 2000). The life-threatening nature of eating disorders has recently been brought to national attention in the controversial case of Terri Schiavo's eating tube being removed. Besides highlighting governmental attempts at regulating families and interesting legal debates over the rights of spouses compared with parents, this case also highlights the devastating effects of eating disorders in that Schiavo's eating tube was first introduced following a heart attack initially assumed to have been brought about by bulimia (her autopsy did not confirm this fact, however). Eating disorders present life-threatening illnesses that can be extremely frightening for family members.

Researchers agree that anorexia and bulimia remain a persistent problem, particularly for young, middle-class, white women. The two most prevalent eating disorders are anorexia nervosa and bulimia. **Anorexia** is characterized by extreme fasting, a refusal to maintain a normal body weight, an intense fear of gaining weight, and a significant disturbance in one's body evaluation. **Bulimia** involves cycles of binge eating, followed by compensatory purging behaviors to prevent weight gain (APA, 2000). Although there are various combinations of these eating disorders (e.g., purging anorexics), these are the central types of eating disorders.

Research supports the negative effects of compulsive behavior in families, including those with eating disorders. Specifically, in families with an anorexic member, research suggests *greater enmeshment* (dependence and entanglement; Kog & Vandereycken, 1989), *greater incongruent communication* (Humphrey, Apple & Kirschenbaum, 1986), and *greater hostility and withholding between members* (Humphrey & Stern, 1988). Thus, communication patterns of families that include a family member with an eating disorder show some consistent patterns surrounding the ideas of *nurturing* and *controlling* communication. In terms of nurturing, mothers of daughters with eating disorders may be overly nurturing to the point of creating extreme patterns of dependence of the daughter on the mother. In a similar vein, families of anorexics are significantly overenmeshed and overprotective (Kadambari, Gowers, & Crisp, 1986); 75% of anorexics and bulimics reported a mother-child overinvolvement or overdependent relationship (Kaffman & Sadah, 1989).

In terms of incongruent communication behavior, Humphrey (1989) found that mothers of anorexics were *both* more nurturing and comforting *and* more ignoring and neglecting than mothers of daughters without eating disorders. The ignoring and neglecting side of the equation may be an attempt to control daughters' behavior. This pattern of negative communication is supported by several research studies that evidence harsh and judgmental tones in mother-daughter relationships from the mother toward the daughter (e.g., Pike & Rodin, 1991). Mothers of daughters with eating disorders may attempt to be overly close to their daughters while they are at the same time overly harsh and judgmental in their communication. This increased closeness may cause the harsh and judgmental comments to have even more impact on the relationship.

Mother involvement is not the only factor related to daughters with eating disorders, however; this mother overinvolvement has been attributed in part to a peripheral-disengaged father. Similar to the concept of triangulation, mothers of daughters with eating disorders appear to be substituting the intimacy of the marital relationship with closeness in the mother-daughter relationship. This is consistent with Humphrey's (1988) finding that mothers of anorexics reported significant marital distress, describing their husbands as unaffectionate, unsupportive, sulky, withdrawn, and neglectful toward them. In the same study, mothers reported positive relationships with their daughters, and the daughters were found to be submissive toward their mothers. In sum, families that include daughters with eating disorders appear to include overenmeshment, incongruent communication, neglectful or hostile communication, distant relationships between parents, disengaged fathers, and compensatory closeness between mothers and daughters.

These family communication patterns are not the only way that families may affect eating disorders, however. Traumatic episodes such as sexual abuse have also been associated with eating disorders (e.g., Wonderlich, Brewerton, Jocic, Dansky, & Abbott, 1997). In addition, eating disorders have been associated with other early familial traumatic episodes such as high levels of parental discord and physical abuse (e.g., Graber, Archibald, & Brooks-Gunn, 1999). Furthermore, parents may contribute to eating disorders through their communicated desire for thinness in the modeling of dieting behavior (e.g, Paxton et al., 1991; Pike & Rodin, 1991) and through fathers' communicated preference for thinner ideals of female attractiveness (e.g., Ogden & Chanana, 1998). In a similar vein, parents' direct comments regarding their children's weight may contribute to eating disorders (e.g., Smolak, Levine, & Schermer, 1999). Finally, a family's history with eating disorders may also be a contributing factor to eating disorders (e.g., Strober, Lampert, Morell, Borroughs, & Jacobs, 1990). Although eating disorders have been associated with a whole host of biological, sociological, and familial processes, this review highlights the important role of family communication in potentially contributing to eating disorders in the family.

Depression and Communication in the Family

While having a family member with a substance abuse or eating disorder can produce much stress in the family, other mental health issues may present similarly troubling issues for the family. Depression is one such mental health problem. Although depression presents a different type of problem than the obvious compulsive behavioral tendencies of substance abusers and individuals with eating disorders, depressed individuals are likely to similarly present their family members with communication challenges. The National Institute of Mental Health (NIMH, 2003b) reports that over 6 million men suffer from depression each year and that the number reaches 19 million, or about 9.5% of the adult population when one includes women (NIMH, 2003a). Because **depression** can result in feelings of hopelessness, guilt, loss of interest in previously enjoyable activities (including sex), and decreased energy or fatigue,

Figure 9.1   Depression can have serious consequences on the communication between children and their parents.

SOURCE: Photo courtesy of Michele Berry and her daughter Tory.

depression in one or more partners in a marriage can have serious consequences on the relationship and on communication in the family.

Similar to families with substance abusers, families with a depressed member evidence *greater marital distress, less affection,* and *more destructive conflict strategies* (Coyne, Thompson, & Palmer, 2002). The work on negativity affect in marriages presented in Chapter 7 is consistent with work on depression and marriages. In other words, depression is consistently associated with *lower marital satisfaction* (e.g., Davila, Karney, Hall, & Bradbury, 2003). Communicationally, depressed individuals engage in *more negative and less supportive communication* with others (Segrin, 1993b; Segrin & Abramson, 1994), receive less social support, and have more problems in social relationships—especially with intimates (Wade & Kendler, 2000). Consistently, families including depressed individuals are *less cohesive and supportive, less able to communicate effectively,* and *have higher levels of conflict, hostility, criticism,* and *overinvolvement* than do families with nondepressed individuals (Downey & Coyne, 1990).

Depressed individuals also make more negative statements about themselves and their partners (Vettese & Mongrain, 2000). Unfortunately, their partners reciprocate with more negative feedback (Segrin & Dillard, 1992; Vettese & Mongrain, 2000), which may exacerbate depressive symptoms

(Coyne, 1976), because depressed people are aware of rejection and internalize the negative mood state further when negative interpersonal feedback occurs (Segrin, 1993a). Thus, depressed individuals may negatively affect others through their aversive communication (Strack & Coyne, 1983) and ultimately may reinforce their own depression through the responses others have to them. There may be a sort of contagion effect operating here whereby depressed individuals share their mood by communicating negatively with those to whom they are closest.

With specific regard to marital satisfaction, those married individuals with low-level depression were found to be more reactive to stress within marriage and accompanying changes in marital satisfaction and stability (Beach & O'Leary, 1993). Thus, depression in one partner can have a strong negative effect on marital satisfaction and communication for both partners. Although depression might *lead* to marital dissatisfaction as alluded to previously, it is also the case that lack of marital satisfaction may *contribute* to major episodes of depression (Beach, 2001). Steven Beach's *marital discord model of depression* argues that depression may be the *result* of marital discord and dissatisfaction instead of the *cause* of it. One study that clearly examined the directionality of this relationship found that not only did spouses' earlier marital quality predict their own later depression, but it also predicted their partners' later depression as well (Beach, Katz, Kim, & Brody, 2003). Not only can marital satisfaction affect physical health (as reported in earlier chapters), but marital satisfaction can affect the mental health of both oneself and one's spouse in the marital relationship. More important, depression may not be a cause of marital dissatisfaction but may in fact be the result of it.

In a similar vein, depression has also been related to the communication and expression of anger in families. Specifically, Cheng, Mallinckrodt, and Wu (2005) indicate that there is a strong relationship between the way anger is expressed in families and depression. Specifically, daughters who preferred expressing anger were less depressed, whereas sons who preferred acting out as an alternative to expressing anger were more depressed. In other words, the strong cultural and familial pressures to express or withhold anger expression can have important consequences on the long-term depression of family members. The sample here was Taiwanese, with the expectation that these participants would hold strong beliefs in *filial piety*, or the tendency to consider the long-term consequences of one's actions for the entire family. Such filial piety may result in the suppression of anger, which has been associated with greater depressive symptoms across a whole range of studies in the Western culture. The communication (or suppression) of anger within families may therefore be associated with depression.

Furthermore, children of depressed parents seem to experience a wide range of negative outcomes and psychiatric diagnoses (Downey & Coyne, 1990). Children of depressed parents are at increased risk for a whole host of emotional and behavioral problems, including deficits in academic and social competencies, greater externalization and internalization, and greater psychiatric difficulties (for a review, see Garber & Little, 1999). These emotional and behavioral problems may manifest themselves in the communication behavior of the children. In other words, deficits in social competencies may be manifested in communication behaviors that make it more problematic for these children to assimilate with their peers. Because better peer relations have been associated with better academic performance (see Chapter 6), it is also possible that the communication behavior of children of depressed parents influences outcomes at both social and academic competence levels.

The Potential Role of Communication and Problematic Behavior in Families

As the previous review clearly demonstrates, substance abuse, eating disorders, and depression can have long-term devastating effects on families. What is unique about all these maladies in families is that one family member perpetuates the problem that acts as a stressor for the entire family. What is likely to happen, then, is that most of the family members want the problematic or stressful behavior to stop. Therefore, family members in a family where substance abuse, eating disorders, and depression exist are likely to make attempts to alter the behavior of the family member who perpetuates the problem. Family members, therefore, may have a potential positive intervening effect on the compulsive behavior of substance abusers, individuals with eating disorders, and depressed persons.[1] With respect to alcoholics, behavioral couples therapy (in combination with remission after individual treatment) has been associated with improved family functioning in the form of reduced family stressors, improved marital adjustment, reduced domestic violence and conflict, reduced risk of separation and divorce, reduced emotional distress in spouses, and improved cohesion and caring (O'Farrell & Feehan, 1999). In addition, greater family involvement in treatment has also been associated with abstinence, better family relations, and positive feelings about self (e.g., McCrady, et al., 1986; McNabb, Der-Karabetian, & Rhoads, 1989). Family members can not only aid their partners in recovery from their compulsion or mental health issue, but they can also improve their family's functioning simultaneously. Thus, it behooves family members to be involved in trying to get their family member to recover. It is important to consider the impact that family members can have communicationally in not only influencing continued substance abuse, eating disorders, and depression but also in increasing the helping family member's own mental health and overall family functioning.

Family Systems Theory

You remember from Chapter 3 that family systems theory argues that family members are interdependent and that you can never understand the communication behavior within a family unless you understand the whole of the family. Family systems theorists are as interested in how family members perpetuate problems as they are in how family members can assist in recovery from the problem. In other words, they argue that family members are mutually influential in that one member's behavioral compulsion may be symptomatic of underlying dysfunction in the family. This family systems theorizing is consistent with theorizing, for instance, that wives unconsciously encourage substance-dependent behavior because of their own pathological problems of martyrdom or domination desires (e.g., Paige, La Pointe, & Krueger, 1971; Rae & Drewery, 1972). Although this theorizing has often been discounted as overly blaming the spouse, the later theorizing of family systems is also consistent with this line of reasoning (Kaufman, 1979, 1985; Steinglass, 1976). The communication model of family therapy served as foundational thinking for this movement (e.g., Satir, 1967), which led Jackson (1968) to develop a theory of homeostasis in the family. Ewing and Fox (1968) argue that this homeostasis (i.e., balance) is used in the alcoholic family to resist change and that alterations by one spouse (e.g., reduction in drinking behavior) prompt the other spouse to attempt to maintain status quo. Fundamentally, the systems approach discounts the "disease model" of alcoholism and proffers instead that the "sickness" of the family may be causing or maintaining the drinking. Certainly, the etiology of drinking cannot be purely familially based, but there may be support for the systems theory contention that a wife may *unwittingly* attempt to control the substance-dependent behavior of her husband in ways that are not only ineffective but that do, in fact, serve to actually strengthen the substance-dependent behavior.

Coercion Theory

Familial interactions including problematic behavior have also been studied through coercion theory (Patterson, 1982; Patterson, Hops, & Weiss, 1975), which has accounted for interactive patterns of families including aggressive children (Patterson & Reid, 1970), distressed marital dyads (Patterson & Hops, 1972), and problem-solving interactions of depressed women and their husbands (Biglan et al., 1985; Hops et al., 1987). Coercion theory is specifically concerned with aversive stimulation (punishment) as an effort to control. For instance, aversive behavior (i.e., negative communication behavior) presented by one partner elicits yielding behavior from his or her counterpart. That is, the aversive person receives positive reinforcement for his or her behavior, and the yielding partner receives negative reinforcement for his or her behavior by the reduction in the first person's aversive behavior. For example, a partner of a substance abuser or an individual with an eating disorder might verbally harass and harangue that person until he or she alters the substance abuse or eating-disordered behavior. The reduction in the disordered behavior is thought to reinforce the aversive behavior of the helping partner. Although future theorizing will likewise be interested in the presentation of reinforcing and punishing behavior, it takes a conceptual step forward in terms of both applying these ideas to partners of substance-dependent individuals, individuals with eating disorders, and depressed individuals and examining the effects of *intermittent* reinforcement and punishment schedules.

Inconsistent Nurturing as Control Theory

Most of you remember that the basic premise of this book is that all families, regardless of family form, consistently offer *nurturing* and *control* to their family members. What you may not know is that the idea that all families nurture and control their members was extended from a theory I've been developing called inconsistent nurturing as control (INC) theory (Le Poire, 1992, 1995). Basically, this theory argues that while all family members nurture and control each other simultaneously, families that include a member who is out of control in terms of some undesirable behavioral tendency or another (e.g., drinking, eating disorder, gambling, violence, sex addiction), use *nurturing as a way to control* their family members. The use of nurturing as control is argued to be paradoxical (i.e., logically inconsistent) and is expected to result in less than effective strategies being used in families with members who exhibit undesirable behavior. **INC theory** attempts to explain the communication dynamics underlying these families' nurturing and control mechanisms and how these dynamics ultimately affect how successful family members can be at curtailing their family members' undesirable behavior.[2]

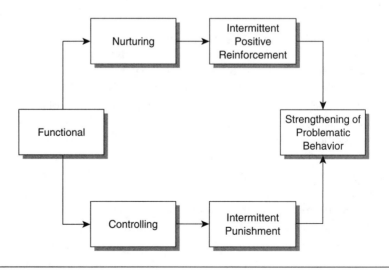

Figure 9.2   Inconsistent Nurturing as Control Theory

Paradoxes

The relational dynamics of this functional (i.e., no behavioral problem) but afflicted (i.e., behavioral compulsion) relationship produce a power structure that is paradoxical. A **paradox** contains two consistent premises that contradict the logical conclusion (Watzlawick, Beavin, & Jackson, 1967). Communicationally, this results in requests that are impossible to carry out. For instance, if I were to ask you not to read this sentence, it would be too late by the time you have read this for you to carry out my request. In other words, the communication makes a request that is impossible. My other favorite example of a paradoxical communication is the parent who says, "Stop obeying me." Obviously, recipients of this request are left in a conundrum because if they do not stop obeying, they have not obeyed the request. However, if they do stop obeying the parent, then they have obeyed the parent. In other words, it is impossible to carry out a paradoxical communication. The effects of these conundrums are evident in the functional-afflicted relationship. The first paradox is about *control*, the second paradox is about *sacrifice and dependency*, and the third paradox is about the *nurturing and control*. Although all three are relevant to the communication of nurturing and control in families including one member with problematic behavior, we focus on the last one here.

Nurturing and Control

The *nurturing and control paradox* concerns the nature of the relationship and is probably the most fundamental in terms of sabotaging functional partners' attempts to help their partners regain control over their behavioral compulsion. In general, the functional partner simultaneously desires to nurture and control his or her partner, two processes that unfortunately result in contradictory communication behavior. These fundamental needs are predicated on the assumption that the functional partner wants to maintain a nurturing relationship with the afflicted partner. There are a lot of reasons why this may be the case. First, the functional loves the afflicted and is committed to the relationship. Second, the functional partner has invested a lot of time and energy in helping the afflicted person regain his or her health. Third, while marital couples choose one another voluntarily, all other familial relationships are nonvoluntary. Fourth, the functional partner may self-identify as nurturing and caring and therefore may help meet this definition by maintaining this relationship with an afflicted who is in need of help and assistance.

At the same time, the functional desires to control or eliminate the substance abuse, eating disorder, or depression of the afflicted. At some point, it is highly likely that the functional gets fed up with the emotional crises surrounding the behavioral compulsion of the afflicted. In the case of substance abusers, the functional partner may get fed up with the afflicted partner's absences, tendency to spend money in pursuit of substances, tendency to commit crimes to get the substances, or lack of attention to the children. However, because the functional nurtures the afflicted during times of crisis, this caretaking behavior is very rewarding for the afflicted. In general, the caregiving behavior of the functional partner provides the support necessary for the afflicted to enact the behavioral compulsion. In other words, it is unlikely that the afflicted could enact the behavioral compulsion without a functional partner to pick up the slack (e.g., provide the money, organize the house, care for the children). If it is the case that the afflicted person actually stays with the functional partner because of this caregiving (and potentially enabling) behavior, then it is possible that extinguishing the afflicted's behavioral compulsions would result in an elimination of this rewarding caretaking behavior. In other words, the functional could not nurture the afflicted in times of crisis if the afflicted actually stopped the behavioral compulsion or tendency. As a result, this paradox suggests that by accomplishing the goal of stopping the substance abuse, the functional partner may actually destroy the relationship.

Paradoxical Outcomes in Learning Theory Terms

This paradox is at the heart of the use of inconsistent patterns of nurturing and control in the relationship. In other words, the *reason* that the functional may use inconsistent patterns of reinforcement and punishment surrounding the compulsive behavior is that the functional has conflicting needs surrounding the substance abuse. That person sincerely desires the diminishment of this crazy-making behavior (*control*), but the functional partner also fears that he or she will not be necessary to the afflicted (for *nurturing)* once the behavioral compulsion is extinguished. Unfortunately, the result of these paradoxes is that the simultaneous enactment of both nurturing and control are likely to contradict each other and make controlling attempts less successful than they otherwise might have been.

To be more specific, nurturing a family member through crises surrounding substance abuse, eating-disordered behavior, or depression is *in effect* supporting or *reinforcing* the behavioral compulsion or tendency. On the other hand, trying to control or extinguish the behavioral compulsion often takes the form of *punishing* the tendency. Thus, nurturing the troubled partner reinforces the problem, and controlling the behavioral compulsion punishes the problem. According to learning theory, reinforcement in essence strengthens the behavior it follows, whereas punishment in essence extinguishes the behavior it follows (Skinner, 1953, 1974). Thus, functional family members contradict themselves by sometimes reinforcing and sometimes punishing the problem. This mix of reinforcement and punishment in combination looks like intermittent reinforcement (i.e., sometimes reinforcing a behavior and sometimes not) *and* intermittent punishment (i.e., sometimes punishing a behavior and sometimes not). Not surprisingly, intermittent reinforcement actually strengthens the behavioral tendency even more because the recipient is never quite sure whether he or she will get the prize or not. Surprisingly, however, intermittent punishment actually strengthens the behavioral tendency as well, because the recipient is never quite sure whether he or she will get away with something or not. So unfortunately, although the functional partner is doing the best he or she can in terms of providing both loving and supportive behavior (i.e., nurturing) for the troubled spouse or child and trying to extinguish (i.e., controlling) the negative behavioral tendency, this nurturing behavior mixed with punishing control attempts actually results in strengthening of the behavioral compulsion. In other words, it is quite possible that functional family members may unknowingly perpetuate the undesired behavior through their nurturing (reinforcing) and controlling (punishing) attempts to decrease this same behavior. It is likely, then, that functional partners will use reinforcement of the compulsive behavior prior to labeling it a problem, increase the use of punishment of the compulsive behavior following the labeling of it as a problem, and revert to a mix of reinforcing and punishing behavior subsequent to frustration with his or her unsuccessful attempts.

An example from a couple with a substance-abusing member may be useful here. You all probably know a couple that includes a heavy drinker. Imagine that this steady-state drinker (someone who drinks heavily every day) is actually a better problem solver and more interpersonally involved when he or she is drinking. In fact, research supports that this in fact the case (Jacob & Leonard, 1988). A wife may therefore be motivated to make her husband a gin and tonic when he gets home because it will make him more pleasant, potentially more affectionate, and more willing to solve problems with her than had he not had the drink. In fact, she might even be motivated to join him with her own G&T. Both making him a G&T and drinking a G&T with him would be considered reinforcing the substance abuse. However, at some point it is likely that she will get fed up with the consequences of his drinking on their lives. He may disappear for awhile, get more aggressive or even violent, or get into trouble with the law. Eventually, her denial of his problem will be broken down, and she will admit he has a problem. This will result in the greater use of punishing strategies. She might hide his booze, lock him out of the house, threaten to leave him, stop having sex with him, and so on. When she eventually realizes that although she is a powerful in-control type of woman who has handled his substance abuse with aplomb, she is not, in fact, in control of his substance-abusive behavior. She might also be tired of nagging him constantly about the substance abuse. At this point, it is likely that the wife will revert to a mix of reinforcing and punishing behavior as she continues to love and support her husband while at the same time punishing his substance-abusive behavior. In other words, she will use inconsistent nurturing as control, presenting a mixture of reinforcing and punishing behaviors, both of which will serve to strengthen the substance abuser's tendencies to abuse substances. Such is the paradox the functional partner faces. She's doing the best she can to stop the compulsive behavior, but unfortunately this is having the opposite effect of what she intends. Let's see how this pattern of reinforcement and punishment plays itself out in research on substance abusers, daughters with eating disorders, and depressed individuals.

Application of INC Theory to Undesirable Behavior in the Family _____

Substance Abusers

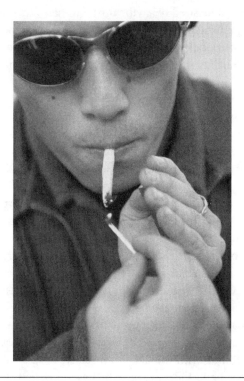

Figure 9.3   Parents' communication style can seriously affect how effective they are at diminishing their children's substance use and abuse.

Because this theory was first developed with substance abusers in mind, my colleagues and I use INC theory to examine how partners of substance abusers attempt to discourage the ongoing substance abuse of their partners. To do this, we interviewed substance abusers and their functional partners in their homes to attain self-reports of both substance abusers and their functional partners (Le Poire, Addis, Duggan, & Dailey, 2003; Le Poire & Cope,

1999; Le Poire, Erlandson, & Hallett, 1998; Le Poire, Hallett, & Erlandson, 2000). Using a timeline procedure, substance abusers and their partners both described behaviors that the partners of substance abusers used surrounding the substance abuse prior to labeling it a problem, subsequent to labeling the substance abuse a problem, and after they became frustrated with their initial attempts to curtail the behavior. Analyses show that partners typically cycle from reinforcing to punishing communication strategies following the labeling of their substance-abusive partners as substance abusive. In fact, the first test of INC theory logic hypothesizes and finds that functional partners change their strategy usage over time, such that (a) they reinforce substance-dependent behavior more before their determination that the behavior was problematic than after, (b) they punish substance-dependent behavior more after they labeled the drinking/drugging behavior as being problematic than before, and (c) in a postfrustration period, they employ a mix of reinforcing and punishing strategies, resulting in an overall pattern of inconsistent reinforcement and punishment (Le Poire et al., 1998). In other words, they might initially drink with their partner (reinforce), then kick their partner out (punish), and then let their partner back in (reinforce) with a strong warning that he or she will never be allowed to see the children again if the substance abusing continues (punish). This cycling is central to the inconsistent nature of reinforcing or punishing communication strategies as postulated by INC theory. Such cycling clearly supports the expected inconsistent nurturing as control communication pattern.

This inconsistent nurturing as control pattern is also supported by a qualitative analysis of the strategies used by functional partners of substance abusers (Le Poire et al., 2003). Functional partners use several macrolevel strategies that include both reinforcement and punishment. Specifically, functional partners report using verbal abuse, making rules pertaining to the addiction, punishment, getting a third party involved, threats, avoidance, ending the relationship, expressing personal feelings, withholding something from the partner as a punishment, supporting abuse by participation, demanding the partner stop and being highly active in attempting to diminish the substance abuse, and confronting. The use of these strategies approximates the hypothesized inconsistent and intermittent use of reinforcement and punishment of the substance abusive behavior.

My colleague Kirstie Cope and I (Le Poire & Cope, 1999) studied the subset of the substance-abusing sample dealing with alcoholics only. Given the research findings that steady drinking may provide more positive functioning for the family unit than the less predictable episodic drinking (e.g., Jacob & Leonard, 1988), we predicted that partners of episodic drinkers (drinkers who binge drink in unpredictable patterns) may be more motivated to stop the alcoholic behavior and thus may use more effective strategies than partners of steady drinkers (drinkers who consistently overindulge in alcohol on a daily basis). Contrary to the prediction, partners of episodic drinkers use less effective strategies (less consistency), whereas partners of steady drinkers use more effective strategies (greater reinforcement of alternative behavior) immediately following the alcoholism labeling. Following frustration with initially unsuccessful persuasive attempts, however, alcoholism subtypes operate as expected in that functional partners of episodic drinkers (afflict-eds) use more effective strategies (greater consistency combined with more punishment of drinking behavior) than do partners of steady drinkers (Le Poire & Cope, 1999).

Evidence of this patterning of strategy usage supports the contention that family members intermittently reinforce and punish the behavior they are trying to extinguish. Of further interest is the effectiveness of the strategies exhibited. Learning theory (Skinner, 1974) suggests that more consistent family members should be more effective in their influence attempts. We found that consistently punishing substance abuse combined with con-sistently reinforcing alternative behavior is predictive of lesser relapse in a substance-abusing sample. In other words, consistently punishing substance abusive behavior (e.g., withholding sex, threatening to leave) while also con-sistently encouraging substance abusers to engage in behaviors that don't include substance use (e.g., going to AA, hanging out with friends who don't abuse substances) is effective in diminishing substance abuse.

These patterns of strategy use and effectiveness also have implications for the mental health of functional family members continuing to live with part-ners with compulsive behavior. Consistent with research cited previously, we found that partners and spouses of substance abusers are less depressed when their partners relapse less (Le Poire & Cope, 1999). This is important for two reasons. First, partners of substance abusers (and partners with other com-pulsive behavioral issues) can assist their partners through consistent punish-ment of undesired behavior and reinforcement of alternative behavior. Second, partners can aid their own mental health in the process, because part-ners of more successfully recovering substance abusers were less depressed.

Children With Eating Disorders

Theoretical application of INC theory successfully applies to mothers of daughters with eating disorder as well. For instance, my colleague Margaret Prescott and I (Prescott & Le Poire, 2002) found that mothers of daughters with eating disorders display similar patterns of reinforcement and punish-ment. Mothers reinforce eating disorders more before they label the behavior problematic, and they punish the eating disorders more after labeling the behaviors. Results indicate that consistently reinforcing alternative behavior immediately following labeling of the eating disorder significantly predicts higher perceptions of the mother's persuasive effectiveness. Finally, reinforc-ing the eating disorder predicts greater amounts of relapse. To make this a bit clearer, a mother might compliment a daughter on her thinness and her ability to wear trendy clothing as she continues to lose weight (inadvertently reinforcing the eating disorder). Following the labeling of the eating disorder, however, she might try to encourage the daughter to join a singing group or some such activity that does not revolve around food (reinforcing alternative behavior). The most important implication of these findings is that significant family members (in this case, mothers) used similar patterns of inconsistent reinforcement and punishment to those used by partners of substance abusers.

Depression

INC theory can also guide research on functional partners living with depressed partners. Similar to the previous studies, Ashley Duggan (2003) found that functional partners of depressed individuals changed their strategy use over time, such that they reinforce the depression more before labeling it as problematic, punish the depression more after labeling it as problematic, and revert to a mix of punishing and reinforcing following frustration with their earlier attempts at diminishing the depressed behaviors. The depressed partners also report that when their partners used positive consistency (using positive reinforcement consistently) throughout the life span of their relationship, they are less depressed. Thus, inconsistency of the functional partner relates to poorer mental health outcomes for the depressed individual as well as for the functional partner. Duggan found that lesser reports of depression are related to greater positive consistency on the part of the functional partner. In other words, more reinforcement and less punishment relate to less depression in the depressed partner. Duggan also found greater mental health outcomes for both depressed and functional partners when functional partners use greater positive consistency.

Summary

In today's world, many families suffer from internal stress brought on by one member's compulsive behavioral tendencies. Today, more adults and children alike are suffering from substance abuse, eating disorders, and depression in the home. These issues create several communication challenges for families that include a member who exhibits problematic compulsive behavior. Specifically, *substance abuse* in the home results in *relational disturbances* (e.g., reduced intimacy and increased conflict) and *negative outcomes for children* (e.g., increased risk of substance abuse, low self-esteem, high anxiety). Families with members who have *eating disorders* face unique challenges in terms of *overly enmeshed relationships* with mothers, *modeling and negativity* from mothers, *disengaged fathers with idealized notions of thinness,* and *potential histories of sexual and family traumas* (i.e., greater family conflict). Families with a *depressed member* suffer from the *aversive communication patterns* of the depressed, *marital instability, low levels of cohesion and marital satisfaction*, and *potential negative outcomes for children*. Several theories attempt to explain the communication behavior in families that include one member with a behavioral compulsion. *Family systems theory* argues that families are interdependent and mutually influential to the extent that family members evidencing some behavioral compulsion are actually symptomatic of a larger underlying problem in the family. They also argue that family members may actually work against each other as they attempt to maintain balance in the family. *Coercion theory* argues that family members may present problematic family members with patterns of negative aversive communication behavior in an attempt to receive yielding or compliant behavior. Building on both perspectives, *inconsistent nurturing as control theory* attempts to understand the unique communication dynamics in families that include a member with an unhealthy behavioral compulsion such as substance abuse, eating disorders, and depression and argues that the paradoxes inherent in such a family relationship make it likely that the functional family members will use patterns of inconsistent reinforcement and inconsistent punishment surrounding the problematic behavior they desire to stop. This inconsistent nurturing as control is likely to lead to strengthening of the behavioral compulsion. Research on substance abusers, individuals with eating disorders, and depressed individuals and their family members shows that functional family members initially reinforce, then punish, then mix reinforcement and punishment surrounding the problematic behavior. This research also shows that consistently punishing the behavior combined with reinforcement of alternative behavior can be related to diminishment of the problematic behavior and the improved mental health of all family members.

KEY TERMS

anorexia

bulimia

coercion theory

consequence of eating disorders

consequences of depression

consequences of substance abuse

controlling

depression

effective communication strategies

family systems theory

inconsistent nurturing as control
   theory

inconsistent punishment

inconsistent reinforcement

nurturing

outcomes for families

paradoxes

punishment

reinforcement

substance abuse

substance dependence

substance use

QUESTIONS FOR APPLICATION

1. From your experiences of families affected by substance abuse, what are the negative consequences for marital partners and children of substance abusers? How does this relate to the literature on these effects?

2. What did your parents do to discourage substance use and abuse when you were younger? How effective was this strategy and why do you think it was or was not effective? Relate this back to the literature on what is more or less effective with adolescents.

3. Think of someone you know who may have an eating disorder. What family dynamics and communication surrounded this life-threatening pattern of behavior? How was his or her family communication similar to that discussed in the text?

4. Think of someone you know who is married and may be depressed. What are the negative consequences of depression for this person's marital partner and children? How is his or her marital satisfaction and marital communication related to the depression?

5. Can you think of relationships in your own life where you have observed inconsistent nurturing as an attempt to control? Describe inconsistent nurturing as control theory. What paradoxes exist in relationships that include one member with undesirable and stress-producing behavior? What patterns of nurturing and control are likely to manifest in this relationship? How do these patterns relate to reinforcement and punishment? What research support exists for this pattern across families that include a substance abusing member, a member with an eating disorder, or a depressed member? What can partners do to assist their family members with problematic behavioral compulsions?

_____ **Endnotes**

1. Although some would argue that depression differs from substance abuse and eating disorders in that a family member might attempt to change the behavior and the disorder itself, it is argued here that depressed individuals are as out of control of the behavior associated with their depression as are individuals who abuse substances or have eating disorders. They are all part of and based in a larger mental health issue.

2. Portions of this chapter were adapted from Le Poire (2004); Le Poire, Prescott, and Shepard (2004); Duggan and Le Poire (2004); and Le Poire and Dailey (2005). The author gratefully acknowledges the contributions and insights of her coauthors.

10

Family Communication: Providing Nurturing and Control in a Changing World

What We Have Learned

Almost all of us want to know how to "do" family communication now and in the future so that we may have the most satisfying family lives and communicative experiences. Many of us come from family situations that were highly satisfying, and we report feeling nurtured, loved, and supported. Some of us are less fortunate and come from families where we experienced high levels of control with less nurturing, and we were dissatisfied with our experiences. This book is based on the premise that regardless of family form (e.g., cohabiting couple; couples with no children; gay couples, with and without children; nuclear families; single-parent families; blended families; and extended families), nurturing and control are the two primary functions that family members provide one another through communication. Through *nurturing* communication, family members provide emotional support, physical sustenance, and developmental assistance to each other across a variety of domains (e.g., physical, socioemotional, intellectual). Simultaneously, family members frequently attempt to *control* one another's behavior in that parents discipline children, and marital partners, parents and children, and siblings engage in conflict to sway each other to their point of view or way of acting. The evidence provided in this textbook supports the fact that nurturance and control are evident across family forms in a variety of developmental phases, especially within communication domains (e.g., intimacy, conflict, violence, interpersonal influence). As such, each topic covered in this book should apply across family types when developmentally relevant. Such is the topic of the first section of this summarizing and concluding chapter: nurturing and controlling communication across our current configuration of families.

Although the concepts of nurturing and control gird the original framework associated with this book on family communication, several new premises about family communication were developed along the way. First and foremost, there is a definite link between *how you think, how you feel*, and *how you communicate* within families. In other words, *cognition, emotion,* and *communication* are linked in fundamental and important ways. Let me be more specific. With regard to **cognition**, your *perceptions, attributions*, and *expectations* provide the frame of reference within which communication episodes within the family occur. Powerful research has been presented here showing that regardless of the "facts," if you *perceive* your family member positively, you will be more satisfied in that relationship and your relationship will be more stable. Conversely, if you see your family member negatively, you will be less satisfied and your relationship is likely to be less stable. It is also likely that you communicate these perceptions to your family members and affect their communication behavior in that way. The most dramatic case in point is that the most severely abused women (in terms of frequency and severity) in intimate terrorism relationships *cognitively framed* their partners in positive ways and were reasonably well-satisfied in their relationships (e.g., Follingstad, Laughlin, Polek, Rutledge, & Hause, 1991). Remember that these severely abused women offered the most excuses for their batterer, attributed external reasons to the man's abuse, minimized the man's responsibility, and felt that no negative effects occurred from the abuse. This positive cognitive framing existed even though these women were frequently and severely abused by their partners. The result was a reasonably satisfying and stable relationship in that they also were able to list several reasons for staying in the relationship. The conclusion here must be that how you perceive your partner is more important than how he or she actually behaves and communicates. Such cognitive framing and its effects on family communication are the focus of the second half of this concluding chapter.

The Current Configuration of Families: Nurturing and Controlling Communication

The current review of the literature on family communication unequivocally supports the notion that nurturing and control are the two primary communicative functions that families, regardless of form, perform for their members. In traditional nuclear families (i.e., one stay-at-home mother, one working father, and biological children), mothers perform traditional sex-typed behavior in that they are the primary nurturers in the family. In other words, mothers continue to provide for the physical (i.e., food preparation, bathing, health maintenance, etc.), emotional (i.e., support and guidance), intellectual (i.e., academic), and social (i.e., friendship encouragement, sexual activity talks) development of their children. Fathers, on the other hand, are valued for their economic contributions to the family. In this way, they provide the resources necessary to allow the children's development to occur. This is evidenced by the fact that husbands are primarily evaluated on their economic potential (e.g., Xie, Raymo, Goyette, & Thornton, 2003), whereas wives are evaluated on factors central to child rearing (e.g., their ability to bear and raise children; Ben Hamida, Mineka, & Bailey, 1998).

Given the ever-changing nature of the family and the persistence of alternative family forms, we must not fail to recognize that these traditional gender roles are manifested in single-parent families, blended families, and families with gay heads of household as well. The fact that single-parent homes continue to be overwhelmingly headed primarily by females (84%) indicates the courts' and society's general recognition that the mother figure is primarily responsible for the *nurturance* of the children. Although many single head-of-household mothers are such because they never married (31%), the remaining mother heads of households are such because of court or familial decisions that the mother was best suited to provide the nurturing for the child. In further support of the male's traditional role of resource provider, unmarried males are expected to provide support for their children, especially in cases where biological paternity has been proven.

For blended and stepfamilies, evidence supports the role of mother *and* stepmother as nurturer as well. Remember that more single-father heads of household are likely to acquire a live-in mate of the opposite gender (33% compared with mothers' 11%). Stepmothers (or their cohabiting equivalents) are expected, more than stepfathers, to contribute to the household in nurturing ways similar to that of the biological mother. Research supports this role further; it indicates that stepmothers are more likely to step into parental monitoring than are stepfathers (e.g., Fisher, Leve, O'Leary, & Leve, 2003) and that biological fathers often rely on stepmothers in this regard (e.g., Fine, Voydanoff, & Donnelly, 1993). This indicates again a preference for females to be involved in the nurturing *and* the control of the children. Because of the social roles of women, stepmothers make attempts to become parental figures earlier than do stepfathers (Brand, Clingempeel, & Bowen-Woodward, 1988), which may account for higher ratings of children's closeness with stepmothers than with stepfathers (Sturgess, Dunn, & Davies, 2001). Further supporting the similarity to nuclear families in terms of nurturing and control, stepparents are very similar to parents in the frequency of private talks, help with homework, transporting children, and enforcement of rules (Mason, Harrison-Jay, Svare, & Wolfinger, 2002). Although there is less research here, research does support the contention that children raised in families with gay or lesbian heads of household develop academically and socially in line with their peers (Patterson, 1992). This indicates that the processes of nurturing and control in nuclear families operate similarly in blended families and families with gay heads of household.

Regardless of family form, many mothers are now reentering the workforce (74% by the time their children are 6 years of age). This workforce participation is in direct conflict with society's and family members' views that the mother is the primary nurturer in the family. Work takes away from time spent in domestic labor and time spent monitoring the activities of the children. To highlight the strength with which society views a mother's role as nurturer, many governmental and religious agencies as well as social science researchers underscore the importance of mothers' work in the home in terms of nurturing their children. Remember, for instance, that the 1996 Personal Responsibility and Work Opportunity Reconciliation Act was designed to increase marriage and reduce out-of-wedlock childbearing, especially among low-income families (Dunifon & Kowaleski-Jones, 2002; Lichter, Graefe, & Brown, 2003). The assumption of this program is that by increasing two-parent households, dependence on public assistance will diminish and children will be better off in a number of ways. In other words, the fathers can go out to work to provide the resources and the mothers can stay at home to nurture the children.

In further support of the mother as nurturer in the family, a number of political factions purport that the difficulties families and children are facing are primarily due to the rise of women in the labor force (Giele, 2003). For instance, the conservative explanation offered by the "new family advocates" argues that the breakdown in two-parent families, which is accompanied by divorce, out-of-wedlock births, and father absence, has put children at greater risk of school failure, unemployment, and antisocial behavior. Proponents of the explanation argue that the cure for these societal ailments is the return to religious faith and family commitment, which would, in essence, encourage mothers to stay at home with their children and fathers to go out and be the resource providers and heads of households. Ironically, such policies that have been put into place (e.g., Temporary Assistance for Needy Families; TANF) have resulted in an overwhelming return to the workforce by single mothers (and lesser reliance on public assistance programs) (Corcoran, Danziger, Kalil, & Seefeldt, 2000; Lichter & Graefe, 2001)—therefore resulting in a greater external focus as mothers work outside the home and rely on alternative sources of child care.

At the same time, mothers who do return to work have been criticized for failing to nurture their children adequately. Specifically, much social science research explores the ill effects of day care programs on children. In a famous example, Belsky's (1986) conclusion that early and extensive nonmaternal care increased the probability of insecure attachments to parents and promoted aggression and noncompliance among toddlers, preschoolers, and early primary schoolers was very controversial because of the pressure it put on working mothers (Belsky, 2001). Once again, the implication is that mothers are, and should be, the primary nurturers of children if we want to raise the most socioemotionally competent children.

Government and religion further delimit the role of mothers as nurturers in that the societal assumption that mothers are the best nurturers is limited to heterosexual mothers. Many lesbian and gay adults have been denied the opportunity to become foster or adoptive parents (Patterson, 1995; Ricketts, 1991; Ricketts & Achtenberg, 1990), and have had custody or visitation with biological children denied or curtailed primarily because of their homosexuality (Cain, 1993; Rivera, 1991). The link between a heterosexual woman and nurturing seems to be predicated on the inherent ability to physiologically produce children—but only if she is in a governmentally sanctioned relationship with a heterosexual man (who it is assumed will provide adequate financial support for the raising of the children). This assumption is evidenced in that 4 of 12 Dutch infertility treatment centers actually withheld infertility treatments from lesbian couples (Hunfeld, Fauser, de Beaufort, & Passchier, 2001) on the grounds that lesbian mothers are inadequate to nurture strong gender identities in their children (Falk, 1989; Green, 1992; Patterson, 1992). According to current courtroom decisions regarding custody and the right to raise children, fathers and lesbian mothers are inadequate nurturers of children. Thus, heterosexual mothers must be expected to carry out this role.

The fact that families nurture each other is not limited to families with children, however. In fact, cohabiting couples with no children appear to nurture each other in similar ways as do marital couples (Bumpass & Sweet, 1995). Furthermore, gay and lesbian couples with no children appear to go through similar relational processes of development as do heterosexual couples (e.g., West & Turner, 1995), and these processes include nurturing and control. In addition, married couples without children who are experiencing infertility issues appear to nurture and support each other through this process, which can be a trying time for couples (e.g., Brothers & Maddux,

2003; Fekkes et al., 2003). Nurturing and control, then, have been evidenced across family forms that do not include children.

The processes of nurturing and control are evident across developmental stages of family relationships as well. With specific regard to courtship, remember that couples first approach each other in very submissive ways and nurture each other through the earliest stages of courtship (e.g., Scheflen, 1965). In addition, as couples become increasingly close, they evidence conflict over interruption of each other's behavioral sequences (e.g., Solomon & Knobloch, 2001), which would seem to indicate some desire for control over each other's behavior. These processes of conflict and interpersonal influence are also evidenced during engagement (e.g., Kelly, Huston, & Cate, 1987) and marriage (e.g., Sillars, Canary, & Tafoya, 2004) and indicate that the processes of control are evident throughout the life span of the family.

Processes of nurturing and control are especially apparent at the stage of family development when children are added. At this point, couples struggle over issues of responsibility of domestic chores (e.g., Huston & Holmes, 2004). Ironically, these struggles for control often focus on issues concerning nurturing or child care responsibilities. These issues of nurturing and control become even more important in families with older children as parents now become authority figures for their children. Issues of nurturing (i.e., responsiveness) and control (i.e., demandingness) are central to perspectives on child rearing (e.g., Baumrind, 1996). Parenting styles and practices have actually been described as varying in nurturing and control, with *authoritarian* parents being high on control and low on nurturing, *permissive* parents being high on nurturing and low on control, and *authoritative* parents being high on both control and nurturing. Differential uses of these nurturing and controlling parenting styles have been associated with various outcomes for children, with the best outcomes being associated with parents who exhibit both high nurturing and high control (i.e., *authoritative parenting*). In addition, siblings have been known to nurture and protect each other in stepparent arrangements.

Within marriages, issues of nurturing and control are paramount to the marital satisfaction and stability of the couple. With regard to nurturing, married couples engage in varying degrees of closeness, which are related to marital satisfaction. Specifically, the extent to which couples self-disclose, display affection, are emotionally vulnerable, socially support one another, and nurture each other sexually have all been related to satisfaction and stability of the couple. Supportive communication in particular may be one of the resources associated with close personal relationships that diminish negative emotions and enhance health in part through their positive impact on immune and endocrine regulation (e.g., Kiecolt-Glaser, McGuire, Robles, & Glaser, 2002b). This may help account for the improved health of those in satisfying marital relationships (Gallo, Troxel, Matthews, & Kuller, 2003); women in highly satisfying marriages had lower levels of biological, lifestyle, and psychosocial risk factors compared with married women in unsatisfying relationships, cohabitants, and single women (single, divorced, or widowed). This interaction between satisfaction and marriage holds true for mental health as well. Married individuals reported the best overall mental health, but if their marriages were classified as unhappy, they actually had poorer mental health than never-married, divorced, or widowed individuals (Gove, Hughes, & Briggs Style, 1983).

On the other hand, how couples handle control and conflict is also related to marital satisfaction and stability. Couples who handle conflict in more nurturing ways (e.g., validators and couples who display five times more positive behavior than negative behavior) tend to be more satisfied and more stable in marriages. In addition, couples who have a tendency to nurture each other through conflict by making kinder attributions about their partner's behavior, tend to be more satisfied and stable as well (e.g., Bradbury & Fincham, 1992). These kinder attributions may translate into more positive communication behavior.

Control in families is particularly salient during violent episodes in families. One explanation for males' violent behavior in *intimate terrorism* type relationships is that they feel a lack of control. Specifically, violent males tend to enact violence when they feel not in control, threatened, and powerless in the family. This feeling of being not in control causes them to try to take control by being violent. Violence is not the only time that control is evident in families, however. Whenever a family member evidences an out-of-control behavioral compulsion, other family members try to step in and control, or stop, the out-of-control behavior. Inconsistent nurturing as control theory attempts to explain the processes of nurturing as control evident in families that include substance abusers, eating disordered individuals, and depressed individuals. It would appear that the processes surrounding behavioral compulsions in the family make it difficult for family members to exercise control over the members with the out-of-control behavior. Paradoxes that exist in these relationships result in inconsistent patterns of intermittent reinforcement and intermittent punishment surrounding the undesirable behavior.

Improving Family Communication

No doubt many of you became interested in taking a family communication course because you are interested in improving the communication within your family of origin or newly formed families. To that end, understanding the nurturing and controlling processes that exist across all family forms is useful in terms of understanding the explanatory mechanisms that underlie the effectiveness of your communication within the family. In addition, understanding the complexities of family communication also requires an appreciation of the cognitive, emotional, and communicative processes that underlie satisfaction and stability in the family. Families are emotionally rich

SOURCE: *Non Sequitur* © 2002 Wiley Miller. Distributed by Unviersal Press Syndicate. Reprinted with permission. All rights reserved.

environments that provide a fertile ground for understanding the relationship between how you feel and how you think about your family members. In turn, how you think and how you feel about your family members influences the ways in which you communicate with them. Specifically, many of the findings reviewed in this text underscore the importance of cognitive, emotive, and communicative processes in ensuring marital satisfaction and marital stability. Thinking and feeling positively about your family members is likely to be related to more positive communication within your family and stronger functioning in terms of family satisfaction and stability. On the other hand, thinking and feeling negatively about your family members is likely to be related to more negative communication within your family and greater marital distress (i.e., lower satisfaction and lower stability).

How you think about, feel about, and communicate with your family members are also likely predicated on factors related to your compatibility. In other words, you came into the family relationship with a greater or lesser likelihood of success. Remember as you form your new family unit that several factors promote greater satisfaction and stability within marital relationships. Several of these are **pre-interactional factors,** or factors that predate your family relationship. Factors that you and your mate bring into the relationship can significantly affect the quality of your family relationships. In sum (from Chapter 7), marital satisfaction has been related to *similarity* (socioeconomic status, religion, race, age, and intelligence), and *economic and personal resources* (greater income, higher education, social class, and better occupational status). In terms of characteristics that emerge after marriages, *marital couples' work* both inside and outside the home is related to marital satisfaction. To be more specific, *dual-earner* couples tend to be more satisfied especially if they *divide the household labor* in ways that are perceived as fair. Relatedly, *role fit* predicts relational satisfaction in that the level of agreement between spouses on decision making, division of household responsibilities, financial issues, and child care also predicts marital satisfaction. Finally, *developmental factors* regarding the natural progression of family life influence marital satisfaction in that the *presence of children* relates to decreases in marital satisfaction, with marital satisfaction appearing highest both before having kids and when the children are adults.

Although marital satisfaction and marital stability are not always related, many of you may also be concerned with how to have an *enduring* marriage. Statistics regarding the divorce rate are confusing, but we know that at least 30% of baby boomers report that they are divorced and that nearly half of all marriages every year are remarriages. Some estimates of divorce are as high as 50% (based on comparison of number of marriages with number of divorces per year). With one third to one half of marriages ending in divorce, many of you may be concerned that you have the ability to maintain a lifelong commitment to marriage. The relationship between the communication of closeness and marital satisfaction and marital stability may be of concern for you.

While all these factors are important because they predict marital satisfaction and marital stability and the communication processes inherent therein, the focus of this section is on the whole host of cognitive, affective, and communication factors that predict marital satisfaction and stability as well. How you perceive your partner and the attributions you make about his or her behavior can have powerful effects on the actual communication behavior that occurs within a family. In addition, how you feel about your family members can also color how you cognitively think about them. In other words, greater feelings of love and closeness are likely to be predicted by, and predict, more positive thinking about your partner. How you think and feel about your partner are likely to influence how you communicate with your family members, and how you communicate with your family members is likely to influence how they communicate with you. Thinking and feeling positively can have important ramifications for interpersonal communication within the family, as can thinking and feeling negatively.

How You Think Is What
You Feel: Or Perception Is Reality

If we have learned one thing together throughout this textbook, it is that cognition plays a powerful role in terms of determining communication behavior and ultimately improving family satisfaction and family stability. The literature is replete with examples of how family members who cognitively frame their communication partners (e.g., marital partners, parents, children, siblings) in positive ways have more satisfying and more stable relationships. Perhaps one of the most striking examples is marital couples who have been married for more than 40 years. These couples were able to maintain marital satisfaction and stability partially because of their ability to *positively distort their perception* of their marital partner (emphasizing positive traits and abilities over negative ones; Pearson, 1992). Remember that they also had *realistic and lowered expectations*. In other words, if you *think* that your partner is wonderful, then you will feel more positively about him or her and feel more satisfied in the relationship. You might remember that this is consistent with research showing that married couples who were more globally satisfied had both positive *and* negative perceptions of their spouse but were more likely to *weight the positive perceptions as more important than the negative perceptions* (Neff & Karney, 2003). Consistently, married couples were more satisfied and had more stable marriages when their partners held *idealized notions* of them (Murray, Holmes, & Griffin, 1996a, 1996b). Thus, positive framing is related to greater satisfaction and stability in marriages.

The Role of Perceptions in the
Successful Development of the Family

This positive framing influences outcomes during the developmental growth of the family as well. Think of the women trying to get pregnant in the face of infertility issues. Of these women, those who perceive their partners to be more supportive report that they also felt closer to their husbands (Pasch, Dunkel-Schetter, & Christensen, 2002). In addition, women who experienced more social support from their partners also had infants with higher birth weights (e.g., Feldman, Dunkel-Schetter, Sandman, & Wadhwa, 2000). Positive framing combined with supportive behavior can actually have positive physical health outcomes. Further illustrating the strength of perceptions, the *perception* that a marital partner is supportive was more important than the actual amount of support provided in terms of predicting marital satisfaction (Dunkel-Schetter & Bennett, 1990). In other words, the perception of the communication may be more important than the *actual* communication.

Also evidencing that the cognitive framing of an event is important during the development of the family, women with unplanned premarital pregnancies or births are more likely to end up divorced than are women who have babies well after they are married (e.g., Graefe & Lichter, 2002). In addition, remember the research showing that couples who became parents just shortly before or shortly after marriage are less satisfied than couples who become parents later in their marital life (Helms-Erikson, 1991). Consistently, Vangelisti and Huston (1994) found that mothers who had infants within 1 year of marriage showed the sharpest decline in satisfaction with the division of the household tasks and loss of leisure time activities. Mothers who had children between 1 and 2 years after marriage were less dissatisfied with the transition. Unplanned and early pregnancies are likely to be *perceived* in more negative ways than are planned pregnancies where women spend much time framing the birth of the baby as a significant and positive part of family life. This negative cognitive framing is likely to be responsible for the significant differences in satisfaction with the transition to parenthood and may even be related to greater marital instability.

Furthermore, *gender role expectations* can significantly influence the smoothness with which family members adapt to adding children to the family. Remember that women consistently do up to two thirds of the domestic child care tasks before they feel that this division of labor is unfair (e.g., Lennon & Rosenfield, 1994). Although *objectively,* the division of labor is unfairly split, the perceptions of the fairness of the family members is what make this division of labor work to establish well-satisfied and more stable unions. This can be attributable only to the role expectations that family members enter the family with. In other words, most couples *expect* that the woman will not only do the primary share of the child care and domestic chores even if she works (e.g., McHale & Huston, 1984; McHale, Bartko, Crouter, & Perry-Jenkins, 1990) but that she will do all this better than the husband (e.g., McHale & Huston, 1984). Remember also that the woman's perception that the division of labor is shared is more important than the actual division of labor in predicting her satisfaction (e.g., Ehrenberg, Gearing-Small, Hunter, & Small, 2001). In addition, mothers' perceptions that their husbands are good at family work actually predicted the amount of housework and child care the husband reports doing (Huston & Holmes, 2004). To fully round out this picture, fathers who perceive that the division of labor is unfair also report being more negative toward their wives and less in love with them (Crouter, Perry-Jenkins, Huston, & McHale, 1987). Thus, perceptions can be highly influential on communication and marital satisfaction and stability during the transition to parenthood.

Perceptions play a role not only in traditionally developing families (e.g., marriage then children) but can also have an impact in blended and stepfamily development as well. Specifically, children and parents in stepfamilies are likely to have divergent perceptions of a stepparent's role in parenting (Fine, Coleman, & Ganong, 1998; Fine, Kurdek, & Hennigen, 1992). These divergent perceptions may be partly responsible for stepfamilies experiencing higher rates of child-rearing conflict, lower levels of cohesion, higher levels of stress, and more problems in child adjustment than families in first marriages (Bray, 1988; Bray & Berger, 1993; Zill, Morrison, & Coiro, 1993). Most strikingly, reconstituted families (or blended families) who frame the development of their families in more positive ways (e.g., *accelerated blended* and *prolonged blended*) have more successful transitions to "feeling like a family" than families who expect to immediately approximate a nuclear family (e.g., *stagnating* and *turbulent blended families;* Braithwaite, Olson, Golish, Soukup, & Turman, 2001). Expectations surrounding roles and the transition to blended families can have powerful effects in terms of family satisfaction and feeling like a family.

The Role of Perceptions in Parent-Child Communication

Cognitive framing is also relevant to outcomes of parent-child interactions. The parenting styles of *authoritarian, permissive,* and *authoritative* can be thought of as cognitive mind-sets, or sets of beliefs on how to raise a child. Authoritarian parents believe that children's impulses need to be controlled through strict adherence to moral guidelines. As reviewed throughout this text, this framing leads to the parenting and communication practices of higher use of rules and lower use of warmth, which generally results in less positive outcomes for the children (e.g., poorer grades, lower self-esteem, greater levels of conflict with parents, more risky sexual behavior, more substance use and abuse).

Alternatively, permissive parents are highly accepting of their children's foibles and do little to try to curb their impulses (Baumrind, 1996). Their communication of low demandingness may be translated to lowered expectations about the child's ability to meet standards. They therefore create a warm and less controlling environment based on their beliefs about the nature of children. As seen throughout this text, the communication of these lower expectations of conduct for children creates generally negative outcomes in the form of poorer academic performance, lower self-esteem, higher conflict with parents over school-related outcomes, more risky sexual behavior, and greater substance use and abuse.

Finally, authoritative parents believe that children need to be guided to internalize standards of behavior through firm guidelines, which the child is encouraged to discuss (Baumrind, 1996). This cognitive framing of children results in the communication of high demandingness and high responsiveness from parents. In other words, how these parents think about their children affects the positivity or warmth they display to their child. As reviewed throughout this text, this positivity combined with high levels of control creates the most positive outcomes for children in terms of better academic performance, more intrinsic motivation, higher self-esteem, less risky sexual behavior, and less substance use and abuse.

A parent's cognitive framing affects not only disciplinary styles, communication, and outcomes but can also affect a child's approach to life. Cognitively and communicatively framing children's failures also helps them learn *mastery orientation*, or the ability to believe that they can be efficacious with regard to the tasks they face in their lives. Therefore, children who learn to frame their failure in positive ways (i.e., attributing successes to positive dispositional traits and failures to negative situational factors) are more likely to be successful. Students with mastery orientations are more confident, persistent, and focused in the face of unexpected difficulties and failure and are less likely to be deterred by critical feedback (e.g., Cain & Dweck, 1995; Strage & Brandt, 1999) compared with their *learned helplessness* peers. In addition, children's perceptions of their parents' expectations (Patrikako, 1997), aspirations, and support (Marjoribanks, 1997) are related to their own educational and career aspirations. Finally, mothers of 3- to 5-year-olds have a direct effect on their children's social competence through their framing of the child's interactions with their peers. Specifically, coaching in the form of resilient framing of negative peer events (i.e., guidance in and support of cooperative, nonconfrontational behavior) and endorsement of prosocial strategies was associated with lower aggression, greater social skills, and higher peer acceptance (Mize & Petit, 1997). Thus, mothers help their children cognitively frame their interactions with their peers in order to have the most socially competent communication outcomes.

In addition, *adolescents who perceive their parents in more positive ways* are likely to communicate in more open ways with their parents. For instance, children who perceive their parents to be more accepting are more likely to approach their parents for information regarding sexually risky behavior and birth control than are children who perceive their parents to be less accepting (Nathanson & Becker, 1986). In addition, closeness within the family has been linked to greater disclosure for adolescents in that adolescents who perceive the family environment as warm, nurturing, and uncritical are more likely to self-disclose to parents (e.g., Papini, Farmer, Clark, Micka, & Barnett, 1990; Searight, Thomas, Manley, & Ketterson, 1995). Not surprisingly and consistent with earlier research presented here, both sons and daughters perceive their mothers to be more responsive than their fathers, and both sons and daughters avoid more topics (such as sex and dangerous behavior) and are less open with their fathers (Golish & Caughlin, 2002; Guerrero & Afifi, 1995). Perception affects satisfaction, which ultimately affects the ongoing communication between parents and children.

As noted earlier (in Chapter 6), adolescents generally perceive communication with their parents less positively than their parents do. Mothers, for instance, often report greater warmth and affection among family members than do adolescent children (Noller & Callan, 1988; Silverberg & Steinberg, 1990). Furthermore, mothers tend to underestimate the degree of conflict in the parent-adolescent relationship and overestimate its severity (Steinberg, 2001) and the extent of conflict's negative repercussions (Silverberg &

Steinberg, 1990). This may indicate that adolescents have more maladaptive attributions regarding their parents and therefore might explain the greater negativity of their perceptions and their communication. In other words, adolescents' desire to individuate from their parents may promote their thinking about their parents in less positive ways. Mothers, alternatively, may have positive expectations that cause them to frame the conflicts with their adolescents in more positive ways but also cause them to be more worried about their negative ramifications.

The Role of Perceptions in Destructive Communication Patterns

Although the research mentioned in the introduction of this chapter highlighted the positive ways that *attributions* can counteract the effects of *actual behavior* on marital satisfaction and stability within violent (intimate terrorism) couples, it is also the case that the negative ways the violent partner perceives his spouse *regardless of her actual behavior* can lead to more violent outcomes. Remember that domestically violent men, compared with nonviolent men, are more likely to perceive their partner's behavior as threatening (Dugan, Umberson, & Anderson, 2001; Holtzworth-Monroe & Hutchinson, 1993). This perception of greater threat is irrespective of the actual objective content of the words and actions (Umberson, Williams, & Anderson, 2002). It is possible that these maladaptive attributions, or the tendency to interpret one's spouse's behavior negatively, may lead to violent behavior.

This is similar to the perceptual bias evidenced by physically abusive mothers. Remember that abusive mothers are more likely than nonabusive mothers to view their children's behavior as an intentional attempt to upset them (Bauer & Twentyman, 1985). In addition, they are likely to attribute their frustrating behavior to stable internal traits of the child (Larrance & Twentyman, 1983). Furthermore, the way the mother perceives the child's behavior in terms of complying with requests can have additional communicative effects. Abusive mothers fail to see their children's behavior as compliant even when it is and continue to make requests for compliance *after* the child has already complied (Oldershaw, Walters, & Hall, 1986). Once again, interpreting behavior in a negative way leads to negative communication outcomes in terms of continual requests for compliance and potentially in terms of the use of physical abuse.

These maladaptive attributions are evident not only in family members with a propensity for violence, however. How a person cognitively frames his or her partner during conflict episodes can also determine the constructive or destructive nature of conflict. Remember that distressed couples (or couples with less marital satisfaction and stability) are more likely to attribute the negative causes of conflict to their spouse and are more likely to emphasize their partner's negative behavior and de-emphasize their partner's positive behavior (e.g., Bradbury & Fincham, 1992). In addition, the familiarity in family relationships makes it more likely that family members in conflict will selectively perceive information to conform with existing ideas of the relationship (Sillars, 1998; Sillars, Roberts, Leonard, & Dun, 2000). Positive frames cause family members to seek out positive confirming information, and negative frames cause family members to seek out confirming negative information. Perceptual biases serve as powerful frames for affecting the outcomes of conflict. Relatedly, partners in conflict are most likely to perceive their partner's hostile behavior accurately (compared with the partner's loving behavior) and are thus more likely to reciprocate negative behavior over positive behavior (see Sillars, Canary, & Tafoya, 2004, for review).

Conflicts often include hurtful messages. Furthermore, the *perceived intentionality* of hurtful messages can influence the effect of hurtful messages within a family. Remember that hurtful messages are more hurtful from family as opposed to nonfamily members (Vangelisti & Crumley, 1998) and that individuals who perceive a message to be intentionally hurtful reported that the hurtful message had more of a distancing effect on the relationship than those who perceived that the hurtful message was unintentional (Vangelisti & Young, 2000). They also reported less relationship satisfaction and closeness in the relationship. Thus, in line with attributions during conflict, perceptions of intentionality can actually increase the negative effects of communication.

How You Communicate Is What You Get: Or the Golden Rule of Communication

Although the previous review of the literature on cognitive framing and family satisfaction and family stability clearly emphasizes the role of perceptions, attributions, and expectations in family processes, it is also the case that communication behavior is frequently an outcome of these cognitive (and affective) processes. Moreover, communication, in and of itself, is a powerful agent in families. The power of reciprocation is most evidenced within the actual communication behavior of family members. In other words, the *golden rule of communication* is that what goes around comes around, or you get as good as you give. Not all that surprisingly, in general, positive family communication is met with positive family communication, whereas negative family communication is met with negative family communication. The conflict literature provides the strongest evidence here in that the four horsemen of the apocalypse (i.e., criticism, contempt, defensiveness, and stonewalling) are likely to be met with more of the same from the other partner (Gottman, 1993, 1994). The conflict literature is replete with examples of runaway escalations of conflict, with negative communication behavior escalating and elevating conflict to the next destructive level. Remember the demand-withdraw pattern of conflict in which the wife's demands (relatively negative communication behavior) lead to the husband's withdrawal (an equally negative communication behavior; Caughlin & Vangelisti, 1999).

Alternatively, the interpersonal influence literature evidences that positive attempts at interpersonal influence in marital relationships (i.e., content validation, other support, and self-assertions) were met with similarly positive behaviors from one's partner (e.g., Newton & Burgoon, 1990). Similarly, *matching* on the conflict styles of *avoiders, volatiles,* and *validators* and their ensuing communication behaviors has been associated with both marital satisfaction and marital stability (e.g., Gottman & Levenson, 1988). Furthermore, matching on romantic attachment styles also results in reciprocation of nonverbal involvement behaviors (e.g., Le Poire, Dailey, Duggan, & Moloney, 2004).

Gottman and Levenson (1992) indicate that *actual communication* behavior is important to predicting marital satisfaction and stability. They argue based on numerous behavioral investigations that successful marriages have a 5:1 ratio in terms of positive to negative behaviors. They find that couples who display more positivity than negativity when they speak to each other are more satisfied, less likely to think about divorce, less likely to separate, and less likely to divorce. This is especially important to marriages in which one or both partners are distressed (i.e., less satisfied). Individuals in distressed relationships tend to display more negative affect, less positive affect, and more reciprocity of negative affect (e.g., Noller, 1984). Interestingly, wives are more likely than husbands to reciprocate the negative communication behavior of their spouses (Notarius & Pellegrini, 1987). In turn, negative communication behaviors are the most predictive of marital satisfaction (e.g., Gottman & Levenson, 1986; Huston & Vangelisti, 1991), with negative communication behaviors being more predictive of marital satisfaction than positive communication behaviors (e.g., Broderick & O'Leary, 1986). This is the case even though happier partners display more positive communication behaviors than unhappy partners (e.g., Cutrona, 1996).

This pattern of reciprocated negativity is also obvious in families that include a depressed member. Depressed individuals make more negative statements about themselves and their partners (Vettese & Mongrain, 2000), and their partners reciprocate with more negative feedback (Segrin & Dillard, 1991; Vettese & Mongrain, 2000). Unfortunately, this may exacerbate depressive symptoms (Coyne, 1976) because depressed people are aware of rejection and internalize the negative mood state further when negative interpersonal feedback occurs (Segrin, 1993b). Thus, depressed individuals may negatively affect others through their aversive communication (Strack & Coyne, 1983) and ultimately may reinforce their own depression through the responses others have to them. There may be a sort of contagion effect operating whereby depressed individuals share their mood by communicating negatively with those to whom they are closest. With

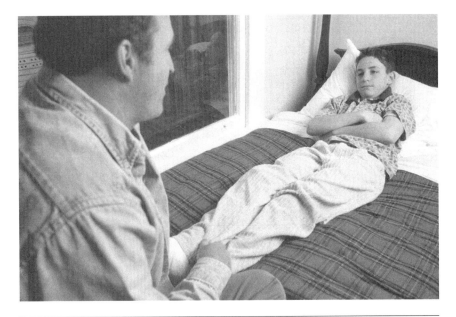

Figure 10.1   The most powerful predictor of communication is reciprocity: Members of families often match the negativity they receive from others.

specific regard for marital satisfaction, those married individuals with low-level depression are found to be more reactive to stress within marriage and accompanying changes in marital satisfaction and stability (Beach & O'Leary, 1993). Depression in one partner, therefore, can have a strong effect on marital satisfaction and communication for both partners. It is also possible that low marital satisfaction can *predict* depression and the accompanying negativity of communication behavior.

Like most relationships, family relationships display a strong tendency for communication reciprocity (e.g., interaction adaptation theory; Burgoon, Dillman, & Stern, 1993; Burgoon, Stern, & Dillman, 1995). In other words, positive communication is met with positive communication, and negative communication is met with negative communication. A strong contagion effect appears to operate in families, in that family members have a strong tendency to match the communication behaviors exhibited by their family members. This reciprocity seems just as likely for positive communication behavior (e.g., intimacy, support, expressiveness) as for negative communication (e.g., hostility, contempt, disgust). However, negative behavior appears to have more long-term effects in terms of affecting marital satisfaction and stability. The bottom line here is that if you want more positive communication in your family, you must communicate more positively to increase the probability that reciprocity of your positive communication occurs.

Figure 10.2   Reciprocity of positive communication is common; couples tend to reinforce each other's inclinations to be pleasant with one another.

Summary

Although family forms are increasingly complex in our society, the research presented throughout this textbook on family communication supports the claim that families are united through the processes of *relatedness, nurturing,* and *control.* Relatedness (biological, legal, and marriage-like commitments), nurturing, and control continue to define our families as families regardless of family form (e.g., *cohabiting couples; couples with no children; gay couples, with and without children; nuclear families; single-parent families; blended families;* and *extended families*). In sum, besides evidencing relatedness (biological, legal, or marriage-like commitments), family members across all family types enact nurturing and control within their families. Marital partners, cohabiting couples, gay couples, and couples without children all nurture and control each other in positive and negative ways. The addition of children to a family makes nurturing and control especially evident as parents provide nurturing child care and adequate levels of control to raise socioemotionally competent children. In fact, many governmental and religious agencies particularly support the role of mother as nurturer. Nurturing and control are also evidenced across the developmental life span of the family in that newly forming relationships use nurturing to entice each other and evidence control at tricky turning points in the relationship. In general, nurturing is especially apparent in the communication of closeness in the family (e.g., self-disclosure, expression of affection, emotional regulation, social support, and sexual intimacy), whereas control is more evidenced through disciplinary encounters, conflict, interpersonal influence, and violence. Control becomes especially apparent in families that include problematic members in that the use of inconsistent nurturing as control surrounding substance abuse, eating disorders, and depression (and the like) make it less likely that family members are effective at diminishing the undesirable behavior. It is therefore evident that nurturing and control can provide a unifying defining theme across the various and diverse family forms that exist in our society today.

Several principles regarding family communication become apparent from this review of family forms, theories of family communication, courtship rituals, marriage, adding children, raising children, intimacy, conflict, violence, and inconsistent nurturing as control in families. Specifically, *how you think is what you feel* (or perception is reality) and *reciprocation of communication* (or the golden rule of communication) operates in families. Cognitive processes are powerful in terms of determining perceptual biases in family relationships. Family satisfaction and stability are predicted by, and/or predict, positive perceptual biases in relationships across marital relationships, cohabiting relationships, gay relationships, parent-child relationships, and sibling relationships. In sum, cognitive framing can have significant effects on the communicative processes in the family. Marital couples who display positive distortion, or the tendency to weight positive information more heavily than negative information, are more satisfied, and their relationships are more stable. This is evidenced across positive intimacy behaviors, supportive behaviors, and conflict behaviors. This pattern holds for families as they develop as well; positive framing and perceived support can enhance family functioning during infertility treatment and the addition of children to the family, for example. Furthermore, the communication of expectations to children in terms of parenting styles can influence important developmental processes of children. In addition, children who perceive their parents more positively are more likely to report being closer to them and are more likely to approach them in critical times (e.g., when they need birth control information). On the flip side, maladaptive negative attributions are likely to contribute to negative outcomes associated with conflict, spousal abuse, and child abuse. In conclusion, how you feel and think about your family members can have well-substantiated effects on how you communicate with them and on how satisfied you are in the family relationship.

These perceptual biases have strong effects on the communication behavior evidenced in families. Thinking and feeling positively results in greater positive communication, whereas thinking and feeling negatively results in greater negative communication. In turn, this communication behavior has strong impacts on subsequent communication. In other words, there is a powerful tendency for communicators within families to reciprocate the communication behavior they receive. Positive communication behavior is more likely to be met with more positive communication, and negative communication is more likely to be met with more negative communication. Thus, in families, thinking and communicating positively predicts more satisfying and more stable family relationships in that more positive evaluations and more positive communication behavior is likely to result and to be reciprocated.

KEY TERMS

attributional biases   perceptual biases
communication reciprocity   positive distortion
control   relatedness
nurturing

QUESTIONS FOR APPLICATION

1. In what ways do nurturing and control operate in your family? How do you suspect that nurturing and control in your family differ from other family forms? How is nurturing and control evidenced in married couples, cohabiting couples with no children, and gay couples? How is nurturing and control evidenced in families that add children? How does nurturing and control operate within parent-child relationships?

2. Think of examples when the ways in which you were thinking about your family members affected how you communicated with them. How is this consistent with the evidence that exists to support the claim that cognitive framing determines communicative outcomes and marital satisfaction and marital stability?

3. In your own or your friends' experiences, what are the effects of cognitive framing on communication outcomes evident in developing families (e.g., families adding children and blended families)? How did the use of cognitive framing affect communication outcomes in your own relationship with your parent(s)?

4. Think of a recent conflict you have had with someone in your family. In what ways were the effects of negative cognitive framing evident during this conflict? If you are aware of violence in a relationship, in what ways are the effects of negative cognitive framing evident within that relationship?

5. Give examples of times when you communicated more or less positively in your family relationships. How did this affect how your family members communicated with you? In what ways was your own positive communication reciprocated? In what ways was your own negative communication reciprocated? Were the effects of negative reciprocity of communication behavior stronger than the effects of positive reciprocity on communication outcomes?

Glossary

abandonment fear: the level of anxiety one experiences about potentially being left by one's relationship partner.

anorexia: characterized by extreme fasting, a refusal to maintain a normal body weight, an intense fear of gaining weight, and a significant disturbance in one's body evaluation.

anxious-ambivalent attachment (parental): has low trust in others and feels negatively about self.

artifacts: communication through the use of physical objects.

attachment style: a working model or orientation toward bonding in relationships.

attention-gaining cues: aimed at increasing the recognition and interest of others.

attraction: forces that pull two interacts toward one another.

attributed communication: where the receiver attributed communicative intent where there was none.

authoritarian parent: positioned at the intersection of high demandingness/control and low responsiveness/warmth; overtly attempts to shape, control and evaluate the behavior of the child in accordance with an absolute standard of conduct from some higher authority (e.g., religion).

authoritative parent: attempts to be both nurturing and warm (*responsive*) and highly controlling *(demanding)* of has or her children's behavior.

autonomy: having an independent sense of self, directing one's own behavior, controlling one's own activities.

avoidant attachments (parental): has low trust in others and feels positive about self.

back stage: where one does not feel the pressure to perform a primary role.

battered woman's syndrome/learned helplessness: women in violent relationships feel that they are responsible for the abuse they receive and that they are unable to do anything about it.

behavior: actions that were not intended to communicate and no intention was perceived.

behavior control: setting guidelines and disciplining.

binuclear families: families in which children share their time relatively equally between their mother and stepfather's and father and stepmother's houses.

biological ties: genetic links between family members.

blended families: families that include legal-only (e.g., stepparents), biological only (e.g., parents) and some biological-legal (e.g., half-siblings) relationships.

boundary maintenance: deciding who is in or out of one's family circle.

bulimia: involves cycles of binge eating, followed by compensatory purging behaviors to prevent weight gain.

chronemics: communication through the use of time.

climate: the pleasantness or unpleasantness of interactions typically set by the nature of the nonverbal and verbal communication used.

closeness: refers to psychological distance in the relationship, with couples experiencing closeness feeling less psychologically distant from one another and couples not experiencing closeness feeling greater psychological distance from their partners.

coercive communication model: argues that the batterer is attempting to coerce his/her partner and when attempts fail, violence occurs.

cognitions: thoughts—includes perceptions, attributions, evaluations, and expectations.

cohabiting couples: opposite-sex partners living together but are not married.

cohabitating parent: a parent who is now cohabitating but not married.

communication attempts: communication where the sender intended to send a message but it was not received.

communication: messages that are typically sent with intent between two or more persons, messages that are typically seen as intentional, and messages that have consensually shared meaning.

communicative intent: the goal to send a message.

competence: ability to complete tasks well.

complementary roles: roles with behaviors that help facilitate the opposite role (e.g., nurturer vs. resource provider).

conflict: "struggle between at least two interdependent parties who perceive incompatible goals, scarce rewards, and interference from the other parties in achieving their goals" (Hocker & Wilmot, 2000, p. 9).

conflict interaction: the interpersonal influence strategies, tactics, and communication patterns that individuals use during the conflict itself.

conservative explanation for family "decline":   argues that the breakdown in two-parent families, which is accompanied by divorce, out-of-wedlock births, and father absence, has put children at greater risk of school failure, unemployment, and antisocial behavior.

constructive conflict: conflict that builds on the strengths of the relationship (i.e., enhances closeness, increases understanding, results in a net gain in positive feelings).

contempt: expressions of extremely negative affect toward a partner; often includes psychological abuse and intentional insults.

content invalidation: conflict strategies that reject the arguments put forth by the other.

content validation: conflict strategies that accept the arguments put forth by the other.

contradiction: refers to the unity of opposites in that two concepts are wed together at the same time that they compete with, or diminish, one another.

control: communication that guides, influences, and limits the types of behaviors evidenced by family members.

control (theory function):   help to control outcomes.

criticism: negative evaluations and attacks on the partner's behavior and personality.

decision making: choosing among options available to the family.

Defense of Marriage Act: gives all states the right to refuse recognition of same-sex marriages from *other* states and defines marriage as heterosexual unions for federal law purposes.

defensiveness: self-justification of behavior in an attempt to maintain one's sense of self.

depression: can result in feelings of hopelessness, guilt, loss of interest in previously enjoyable activities (including sex), and decreased energy or fatigue.

describe (theory function):   answer the "what?" question.

destructive conflict: conflict that is damaging to the relationship (e.g., results in hurt, reduces closeness, damages trust).

developer: in charge of ensuring growth and development as a human across physical, social, emotional, and intellectual realms.

dialectic model: explains how partners vacillate through periods of closeness and distance in relationships.

distal context: the more historical factors that predict conflict.

distal outcomes: the long-term consequences of the conflict that are either removed or delayed.

emotional bids: a marital partner's direct or indirect request for attention, interest, conversation or emotional support.

emotional development: growth with regard to appropriate rules and expressions for various emotions.

evolutionary psychology: individuals are assumed to select partners who will enable their reproductive success and promote survival of their offspring.

explain (theory function):   answer the "why" question.

extended families: families that include grandparents in residence.

family communication: messages that are typically sent with intent, that are typically perceived as intentional, and that have consensually shared meaning among individuals who are related biologically, legally, or through marriage-like commitments and who nurture and control each other.

family of origin: the family in which one grows up.

family of procreation: a newly formed family.

family systems theory: attempts to explain the communication between family members as a function of the systems theory concepts of interdependence, balance, equifinality, and wholeness.

fearful (romantic):   individuals who avoid relationships because they do not trust others and do not believe they are worthy of love.

feedback: evaluative responses to performances.

feminist view of family change: supports the family as an institution, but it also has an appreciation for modernity.

financial organization: managing the funds available to the family.

front stage: where a role is performed.

frustration-aggression model: argues that when batterers become frustrated, this frustration gets channeled into violence.

gay couples with children: same-sex couples (lesbians or gays) who are committed to one another with the same level of commitment as married individuals and assume the role of parent (*nurturer/controllers*) to at least one child.

haptics: communication through the use of touch.

health care provider: maintains family members' health through arranging for doctors' visits, applying bandages, dispensing medicine, and the like.

homeostasis: emphasizes the balance that families attempt to achieve as they set about attaining goals such as well-raised children, social and emotional well-being, family satisfaction.

INC (inconsistent nurturing as control) theory: argues that families that include a member who is out of control in terms of some undesirable behavioral tendency or another (e.g., drinking, eating disorder, gambling, violence, sex addiction), use *nurturing as a way to control* their family members.

inconsistent nurturing as control theory: attempts to understand the paradoxes in a relationship that make it difficult for partners to assist their partners through substance abuse, eating disorders, depression, and violence.

infertility: inability to conceive after 12 months of regular unprotected intercourse.

information: anything that reduces uncertainty.

inputs: include the quantity and the difficulty level of the information a child is expected to understand.

intellectual development: growth with regard to learning.

interdependence: intricate and necessary interrelationships of family members; family members rely on one another to promote the functioning of the family.

interpersonal model: argues that violence does not begin in all relationships with the batterer because the partner in this case provokes the violence.

interrole conflict: when the performance of one role interferes with the performance of another role.

intimacy fear: anxiety level one experiences regarding being smothered by one's relational partner's demands for closeness.

kinesics: overall use of the body, including gestures and posture, to communicate.

learned hopefulness: argues that women may stay in violent relationships because they are hopeful that their partner will eventually change his violent behavior.

legal ties: connections among family members that are based on laws.

liberal analysis of family change: argues that the negative effects of family change are the result of economic and structural changes that have placed new demands on the family while failing to provide necessary social supports.

logical consequences: related to outcomes associated with a behavior but not naturally occurring.

marital type: *Traditionals* hold conventional values, value stability over spontaneity, and are highly interdependent. *Independents* hold unconventional values, including that marriage should not constrain individual freedoms. *Separates* hold the viewpoint both of the traditional and the independent couples in that they have conventional values and value stability over spontaneity, but they do not believe in a high amount of interdependence among the couple.

married couple with no children: two opposite-sex individuals who have legalized their commitment to one another through the bonds of marriage but who have no children.

naive theory of affection: siblings perceive the affection that parents have as a finite resource that must be competed for.

natural consequences: the direct and contingent effects of a behavior.

negative strategies: content invalidation, other accusations, and self-defense\.

nuclear: with two parents, who may or may not be working outside the home, and children residing together.

nurture, nurturing: both verbal and nonverbal behaviors that are encouraging and supportive; encouraging physical, social, emotional, and intellectual growth.

other accusations: conflict strategies that invalidate and disconfirm the other through attempts to negate the other.

other support: conflict strategies that validate and confirm the other through acknowledgement, recognition, and endorsement.

outputs: include the number of, and level of sophistication of, the products that are completed by the child.

paradox: contains two consistent premises that contradict the logical conclusion.

parenting practices: patterns of communication behavior parents use to enact parenting styles, specifically aimed at guiding the development of the child.

parenting styles: patterns of responsiveness (high or low) and demandingness (high or low) that parents adopt in their interactions with their children.

performance expert: people to consult for advice about performing a particular role.

performances: all behaviors associated with a particular role.

permissive parent: positioned at the intersection of high responsiveness/warmth and low demandingness/control; behaves in nonpunitive, accepting, and affirmative ways toward their child's actions, impulses, and desires.

physical growth and development: bodily development.

positioning for courtship: Placing one's body in relation to significant others in order to exclude others.

positive strategies: content validation, other support, self-assertions.

predict (theory function): answer the "how?" question.

pre-interactional factors: factors that predate your family relationship.

preoccupied (romantic): a person is preoccupied with others to determine his or her own sense of self-worth.

provider: supplies the resources required to allow for the types of activities necessary to encourage growth and development; in charge of provision of resources, supplies the money, food, clothes and other durable items that maintain the household.

proximal context: the more immediate factors preceding the conflict episode; goals, rules, emotions, and attributions that individuals make immediately prior to the conflict.

proximal outcomes: the immediate consequences or results of the conflict.

proximity: communication through the use of space.

punishment: the presentation of aversive stimuli in contingent response to behaviors a parent wishes to eliminate.

racial and ethnic endogamy: the tendency to marry within a group.

receiver orientation: the receiver's perception of intent is more important than the source's intent to communicate.

reciprocal roles: reciprocal role holders alternate complementary tasks so that each is performing only one role at a time.

recognition or courtship readiness: indicates the communicator's interest and availability.

relatedness: biological, legal, or marriage-like commitment.

resolution: final stage of courtship, which includes sexual intercourse.

role expectations: anticipated behaviors associated with a particular role.

role reversed (parental): expected to give care to their caregivers.

role strain: when one either feels uncomfortable with one's role or does not entirely know how to enact the behaviors associated with one's roles.

roles: various positions we hold in relation to others.

roles theory: assumes that the roles one holds are powerful dictators of the behaviors one enacts.

rule: "a followable prescription that indicates what behavior is obligated, preferred, and prohibited" (Shimanoff, 1980, p. 57).

rules theory: attempts to explain the rules—verbal and nonverbal—in communication.

satisfying marriages: marriages that partners evaluate positively.

secure attachment: has high trust in others and feels positive about self.

self-assertions: conflict strategies that validate or promote the self.

self-defense: conflict strategies that excuse or justify one's behavior.

sender orientation: the source's intent to communicate is more important than the receiver's perception of intent.

similarity hypothesis: Individuals have a strong desire to communicate with and be with other individuals whom they see as similar.

single-parent homes: where children live with and are cared for by one parent only.

skills deficits models: argue that violent partners lack the communication skills to deal with conflict, and thus, violence occurs.

social development: becoming a socioemotionally competent communicator.

social exchange theory: individuals consider the potential rewards of the relationship relative to its potential costs.

social penetration theory: individuals in relationship development go through various communication phases, or stages, in their movement toward greater relationship stability.

stable marriages: marriages that endure and do not end in divorce.

stepfamilies: families that include some legal and some biological connectedness.

stonewalling: responding to an onslaught of negative affect with withdrawal and flat facial affect.

symmetrical roles: When two members of the same family perform the same role.

true communication: the sender intended to send a message and the receiver perceived the intention of the communication.

uncertainty reduction theory: predicts that the uncertainty associated with early stages of a relationship prompts increases in information gathering.

vocalics: communication through the use of voice.

wholeness: "the sum of the whole is greater than the individual parts" (from family systems theory).

wings: those areas where role holders prepare for their roles.

working models: schemas about relationships.

References

Afifi, T. D., & Keith, S. (2004). A risk and resiliency model of ambiguous loss in post-divorce stepfamilies. *Journal of Family Communication, 4,* 65–98.

Afifi, T. D., & Schrodt, P. (2003). "Feeling caught" as a mediator of adolescents' and young adults' avoidance and satisfaction with their parents in divorced and non-divorced households. *Communication Monographs, 70,* 142–173.

Afifi, W. A., & Metts, S. (1998). Characteristics and consequences of expectation violations in close relationships. *Journal of Social and Personal Relationships, 15,* 365–393.

Ainsworth, M. D. S. (1991). Attachments and other affectional bonds across the life cycle. In C. M. Parkes, J. Stevenson-Hinde, & P. Marris (Eds.), *Attachment across the life cycle* (pp. 33–51). New York: Tavistock/Routledge.

Alan Guttmacher Institute. (1999). Teenage pregnancy: Overall trends and state-by-state information, 1999. In *U.S. Teenage pregnancy statistics with comparative statistics for women aged 20–24* (p. 5). New York: Author.

Albrecht, T. L., Burleson, B. R., & Goldsmith, D. J. (1994). Supportive communication. In M. L. Knapp & G. R. Miller (Eds.), *Handbook of interpersonal communication* (2nd ed., pp. 419–449). Thousand Oaks, CA: Sage.

Allen, J. G., & Haccoun, D. M. (1976). Sex differences in emotionality: A multidimensional approach. *Human Relations, 8,* 711–722.

Allen, S. M., & Hawkins, A. J. (1999). Maternal gatekeeping: Mothers' beliefs and behaviors that inhibit greater father involvement in family work. *Journal of Marriage and the Family, 61,* 199–212.

Altman, I., & Taylor, D. A. (1973). *Social penetration: The development of interpersonal relationships.* New York: Holt, Rinehart & Winston.

Altman, I., Vinsel, A., & Brown, B. B. (1981). Dialectic conceptions in social psychology: An application to social penetration and privacy regulation. *Advances in Experimental Social Psychology, 14,* 107–160.

Alwin, D. F., Converse, P. E., & Martin, S. S. (1985). Living arrangements and social integration. *Journal of Marriage and the Family, 47,* 319–334.

Amanat, E., & Butler, C. (1984). Oppressive behaviors in the families of depressed children. *Family Therapy, 11,* 65–77.

Amato, P. R. (1986). Father involvement and the self-esteem of children and adolescents, *Australian Journal of Sex, Marriage & Family, 7,* 6–16.

Amato, P. R. (1989). Family processes and the competence of adolescent and primary school children. *Journal of Youth and Adolescence, 18,* 39–53.

American Law Institute. (2000). *Principles of the law of family dissolution: Analysis and recommendations* (Tentative Draft No. 4.). Philadelphia: Author.

American Psychiatric Association Work Group on Eating Disorders. (2000). Practice guideline for the treatment of patients with eating disorders (revision). *American Journal of Psychiatry, 157,* 1–39.

American Psychological Association. (1996). *Violence and the family: Report of the American Psychological Association Presidential Task Force on Violence and the Family*. Washington, DC: Author.

Anderson, E. R., & Rice, A. M. (1992). Sibling relationships during remarriage. *Coping with marital transitions: A family systems perspective. Monographs for the Society for Research in Child Development, 57*(2–3, Serial No. 227).

Anderson, K. L., Umberson, D., & Elliott, S. (2004). Violence and abuse in families. In A. L. Vangelisti (Ed.), *Handbook of family communication* (pp. 629–645). Thousand Oaks, CA: Sage.

Anderson, K. M., Sharpe, M., Rattray, A., & Irvine, D. S. (2003). Distress and concerns in couples referred to a specialist infertility clinic. *Journal of Psychosomatic Research, 54*, 353–355.

Angrist, S. S., & Almquist, E. M. (1993). The Carnegie Mellon class of 1968: Families, careers, and contingencies. In K. D. Hulbert & D. T. Schuster (Eds.), *Women's lives through time: Educated American women of the twentieth century* (Jossey-Bass Social and Behavioral Science Series and Jossey-Bass Higher and Adult Education Series, pp. 282–300). San Francisco: Jossey-Bass.

Antill, J. K., Goodnow, J. J., Russell, G., & Cotton, S. (1996). The influence of parents and family context on children's involvement in household tasks. *Sex Roles: A Journal of Research, 34*, 215–236.

Arendell, T. (1996). *Co-parenting: A review of the literature*. Philadelphia, PA: National Center on Fathers and Families.

Arnold, K. D. (1993). Undergraduate aspirations and career outcomes of academically talented women: A discriminant analysis. *Roeper Review, 15*, 169–175.

Aune, K. S., Aune, R. K., & Buller, D. G. (1994). The experience, expression, and perceived appropriateness of emotions across levels of relationship development. *Journal of Social Psychology, 134*, 141–150.

Australian Bureau of Statistics. (1999). Census 96: Customized Matrix Tables.

Babcock, J. C., Waltz, J., Jacobson, N. S., & Gottman, J. M. (1993). Power and violence: The relation between communication patterns, power discrepancies, and domestic violence. *Journal of Consulting and Clinical Psychology, 61*, 40–50.

Bachman, R., & Saltzman, L. E. (1996). *Violence against women* (NCJ No. 154348). Rockville, MD: U.S. Department of Justice.

Bachu, A., & O'Connell, M. (2001). *Fertility of American women: June 2000* (Current Population Reports, P20–543RV). Washington, DC: U.S. Bureau of the Census.

Baetens, P., & Brewaeys, A. (2001). Lesbian couples requesting donor insemination: An update of the knowledge with regard to lesbian mother families. *Human Reproduction Update, 7*, 512–519.

Bagarozzi, D. A., & Giddings, C. W. (1983). Conjugal violence: A critical review of the current research and clinical practices. *American Journal of Family Therapy, 11*, 3–15.

Bank, S., & Kahn, N. (1982). *The sibling bond*. New York: Basic Books.

Barbee, A. P., & Cunningham, M. (1995). An experimental approach to social support communications: Interactive coping in close relationships. In B. Burleson (Ed.), *Communication yearbook* (Vol. 18, pp. 381–413). Thousand Oaks, CA: Sage.

Barnett, O. W., & LaViolette, A. D. (1993). *It could happen to anyone: Why battered women stay*. Newbury Park, CA: Sage.

Barnett, R. C., & Baruch, G. K. (1987). Determinants of fathers' participation in family work. *Journal of Marriage and the Family, 49*, 29–40.

Barnett, R. C., & Shen, Y. C. (1997). Gender, high- and low-schedule-control housework tasks and psychological distress: A study of dual-earner couples. *Journal of Family Issues, 18*, 423–428.

Barrile, M., Armstrong, E. S., & Bower, T. G. R. (1999). Novelty and frequency as determinants of newborn preference. *Developmental Science, 2*, 47–52.

Bartholomew, K., & Horowitz, L. M. (1991). Attachment styles among young adults: A test of a four-category model. *Journal of Personality and Social Psychology, 61*, 226–244.

Baucom, D. H., Notarius, C. I., Burnett, C. K., & Haefner, P. (1990). Gender differences and sex-role identity in marriage. In F. D. Fincham & T. N. Bradbury (Eds.), *the psychology of marriage* (pp. 150–171). New York: Guilford.

Bauer, W. D., & Twentyman, C. T. (1985). Abusing, neglectful, and comparison mothers' responses to child-related and non-child-related stressors. *Journal of Consulting and Clinical Psychology, 53*, 335–343.

Baumrind, D. (1966). Effects of authoritative parental control on behavior. *Child Development, 37*, 887–907.

Baumrind, D. (1967). Child care practices anteceding three patterns of preschool behavior. *Genetic Psychology Monographs, 75*, 43–88.

Baumrind, D. (1971). Current patterns of parental authority. *Developmental Psychology Monographs, 4*, 99–102.

Baumrind, D. (1978). Parental disciplinary patterns and social competence in children. *Youth and society, 9*, 239–276.

Baumrind, D. (1991). The influence of parenting style on adolescent competence and substance use. *Journal of Early Adolescence, 11*, 56–95.

Baumrind, D. (1996). Parenting: The discipline controversy revisited. *Family Relations, 45*, 405–414.

Baxter, L. A. (1988). A dialectical perspective on communication strategies in relationship development. In S. W. Duck (Ed.), *A handbook of personal relationships* (pp. 257–273). New York: Wiley.

Baxter, L. A. (1990). Dialectical contradictions in relationship development. *Journal of Social and Personal Relationships, 7*, 69–88.

Baxter L. A., Braithwaite, D. O., & Nicholson, J. (1999). Turning points in the development of blended family relationships. *Journal of Social and Personal Relationships, 16*, 291–313.

Baxter, L. A., & Ebert, L. A. (1999). Perceptions of dialectical contradictions in turning points of development in heterosexual romantic relationships. *Journal of Social and Personal Relationships, 16*, 547–569.

Baxter, L. A., & Montgomery, B. M. (1996). *Relating: Dialogues and dialectics.* New York: Guilford Press.

Baxter, L. A., & West, L. (2003). Couple perceptions of their similarities and differences: A dialectic perspective. *Journal of Personal and Social Relationships, 20*, 491–514.

BBC News (2003a). *Australian church accepts gay priests.* Retrieved July 30, 2003, from http://newsvote.bbc.co.uk/mpapps/pagetools/print/news.bbc.co.uk/2/h1/asia-pacific/307573.stm

BBC News (2003b). *Gay showdown for US Church.* Retrieved July 30, 2003, from http://newsvote.bbc.co.uk/mpapps/pagetools/print/news.bbc.co.uk/2/hi/americas/3110581.stm

BBC News. (2003c). *Vatican denounces gay marriage*. Retrieved July 30, 2003, from http://news.bbc.co.uk/go/pr/fr/-/2/hi/europe/3108349.stm

Beach, S. R. H. (2001). *Marital and family processes in depression: A scientific foundation for clinical practice*. Washington, DC: American Psychological Association.

Beach, S. R. H., Katz, J., Kim, S., & Brody, G. H. (2003). Prospective effects of marital satisfaction on depressive symptoms in established marriages: A dyadic model. *Journal of Social and Personal Relationships, 20*, 355–371.

Beach, S. R. H., & O'Leary, K. D. (1993). Marital discord and dysphoria: For whom does the marital relationship predict depressive symptomatology? *Journal of Social and Personal Relationships, 10*, 405–420.

Bean, R. A., Bush, K. R., McKenry, P. C., & Wilson, S. M. (2003). The impact of parental support, behavioral control, and psychological control on the academic achievement and self-esteem of African American and European American adolescents. *Journal of Adolescent Research, 18*, 523–541.

Beebe, B., & Stern, D. N. (1977). Engagement-disengagement and early object experiences. In N. Freedman & S. Granel (Eds.), *Communicative structures and psychic structures* (pp. 35–55). New York: Plenum Press.

Bell, K. L., Allen, J. P., Hauser, S. T., & O'Connor, T. G. (1996). Family factors and young adult transitions: Educational attainment and occupational prestige. In J. A. Grabner & J. Brooks-Gunn (Eds.), *Transitions through adolescence: Interpersonal domains and contexts* (pp. 345–366). Mahwah, NJ: Erlbaum.

Bellavia, G., & Murray, S. (2003). Did I do that? Self-esteem-related differences in reactions to romantic partners' moods. *Personal Relationships, 10*, 77–95.

Belsky, J. (1986). The "effects" of infant day care reconsidered. *Child Development, 57*, 202–216.

Belsky, J. (1999). Quantity of nonmaternal care and boys' problematic behavior/adjustment at ages 3 and 5: Exploring the mediating role of parenting. *Psychiatry Interpersonal and Biological Processes, 62*, 1–20.

Belsky, J. (2001). Emanuel Miller lecture developmental risks (still) associated with early childcare. *Journal of Child Psychology and Psychiatry and Allied Disciplines, 42*, 845–859.

Belsky, J., & Kelly, J. (1994). *The transition to parenthood: How a first child changes a marriage*. London: Vermillion.

Belsky, J., Lang, M. E., & Rovine, M. (1985). Stability and change in marriage across the transition to parenthood: A second study. *Journal of Marriage and the Family, 47*, 855–865.

Belsky, J., & Volling, B. (1987). Mothering, fathering, and marital interaction in the family triad during infancy: Exploring family system's processes. In P. W. Berman & F. A. Pedersen (Eds.), *Men's transitions to parenthood: Longitudinal studies of early family experience* (pp. 37–63). Hillsdale, NJ: Erlbaum.

Ben Hamida, S., Mineka, S., & Bailey, J. M. (1998). Sex differences in perceived controllability of mate value: An evolutionary perspective. *Journal of Personality and Social Psychology, 75*, 953–966.

Benin, M. H., & Agostinelli, J. (1988). Husbands' and wives' satisfaction with the division of labor. *Journal of Marriage and the Family, 50*, 349–361.

Benin, M. H., & Robinson, L. B. (1997, August). *Marital happiness across the family life cycle: A longitudinal analysis*. Paper presented at the American Sociological Association, Toronto.

Bennett, N. G., Bloom, D. E., & Miller, C. K. (1995). The influence of nonmarital childbearing on the formation of first marriages. *Demography, 32*, 47–62.

Benoit, W. J., & Benoit, P. J. (1987). Everyday argument practices of native social actors. In J. W. Wenzel (Ed.), *Argument and critical practices* (pp. 465–473). Annandale, VA: Speech Communication Association.

Berger, C. R., & Calabrese, R. J. (1975). Some explorations in initial interaction and beyond: Toward a developmental theory of interpersonal communication. *Human Communication Research, 1*, 99–112.

Berger, C. R., & Kellermann, K. (1994). Acquiring social information. In J. A. Daly & J. M. Wiemann (Eds.), *Strategic interpersonal communication* (pp. 1–31). Hillsdale, NJ: Erlbaum.

Berglund, M., & Tunving, K. (1985). Assaultive alcoholics 20 years later. *Acta Psychiatrica Scandinavica,, 71*, 141–147.

Berman, P. W., & Pederson, F. A. (1987). *Men's transitions to parenthood: Longitudinal studies of early family experience*. Hillsdale, NJ: Erlbaum.

Berns, S. B., Jacobsen, N. S., & Gottman, J. M. (1999). Demand-withdraw interaction patterns between different types of batterers and their spouses. *Journal of Marital and Family Therapy, 25*, 337–348.

Bernstein, A. C. (1989). *Yours, mine and ours: How families change when remarried parents have a child together*. New York: Scribner.

Berry, D. B. (1998). *The domestic violence sourcebook*. Los Angeles: Lowell House.

Berscheid, E., Dion, K. K., Walster, E. H., & Walster, G. W. (1971). Physical attractiveness and dating choice: Tests of the matching hypothesis. *Journal of Experimental Social Psychology, 7*, 173–189.

Berscheid, E., & Walster, E. H. (1972). Beauty and the best. *Psychology Today, 5*, 42–46, 74.

Berscheid, E., & Walster, E. H. (1974). Physical attractiveness. In L. Berkowitz (Ed.), *Advances in experimental social psychology* (Vol. 7, pp. 158–215). New York: Academic.

Berscheid, E., & Walster, E. H. (1978). *Interpersonal attraction* (2nd ed.). Reading, MA: Addison-Wesley.

Biaggio, M. K., Mohan, P. J., & Baldwin, C. (1985). Relationships among attitudes toward children, women's liberation, and personality characteristics. *Sex Roles, 12*, 47–62.

Bianchi, S. M., & Casper, L. M. (2000). American families. *Population Bulletin, 55*(4), 17.

Bianchi, S. M., & Spain, D. (1996). Women, work, and family in America. *Population Bulletin, 51*, 2–48.

Biglan, A., Hops, H., Sherman, L., Friedman, L. S., Arthur, J., & Osteen, V. (1985). Problem-solving interactions of depressed women and their husbands. *Behavior therapy, 16*, 431–451.

Billingham, R. E., & Sack, A. R. (1987). Conflict tactics and the level of emotional commitment among unmarried. *Human Relations, 40*, 59–74.

Birchler, G. R., Clopton, P. L., & Adams, N. L. (1984). Marital conflict resolution: Factors influencing concordance between partners and trained coders. *American Journal of Family Therapy, 12*, 15–28.

Bird, G. W., Stith, S. M., & Schladale, J. (1991). Psychological resources, coping strategies, and negotiation styles as discriminators of violence in dating relationships. *Family Relations, 41*, 318–323.

Blair, S. L. (1992). Children's participation in household labor: Child socialization versus the need for household labor. *Journal of Youth and Adolescence, 21,* 241–258.

Blair, S. L., & Johnson, M. P. (1992). Wives' perceptions of fairness of the division of household labor: The intersection of housework and ideology. *Journal of Marriage and the Family, 54,* 570–581.

Blank, R. M., & Schmidt, L. (2001). Work, wages, and welfare. In R. Blank & R. Haskins (Eds.), *The new world of welfare* (pp. 70–102). Washington, DC: Brookings.

Blood, R. O., & Wolfe, D. M. (1960). *Husbands and wives: The dynamics of married living.* New York: Free Press.

Boer, F., & Dunn, J. (Eds.). (1992). *Children's sibling relationships: Developmental and clinical issues.* Hillsdale, NJ: Erlbaum.

Bond, J. T., Galinsky, E., & Swanberg, J. E. (1998). *The 1997 national study of the changing workforce.* New York: Families and Work Institute.

Bonney, J. F., Kelley, M. L., & Levant, R. F. (1999). A model of fathers' behavioral involvement in child care in dual-earner families. *Journal of Family Psychology, 13,* 401–415.

Borawski, E. A., Ievers-Landis, C. E., Lovegreen, L. D., & Trapl, E. S. (2003). Parental monitoring, negotiated unsupervised time, and parental trust: The role of perceived parenting practices in adolescent health risk behaviors. *Society for Adolescent Medicine, 33,* 60–70.

Bottoms v. Bottoms, No. 941166 (Va. 1995).

Bowers, J. W., & Bradac, J. J. (1982). Issues in communication theory: A metatheoretical analysis. In M. Burgoon (Ed.), *Communication yearbook* (Vol. 5, pp. 1–27). New Brunswick, NJ: Transaction Books.

Bowlby, J. (1973). *Attachment and loss: Vol. 2. Separation: Anxiety and anger.* New York: Basic Books.

Bowlby, J. (1980). *Attachment and loss: Vol. 3. Loss.* New York: Basic Books.

Bowlby, J. (1982). *Attachment and loss: Vol. 1. Attachment* (2nd ed.). New York: Basic Books.

Bradbury, T. N., & Fincham, F. D. (1992). Attributions and behavior in marital interaction. *Journal of Personality and Social Psychology, 63,* 613–628.

Braiker, H. B., & Kelley, H. H. (1979). Conflict in the development of close relationship. In R. L. Burgess & T. L. Huston (Eds.), *Social exchange in developing relationships* (pp. 135–168). New York: Academic Press.

Braithwaite, D. O., McBride, C., & Schrodt, P. (2003). Parent teams and the everyday interactions of co-parenting children in stepfamilies. *Communication Reports, 16,* 93–112.

Braithwaite, D. O., Olson, L., Golish, T., Soukup, C., & Turman, P. (2001). Becoming a family: Developmental processes represented in blended family discourse. *Journal of Applied Communication Research, 29,* 221–247.

Brand, E., Clingempeel, W. G., & Bowen-Woodward, K. (1988). Family relationships and children's psychological adjustment in stepmother and stepfather families: Findings and conclusions for the Philadelphia Stepfamily Research Project. In E. M. Hetherington & J. D. Arasteh (Eds.), *Separate worlds of siblings: The impact of nonshared environment on development* (pp. 299–324). Hillsdale, NJ: Erlbaum.

Bray, J. T. (1988). Children's development during early remarriage. In E. M. Hetherington & J. D. Arasteh (Eds.), *Impact of divorce, singles parenting and stepparenting on children* (pp. 279–298). Hillsdale, NJ: Erlbaum.

Bray, J. T., & Berger, S. H. (1993). Developmental issues in stepfamilies research project: Family relationships and parent-child interactions. *Journal of Family Psychology, 7*, 1–17, 76–90.

Brennan, R. T., Chait Barnett, R., & Gareis, K. C. (2001). When she earns more than he does: A longitudinal study of dual-earner couples. *Journal of Marriage and Family, 63*, 168–182.

Bretherton, I. (1992). Open communication and internal working models: Their role in the development of attachment relationships. In R. A. Thompson (Ed.), *Nebraska Symposium on Motivation: Socioemotional development* (pp. 59–113). Lincoln: University of Nebraska Press.

Brewaeys, A. (2001). Review: Parent-child relationships and child development in donor insemination families. *Human Reproduction Update, 7*, 38–46.

Broderick, C. B. (1993). *Understanding family process: Basics of family systems theory.* Thousand Oaks, CA: Sage.

Broderick, J. E., & O'Leary, K. D. (1986). Contributions of affect, attitudes, and behavior to marital satisfaction. *Journal of Consulting and Clinical Psychology, 54*, 514–517.

Brook, J. S., Brook, D. W., & Whiteman, M. (1999). Older sibling correlates of younger sibling drug use in the context of parent-child relations. *Genetic, Social and General Psychology Monographs, 125*, 451–468.

Brook, J. S., Whiteman, M., Gordon, A. S., & Brook, D. W. (1990). The role of older brothers in younger brothers' drug use viewed in the context of parent and peer influences. *Journal of Genetic Psychology, 151*, 59–75.

Brookoff, D., O'Brien, K., Cook, C., Thompson, T., & Williams, C. (1997). Characteristics of participants in domestic violence: Assessment at the scene of domestic assault. *Journal of the American Medical Association, 277*, 17, 1369–1373.

Brooks, C. (2002). Religious influence and the politics of family decline concern: Trends, sources, and US political behavior. *American Sociological Review, 67*, 191-211.

Brooks, J. H. (1996). *The process of parenting.* Mountain View, CA: Mayfield.

Brothers, S. C., & Maddux, J. E. (2003). The goal of biological parenthood and emotional distress from infertility: Linking parenthood to happiness. *Journal of Applied Social Psychology, 33*, 248–262.

Brown, S. L. (2000). The effect of union type on psychological well-being: Depression among cohabitors versus marrieds. *Journal of Health and Social Behavior, 41*, 241–255.

Brown, S. L., & Booth, A. (1996). Cohabitation versus marriage: A comparison of relationship quality. *Journal of Marriage and the Family, 58*, 668–678.

Brownridge, D. A., & Halli, S. S. (2000). "Living in sin and sinful living": Toward filling a gap in the explanation of violence against women. *Aggressive and violent behavior, 5*, 565–583.

Brush, L. D. (1993). Violent acts and injurious outcomes in married couples: Methodological issues in the National Survey of Families and Households. In P. B. Bart & E. G. Moran (Eds.), *Violence against women: The bloody footprints* (pp. 240–251). Newbury Park, CA: Sage.

Buber, M. (1965). *The knowledge of man.* New York: Harper & Row.

Buck, R. (1975). Nonverbal communication of affect in children. *Journal of Personality and Social Psychology, 31*, 644–653.

Buehlman, K. T., Gottman, J. M., & Katz, L. F. (1992). How a couple views their past predicts their future: Predicting divorce from an oral history interview. *Journal of Family Psychology, 5*, 295–318.

Buhrmester, D. (1992). The developmental course of sibling and peer relationships. In F. Boer & J. Dunn (Eds.), *Children's sibling relationships* (pp. 19–40). Hillsdale, NJ: Erlbaum.

Buhrmester, D., & Furman, W. (1987). The development of companionship and intimacy. *Child Development, 58*, 1101–1113.

Bulcroft, R. A., & Bulcroft, K. A. (1993). Race differences in attitudinal and motivational factors in the decision to marry. *Journal of Marriage and Family, 55*, 338–355.

Bumpass, L. L. (1984). Some characteristics of children's second families. *American Journal of Sociology, 90*, 608–623.

Bumpass, L. L. (1990). What's happening to the family? Interactions between demographic and institutional change. *Demography, 27*, 483–498.

Bumpass, L. & Lu, H. H. (1998). *Trends in cohabitation and implications for children's family contexts.* Unpublished manuscript, University of Wisconsin–Madison, Center for Demography.

Bumpass, L. L., & Sweet, J. A. (1989). National estimates of cohabitation. *Demography, 26*, 615–625.

Bumpass, L. L., & Sweet, J. A. (1995). *Cohabitation, marriage and union stability: Preliminary findings from the NSFH2* (Working paper No. 65). Madison, WI: National Survey of Families and Households.

Bumpass, L. L, Sweet, J. A., & Cherlin, A. (1991). The role of cohabitation in declining rates of marriage. *Journal of Marriage and Family, 53*, 913–927.

Burgoon, J. K., Buller, D. B., & Woodall, W. G. (1996). *Nonverbal communication: The unspoken dialogue* (2nd ed.). New York: McGraw-Hill.

Burgoon, J. K., Dillman, L. A., & Stern, L. (1993). Adaptation in dyadic interaction: Defining and operationalizing patterns of reciprocity and compensation. *Communication Theory, 3*, 295–316.

Burgoon, J. K., Stern, L., & Dillman, L. A. (1995). *Interpersonal adaptation: Dyadic interaction patterns.* New York: Cambridge University Press.

Burgoon, M., & Ruffner, M. (1978). *Human communication.* Austin, TX: Holt, Rinehart & Winston.

Buri, J. R., Kirchner, P.A., & Walsh, J. M. (1987). Familial correlates of self-esteem in young American adults. *Journal of Social Psychology, 127*, 583–588.

Buri, J. R., Louiselle, P. A., Misukanis, T. M., & Mueller, R. A. (1988). Effects of parental authoritarianism and authoritativeness on self-esteem. *Personality and Social Psychology Bulletin, 14*, 271–282.

Burke, R. J., & Weir, T. (1976). Some personality differences between members of one-career and two-career families. *Journal of Marriage and the Family, 38*, 453–459.

Burleson, B. R. (1994). Comforting messages: Features, functions and outcomes. In J. A. Daly & J. M. Wiemann (Eds.), *Strategic interpersonal communication* (pp. 135–161). Hillsdale, NJ: Erlbaum.

Burleson, B. R., Delia, J. G., & Applegate, J. L. (1995). The socialization of person-centered communication: Parents' contributions to their children's social-cognitive and communication skills. In M. A. Fitzpatrick & A. L. Vangelisti (Eds.), *Explaining family interaction* (pp. 34–76). Thousand Oaks, CA: Sage.

Burleson, B. R., & Mortenson, S. R. (2003). Explaining cultural differences in evaluations of emotional support behaviors: Exploring the mediating influences of value systems and interaction goals. *Communication Research, 30,* 113–146.

Burroughs, L. V., Turner, B. F., & Turner, C. B. (1984). Careers, contingencies, and locus of control among white college women. *Sex Roles, 11,* 289–302.

Bushman, B. (1993). Human aggression while under the influence of alcohol and other drugs: An integrative research review. *Current Directions in Psychological Science, 2,* 148–152.

Butterworth, G., & Morissette, P. (1996). Onset of pointing and the acquisition of language in infancy. *Journal of Reproductive and Infant Psychology, 14,* 219–231.

Cain, K. M., & Dweck, C. (1995). The relation between motivational patterns and achievement cognitions through elementary school years. *Merrill-Palmer Quarterly, 41,* 25–52.

Cain, P. (1993). Litigating for lesbian and gay rights: A legal history. *Virginia Law Review, 79,* 1551–1642.

Cancian, M., & Reed, D. (2001). Changes in family structure: Implications for poverty and related policy. In S. Danziger & R. Haveman (Eds.), *Understanding poverty in America: Progress and problems* (pp. 69–97). New York: Harvard University Press & Russell Sage.

Carlson, M. J., Harris, S. D., & Holden, G. W. (1999). Protective orders and domestic violence: Risk factors for re-abuse. *Journal of Family Violence, 14,* 205–226.

Carroll, J. J, Robinson, B. E., & Flowers, C. (2002). Marital estrangement, positive feelings toward partners and locus of control: Female counselors married to alcohol-abusing and non-alcohol-abusing spouses. *Journal of Addictions & Offender Counseling, 23,* 30–40.

Cartier, M. (1995). Nuclear versus quasi-stem families: The new Chinese family. *Journal of Family History, 20,* 307–327.

Caughlin, J. P. (2002). The demand/withdraw pattern of communication as a predictor of marital satisfaction over time: Unresolved issues and future directions. *Human Communication Research, 28,* 49–86.

Caughlin, J. P., & Petronio, S. (2004). Privacy in families. In A. Vangelisti (Ed.), *Handbook of family communication* (pp. 379–412). Thousand Oaks, CA: Sage.

Caughlin, J. P., & Ramey, M. (in press). The demand/withdraw pattern of communication in parent-adolescent dyads. *Personal Relationships.*

Caughlin, J. P., & Vangelisti, A. L. (1999). Desire for change in one's partner as predictor of the demand/withdraw pattern of marital communication. *Communication Monographs, 66,* 66–89.

Center for Family Policy and Practice. (2005, March). Lawsuit challenges state law criminalizing cohabitation. *National Policy Briefings, 7*(2). Retrieved July 18, 2005, from www.cffpp.org/briefings/brief_0503.html

Cerezo, M. A., D'Ocon, A., & Dolz, L. (1996). Mother-child interactive patterns in abusive families versus nonabusive families: An observational study. *Child Abuse and Neglect, 20,* 573–584.

Chait Barnett, R., Gareis, K. C., Boone James, J., & Steele, J. (2003). Planning ahead: College seniors' concerns about career-marriage conflict. *Journal of Vocational Behavior, 62,* 305–319.

Chambers, D. L., & Polikoff, N. D. (1999). Family law and gay and lesbian family issues in the twentieth century. *Family law quarterly, 33,* 523–542.

Chase Goodman, C., & Silverstein, M. (2001). Grandmothers who parent their grandchildren: An exploratory study of close relations among three generations. *Journal of Family Issues, 22,* 557–578.

Cheng, H. L., Mallinckrodt, B., & Wu, L. C. (2005). Anger expression toward parents and depressive symptoms among undergraduates in Taiwan. *The Counseling Psychologist, 33,* 72–97.

Chevan, A. (1996). As cheaply as one: Cohabitation in the older population. *Journal of Marriage and Family, 58,* 656–667.

Christensen, A., & Shenk, J. L. (1991). Communication, conflict, and psychological distance in nondistressed, clinic, and divorcing couples. *Journal of Consulting and Clinical Psychology, 59,* 458–463.

Christopher, F. S., & Cate, R. M. (1985). Premarital sexual pathways and relationship development. *Journal of Social and Personal Relationships, 2,* 271–288.

Cicirelli, V. G. (2003). Mothers' and daughters' paternalism beliefs and caregiving decision making. *Research on Aging, 25,* 3–21.

Clark, V. (2001). What about the children? Arguments against lesbian and gay parenting. *Women's Studies International Forum, 24,* 555–570.

Clarke-Stewart, K. A. (1978). And daddy makes three: Father's impact on mother and young child. *Child Development, 49,* 466–478.

Clay, J. W. (1991). Respecting and supporting gay and lesbian parents. *Education Digest, 56*(8), 51.

Clingempeel, W. G., Brand, E., & Segal, S. (1987). A multilevel-multivariable-developmental perspective for future research on stepfamilies. In K. Pasley & M. Ihinger-Tallman (Eds.), *Remarriage and stepparenting today: Current research and theory* (pp. 65–93). New York: Guilford.

Clingempeel, W. G., Ievoli, R., & Brand, E. (1984). Structural complexity and the quality of stepfather-stepchild relationships. *Family Process, 23,* 547–556.

Cloninger, C. R. (1987). A systematic method for clinical description and classification of personality variants: A proposal. *Archives of General Psychiatry, 44,* 573–588.

Cloven, D. H., & Roloff, M. E. (1994). A developmental model of decisions to withhold relational irritations in romantic relationships. *Personal Relationships, 1,* 143–164.

Coker, D. A., & Burgoon, J. K. (1987). The nature of conversational involvement and nonverbal encoding patterns. *Human Communication Research, 13,* 463–494.

Collins, N. L., & Read, S. J. (1990). Adult attachment, working models, and relationship quality in dating couples. *Journal of Personality and Social Psychology, 58,* 644–663.

Collins, W. A., & Luebker, C. (1994). Parent and adolescent expectancies: Individual and relational significance. In J. G. Smetana (Ed.), *Beliefs about parenting: Origins and developmental implications* (New Directions for Child Development, Vol. 66, pp. 65–80). San Francisco: Jossey-Bass.

Collins, W. A., Maccoby, E., Steinberg, L., Hetherington, E. M., & Bornstein, M. (2000). Contemporary research on parenting: The case for nature *and* nurture. *American Psychologist, 55,* 218–232.

Coltrane, S. (2000). Research on household labor: Modeling and measuring social embeddedness of routine family work. *Journal of Marriage and the Family, 62,* 1208–1233.

Connecticut Health Policy Project. (2003). *2003 federal poverty levels effective April 1, 2003.* Retrieved June 16, 2005, from www.cthealthpolicy.org/pubs/fpl2003.htm

Coombs, R. H., Paulson, M. J., & Richardson, M. A. (1991). Peer vs. parental influence in substance use among Hispanic and Anglo children and adolescents. *Journal of Youth and Adolescence, 20,* 73–88.

Cooney, T. M., & Hogan, D. P. (1991). Marriage as an institutionalized life course: First marriage among American men in the twentieth century. *Journal of Marriage and the Family, 53,* 178–190.

Coontz, S. (1992). *The way we never were: American families and the nostaligia trap.* New York: Basic Books.

Cooper, R. P., & Aslin, R. N. (1989). The language environment of the young infant: Implications for early perceptual development. *Canadian Journal of Psychology, 43,* 247–265.

Cooper, R. P., & Aslin, R. N. (1994). Developmental differences in infant attention to the spectral properties of infant-directed speech. *Child Development, 65,* 1633–1677.

Corcoran, M., Danziger, S. K., Kalil, A., & Seefeldt, K. S. (2000). How welfare reform is affecting women's work. *Annual Review of Sociology, 26,* 241–269.

Cowan, C. P., & Cowan, P. A. (1987). Men's involvement in parenthood: Identifying the antecedents and understanding the barriers. In P. W. Berman & F. A. Pedersen (Eds.), *Men's transitions to parenthood: Longitudinal studies of early family experience* (pp. 145–171). Hillsdale, NJ: Erlbaum.

Cowan, C. P., & Cowan, P. A. (2000). *When partners become parents: The big life change for couples.* Mahwah, NJ: Erlbaum.

Cowan, P. A. (1988). Becoming a father: A time of change, an opportunity for development. In P. Bronstein & C. P. Cowan (Eds.), *Fatherhood today: Men's changing role in the family* (pp. 13–35). New York: Wiley.

Cowan, P. A., & Cowan, C. P. (1988). Changes in marriage during the transition to parenthood: Must we blame the baby? In G. Michaels & W. Goldberg (Eds.), *The transition to parenthood: Current theory and research* (pp. 114–154). Cambridge, UK: Cambridge University Press.

Cox, M. J., Owen, M., Lewis, J., & Henderson, V. K. (1989). Marriage, adult adjustment and early parenting. *Child Development, 60,* 1015–1024.

Coyne, J. C. (1976). Toward an interactional description of depression. *Psychiatry, 39,* 28–40.

Coyne, J. C., Thompson, R., & Palmer, S. C. (2002). Marital quality, coping with conflict, marital complaints, and affection in couples with a depressed wife. *Journal of Family Psychology, 16,* 26–37.

Crawford, D. W., & Huston, T. L. (1993). The impact of the transition to parenthood on marital leisure. *Personality and Social Psychology Bulletin, 19,* 39–46.

Crohan, S. E. (1996). Marital quality and conflict across the transition to parenthood in African American and White couples. *Journal of Marriage and Family, 58,* 933–944.

Crouter, A. C., McHale, S. M., & Bartko, W. T. (1993). Gender as an organizing feature in parent-child relationships. *Journal of Social Issues,* 161–174.

Crouter, A. C., Perry-Jenkins, M., Huston, T. L., & McHale, S. M. (1987). Processes underlying father involvement in dual-earner and single-earner families. *Developmental Psychology, 23,* 431–440.

Crowder, K. D., & Tolnay, S. E. (2000). A new marriage squeeze for black women: The role of interracial marriage by black men. *Journal of Marriage and the Family, 62*, 792–807.

Crowther, J. H., Lilly, R. S., Crawford, P. A., Shepard, K. L. (1992). The stability of the eating disorder inventory. *International Journal of Eating Disorders, 12*, 97–101.

Cuber, J. F., & Haroff, P. (1965). *Sex and the significant Americans*. Baltimore: Penguin.

Cunningham, M. R., & Barbee, A. P. (2000). Social support. In C. Hendrick & S. S. Hendrick (Eds.), *Close relationships: A sourcebook* (pp. 272–285). Thousand Oaks, CA: Sage.

Cupach, W. R. (2000). Advancing understanding about relational conflict. *Journal of Social and Personal Relationships, 17*, 697–703.

Cupach, W. R., & Canary, D. G. (1997). *Competence in interpersonal conflict*. New York: McGraw-Hill.

Cupach, W. R., & Metts, S. (1995). The role of sexual attitude similarity in romantic heterosexual relationships. *Personal Relationships, 2*, 287–300.

Curran, P. J., & Chassin, L. (1996). A longitudinal study of parenting as a protective factor for children of alcoholics. *Journal of Studies on Alcohol, 57*, 305–313.

Cushman, D. (1977). The rules perspective as a theoretical basis for the study of human communication. *Communication Quarterly, 25*, 30–45.

Cutrona, C. E. (1996). *Social support in couples*. Thousand Oaks, CA: Sage.

Dainton, M. (1993). The myths and misconceptions of the stepmother identity: Descriptions and prescriptions for identity management. *Family Relations, 42*, 93–98.

Darling, N., & Steinberg, L. (1993). Parenting style as context: An integrative model. *Psychological Bulletin, 113*, 487–496.

Davidson, B., Balswick, J., & Halverson, C. (1983). Affective self-disclosure and marital adjustment: A test of equity theory. *Journal of Marriage and the Family, 45*, 93–102.

Davidson, J. K., & Moore, N. B. (1996). *Marriage and family: Change and continuity*. Boston: Allyn & Bacon.

Davila, J., Karney, B. R., Hall, T. W., & Bradbury, T. N. (2003). Depressive symptoms and marital satisfaction: Within-subject associations and the moderating effects of gender and neuroticism. *Journal of Family Psychology, 17*, 557–570.

DeCasper, A. J., & Fifer, W. P. (1980). Of human bonding: Newborns prefer their mothers' voices. *Science, 208*, 1174–1176.

Deiner, C. I., & Dweck, C. S. (1978). An analysis of learned helplessness: Continuous changes in performance, strategy, and achievement cognitions following failure. *Journal of Personality and Social Psychology, 36*, 451–462.

Dekovic, M., & Janssens, J. M. A. M. (1992). Parents' child-rearing style and child's sociometric status. *Developmental Psychology, 28*, 925–932.

DeLuccie, M. F. (1995). Mothers as gatekeepers: A model of maternal mediators of father involvement. *Journal of Genetic Psychology, 156*, 115–131.

DeMaris, A. (2000). Till discord do us part: The role of physical and verbal conflict in union disruption. *Journal of Marriage and the Family, 62*, 683–692.

Demo, D. H., & Acock, A. C. (1993). Family diversity and the division of domestic labor: How much have things really changed? *Family Relations, 42*, 323–331.

Dempsey, K. C. (1997). Trying to get husbands to do more work at home. *Australian & New Zealand Journal of Sociology, 33*, 216–225.

DeTurck, M. (1987). When communication fails: Physical aggression as a compliance-gaining strategy. *Communication Monographs, 54*, 106–112.

Dickson, K. L., Walker, H., & Fogel, A. (1997). The relationship between smile type and play during parent-infant play. *Developmental Psychology, 33*, 925–933.

DiIorio, C., Kelley, M., & Hockenberry-Eaton, M. (1999). Communication about sexual issues: Mothers, fathers and friends. *Journal of Adolescent Health, 24*, 181–189.

Dindia, K., & Allen, M. (1992). Sex differences in self-disclosure: A meta-analysis. *Psychological Bulletin, 112*, 106–124.

Dixson, M. (1995). Models and perspectives of parent-child communication. In T. J. Socha & G. H. Stamp (Eds.), *Parents, children, and communication: Frontiers of theory and research* (pp. 43–61). Mahwah, NJ: Erlbaum.

Dobash, R. E., & Dobash, R. P. (1998). Violent man and violent contexts. In R. E. Dobash & R. P. Dobash (Eds.), *Rethinking violence against women* (pp. 141–168). Thousand Oaks, CA: Sage.

Dominguez, M. M., & Carton, J. S. (1997). The relationship between self-actualization and parenting style. *Journal of Social Behavior and Personality, 12*, 1093–1100.

Dontas, C., Maratos, O., Fafoutis, M., & Karangelis, A. (1985). Early social development in institutionally reared Greek infants: Attachment and peer interaction. *Monographs of the Society for Research in Child Development, 50*, 136–146.

Dore, M. M., Doris, J. M., & Wright, P. (1995). Identifying substance abuse in maltreating families: A child welfare challenge. *Child Abuse and Neglect, 19*, 531–543.

Dornbusch, S. M., Ritter, P. L., Mont-Reynaud, R., & Chen, Z. (1990). Family decision making and academic performance in a diverse high school population. *Journal of Adolescent Research, 5*, 143–160.

Dornbusch, S. M., Ritter, R. L, Leiderman, P. H., Roberts, D. F., & Fraleigh, M. J. (1987). The relation of parenting style to adolescent school performance. *Child Development, 58*, 1244–1257.

Dosser, D. A., Balswick, J. O., & Halverson, C. F. (1986). Male inexpressiveness and relationships. *Journal of Social and Personal Relationships, 3*, 241–258.

Doumas, D. M., Margolin, G., & John, R. S. (2003). The relationship between daily marital interaction, work, and health-promoting behaviors in dual-earner couples: An extension of the work-family spillover model. *Journal of Family Issues, 24*, 3–20.

Downey, G., & Coyne, J. C. (1990). Children of depressed parents: An integrative review. *Psychological Bulletin, 108*, 50–76.

Downie, J., & Coates, R. (1999). The impact of gender on parent-child sexuality and communication: Has anything changed? *Sexual and marital therapy, 14*, 109–121.

Doyle, J. A., & Paludi, M. A. (1991). *Sex and gender: The human experience.* Dubuque, IA: William. C. Brown.

Drigotas, S. M., & Rusbult, C. E. (1992). Should I stay or should I go? A dependence model of breakups. *Journal of Personality and Social Psychology, 62*, 62–87.

Dugan, S., Umberson, D., & Anderson, K. L. (2001). The batterer's view of the self and others in domestic violence. *Sociological Inquiry, 71*, 221–240.

Duggan, A. (2003). *One-up, Two-Down: An application of inconsistent nurturing as control theory to depressed individuals and their partners.* Unpublished doctoral dissertation, University of California, Santa Barbara.

Duggan, A., & Le Poire, B. A. (2004). *One Down, Two Involved: An application and extension of Inconsistent Nurturing as Control theory to couples including one depressed individual*. Manuscript submitted for publication.

Dunifon, R., & Kowaleski-Jones, L. (2002). Who's in the house? Race differences in cohabitation, single parenthood, and child development. *Child Development, 73*, 1249–1264.

Dunkel-Schetter, C., & Bennett, T. L. (1990). Differentiating the cognitive and behavioral aspects of social support. In I. G. Sarason, B. R. Sarason, & G. R. Pierce (Eds.), *Social support: An interactional view* (pp. 267–296). New York: John Wiley.

Dunn, J., & Kendrick, C. (1982). Social behavior of young siblings in the family context: Differences between same-sex and different-sex dyads. *Annual Progress in Child Psychiatry & Child Development, 21*, 166–181.

Dunn, J., O'Connor, T. G., & Levy, I. (2002). Out of the picture: A study of family drawings by children from step-, single-parent, and non-step families. *Journal of Clinical Child and Adolescent Psychology, 31*, 505–512.

Durlak, J. A. (2001). School problems of children. In C. Walker & M. C. Roberts (Eds.), *Handbook of clinical child psychology* (3rd ed., pp. 561–575). New York: Wiley.

Dutton, D. G. (1998). *The abusive personality*. New York: Guilford Press.

Ehrenberg, M. F., Gearing-Small, M., Hunter, M. A., & Small, B. J. (2001). Childcare task division and shared parenting attitudes in dual-earner families with young children. *Family Relations, 50*, 143–153.

Erickson, M. F., Sroufe, L. A., & Egeland, B. (1985). The relationship between quality of attachment and behavior problems in preschool in a high-risk sample. *Monographs of the Society for Research in Child Development, 50*(1-2), 147–166.

Eskilson, A., Wiley, M. G., Muehlbauer, G., & Dodder, L. (1986). Parental pressure, self-esteem and adolescent reported deviance: Bending the twig too far. *Adolescence, 2*, 501–515.

Ewing, J. A., & Fox, R. E. (1968). Family therapy of alcoholism. In J. Masserman (Ed.), *Current psychiatric therapies* (Vol. 18, pp. 86–91). New York: Grune & Stratton.

Falk, P. J. (1989). Psychosocial assumptions in family law. *American Psychologist, 44*, 941–947.

Fals-Stewart, W., & Birchler, G. R. (1998). Marital interactions of drug-abusing patients and their partners: Comparisons with distressed couples and relationship to drug-using behavior. *Psychology of Addictive Behaviors, 12*, 28–38.

Feeney, J. A., Hohaus, L., Noller, P., & Alexander, R. P. (2001). *Becoming parents: Exploring the bonds between mothers, fathers, and their infants*. Cambridge, UK: Cambridge University Press.

Feeney, J. A., & Noller, P. (1991). Attachment style and verbal descriptions of romantic partners. *Journal of Social and Personal Relationships, 8*, 187–215.

Feigelman, W. (1987). Day-care treatment for multiple drug abusing adolescents: Social factors linked with completing treatment. *Journal of Psychoactive Drugs, 19*, 335–344.

Fekkes, M., Buitendijk, S. E., Verrips, G. H. W., Braat, D. D. M., Brewaeys, A. M. A., Dolfing, J. G., Kortman, M., Leerentveld, R. A., & Macklon, N. S. (2003). Health-related quality of life in relation to gender and age in couples planning IVF treatment. *Human Reproduction, 18*, 1536–1543.

Feldman, C. M., & Ridley, C. A. (2000). The role of conflict-based communication responses and outcomes in male domestic violence towards female partners. *Journal of Social and Personal Relationships, 17*, 552–573.

Feldman, P. J., Dunkel-Schetter, C., Sandman, C. A., & Wadhwa, P. D. (2000). Maternal social support predicts birth weight and fetal growth in human pregnancy. *Psychosomatic Medicine, 62*, 715–725.

Feldman, S. S., Nash, S. C., & Aschenbrenner, B. G. (1983). Antecedent of fathering. *Child Development, 54*, 1628–1636.

Fichten, C. S., & Wright, J. (1983). Problem-solving skills in happy and distressed couples: Effects of videotape and verbal feedback. *Journal of Clinical Psychology, 39*, 340–352.

Fields, R. (2001, August 20). Virginia and six other states still classify cohabitation as illegal. *LA Times*. Retrieved July 3, 2005, from www.sullivan-county.com/news/deist1999/7_states.htm

Fincham, F. D. (2004). Communication in marriage. In A. Vangelisti's (Ed.), *Handbook of family communication* (pp. 83–103). Mahwah, NJ: Erlbaum.

Fine, M. A., Coleman, M., & Ganong, L. H. (1998). Consistency in perceptions of the step-parent role among step-parents, parents and stepchildren. *Journal of Social and Personal Relationships, 15*, 810–828.

Fine, M. A., Kurdek, L. A., & Hennigen, L. (1992). Perceived self-competence, stepfamily myths, and (step)parent role ambiguity in adolescents from stepfather and stepmother families. *Journal of Family Psychology, 6*, 69–76.

Fine, M. A., Voydanoff, P., & Donnelly, B. W. (1993). Relations between parental control and warmth and child well-being in stepfamilies. *Journal of Family Psychology, 9*, 222–232.

Fisher, P. A., Leve, L. D., O'Leary, C. C., & Leve, C. (2003). Parental monitoring of children's behavior: Variation across stepmother, stepfather, and two-parent biological families. *Family Relations, 52*, 45–52.

Fitzpatrick, M. A. (1988). *Between husbands and wives: Communication in marriage*. Beverly Hills, CA: Sage.

Fitzpatrick, M. A., & Caughlin, J. P. (2002). Interpersonal communication in family relationships. In M. L. Knapp & J. A. Daly (Eds.), *Handbook of interpersonal communication* (3rd ed., pp. 726–777). Thousand Oaks, CA: Sage.

Fitzpatrick, M. A., Vangelisti, A. L., & Firman, S. M. (1994). Perceptions of marital interaction and change during pregnancy: A typological approach. *Personal Relationships, 1*, 101–122.

Fitzpatrick, M. A., & Winke, J. (1979). You always hurt the one you love: Strategies and tactics in interpersonal conflict. *Communication Quarterly, 29*, 3–11.

Fletcher, A. C., & Jeffries, B. C. (1999). Parental mediators of associations between perceived authoritative parenting and early adolescent substance use. *Journal of Early Adolescence, 19*, 465–487.

Flora, J., & Segrin, C. (2003). Relational well-being and perceptions of relational history in married and dating couples. *Journal of Social and Personal Relationsips, 20*, 515–536.

Flouri, E., & Buchanan, A. (2002). What predicts good relationships with parents and adolescence and partners in adult life: Findings from the 1958 British birth cohort. *Journal of Family Psychology, 16*, 186–198.

Floyd, K. (1997). Communicating affection in dyadic relationships: An assessment of behavior and expectancies. *Communication Quarterly, 45*, 68–81.

Floyd, K., & Morman, M. T. (2005a). Fathers' and sons' reports of fathers' affectionate communication: Implications of a naïve theory of affection. *Journal of Social and Personal Relationships, 22,* 99–109.

Floyd, K., & Morman, M. T. (2005b). (Eds.). *Widening the family circle.* Thousand Oaks, CA: Sage.

Floyd, K., & Morr, M. C. (2003). Human affection exchange: VII. Affectionate communication in the sibling/spouse/sibling-in-law triad. *Communication Quarterly, 51,* 247–261.

Follingstad, D. R., Laughlin, J. E., Polek, D. S., Rutledge, L. L., & Hause, E. S. (1991). Identification of patterns of wife abuse. *Journal of Interpersonal Violence, 6,* 187–204.

Ford, F. R. (1983). Rules: The visible family. *Family Process, 22,* 135–145.

Fossett, M. A., & Kiecolt, K. J. (1991). A methodological review of the sex ratio: Alternatives for comparative research. *Journal of Marriage and the Family, 53,* 941–957.

Francis-Connolly, E. (2003). Constructing parenthood: Portrayals of motherhood and fatherhood in popular American magazines. *Journal of the Association for Research on Mothering, 5,* 179–185.

Frazier, P. A., Tix, A. P., & Barnett, C. L. (2003). The relational context of social support: Relationship satisfaction moderates the relations between enacted support and distress. *Personality and Social Psychology Bulletin, 29,* 1133–1146.

Freeman, E. W., Boxer, A. S., Rickels, K., Tureck, R., & Mastroiani, L. (1985). Psychological evaluation and support in a program of *in vitro* fertilization and embryo transfer. *Fertility Sterilization, 43,* 48–53.

Frei, J. R., & Shaver, P. R. (2002). Respect in close relationships: Prototype definition, self-report assessment, and initial correlates. *Personal Relationships, 9,* 121–139.

Galinsky, E. (1981). *Between generations: The six stages of parenthood.* New York: Times Books.

Gallo, L. C., Troxel, W. M., Matthews, K. A., & Kuller, L. H. (2003). Marital status and quality in middle-aged women: Associations with levels and trajectories of cardiovascular risk factors. *Health Psychology, 22,* 453–463.

Galvin, K. M., Bylund, C. L., & Brommel, B. J. (2003). *Family communication: Cohesion and change* (6th ed.). New York: Allyn & Bacon.

Ganong, L., & Coleman, M. (1987). Effects of parental remarriage on children: An updated comparison of theories, methods and findings from clinical and empirical research. In K. Pasley & M. Ihinger-Tallman (Eds.), *Remarriage and stepparenting today: Current research and theory* (pp. 94–140). New York: Guilford.

Ganong, L., & Coleman, M. (1994). *Remarried family relationships.* Newbury Park, CA: Sage.

Garber, J., & Little, S. (1999). Predictors of competence among offspring of depressed mothers. *Journal of Adolescent Research, 14,* 44–71.

Garcia-Pindado, G. (1992). The family effect on adolescent drug use: Environmental and genetic factors. *Psiquis: Revisita de Psiquiatria, Psicologia y Psicosomatica, 13,* 39–48.

Gavanas, A. (2004). *Fatherhood politics in the United States: Masculinity, sexuality, race, and marriage.* Champaign-Urbana: University of Illinois Press.

Gerson, L. W. (1978). Alcohol-related acts of violence: Who was drinking and where the acts occurred. *Journal of Studies on Alcohol, 39,* 1294–1296.

Gerzi, S., & Berman, E. (1981). Emotional reactions of expectant fathers to their wives' first pregnancy. *British Journal of Medical Psychology, 54,* 259–265.

Gest, S. D., Freeman, N. R., Domitrovich, C. E., & Welsh, J. A. (2004). Shared book reading and children's language comprehension skills: The moderating role of parental discipline practices. *Early Childhood Research Quarterly, 19*, 319–336.

Gibbs, N. (1995, October 2). The EQ factor. *Time*, pp. 60–88.

Giele, J. Z. (2003). Decline of the family: Conservative, liberal, and feminist views. In A. S. Skolnick & J. H. Skolnick's (Eds.), *Family in transition* (12th ed., pp. 57–75). Boston: Allyn & Bacon.

Gilbert, L. A. (1994). Current perspectives on dual-career families. *Current Direction in Psychological Science, 3*, 101–105.

Ginsburg, G., & Bronstein, P. (1993). Family factors related to children's intrinsic/extrinsic motivational orientation and academic performance. *Child Development, 64*, 1461–1471.

Glass, J., & Fujimoto, T. (1994). Housework, paid work, and depression among husbands and wives. *Journal of Health and Social Behavior, 35*, 179–191.

Glenn, N. D. (1998). The course of marital success and failure in five American 10-year marriage cohorts. *Journal of Marriage and the Family, 60*, 569–576.

Goffman, E. (1959). *The presentation of self in every day life*. New York: Doubleday, Anchor.

Goldenberg, I., & Goldenberg, H. (1991). *Family therapy: An overview*. Pacific Grove, CA: Brooks/Cole.

Golding, J. M. (1990). Division of household labor, strain, and depressive symptoms among Mexican Americans and non-Hispanic Whites. *Psychology of Women Quarterly, 14*, 103–117.

Goldscheider, F. K., & Waite, L. J. (1991). *New families, no families? The transformation of the American home*. Berkeley: University of California Press.

Goldsmith, D. J., & Baxter, L. A. (1996). Constituting relationships in talk: A taxonomy of speech events in social and personal relations. *Human Communication Research, 1*, 106–127.

Goldsmith, D. J., McDermott, V. M., & Alexander, S. C. (2000). Helpful, supportive and sensitive: Measuring the evaluation of enacted social support in personal relationships. *Journal of Social and Personal Relationships, 17*, 369–391.

Goldstein, J. R., & Kenney, C. T. (2001). Marriage delayed or marriage forgone? New cohort forecasts of first marriage for U.S. women. *American Sociological Review, 66*, 506–519.

Goleman, D. (1995). *Emotional intelligence: Why it can matter more than IQ*. New York: Bantam.

Golombok, S. (1998). New families, old values: Considerations regarding the welfare of the child. *Human Reproduction, 13*, 1146–1150.

Gondolf, E. W. (with Fisher, E. R.). (1988). *Battered women as survivors: An alternative to treating learned helplessness*. Lexington, MA: Lexington Books.

Goodnow, J. J., Bowes, J. M., Warton, P. M., Dawes, L. J., & Taylor, A. J. (1991). Would you ask someone else to do this task? Parents' and children's ideas about household work requests. *Developmental Psychology, 27*, 817–828.

Goodwin, D. W. (1985). Alcoholism and genetics: The sins of the fathers. *Archives of General Psychiatry, 42*, 171–174.

Gottman, J. M. (1979). *Marital interaction*. New York: Academic Press.

Gottman, J. M. (1993). The roles of conflict engagement, escalation, and avoidance in marital interaction: A longitudinal view of five types of couples. *Journal of Consulting and Clinical Psychology, 61*, 6–15.

Gottman, J. M. (1994). *What predicts divorce? The relationship between marital processes and marital outcomes.* Hillsdale, NJ: Erlbaum.

Gottman, J. M. (1995). *Why marriages succeed or fail: And how you can make yours last.* New York: Simon & Schuster.

Gottman, J. M. (2001). What the study of relationships has to say about emotion research. *Social Science Information, 40,* 79–94.

Gottman, J. M., Coan, J., Carrere, S., & Swanson, C. (1998). Predicting happiness and stability from newlywed interactions. *Journal of Marriage and the Family, 60,* 5–22.

Gottman, J. M., & Krokoff, L. J. (1989). Marital interaction and satisfaction: A longitudinal view. *Journal of Consulting and Clinical Psychology, 57,* 47–52.

Gottman, J. M., & Levenson, R. W. (1986). Assessing the role of emotion in marriage. *Behavioral Assessment, 8,* 31–48.

Gottman, J. M., & Levenson, R. W. (1988). The social psychophysiology of marriage. In P. Noller & M. A. Fitzpatrick (Eds.), *Perspectives on marital interaction* (pp. 182–200). Philadelphia: Multilingual Matters.

Gottman, J. M., & Levenson, R. W. (1992). Marital processes predictive of later dissolution: Behavior, physiology, and health. *Journal of Personality and Social Psychology, 63,* 221–233.

Gottman, J. S. (1989). Children of gay and lesbian parents. *Marriage and Family Review, 14,* 177–196.

Gove, W. R., Hughes, M., & Briggs Style, C. (1983). Does marriage have positive effects on the psychological well-being of the individual? *Journal of Health and Social Behavior, 24,* 122–131.

Graber, J. A., Archibald, J. B., & Brooks-Gunn, J. (1999). The role of parents in the emergence, maintenance and prevention of eating problems and disorders. In N. Piran, M. P. Levine, & C. Steiner Adair (Eds.), *Preventing eating disorders: A handbook of interventions and special challenges* (pp. 44–62). New York: Brunner/Mazel.

Graefe, D. R., & Lichter, D. T. (2002). *When unwed mothers marry: The men in women's lives at mid-life* (Population Research Institute Working Paper 02–01). University Park: Pennsylvania State University.

Greeff, A. P. (2000). Characteristics of families that function well. *Journal of Family Issues, 21,* 948–962.

Green, R. (1992). *Sexual science and the law.* Cambridge, MA: Harvard University Press.

Greenfield, L. A., Rand, M. R., Craven, D., Klaus, P. A., Perkins, C. A., Ringel, C., Warchol, G., Maston, C., & Fox, J. A. (1998). *Violence by intimates: Analysis of data on crimes by current or former spouses, boyfriends, and girlfriends* (NCJ-167237). Washington, DC: U.S. Department of Justice.

Greenstein, T. N. (1990). Marital disruption and the employment of married women. *Journal of Marriage and Family, 52,* 657–676.

Grisso, J. A., Schwartz, D. F., Hirschinger, N., Sammel, M., Brensigner, C., Santanna, J., Lowe, R. A., Anderson, E., Shaw, L. M., Bethel, C. A., & Teelpe, L. (1999). Violent injuries among women in an urban area. *New England Journal of Medicine, 341,* 1899–1905.

Griswold, R. L. (1993). *Fatherhood in America: A history.* New York: Basic Books.

Grolnick, W. S., & Ryan, R. M. (1989). Parent style associated with children's self-regulation and competence in school. *Journal of Educational Psychology, 81,* 143–154.

Grote, N. K., Naylor, K., & Clark, M. S. (2002). Perceiving the division of family work to be unfair: Do social comparisons, enjoyment and competence matter? *Journal of Family Issues,* 16, 510–522.

Grusec, J. E., & Lytton, H. (1988). *Social development: History, theory, and research.* New York: Springer Verlag.

Guerrero, L. (1996). Attachment-style differences in intimacy and involvement: A test of the four-category model. *Communication Monographs, 63,* 269–292.

Guerrero, L. K. (1994, November). *Nonverbal immediacy and involvement in friendships and romantic relationships: Untangling the effects of communicator sex, target sex, and relationship type.* Paper presented at the annual meeting of the Speech Communication Association, New Orleans.

Guerrero, L. K., & Afifi, W. A. (1995). What parents don't know: Topic avoidance in parent-child relationships. In T. J. Socha & G. H. Stamp (Eds.), *Parents, children, and communication: Frontiers of theory and research* (pp. 219–245). Hillsdale, NJ: Erlbaum.

Guerrero, L. K., & Burgoon, J. K. (1996). Attachment styles and reactions to nonverbal involvement change in romantic dyads: Patterns of reciprocity and compensation. *Human Communication Research, 22,* 335–370.

Hahlweg, K., Revenstorf, D., & Schindler, L. (1984). Effects of behavioral marital therapy on couples' communication and problem-solving skills. *Journal of Consulting and Clinical Psychology, 52,* 553–366.

Hall, D. R., & Zhao, J. Z. (1995). Cohabitation and divorce in Canada: Testing the selectivity hypothesis. *Journal of Marriage and the Family, 57,* 421–427.

Hall, J. A., & Briton, N. J. (1993). Gender, nonverbal behavior and expectations. In P. D. Blanck (Ed.), *Interpersonal expectations: Theory, research, and applications* (pp. 276–295). New York: Cambridge University Press.

Hall, J. A., & Henggeler, S. W., Ferreira, D. K., & East, P. L. (1992). Sibling relations and substance use in high-risk female adolescents. *Family Dynamics of Addiction Quarterly, 2,* 44–51.

Halpin, G., Halpin, G., & Whiddon, T. (1980). The relationship of perceived parental behaviors to locus of control and self-esteem among American Indian and White Children. *Journal of Social Psychology, 111,* 189–195.

Handelsman, L., Branchey, M. H., Buydens-Branchey, L., Gribomont, B., Holloway, K., & Silverman, J. (1993). Morbidity risk for alcoholism and drug abuse in relatives of cocaine addicts. *American Journal of Drug and Alcohol Abuse, 19,* 347–357.

Hanson, S. M. H., & Sporakowski, M. J. (1986). Single parent families. *Family Relations, 35,* 3–8.

Harmer, A. L. M., Sanderson, J., & Mertin, P. (1999). Influence of negative childhood experiences on psychological functioning, social support, and parenting for mothers recovering from addiction, *Child Abuse and Neglect, 23,* 421–433.

Harrington Cleveland, H., Udry, J. R., & Chantala, K. (2001). Environmental and genetic influences on sex-typed behaviors and attitudes of male and female adolescents. *Personality and Social Psychology Bulletin, 27,* 1587–1598.

Hart, C. H., Newell, L. D., & Olsen, S. F. (2003). Parenting skills and social-communicative competence in childhood. In J. O. Greene & B. R. Burleson (Eds.), *Handbook of communication and social interaction skills* (pp. 753–797). Mahwah, NJ: Erlbaum.

Hartos, J. L., Eitel, P., Haynie, D. L., & Simons-Morton, B. G. (2000). Can I take the car? Relations among parenting practices and adolescent problem-driving practices. *Journal of Adolescent Research, 15,* 352–367.

Hartup, W. W., & Laursen, B. (1991). Relationships as developmental contexts. In R. Cohen & A. W. Siegel (Eds.), *Context and development* (pp. 253–279). Hillsdale, NJ: Erlbaum.

Hauser, S. T., Powers, S. I., & Noam, G. G. (1991). *Adolescents and their families.* New York: Free Press.

Havey, J. M., & Dodd, D. K. (1993). Variables associated with alcohol-abuse among self-identified collegiate COAS and their peers. *Addictive Behaviors, 18,* 567–575.

Hawkins, A. J., Marshall, C. M., & Allen, S. M. (1998). The orientation toward domestic labor questionnaire: Exploring dual-earner wives' sense of fairness about family work. *Journal of Family Psychology, 12,* 244–258.

Hayghe, H. V. (1990, March). Family members in the work force. *Monthly Labor Review,* pp. 14–19.

Haynes, H., White, B. L., & Held, R. (1965). Visual accommodation in human infants. *Science, 148,* 528–530.

Hazan, C., & Hutt, M. J. (1990, July). *Continuity and change in inner working models of attachment.* Paper presented at the Fifth International Conference on Personal Relationships, Oxford, UK.

Hazan, C., & Shaver, P. (1987). Romantic love conceptualized as an attachment process. *Journal of Personality and Social Psychology, 52,* 511–524.

Healthy Parenting Initiative. (2004, July 2). *Questions and answers about natural and logical consequences.* Retrieved September 15, 2004, from www.mfrc-dod-qol.org/healthyparenting/factsheets/QAP12naturalandlogical.cfm

Heaton, T. B. (2002). Factors contributing to increasing marital stability in the United States. *Journal of Family Issues, 23,* 392–409.

Heavey, C. L., Christensen, A., & Malamuth, N. M. (1995). The longitudinal impact of demand and withdrawal during marital conflict. *Journal of Consulting and Clinical Psychology, 63,* 797–801.

Heavey, C. L., Layne, C., & Christensen, A. (1993). Gender and conflict structure in marital interaction: A replication and extension. *Journal of Consulting and Clinical Psychology, 61,* 16–27.

Helms-Erikson, H. (2001). Marital quality ten years after the transition to parenthood: Implications of the timing of parenthood and the division of housework. *Journal of Marriage and Family, 63,* 1099–1110.

Henderson, V. L., & Dweck, C. S. (1990). Motivation and achievement. In S. S. Feldman & G. R. Elliott (Eds.), *At the threshold: The developing adolescent* (pp. 308–329). Cambridge, MA: Harvard University Press.

Hendrick, S. S. (1981). Self-disclosure and marital satisfaction. *Journal of Personality and Social Psychology, 40,* 1150–1159.

Hendrick, S. S., Hendrick, C., & Adler, N. L. (1988). Romantic relationships: Love, satisfaction, and staying together. *Journal of Personality and Social Psychology, 54,* 930–988.

Henry, W. A. (1990, November 1). The lesbians next door. *Time*, pp. 78–79.

Henton, J., Cate, R., Koval, J., Lloyd, S., & Christopher, S. (1983). Romance and violence in dating relations. *Journal of Family Issues, 4*, 467–482.

Hess, U., & Kirouac, G., (2000). Emotional expressivity in men and women: Stereotypes and self-perceptions. *Cognition & Emotion, 14*, 609–642.

Hetherington, E. M. (1989). Coping with transitions: Winners, losers, and survivors. *Child Development, 60*, 1–14.

Hetherington, E. M. (1993). An overview of the Virginia Longitudinal Study of Divorce and Remarriage: A focus on early adolescence. *Journal of Family Psychology, 7*, 39–56.

Hetherington, E. M. (1999). Should we stay together for the sake of the children? In E. M. Hetherington (Ed.), *Coping with divorce, single parenting and remarriage: A risk and resiliency perspective* (pp. 93–116). Mahwah, NJ: Erlbaum.

Hetherington, E. M., & Clingempeel, W. G. (1992). Coping with marital transitions: A family systems perspective. *Monographs of the Society for Research in Child Development, 57*(2–3 Serial No. 227).

Hetherington, E. M., Cox, M., & Cox, R. (1978). The aftermath of divorce. In J. H. Stevens, Jr., & M. Matthews (Eds.), *Mother-child, father-child relations* (pp. 38–50). Washington: National Association for the Education of Young Children.

Hetherington, E. M., Henderson, S. H., & Reiss, D. (1999). Adolescent siblings in stepfamilies: Family functioning and adolescent adjustment. *Adolescent Siblings in Stepfamilies, 64*, 1–222.

Hetherington, E. M., & Jodl, K. M. (1994). Stepfamilies as setting for child development. In A. Booth & J. Dunn (Eds.), *Stepfamilies: Who benefits? Who does not?* (pp. 55–79). Hillsdale, NJ: Erlbaum.

Hickman, G. P., Bartholomae, S., & McKenry, P. C. (2000). Influence of parenting styles on the adjustment and academic achievement of traditional college freshmen. *Journal of College Student Development, 41*, 41–54.

Hill, J. P. (1988). Adapting to menarche: Familial control and conflict. In M. R. Gunnar & W. A. Collins (Eds.), *The Minnesota Symposia on Child Psychology: Vol. 21. Development during the transition to adolescence* (pp. 43–77). Hillsdale, NJ: Erlbaum.

Hocker, J. L., & Wilmot, W. W. (2000). *Interpersonal conflict* (6th ed.). New York: McGraw-Hill.

Holland Benin, M., & Edwards, D. A. (1990). Adolescents' chores: The difference between dual- and single-earner families. *Journal of Marriage and Family, 52*, 361–373.

Holtzworth-Munroe, A., & Hutchinson, G. (1993). Attributing negative intent to wife behavior: The attributions of maritally violent vs. nonviolent men to problematic marital situations. *Journal of Abnormal Psychology, 102*, 206–211.

Holtzworth-Munroe, A., & Jacobson, N. S. (1985). Causal attributions of married couples: When do they search for causes? What do they conclude when they do? *Journal of Personality and Social Psychology, 48*, 1398–1412.

Holtzworth-Munroe, A., Smutzler, N., & Stuart, G. L. (1998). Demand and withdraw communication among couples experiencing husband violence. *Journal of Consulting and Clinical Psychology, 66*, 731–743.

Hops, H., Biglan, A., Sherman, L., Arthur, J., Friedman, L. S., & Osteen, V. (1987). Home observations of family interactions of depressed women. *Journal of Consulting and Clinical Psychology, 55*, 341–346.

Horwitz, A. V., & White, H. R. (1998). The relationship of cohabitation and mental health: A study of a young adult cohort. *Journal of Marriage and the Family, 80,* 505–514.

Houston, R. G., & Toma, R. F. (2003). Home schooling: An alternative school choice. *Southern Economic Journal, 69,* 920–936.

Huberty, D. J., & Huberty, C. E. (1986). Sabotaging siblings: An overlooked aspect of family therapy with drug dependent adolescents. *Journal of Psychoactive Drugs, 18,* 31–41.

Humphrey, L. L. (1988). Relationships within subtypes of anorexic, bulimic, and normal families. *Journal of the American Academy of Child and Adolescent Psychiatry, 27,* 544–551.

Humphrey, L. L. (1989). Observed family interactions among subtypes of eating disorders using structural analysis of social behavior. *Journal of Consulting and Clinical Psychology, 57,* 206–214.

Humphrey, L. L., Apple, R. F., & Kirschenbaum, D. S. (1986). Differentiating bulimic-anorexic from normal families using interpersonal and behavioral observational systems. *Journal of Consulting and Clinical Psychology, 54,* 190–195.

Humphrey, L. L., & Stern, S. (1988). Object relations and the family system in bulimia. *Journal of Marital and Family Therapy, 14,* 337–350.

Hunfeld, J. A. M., Fauser, B. C. M. M., de Beaufort, I. D., & Passchier, J. (2001). Child development and quality of parenting in lesbian families: No psychosocial indications for a-priori withholding of infertility treatment. A systematic review. *Human Reproduction Update, 7,* 579–590.

Hurcom, C., Copello, A., & Orford, J. (2000). The family and alcohol: Effects of excessive drinking and conceptualizations of spouses over recent decades. *Substance use and misuse, 35,* 473–502.

Hurrelmann, K. (1990). Parents, peers, teachers and other significant partners in adolescence. *International Journal of Adolescence and Youth, 2,* 211–236.

Hussong, A. M., & Chassin, L. (1997). Substance use initiation among adolescent children of alcoholics: Testing protective factors. *Journal of Studies on Alcohol, 58,* 272–279.

Huston, T. L., Caughlin, J. P., Houts, R. M., Smith, S. E., & George, L. J. (2001). The connubial crucible: Newlywed years as predictors of marital delight, distress, and divorce. *Journal of Personality and Social Psychology, 80,* 237–252.

Huston, T. L., & Holmes, E. K. (2004). Becoming parents. In A. Vangelisti (Ed.), *Handbook of family communication* (pp. 105–133). Mahwah, NJ: Erlbaum.

Huston, T. L., McHale, S., & Crouter, A. (1986). When the honeymoon's over: Changes in the marital relationship over the first year. In R. Gilmour & S. Duck (Eds.), *The emerging field of personal relationships* (pp. 109–132). Hillsdale, NJ: Erlbaum.

Huston, T. L., Robins, E., Atkinson, J., & McHale, S. M. (1987). Surveying the landscape of marital behavior: A behavioral self-report approach to studying marriage. In S. Oskamp (Ed.), *Family processes and problems: Social psychological aspects* (pp. 45–72). Newbury Park, CA: Sage.

Huston, T. L., & Vangelisti, A. L. (1991). Socioemotional behavior and satisfaction in marital relationships. *Journal of Personality and Social Psychology, 61,* 721–733.

Huston, T. L., & Vangelisti, A. L. (1995). How parenthood affects marriage. In M. A. Fitzpatrick & A. L. Vangelisti (Eds.). *Explaining family interactions* (pp. 147–176). Thousand Oaks, CA: Sage.

Hutchinson, M. K. (1999). Individual, family, and relationship predictors of young women's sexual risk perceptions. *Journal of Obstetric, Gynecologic, and Neonatal Nursing, 28*, 60–66.

Hutchinson, M. K. (2002). The influence of sexual risk communication between parents and daughters on sexual risk behaviors. *Family Relations, 51*, 238–247.

Hutchinson, M. K., & Cooney, T. M. (1998). Patterns in parent-teen sexual risk communication: Implications for intervention. *Interdisciplinary Journal of Applied Family Studies, 47*, 185–194.

Hutchinson, M. K., Jemmott, J. B., Jemmott, L. S., Braverman, P., & Fong, G. T. (2003). The role of mother-daughter sexual risk communication in reducing sexual risk behaviors among urban adolescent females: A prospective study. *Journal of Adolescent Health, 33*, 98–107.

Ihinger-Tallman, M. (1987). Sibling and step sibling bonding in stepfamilies. In K. Pasley & M. Ihinger-Tallman (Eds.), *Remarriage and stepparenting today: Current research and theory*. New York: Guilford.

Infante, D., A., Chandler, T. A., & Rudd, J. E. (1989). Tests of an argumentative skill deficiency model of interspousal violence. *Communication Monographs, 56*, 163–177.

Israelson, C. L. (1989). Family resource management. *Family Perspective, 23*, 311–331.

Jaccard, J., Dittus, P. J., & Gordon, V. V. (2000). Parent-teen communication about premarital sex: Factors associated with the extent of communication. *Journal of Adolescent Research, 15*(2), 187–208.

Jackson, D. (1968). *Communication, family and marriage*. Palo Alto, CA: Science and Behavior.

Jackson, S., Bijstra, J., Oostra, L., & Bosma, H. (1998). Adolescents' perceptions of communications with parents relative to specific aspects of relationships with parents and personal development. *Journal of Adolescence, 21*, 305–322.

Jacob, T., & Leonard, K. (1988). Alcoholic spouse interaction as a function of alcoholism subtype and alcohol consumption interaction. *Journal of Abnormal Psychology, 97*, 231–237.

Jacobson, N. S. (1984). A component analysis of behavioral marital therapy: The relative effectiveness of behavior exchange and communication/problem-solving training. *Journal of Consulting and Clinical Psychology, 52*, 295–305.

Jacobson, N. S. (1990). Contributions from psychology to an understanding of marriage. In F. D. Fincham & T. N. Bradbury (Eds.), *The psychology of marriage* (pp. 258–275). New York: Guilford.

Jacobson, N. S., Follette, W. C., & Pagel, M. (1986). Predicting who will benefit from behavioral therapy. *Journal of Consulting and Clinical Psychology, 54*, 518–522.

Jacobson, N. S., Gottman, J. M., Gortner, E., Berns, S., & Shortt, J. W. (1996). Psychological factors in the longitudinal course of battering: When do the couples split up? When does the abuse decrease? *Violence & Victims, 11*, 371–392.

Jacobson, N. S., Gottman, J. M., Waltz, J., Rushe, R., & Holtzworth-Munroe, A. (1994). Affect, verbal content, and psychophysiology in the arguments of couples with a violent husband. *Journal of Consulting and Clinical Psychology, 62*, 982–988.

Jaffe, J. G., Babor, T. F., & Fishbein, D. H. (1988). Alcoholics, aggression, and antisocial personality. *Journal of Studies on Alcohol, 49*, 211–218.

Jagacinski, C. (1992). The effects of task involvement and ego involvement on achievement-related cognitions and behaviors. In D. H. Schunk & J. L. Meece (Eds.), *Student perceptions in the classroom* (pp. 307–326). Hillsdale, NJ: Erlbaum.

Johnson, M. P., & Leone, J. M. (2005). The differential effects of intimate terrorism and situational couple violence: Findings from the National Violence Against Women Survey. *Journal of Family Issues, 26,* 322–349.

Josephs, R. A., Markus, H. R., & Tafarodi, R. W. (1992). Gender and self-esteem. *Journal of Personality and Social Psychology, 63,* 391–402.

Jusczyk, P. W., & Bertoncini, J. (1988). Viewing the development of speech perception as an innately guided learning process. *Language and Speech, 31,* 217–238.

Kadambari, R., Gowers, S., & Crisp, A. (1986). Some correlates of vegetarianism in anorexia nervosa. *International Journal of Eating Disorders, 5,* 539–544.

Kaffman, M., & Sadeh, T. (1989). Anorexia nervosa in the kibbutz: Factors influencing the development of a monoideistic fixation. *International Journal of Eating Disorders, 8,* 33–53.

Kagan, S. L., & Cohen, N. E. (1995). *Solving the quality problem: A vision for America's early care and education system. A final report of the Quality 2000 initiative.* New Haven, CT: Yale University Press.

Kaiser Family Foundation. (1996). *The entertainment media as "sex educators?" and other ways teens learn about sex, contraception, STDs and AIDS. A report to the Kaiser Family Foundation.* Menlo Park, CA: Author.

Kaiser Family Foundation. (1998). *Sexually transmitted diseases in America: How many cases and at what cost?* Menlo Park, CA: Author.

Kaiser Family Foundation. (2000). *Sex smarts: Decision making: A series of national surveys of teens about sex. A report to the Kaiser Family Foundation.* Menlo Park, CA: Author.

Kaiser Family Foundation. (2001). *MTV, teen people, national survey of teens: What they know and don't (but should) about STDs. A report to the Kaiser Family Foundation.* Menlo Park, CA: Author.

Kalish, S. (1994, November). Fewer and fewer "traditional" U.S. households. *Population Today,* p. 3.

Kantor, G., & Straus, M. A. (1987). The drunken bum theory of wife beating. *Social Problems, 34,* 213–230.

Kantor, G., & Straus, M. A. (1989). Substance abuse as a precipitant of family violence victimization. *American Journal of Drug and Alcohol Abuse, 15,* 173–189.

Karney, B. R., & Bradbury, T. N. (1997). Neuroticism, marital interaction, and the trajectory of marital satisfaction. *Journal of Personality and Social Psychology, 72,* 1075–1092.

Karney, B. R., Bradbury, T. N., Fincham, F. D., & Sullivan, K. T. (1994). The role of negative affectivity in the association between attributions and marital satisfaction. *Journal of Personality and Social Psychology, 66,* 413–424.

Kashubeck, S., & Christensen, S. A. (1995). Parental alcohol use, family relationship quality, self-esteem, and depression in college students. *Journal of College Student Development, 36,* 431–443.

Kaufman, E. (1979). The application of the basic principles of family therapy to the treatment of drug and alcohol abusers. In E. Kaufman & P. Kaufman (Eds.), *Family therapy of drug and alcohol abuse* (pp. 255–272). New York: Gardner Press.

Kaufman, E. (1985). Family systems and family therapy of substance abuse: An overview of two decades of research and clinical experience. *The International Journal of the Addictions, 20,* 897–916.

Keller, H., Chasiotis, A., Risau Peters, J., Voelker, S., Zach, U., & Restemeier, R. (1996). Psychobiological aspects of infant crying. *Early Development and Parenting, 5,* 1–13.

Kelly, A. B., Halford, W. K., & Young, R. M. (2002). Couple communication and female problem drinking: A behavioral observation study. *Psychology of Addictive Behaviors, 16,* 269–271.

Kelly, A. E. (2002). *The psychology of secrets.* New York: Kluwer Academic/Plenum.

Kelly, C., Huston, T. L., & Cate, R. M. (1985). Premarital relationship correlates of erosion of satisfaction in marriage. *Journal of Social and Personal Relationships, 2,* 167–178.

Kenrick, D. T., Groth, G. E., Trost, M. R., & Sadalla, E. K. (1993). Integrating evolutionary and social exchange perspectives on relationships: Effects of gender, self-appraisal, and involvement level on mate selection criteria. *Journal of Personality and Social Psychology, 64,* 951–969.

Kessler, R. C., & McRae, J. A. (1982). The effect of wives' employment on the mental health of married men and women. *American Sociological Review, 47,* 216–227.

Kiecolt-Glaser, J. K., McGuire, L., Robles, T. F., & Glaser, R. (2002a). Emotions, morbidity, and mortality: New perspectives from psychoneuroimmunology. *Annual Reviews of Psychology, 53,* 83–107.

Kiecolt-Glaser, J. K., McGuire, L., Robles, T. F., & Glaser, R. (2002b). Psychoneuroimmunology: Psychological influences on immune function and health. *Journal of Consulting and Clinical Psychology, 70,* 537–547.

Kirchler, E., Rodler, C., Hölzl, E., & Meier, K. (2001). *Conflict and decision making in close relationships: Love, money, and daily routines.* East Sussex, UK: Psychology Press.

Kirkwood, C. (1993). *Leaving abusive partners: From the scars of survival to the wisdom for change.* Newbury Park, CA: Sage.

Klein, R. C. A., & Johnson, M. P. (1997). Strategies of couple conflict. In S. Duck (Ed.), *Handbook of personal relationships* (2nd ed., pp. 469–486). New York: Wiley.

Knapp, M. L. (1984). *Interpersonal communication and human relationships.* Boston: Allyn & Bacon, 1984).

Knapp, M. L., Stafford, L., & Daly, J. A. (1986). Regrettable messages: Things people wish they hadn't said. *Journal of Communication, 36,* 40–58.

Knaub, P. K. (1986). Growing up in a dual-career family: The children's perceptions. *Family Relations, 35,* 431–437.

Knobloch, L. K., & Solomon, D. H. (2002). Intimacy and the magnitude and experience of episodic relational uncertainty within romantic relationships. *Personal Relationships, 9,* 457–478.

Knobloch, L. K., Solomon, D. H., & Cruz, M. G. (2001). The role of relationship development and attachment in the experience of romantic jealousy. *Personal Relationships, 8,* 205–224.

Kog, E., & Vandereycken, W. (1989). Family interaction in eating disorder patients and normal controls. *International Journal of Eating Disorders, 8,* 11–23.

Kolbo, J. R., Blakely, E. H., & Engleman, D. (1996). Children who witness domestic violence: A review of empirical literature. *Journal of Interpersonal Violence, 11,* 281–293.

Kreider, R. M., & Fields, J. M. (2001). *Number, timing, and duration of marriages and divorces: Fall 1996* (Current population reports, P70–80). Washington, DC: U.S. Census Bureau.

Krogh, K. M. (1985). Women's motives to achieve and to nurture in different life stages. *Sex Roles, 12,* 75–90.

Krusiewicz, E. S., & Wood, J. T. (2001). "He was our child from the moment we walked in that room": Entrance stories of adoptive parents. *Journal of Social and Personal Relationships, 18,* 785–803.

Kurdek, L. (1993). Nature and prediction of changes in marital quality for first-time parent and non-parent husbands and wives. *Journal of Family Psychology, 6,* 255–265.

Laakso, M. L., Poikkeus, A. M., Eklund, K., & Lyytenin, P. (2004). Interest in early shared reading: Its relation to later reading and letter knowledge in children with and without risk for reading difficulties. *First Language, 24,* 323–345.

Lachner, G., & Wittchen, H. U. (1995). Familial transmission of vulnerability factors in alcohol-abuse and dependence. *Zeitschrift fur Klinishche Psychologie-Forschung und Praxis, 24,* 118–146.

Laing, R. D. (1961). *The self and others.* London: Tavistock.

Lamb, M. E. (1997). The development of father-infant relationships. In M. E. Lamb (Ed.), *The role of the father in child development* (3rd ed., pp. 104–120). New York: Wiley.

Lamborn, S. D., Mounts, N. S., Steinberg, L., & Dornbusch, S. M. (1991). Patterns of competence and adjustment among adolescents from authoritative, authoritarian, indulgent, and neglectful families. *Child Development, 62,* 1049–1065.

Lanz, M., Iafrate, R., Rosnati, R., & Scabini, E. (1999). Parent-child communication and adolescent self-esteem in separated, intercountry adoptive and intact non-adoptive families. *Journal of Adolescence, 22,* 785–794.

Larrance, D. T., & Twentyman, C. T. (1983). Maternal attributions and child abuse. *Journal of Abnormal Psychology, 92,* 449–457.

Larson, R. W., Richards, M. H., Moneta, G., Holmbeck, G., & Duckett, E. (1996). Changes in adolescents' daily interactions with their families from ages 10 to 18: Disengagement and transformation. *Developmental Psychology, 32,* 744–754.

Larson, R. W., & Almeida, D. M. (1999). Emotional transmission in the daily lives of families: A new paradigm for studying family process. *Journal of Marriage and the Family, 61,* 5–20.

Laumann, E. O., Gagnon, J. H., Michael, R. T., & Michaels, S. (1994). *The social organization of sexuality.* Chicago: University of Chicago Press.

Laursen, B. (1993). The perceived impact of conflict on adolescent relationships. *Merrill-Palmer Quarterly, 39,* 535–550.

Laursen, B., & Collins, W. A. (1994). Interpersonal conflict during adolescence. *Psychological Bulletin, 115,* 197–209.

Laursen, B., & Collins, W. A. (2004). Parent-child communication during adolescence. In A. L. Vangelisti (Ed.), *Handbook of Family Communication* (pp. 333–348). Mahwah, New Jersey: Erlbaum.

Laursen, B., & Williams, V. (1997). Perceptions of interdependence and closeness in family and peer relationships among adolescents with and without romantic partners. In S. Shulman & W. A. Collins (Eds.), *Romantic relationships in adolescence: Developmental perspectives* (New Directions for Child Development, Vol. 78, pp. 3–20). San Francisco: Jossey-Bass.

Lawrance, K. A., & Byers, E. S. (1995). Sexual satisfaction in long-term heterosexual relationships: The interpersonal exchange model of sexual satisfaction. *Personal Relationships, 2*, 267–285.

Le Poire, B. A. (1992). Does the codependent encourage substance dependent behavior? Paradoxical injunctions in the codependent relationship. *International Journal of Addictions, 27*, 1465–1474.

Le Poire, B. A. (1995). Inconsistent nurturing as control theory: Implications for communication-based research and treatment programs. *Journal of Applied Communication Research, 23*, 1–15.

Le Poire, B. A. (2004). The influence of drugs and alcohol on family communication: The effects that substance abuse has on family members and the effects that family members have on substance abuse. In A. Vangelisti (Ed.), *Handbook of family communication* (pp. 609–628). Thousand Oaks, CA: Sage.

Le Poire, B. A., Addis, K. A., Duggan, A. P., & Dailey, R. M. (2003). *Communicative strategies used by partners of drug abusers.* Manuscript submitted for publication.

Le Poire, B. A., & Cope, K. (1999). Episodic versus steady state drinkers: Evidence of differential reinforcement patterns. *Alcoholism Treatment Quarterly, 17*, 79–90.

Le Poire, B. A., & Dailey, R. (2005). A new theory in family communication: Inconsistent nurturing as control theory. In D. O. Braithwaite & L. A. Baxter (Eds.), *Engaging theories in family communication* (pp. 82–98). Thousand Oaks, CA: Sage.

Le Poire, B. A., Dailey, R. M., Duggan, A. P., & Moloney, E. (2004, November). *Reciprocity and compensation of nonverbal involvement behavior in romantic couples: Interactions of parental and partner attachment styles.* Paper presented to the interpersonal division of the National Communication Association, Chicago.

Le Poire, B. A., Erlandson, K. T., & Hallett, J. S. (1998). Punishing versus reinforcing strategies of drug discontinuance: Effect of persuaders' drug use. *Health Communication, 10*, 293–316.

Le Poire, B. A., Hallett, J. S., & Erlandson, K. T. (2000). An initial test of inconsistent nurturing as control theory: How partners of drug abusers assist their partners' sobriety. *Human Communication Research, 26*, 432–457.

Le Poire, B. A., Haynes, J., Driscoll, J., Driver, B. N., Wheelis, T. F., Hyde, M. K., Prochaska, M., & Ramos, L. (1997). Attachment as a function of parental and partner approach-avoidance tendencies. *Human Communication Research, 23*, 413–441.

Le Poire, B. A., Prescott, M., & Shepard, C. (in press). Understanding the role of the helper: The role of codependency in health care and health care outcomes. In D. E. Brashers & D. Goldsmith (Eds.), *Communication in the management of health and illness.*

Le Poire, B., Shepard, C., & Duggan, A. (1999). Nonverbal involvement, expressiveness, and pleasantness as predicted by parental and partner attachment style. *Communication Monographs, 66*, 293–311.

Lee, G. R., Seccombe, K., & Shehan, C. L. (1991). Marital status and personal happiness: An analysis of trend data. *Journal of Marriage and the Family, 53*, 839–844.

Lefebvre, P., & Merrigan, P. (1998). The impact of welfare benefits on the conjugal status of single mothers in Canada: Estimates from a hazard model. *Journal of Human Resources, 33*, 742–757.

Legerstee, M. (1991). Changes in the quality of infant sounds as a function of social and nonsocial stimulation. *First Language, 11*, 327–343.

Lehmann, N., & Krupp, S. L. (1983). Incidence of alcohol-related domestic violence: An assessment. *Alcohol Heath Research World, 39*, 23–27.

LeMasters, E. E. (1957). Parenthood as crisis. *Marriage and Family Living, 19*, 352–355.

Lennon, M. C., & Rosenfield, S. (1994). Relative fairness and the division of housework: The importance of options. *American Journal of Sociology, 100*, 506–531.

Levenson, R. W., & Gottman, J. M. (1985). Physiological and affective predictors of change in relationship satisfaction. *Journal of Personality and Social Psychology, 49*, 85–94.

Levy, E. F. (1992). Strengthening the coping resources of lesbian families. *Journal of Contemporary Human Services, 73*, 23–31.

Lewis, R. A., & Spanier, G. (1979). Theorizing about the quality and stability of marriage. In W. R. Burr, R. Hill, F. I. Nye, & I. Reiss (Eds.), *Contemporary theories about the family* (Vol. 1, pp. 268–294). New York: Free Press.

Lichter, D. T., & Graefe, D. R. (2001). Finding a mate? The marital and cohabitation histories of unwed mothers. In L. L. Wu & B. Wolfe (Eds.), *Out of wedlock: Trends, causes, and consequences of nonmarital fertility* (pp. 317–342). New York: Russell Sage.

Lichter, D. T., Graefe, D. R., & Brown, J. B. (2003). Is marriage a panacea? Union formation among economically disadvantaged unwed mothers. *Social Problems, 50*, 60–86.

Lichter, D. T., LeClere, F. B., & McLaughlin, D. K. (1991). Local marriage markets and the marital behavior of black and white women. *American Journal of Sociology, 96*, 843–867.

Lieberman, P. (1984). *The biology and evolution of language*. Cambridge, MA: Harvard University Press.

Linker, J. S., Stolberg, A. L., & Green, R. G. (1999). Family communication as a mediator of child adjustment to divorce. *Journal of Divorce and Remarriage, 30*, 83–97.

Littlejohn, S., & Foss, K. (2005). *Theories of human communication* (8th ed.). Belmont, CA: Thomson Wadsworth.

Livia, A. (2000). Snapshots from a family album. *International Journal of Sexuality and Gender Studies, 5*, 215–219.

Lloyd, C. (1998). Risk factors for problem drug use: Identifying vulnerable groups. *Drugs: Education, Prevention, and Policy, 5*, 217–232.

Lloyd, S. A., & Cate, R. M. (1985). The developmental course of conflict in dissolution of premarital relationships. *Journal of Social and Personal Relationships, 2*, 179–194.

Lollis, S. Ross, H., & Leroux, L. (1996). An observational study of parents' socialization of moral orientation during sibling conflicts. *Merrill Palmer Quarterly, 42*, 475–494.

Lott, B. (1987). *Women's lives: Themes and variations in gender learning*. Pacific Grove, CA: Wadsworth.

Luster, T., & Small, S. A. (1994). Factors associated with sexual risk-taking behaviors among adolescents. *Journal of Marriage and Family, 56*, 622–632.

Lytton, H. (1980). *Parent-child interaction: The socialization process observed in twin and singleton families*. New York: Plenum.

MacCallum, F., Lycett, E., Murray, C., Jadva, V., & Golombok, S. (2003). Surrogacy: The experience of commissioning couples. *Human Reproduction, 18*, 1334–1342.

Maccoby, E. E., & Martin, J. A. (1983). Socialization in the context of the family: Parent-child interaction. In P. H. Mussen (Series Ed.) & E. M. Hetherington (Vol. Ed.), *Handbook of child psychology: Vol. 4. Socialization, personality, and social development* (4th ed., pp. 1–101). New York: Wiley.

MacDermid, S. M., Huston, T. L., & McHale, S. M. (1990). Changes in marriage associated with the transition to parenthood: Individual differences as a function of sex-role attitudes and changes in the division of labor. *Journal of Marriage and the Family, 52,* 475–485.

MacDonald, D., & Parke, R. D. (1986). Parent-child physical play: The effect of sex and age of children and parents. *Sex Roles, 15,* 367–378.

Mahlstedt, P. P., Macduff, S., & Bernstein, J. (1987). Emotional factors and the *in vitro* fertilization and embryo transfer process. *Journal of In Vitro Fertilization Embryo Transfer, 4,* 232–236.

Mahoney, M. (1994). *Stepfamilies and the law.* Ann Arbor: University of Michigan.

Main, M., Kaplan, N., & Cassidy, J. (1985). Security in infancy, childhood, and adulthood: A move to the level of representation. *Monographs of the Society for Research in Child Development, 50*(1-2), 60–104.

Manning, W. D., & Lichter, D. T. (1996). Parental cohabitation and the children's economic well-being. *Journal of Marriage and the Family, 58,* 998–1010.

Mare, R. D. (1991). Five decades of educational assortative mating. *American Sociological Review, 56,* 15–32.

Marjoribanks, K. (1997). Family contexts, immediate settings, and adolescents' aspirations. *Journal of Applied Developmental Psychology, 18,* 119–132.

Markman, H. J., & Kraft, S. (1989). Men and women in marriage: Dealing with gender differences in marital therapy. *Behavior Therapist, 12,* 51–56.

Martin, A. (1993). *The lesbian and gay parenting handbook: Creating and raising our families.* New York: Harper Perennial.

Masataka, N. (1993). Effects of contingent and noncontingent maternal stimulation on the vocal behaviour of three- to four-month-old Japanese infants. *Journal of Child Language, 20,* 303–312.

Mason, M. A. (2000). *The custody wars.* New York: Basic Books.

Mason, M. A., Fine, M. A., & Carnochan, S. (2003). Family law in the new millennium: For whose families? In A. S. Skolnick & J. H. Skolnick (Eds.), *Family in transition* (12th ed., pp. 76–89). Boston: Allyn & Bacon.

Mason, M. A., Harrison-Jay, S., Svare, G. M., & Wolfinger, N. H. (2002). Stepparents: De facto parents or legal strangers? *Journal of Family Issues, 23,* 507–522.

Mason, M. A., & Zaya, N. (2002). Rethinking stepparent rights: Has the ALI found a better definition? *Family Law Quarterly, 36,* 227–253.

Mayer, J., & Salovey, P. (1997). What is emotional intelligence? In P. Salovey & D. J. Sluyter (Eds.), *Emotional development and emotional intelligence: Educational implications* (pp. 3–32). New York: Basic Books.

McCrady, B. S., Noel, N. E., Abrams, D. B., Stout, R. L., Nelson, H. F., & Hay, W. M. (1986). Comparative effectiveness of three types of spouse involvement in outpatient behavioral alcoholism treatment. *Journal of Studies on Alcohol, 47,* 459–465.

McGonagle, K. A., Kessler, R. C., & Schilling, E. A. (1992). The frequency and determinants of marital disagreements in a community sample. *Journal of Social and Personal Relationships, 9,* 507–524.

McGovern, M. P., & Morrison, D. H. (1992). The chemical use, abuse, and dependence scale (CUAD): Rationale, reliability, and validity. *Journal of Substance Abuse Treatment, 9,* 27–38.

McHale, S. M., Bartko, W. T., Crouter, A. C., & Perry-Jenkins, M. (1990). Children's housework and psychosocial functioning: The mediating role of parents' sex-role behaviors and attitudes. *Child Development, 61,* 1413–1426.

McHale, S. M., & Huston, T. L. (1984). Men and women as parents: Sex role orientations, employment, and parental roles with infants. *Child Development, 55,* 1349–1361.

McHale, S. M., & Huston, T. L. (1985). The effect of the transition to parenthood on the marriage relationship: A longitudinal study. *Journal of Family Issues, 6,* 409–433.

Mackay, J. (2000). *The Penguin atlas of human sexual behavior.* New York: Penguin Reference.

Maricopa Association of Governments, Regional Domestic Violence Council. (nd). *Profiles of a victim and batterer.* Retrieved October 14, 2004, from www.mag. maricopa.gov/dv/About_DV/Profile/profile.html

McHale, S. M., & Huston, T. L. (1985). The effect of the transition to parenthood on the marriage relationship: A longitudinal study. *Journal of Family Issues, 6,* 409–433.

McLanahan, S., & Sandefur, G. (1994). *Growing up with a single parent: What hurts, what helps?* Cambridge, MA: Harvard University Press.

McNabb, J., Der-Karabetian, A., & Rhoads, J. (1989). Family involvement and outcome in treatment of alcoholism. *Psychological Reports, 65,* 1327–1330.

McNulty, J. K., & Karney, B. R. (2004). Positive expectations in the early years of marriage: Should couples expect the best or brace for the worst? *Journal of Personality and Social Psychology, 86,* 729–743.

Melender, H. L. (2002). Experiences of fears associated with pregnancy and childbirth: A study of 329 pregnant women. *Birth: Issues in perinatal care, 29,* 101–111.

Menaghan, E. (1982). Assessing the impact of family transitions on marital experience. In H. I. McCubbin, A. E. Cauble, & J. M. Patterson (Eds.), *Family stress, coping and social support* (pp. 90–108). Springfield, IL: Charles C Thomas.

Merikangas, K. R., Dierker, L. C., & Szamari, P. (1998). Psychopathology among offspring of parents with substance abuse and/or anxiety disorders: A high risk study. *Journal of Child Psychology and Psychiatry and Allied Disciplines, 39,* 711–720.

Merikangas, K. R., Rounsaville, B. J., & Prusoff, B. A. (1992). Familial factors in vulnerability to substance abuse. In M. G. Glantz & R. W. Pickens (Eds.), *Vulnerability to drug abuse* (pp. 75–97). Washington DC: American Psychological Association.

Meschke, L. L., Bartholomae, S., & Zentall, S. R. (2002). Adolescent sexuality and parent-adolescent processes: Promoting healthy teen choices. *Journal of Adolescent Health, 31,* 264–279.

Mikhailovich, K., Martin, S., & Lawton, S. (2001). Lesbian and gay parents: Their experiences of children's health care in Australia. *International Journal of Sexuality and Gender Studies, 6,* 181–191.

Mikulincer, M., & Nachshon, O. (1991). Attachment styles and patterns of self-disclosure. *Journal of Personality and Social Psychology, 61,* 321–331.

Mikulincer, M., Shaver, P. R., & Pereg, D. (2003). Attachment theory and affect regulation: The dynamics, development, and cognitive consequences of attachment-related strategies. *Motivation and Emotion, 27*(2), 77–102.

Miller, B. A., Downs, W. R., & Gondoli, D. M. (1989). Spousal violence among alcoholic women as compared to a random household sample. *Journal of Studies on Alcohol, 50,* 533–540.

Miller, B. C., Benson, B., & Galbraith, K. A. (2001). Family relationships and adolescent pregnancy risk: A research synthesis. *Developmental Review, 21,* 1–38.

Miller, C. L. (1983). Developmental changes in male/female voice classification by infants. *Infant Behavior and Development, 6,* 313–330.

Miller, L. C. (1990). Intimacy and liking: Mutual influence and the role of unique relationships. *Journal of Personality and Social Psychology, 59,* 50–60.

Miller, L. C., & Read, S. J. (1991). On the coherence of mental models of persons and relationships: A knowledge structure approach. In G. O. Fletcher & F. D. Fincham (Eds.), *Cognition in close relationships* (pp. 69–99). Hillsdale, NJ: Erlbaum.

Mitchell, B. A., & Gee, E. M. (1996). "Boomerang kids" and midlife parental marital satisfaction. *Family Relations, 45,* 442–448.

Mize, J., & Petit, G. S. (1997). Mother's social coaching, mother child relationship style, and children's peer competence: Is the medium the message? *Child Development, 68,* 312–332.

Moen, P. (1999). *The Cornell couples and career study.* Ithaca, NY: Cornell University, Cornell Employment and Family Careers Institute.

Mohr, J., Eiche, K., & Sedlacek, W. (1998). So close, yet so far: Predictors of attrition in college seniors. *Journal of College Student Development, 39,* 343–354.

Mondloch, C. J., Lewis, T. L., Budreau, D. R., Maurer, D., Dannemiller, J. L., Stephens, B. R., & Kleiner-Gathercoal, K. A. (1999). Face perception during early infancy. *Psychological Science, 10,* 419–422.

Monroe, P. A., & Tiller, V. V. (2001). Commitment to work among welfare-reliant women. *Journal of Marriage and the Family, 63,* 816–828.

Montemayor, R. (1986). Parents and adolescents in conflict. All forms some of the time and some forms most of the time. *Journal of Early Adolescence, 3,* 83–103.

Montgomery, M. J., Anderson, E. R., Hetherington, E. M., & Clingempeel, W. G. (1992). Patterns of courtship for remarriage: Implications for child adjustment and parent-child relationships. *Journal of Marriage and the Family, 54,* 686–698.

Moore, K. A., & Waite, L. J. (1981). Marital dissolution, early motherhood and early marriage. *Social Forces, 60,* 20–40.

Morris, D. (2004, May 13). *Courting gay marriage.* Retrieved July 18, 2005, from www.alternet.org/story/18694

Mothersead, P. K., Kivlighan, D. M., & Wynkoop, T. F. (1998). Attachment, family dysfunction, parental alcoholism, and interpersonal distress in late adolescence: A structural model. *Journal of Counseling Psychology, 45,* 196–203.

Mulac, A., Studley, L. B., Wiemann, J. W., & Bradac, J. J. (1987). Male/female gaze in same-sex and mixed-sex dyads: Gender-linked differences and mutual influence. *Human Communication Research, 13,* 323–344.

Murphy, C. M., & O'Farrell, T. J. (1997). Couple communication patterns and aggressive and nonaggressive male alcoholics. *Journal of Studies on Alcohol, 58,* 83–90.

Murray, S. L., Holmes, J. G., & Griffin, D. W. (1996a). The benefits of positive illusions: Idealization and the construction of satisfaction in close relationships. *Journal of Personality and Social Psychology, 70,* 79–98.

Murray, S. L., Holmes, J. G., & Griffin, D. W. (1996b). The self-fulfilling nature of positive illusions in romantic relationships: Love is not blind but prescient. *Journal of Personality and Social Psychology, 71,* 1155–1180.

Nathanson, C. M., & Becker, M. H. (1986). Family and peer influence on obtaining a method of contraception. *Journal of Marriage and Family, 48,* 513–525.

National Association of Anorexia Nervosa and Associated Disorders. (2000). *General information.* Retrieved July 14, 2005, from www.anad.org/site/anadweb/content.php?type=1&id=6982

National Center for Health Statistics. (1995). Advance report of final divorce statistics, 1989 and 1990. *Monthly Vital Statistics Report, 43*(9).

National Institute of Mental Health. (2003a). *Depression: A treatable illness* (NIH Publication No. 03-5299). Bethesda, MD: Author. Retrieved November 2, 2004, from http://menanddepression.nimh.nih.gov/infopage.asp?id=15

National Institute of Mental Health. (2003b). *Real men, Real depression: Men and depression* (NIH Publication No. 03-4972). Bethesda, MD: Author. Retrieved November 2, 2004, from http://menanddepression.nimh.nih.gov/infopage.asp?ID=1

Neff, L. A., & Karney, B. R. (2003). The dynamic structure of relationship perceptions: Differential importance as a strategy of relationship maintenance. *Personality and Social Psychology Bulletin, 29,* 1433–1446.

Newton, D. A., & Burgoon, J. K. (1990). The use and consequences of verbal influence strategies during interpersonal disagreements. *Human Communication Research, 16,* 477–518.

Newton, T. L., Kiecolt-Glaser, J. K., & Malarkey, W. (1995). Conflict and withdrawal during marital interaction: Theories of hostility and defensiveness. *Personality and Social Psychology Bulletin, 21,* 512–524.

Niehuis, S. (2001). Premarital predictors of marital outcomes. *Dissertation Abstracts, 62,* 4350.

Noller, P. (1984). *Nonverbal communication and marital interaction.* Elmsford, NY: Pergamon Press.

Noller, P. (1985). Negative communications in marriage. *Journal of Social and Personal Relationships, 11,* 233–252.

Noller, P., & Callan, V. J. (1988). Understanding parent-adolescent interactions: Perceptions of family members and outsiders. *Developmental Psychology, 24,* 707–714.

Noller, P., Feeney, J. A., Bonnell, D., & Callan, V. (1994). A longitudinal study of conflict in early marriage. *Journal of Social and Personal Relationships, 11,* 233–253.

Nolin, M. J., & Petersen, K. K. (1992). Gender differences in parent-child communication about sexuality: An exploratory study. *Journal of Adolescent Research, 7,* 59–79.

Notarius, C. I., Benson, P. R., Sloane, D., Vanzetti, N., & Hornyak, L. M. (1989). Exploring the interface between perception and behavior: An analysis of marital interaction in distressed and nondistressed couples. *Behavioral Assessment, 11,* 39–64.

Notarius, C. I., & Johnson, J. S. (1982). Emotional expression in husbands and wives. *Journal of Marriage and the Family, 45,* 483–489.

Notarius, C. I., & Pellegrini, D. S. (1987). Differences between husbands and wives: Implications for understanding marital discord. In K. Hahlweg & M. J. Goldstein (Eds.), *Understanding major mental disorder: The contribution of family interaction research* (pp. 231–249). New York: Family Process Press.

Novack, L. L., & Novack, D. R. (1996). Being female in the eighties and nineties: Conflicts between new opportunities and traditional expectations among White, middle class, heterosexual women. *Sex Roles: A Journal of Research, 35*, 57–72.

Novello, A., Rosenberg, M., Saltzman, L., & Shosky, J. (1992). From the Surgeon General, U.S. Public Health Service. *Journal of the American Medical Association, 267*, 3132.

O'Brien, K. O., & Zamostny, K. P. (2003). Understanding adoptive families: An integrative review of empirical research and future directions for counseling psychology. *The Counseling Psychologist, 31*, 679–710.

O'Brien, R. (2001). *How much should a stay-at-home mom be earning?* Retrieved July 18, 2005, from http://aol.salary.com/careersandwork/salary/articles/atcl_careeradvice.asp?atc=358

Ochs, E., & Schieffelin, B. B. (1984). Language acquisition and socialization: Three developmental stories and their implications. In R. Schweder & R. A. LeVine (Eds.), *Culture theory: Essays on minds, self, and emotion* (pp. 276–332). New York: Cambridge University Press.

Ockleford, E. M., Vince, M. A., Layton, C., & Reader, M. R. (1988). Responses of neonates to parents' and others' voices. *Early Human Development, 18*, 27–36.

O'Farrell, T. J., & Feehan, M. (1999). Alcoholism treatment and the family: Do family and individual treatments for alcoholic adults have preventive effects for children? *Journal of Studies on Alcohol, 13*, 125–129.

Office of National AIDS Policy. (2003). *HIV/AIDS surveillance report*. Atlanta, GA: Centers for Disease Control.

Ogden, J., & Chanana, A. (1998). Explaining the effect of ethnic group on weight concern: Finding a role for family values. *International Journal of Obesity and Related Metabolic Disorders, 22*, 641–647.

Oldershaw, L., Walters, G. C., & Hall, D. K. (1986). Control strategies and noncompliance in abusive mother-child dyads: An observational study. *Child Development, 57*, 722–732.

Oller, D. K. (1986). Metaphonology and infant vocalizations. In R. A. B. Lindblom & R. Zetterström (Ed.), *Precursors of early speech* (pp. 21–35). New York: Stockton Press.

Olsen, D. H., Russell, C. S., & Sprenkle, D. H. (1989). *Circumplex model: Systematic assessment and treatment of families*. New York: Hayworth.

Olsen, D. H., & Tiesel, J. W. (1991). *Faces II update: Linear scoring and interpretation*. St. Paul: University of Minnesota Press.

Oppenheim, D., Goldsmith, D., & Koren-Karie, N. (2004). Maternal insightfulness and preschoolers' emotion and behavior problems: Reciprocal influences in a therapeutic preschool program. *Infant Mental Health Journal, 25*, 352–367.

Oppenheimer, V. K. (1997). Women's employment and the gain to marriage: The specialization and trading model. *Annual Review of Sociology, 23*, 431–453.

Paasch, K., & Teachmen, J. (1991). Gender of children and receipt of assistance from absent fathers. *Journal of Family Issues, 12*, 450–466.

Pagelow, M. D., (1992). Adult victims of domestic violence. *Journal of Interpersonal Violence, 7*, 87–120.

Paige, P. E., La Pointe, W., & Krueger, A. (1971). The marital dyad as a diagnostic treatment variable in alcohol addiction. *Psychology Savannah, 8*, 64–73.

Pandina, R. J., & Schuele, J. A. (1983). Psychosocial correlates of alcohol and drug use of adolescent students and adolescents in treatment. *Journal of Studies on Alcohol, 44*, 950–973.

Papini, D. R., Farmer, F. F., Clark, S. M., Micka, J. C., & Barnett, C. (1990). Early adolescent age and gender differences in patterns of emotional self-disclosure to parents and friends. *Adolescence, 25, 959–976.*

Papousek, M. (1989). Determinants of responsiveness to infant vocal expression of emotional state. *Infant Behavior and Development, 12, 507–524.*

Papousek, M., Bornstein, M. H., Nuzzo, C., Papousek, H., & Symmes, D. (1990). Infant responses to prototypical melodic contours in parental speech. *Infant Behavior and Development, 13, 539–545.*

Papousek, M., & Papousek, H. (1991). Early verbalizations as precursors of language development. In M. E. Lamb & H. Keller (Eds.), *Infant development: Perspectives from German speaking countries* (pp. 299–328). Hillsdale, NJ: Erlbaum.

Papousek, M., Papousek, H., & Bornstein, M. H. (1985). The naturalistic vocal environment of young infants: On the significance of homogeneity and variability in parent speech. In T. Field & N. Fox (Eds.), *Social perception in infants* (pp. 269–297). Norwood, NJ: Ablex.

Papousek, M., Papousek, H., & Haekel, M. (1987). Didactic adjustments in fathers' and mothers' speech to their 3-month old infants. *Journal of Psycholinguistic Research, 16, 491–516.*

Papousek, M., Papousek, H., & Symmes, D. (1991). The meanings of melodies in motherese in tone and stress languages. *Infant Behavior and Development, 14, 415–440.*

Parke, R. D. (1981). *Fathers.* Cambridge, UK: Cambridge University.

Parke, R. D., & Brott, A. A. (1999). *Throwaway dads: The myths and barriers that keep men from being the fathers they want to be.* Boston: Houghton Mifflin.

Pasch, L. A., Dunkel-Schetter, C., & Christensen, A. (2002). Differences between husbands' and wives' approach to infertility affect marital communication and adjustment. *Fertility and Sterility, 77, 1241–1247.*

Patrikako, E. (1997). A model of parental attitudes and the academic achievement of adolescents. *Journal of Research and Development in Education, 31, 7–26.*

Patterson, C. J. (1992). Children of lesbian and gay parents. *Child Development, 63,* 1025–1042.

Patterson, C. J. (1995). Adoption of minor children by lesbian and gay adults: A social science perspective. *Duke Journal of Gender Law and Policy, 2, 191–205.*

Patterson, C. J., & Redding, R. E. (1996). Lesbian and gay families with children: Implications of social science research for policy. *Journal of Social Issues, 52(3),* 29–50.

Patterson, G. R. (1982). *A social learning approach to family intervention: Vol. 3. Coercive family process.* Eugene, OR: Castalia.

Patterson, G. R., & Hops, H. (1972). Coercion, a game for two: Intervention techniques for marital conflict. In R. E. Ulrich & P. Mountjoy (Eds.), *The experimental analysis of social behavior.* New York: Appleton-Century-Crofts.

Patterson, G. R., Hops, H., & Weiss, R. L. (1975). Interpersonal skill training for couples in early stages of conflict. *Journal of Marriage and the Family, 37, 295–303.*

Patterson, G. R., & Reid, J. B. (1970). Reciprocity and coercion: Two facets of social systems. In C. Neuringer & J. Michael (Eds.), *Behavior modification in clinical psychology.* (pp. 133–177). New York: Appleton-Century-Crofts.

Paxton, S. J., Wertheim, E. H., Gibbons, K., Szmuckler, G. I., Hiller, L., & Petrovich, J. C. (1991). Body image satisfaction, dieting beliefs and weight loss behaviors in adolescent girls and boys. *Journal of Youth and Adolescence, 20,* 361–379.

Pearson, J. C. (1992). *Lasting love: What keeps couples together.* Dubuque, IA: William C. Brown.

Pearson, J. C. (1993). *Communication in the family: Seeking satisfaction in changing times* (2nd ed.). New York: Harper Collins.

Peery, J. C., Jensen, L., & Adams, G. H. (1985). The relationships between parents' attitudes toward child rearing and the sociometric status of their preschool children. *Journal of Psychology, 119,* 567–574.

Pence, E., & Paymar, M. (1993). *Education groups for men who batter: The Duluth model.* New York: Springer.

Perlman, M., & Ross, H. S. (1997). Who's the boss? Parents' failed attempts to influence the outcomes of conflicts between their children. *Journal of Social and Personal Relationships, 14,* 463–480.

Perry-Jenkins, M., Pierce, C. P., & Goldberg, A. E. (2004). Discourses on diapers and dirty laundry: Family communication about child care and housework. In A. Vangelisti (Ed.), *Handbook of family communication* (pp. 541–561). Mahwah, NJ: Erlbaum.

Pianta, R., Egeland, B., & Erikson, M. F. (1989). The antecedents of maltreatment: Results of the mother-child interaction research project. In D. Cicchetti & V. Carlson (Eds.), *Child maltreatment: Theory and research on the causes and consequences of child abuse and neglect* (pp. 203–253). New York: Cambridge University Press.

Pihl, R. O., Peterson, J., & Finn, P. R. (1990). An heuristic model for the inherited predisposition to alcoholism. *Psychology of Addicted Behavior, 4,* 12–25.

Pike, K. M., & Rodin, J. (1991). Mothers, daughters, and disordered eating. *Journal of Abnormal Psychology, 100,* 198–204.

Ponsford, L. (2004). *Parent-adolescent sexual communication: The role of expectancies in affecting teen evaluations and sexual behavior.* Unpublished Senior's Honors Thesis, University of California, Santa Barbara.

Pratt, M. Green, D., MacVicar, J., & Bountrogianni, M. (1993). The mathematical parent: Parental scaffolding, parenting style, and learning outcomes in long-division mathematic homework. *Journal of Applied Development, 13,* 17–34.

Prescott, M. E., & Le Poire, B. A. (2002). Eating disorders and mother-daughter communication: A test of inconsistent nurturing as control theory. *Journal of Family Communication, 2,* 59–78.

Purnine, D. M., & Carey, M. P. (1997). Interpersonal communication and sexual adjustment: The role of understanding and agreement. *Journal of Consulting and Clinical Psychology, 65,* 1017–1025.

Putallaz, M., & Heflin, A. H. (1990). Parent-child interaction. In S. R. Asher & J. D. Coie (Eds.), *Peer rejection in childhood* (pp. 189–216). Cambridge, UK: Cambridge University Press.

Quigley, B. M., & Leonard, K. E. (2000). Alcohol, drugs, and violence. In V. B. Van Hasselt, & M. Hersen (Eds.), *Aggression and violence: An introductory text* (pp. 259–283). Needham Heights, MA: Allyn & Bacon.

Quinton, D., Pickles, A., Maughan, B., & Rutter, M. (1993). Partners, peers, and pathways: Assortative pairing and continuities in conduct disorder. Special

Issue: Milestones in the development of resilience. *Development and Psychopathology, 5*, 763–783.

Radke-Yarrow, M., Zahn-Waxler, C., & Chapman, M. (1983). Children's prosocial dispositions and behavior. In P. H. Mussen (Ed.), *Handbook of child psychology.* (Vol. 2, pp. 469–545). New York: Wiley.

Rae, J. B., & Drewery, J. (1972). Interpersonal patterns in alcoholic marriages. *British Journal of Psychiatry, 120,* 615–621.

Raffaelli, M., & Green, S. (2003). Parent-adolescent communication about sex: Retrospective reports by Latino college students. *Journal of Marriage and Family, 65,* 474–481.

Read, S. J., & Miller, L. C. (1989). Interpersonalism: Towards a goal-based theory of persons in relationships. In L. Pervin (Ed.), *Goal concepts in personality and social psychology* (pp. 413–472). Hillsdale, NJ: Erlbaum.

Reid, J. B. (1986). Social-interactional patterns in families of abused and nonabused children. In C. Zahn-Waxler, E. M. Cummings, & R. Iannotti (Eds.), *Altruism and aggression: Biological and social origins* (pp. 238–255). New York: Cambridge University Press.

Rennison, C. (2001, March). *Violent victimization and race: 1993 to 1998* (Bureau of Justice Statistics Special Report, NCJ 176354). Washington, DC: U.S. Department of Justice, Office of Justice Programs.

Rennison, C. M., & Welchans, S. (2000, May). *Intimate partner violence* (Bureau of Justice Statistics, NCJ 178247). Washington, DC: U.S. Department of Justice, Office of Justice Programs.

Revenstrof, D., Vogel, B., Wegner, C., Hahlweg, K., & Schindler, L. (1980). Escalation phenomena in interaction sequences: An empirical comparison of distressed and nondistressed couples. *Behavior Analysis and Modification, 4,* 97–115.

Rice, F. P. (1992). *The adolescent: Development, relationships, and culture.* Boston: Allyn & Bacon.

Richards, L. N., & Schmiege, C. J. (1993). Problems and strengths of single-parent families: Implications for practice and policy. *Family Relations, 42,* 277–285.

Richmond, V. P., McCroskey, J. C., & Roach, K. D. (1997). Communication and decision-making styles, power base usage, and satisfaction in marital dyads. *Communication Quarterly, 45,* 410–437.

Ricketts, W. (1991). *Lesbians and gay men and foster parents.* Portland, ME: National Child Welfare Resource Center.

Ricketts, W., & Achtenberg, R. (1990). Adoption and foster parenting for lesbians and gay men: Creating new traditions in family. In F. W. Bozett & M. B. Sussman (Eds.), *Homosexuality and family relations* (pp. 83–118). New York: Harrington Park Press.

Rivera, R. R. (1991). Sexual orientation and the law. In J. C. Gonsiorek & J. D. Weinrich (Eds.), *Homosexuality: Research implications for public policy* (pp. 81–100). Newbury Park, CA: Sage.

Robertson, A. F. (1991). *Beyond the family: The social organization of human reproduction.* Cambridge, UK: Polity Press.

Robey, K. L., Cohen, B. D., & Epstein, Y. M. (1988). The child's response to affection given to someone else: Effects of parental divorce, sex of child, and sibling position. *Journal of Clinical Child Psychology, 17,* 2–7.

Rodriguez, E., Lasch, K. E., Chandra, J., & Lee, P. (2001). Family violence, employment status, welfare benefits, and alcohol drinking in the United States:

What is the relation? *Journal of Epidemiology & Community Health, 55*, 172–178.

Roe v. Roe, 324 S.E.2d 691 (Va. 1985).

Rogers, R. G. (1995). Marriage, sex, mortality. *Journal of Marriage and the Family, 57*, 515–526.

Roggman, L. A., Boyce, L. K., & Cook, J. (2001). Widening the lens: Viewing fathers in infants' lives. In H. E. Fitzgerald, K. H. Karraker, & T. Luster (Eds.), *Infant development: Ecological perspectives* (pp. 193–220). New York: Routledge Falmer.

Roloff, M. E. (1996). The catalyst hypothesis: Conditions under which coercive communication leads to physical aggression. In D. D. Cahn & S. A. Lloyd (Eds.), *Family violence from a communication perspective* (pp. 20–36). Thousand Oaks, CA: Sage.

Roloff, M. E., & Cloven, D. H. (1990). The "chilling effect" in interpersonal relationships: The reluctance to speak one's mind. In D. D. Cahn (Ed.), *Intimates in conflict: A communication perspective* (pp. 49–76). Hillsdale, NJ: Erlbaum.

Rose-Krasnor, L. (1997). The nature of social competence: A theoretical review. *Social Development, 6*, 111–135.

Rosenthal, R. (1973). The mediation of Pygmalion effects: A four-factor "theory." *Papua New Guinea Journal of Education, 9*, 1–12.

Rosenthal, R. (1981). Pavlov's mice, Pfungst's horse, and Pygmalion's PONS: Some models for the study of interpersonal expectancy effects. In T. A. Sebeok & R. Rosenthal (Eds.), *The Clever Hans phenomenon: Communication with horses, whales, apes and people* (pp. 182–198). New York: Annals of the New York Academy of Sciences.

Rubenstein, W. B. (1991). We are family: A reflection on the search for legal recognition of lesbian and gay relationships. *Journal of Law and Politics, 8*, 89–105.

Rubin, R. (1975). Maternal tasks in pregnancy. *Maternal Child Nursing Journal, 4*, 143–153.

Rubin, Z., Hill, C. T., Peplau, L. A., & Dunkel-Schetter, C. (1980). Self-disclosure in dating couples: The ethic of openness. *Journal of Marriage and the Family, 42*, 499–506.

Rubio-Stipec, M., Bird, H., Canino, G., & Bravo, M. (1991). Children of alcoholic parents in the community. *Journal of Studies on Alcohol, 52*, 78–88.

Ruble, D. N., Fleming, A. S., Hackel, L. S., & Stangor, C. (1988). Changes in the marital relationship during the transition to first time motherhood: Effects of violated expectations concerning the division of labor. *Journal of Personality and Social Psychology, 55*, 78–87.

Ruble, D. N., Fleming, A. S., Stangor, C., Brooks-Gunn, J., Fitzmaurice, G., & Deutsch, F. (1990). Transition to motherhood and the self: Measurement, stability, and change. *Journal of Personality and Social Psychology, 58*, 450–463.

Rusbult, C. E. (1980). Commitment and satisfaction in romantic associations: A test of the investment model. *Journal of Experimental Social Psychology, 16*, 172–186.

Rusbult, C. E. (1983). A longitudinal test of the investment model: The development (and deterioration) of satisfaction and commitment in heterosexual involvements. *Journal of Personality and Social Psychology, 45*, 101–117.

Rutter, M., & Quinton, R. (1984). Long-term follow-up of women institutionalized in childhood: Factors promoting good functioning in adulthood. *British Journal of Developmental Psychology, 2*, 191–204.

Sabourin, T. C., Infante, D. A., & Rudd, J. E. (1993). Verbal aggression in marriages: A comparison of violent, distressed but nonviolent, and nondistressed couples. *Human Communication Research, 20,* 245–267.

Sacco, W. P., & Phares, V. (2001). Partner appraisal and marital satisfaction: The role of self-esteem and depression. *Journal of Marriage and the Family, 63,* 504–513.

Sagrestano, L. M., Heavey, C. L., & Christensen, A. (1999). Perceived power and physical violence in marital conflict. *Journal of Social Issues, 55,* 65–79.

Samp, J. A., & Solomon, D. H. (1998). Communicative responses to problematic events in close relationships: I. The variety and facts of goals. *Communication Research, 25,* 66–95.

Sanderson, C. A., & Cantor, N. (2001). The association of intimacy goals and marital satisfaction: A test of four mediational hypotheses. *Personality and Social Psychology Bulletin, 27,* 1567–1577.

Sanderson, C. A., & Evans, S. M. (2001). Seeing one's partner through intimacy-colored glasses: An examination of the processes underlying the intimacy goals-relationship satisfaction link. *Personality and Social Psychology Bulletin, 27,* 463–473.

Sandmaier, M. (1980). *The invisible alcoholics: Women and alcohol abuse in America.* New York: McGraw-Hill.

Sanford, K., & Rowatt, W. C. (2004). When is negative emotion positive for relationships? An investigation of married couples and roommates. *Personal Relationships, 11,* 329–354.

Sarason, B. R., Sarason, I. G., & Gurung, R. A. R. (1997). Close personal relationships in health outcomes: A key to the role of social support. In S. Duck, (Ed.), *Handbook of personal relationships* (2nd ed.). London: Wiley.

Sassler, S., & Schoen, R. (1999). The effect of attitudes on economic activity on marriage. *Journal of Marriage and the Family, 61,* 147–159.

Satir, V. (1967). *Conjoint family therapy.* Palo Alto, CA: Science and Behavior Books.

Scanzoni, J., Polonko, K., Teachman, K., & Thompson, L. (1989). *The sexual bond: Rethinking families and close relationships.* Newbury Park, CA: Sage.

Schaap, C. (1984). A comparison of the interaction of distressed married couples in a laboratory situation: Literature survey, methodological issues, and an empirical investigation. In K. Hahlweg & N. S. Jacobson (Eds.), *Marital interaction: Analysis and modification* (pp. 133–158). New York: Guilford Press.

Schaap, C., Buunk, B., & Kerkstra, A. (1988). Marital conflict resolution. In P. Noller & M. A. Fitzpatrick (Eds.), *Perspectives on family communication* (pp. 203–244). Clevedon, UK: Multilingual Matters.

Scheflen, A. E. (1965). Quasi-courtship behavior in psychotherapy. *Psychiatry, 28,* 245–257.

Schmitt, D. P., & Buss, D. M. (1996). Strategic self-promotion and competitor derogation: Sex and context effects on the perceived effectiveness of mate attraction tactics. *Journal of Personality and Social Psychology, 70,* 1185–1204.

Schoen, R., & Weinick, R. M. (1993). Partner choice in marriages and cohabitations. *Journal of Marriage and the Family, 55,* 408–415.

Schor, E. L. (1996). Adolescent alcohol use: Social determinants and the case for early family-centered intervention. *Bulletin of the New York Academy of Medicine, 73,* 335–355.

Schumm, W. R., Barnes, H. L., Bollman, S. R., Jurich, A. P., & Bugaighis, M. A. (1986). Self-disclosure and marital satisfaction revisited. *Family Relations, 34,* 241–247.

Searight, H. R., Thomas, S. L., Manley, C. M., & Ketterson, T. U. (1995). Self-disclosure in adolescents: A family systems perspective. In K. J. Rotenberg (Ed.), *Disclosure processes in children and adolescents. Cambridge studies in social and emotional development* (pp. 204–225). New York: Cambridge University Press.

Segrin, C. (1993a). Interpersonal reactions to dysphoria: the role of relationship with Partner and perceptions of rejection. *Journal of Social and Personal Relationships, 10,* 83–97.

Segrin, C. (1993b). Social skills deficits and psychosocial problem: Antecedent, concomitant, or consequent? *Journal of Social and Clinical Psychology, 12,* 336–353.

Segrin, C., & Abramson, L. Y. (1994). Negative reactions to depressive behaviors: A communication theories analysis. *Journal of Abnormal Psychology, 103,* 655–668.

Segrin, C., & Dillard, J. P. (1991). (Non)Depressed persons' cognitive and affective reactions to (un)successful interpersonal influence. *Communication Monographs, 58,* 115–134.

Seltzer, J. A. (2000). Families formed outside of marriage. *Journal of Marriage and the Family, 62,* 1247–1268.

Shanley, M. L. (2003). Transracial and open adoption: New forms of family relationships. In A. S. Skonick & J. H. Skolnick (Eds.), *Family in transition* (12th ed., pp. 255–262). San Francisco: Allyn & Bacon.

Shantz, C. U., & Hobart, C. J. (1989). Social conflict and development: Peers and siblings. In T. J. Berndt & G. W. Ladd (Eds.), *Peer relationships in child development* (pp. 71–94). New York: Wiley.

Shapiro, A. F., Gottman, J. M., & Carrere, S. (2000). The baby and marriage: Identifying factors that buffer against decline in marital satisfaction after the first baby arrives. *Journal of Family Psychology, 14,* 59–70.

Shaver, P. R., Schachner, D. A., & Mikulincer, M. (2005). Attachment style, excessive reassurance seeking, relationship processes, and depression. *Personality and Social Psychology Bulletin, 31,* 343–359.

Sher, K. J. (Ed.). (1991). *Children of alcoholics: A critical appraisal of theory and research.* Chicago: University of Chicago Press.

Sheridan, M. J. (1995). A proposed intergenerational model of substance abuse, family functioning, and abuse/neglect. *Child Abuse and Neglect, 19,* 519–530.

Shields, S. (1987). Women, men, and the dilemma of emotion. In P. Shaver (Ed.), *Review of personality and social psychology* (Vol. 7, pp. 229–250). Newbury Park, CA: Sage.

Shimanoff, S. (1980). *Communication rules: Theory and research.* Beverly Hills, CA: Sage.

Shuntich, R. J., Loh, D., & Katz, D. (1998). Some relationships among affection, aggression and alcohol abuse in the family setting. *Perceptual and Motor Skills, 86,* 1051–1060.

Siegert, J. R., & Stamp, G. H. (1994). "Our first big fight" as a milestone in the development of close relationships. *Communication Monographs, 61,* 345–360.

Sillars, A. L. (1986, April). *Procedures for coding interpersonal conflict* (Rev.). Missoula: University of Montana, Department of Interpersonal Communication.

Sillars, A. L. (1998). (Mis)understanding. In B. H. Spitzberg & W. R. Cupach (Eds.), *The dark side of relationships* (pp. 73–102). Mahwah, NJ: Erlbaum.

Sillars, A., Canary, D. J., & Tafoya, M. (2004). Communication, conflict, and the quality of family relationships. In A. L. Vangelisti (Ed.), *Handbook of family communication* (pp. 413–446). Mahwah, NJ: Erlbaum.

Sillars, A., Roberts, L. J., Leonard, K. E., & Dun, T. (2000). Cognition during marital conflict: The relationship of thought and talk. *Journal of Social and Personal Relationships, 17*, 479–502.

Silverberg, S. B., & Steinberg, L. (1990). Psychological well-being of parents with early adolescent children. *Developmental Psychology, 26*, 658–666.

Simmons, T., & O'Connell, M. (2003). *Married-couple and unmarried-partner households: 2000.* Washington, DC: Government Printing Office. Retrieved July 1, 2005 from www.census.gov/prod/2003pubs/censr-5.pdf

Simons, R. L., Beaman, J., Conger, R. D., & Chao, W. (1993). Stress, support, and antisocial behavior trait as determinants of emotional well-being and parenting practices among single mothers. *Journal of Marriage and the Family, 55*, 385–398.

Simpson, J. A., & Gangestad, S. W. (2001). Evolution and relationships: A call for integration. *Personal Relationships, 8*, 341–355.

Simpson, J. A., Gangestad, S. W., & Beik, M. (1993). Personality and nonverbal social behavior: An ethological perspective of relationship initiation. *Journal of Experimental Social Psychology, 29*, 434–461.

Singh, D. (1993). Adaptive significance of female physical attractiveness: Role of waist-to-hip ratio. *Journal of Personality and Social Psychology, 65*, 293–307.

Skinner, B. F. (1953). *Science and human behavior.* New York: Macmillan.

Skinner, B. F. (1974). *About behaviorism.* New York: Knopf.

Slater, A., & Johnson, S. P. (1998). Visual sensory and perceptual abilities of the newborn: Beyond the blooming, buzzing confusion. In F. Simion & G. Butterworth (Eds.), *The development of sensory, motor and cognitive capacities in early infancy: From perception to cognition* (pp. 121–41). Hove, UK: Psychology Press/Lawrence Erlbaum Associates (UK) Taylor & Francis.

Small, S. A., & Riley, D. (1990). Life events and changes in social relationships: Examples, mechanisms, and measurement. *Journal of Marriage and the Family, 52*, 51–61.

Smetana, J. G. (1995). Parenting styles and conceptions of parental authority during adolescence. *Child Development, 66*, 299–316.

Smetana, J., Yau, J., & Hanson, S. (1991). Conflict resolution in families with adolescents. *Journal of Research on Adolescence, 1*, 189–206.

Smith, J., Brooks-Gunn, J., & Klebanov, P. (1997). Consequences of living in poverty for young children's cognitive and verbal ability and early school achievement. In G. J. Duncan & J. Brooks-Gunn (Eds.), *Consequences of growing up poor* (pp. 132–189). New York: Russell Sage.

Smith, M. J. (1982). *Persuasion and human action: A review and critique of social influence theories.* Belmont, CA: Wadsworth.

Smolak, L., Levine, M. P., & Schermer, F. (1999). Parental inputs and weight concerns among elementary children. *International Journal of Eating Disorders, 25*, 266–271.

Smyth, J. M., & Pennebaker, J. W. (2001). What are the health effects of disclosure? In A. Baum, T. A. Renvenson, & J. E. Singer (Eds.), *Handbook of health psychology* (pp. 339–348). Mahwah, NJ: Erlbaum.

Solomon, D. H. (1997). A developmental model of intimacy and date request explicitness. *Communication Monographs, 64*, 99–118.

Solomon, D. H., & Knobloch, L. K. (2001). Relationship uncertainty, partner interference, and intimacy within dating relationships. *Journal of Social and Personal Relationships, 18*, 804–820

Solomon, D. H., & Knobloch, L. K. (2004). A model of turbulence: The role of intimacy, relational uncertainty, and interference from partners in appraisals of irritations. *Journal of Social and Personal Relationships, 21*(6), 795–816.

South, S. J. (2001). The variable effects of family background on the timing of first marriage: United States, 1969–1993. *Social Science Research, 30,* 606–626.

South, S. J., & Lloyd, K. M. (1992). Marriage opportunities and family formation: Further implications of imbalanced sex ratios. *Journal of Marriage and the Family, 54,* 440–451.

Spence, M. J., & Freeman, M. S. (1996). Newborn infants prefer the maternal low-pass filtered voice, but not the maternal whispered voice. *Infant Behavior and Development, 19,* 199–212.

Spence, S. H., Najman, J. M., Bor, W., O'Callaghan, M. J., Williams, G. M. (2002). Maternal anxiety and depression, poverty and marital relationship factors during early childhood as predictors of anxiety and depressive symptoms in adolescence. *Journal of Child Psychology and Psychiatry and Allied Disciplines, 43,* 457–469.

Sprecher, S. (2001). Equity and social exchange in dating couples: Associations with satisfaction, commitment, and stability. *Journal of Marriage and the Family, 63,* 599–613.

Sprecher, S., Metts, S., Burleson, B., Hatfield, E., & Thompson, A. (1995). Domains of expressive interaction in intimate relationships: Associations with satisfaction and commitment. *Family Relations, 44,* 203–210.

Stack, S., & Eshleman, J. R. (1998). Marital status and happiness: A 17-nation study. *Journal of Marriage and Family, 60,* 527–536.

Stafford, L. (2004). Communication competencies and sociocultural priorities of middle childhood. In A. Vangelisti (Ed.), *Handbook of family communication* (pp. 311–332). Mahwah, NJ: Erlbaum.

Stallings, J., Fleming, A. S., Corter, C., Worthman, C., & Steiner, M. (2001). The effects of infant cries and odors on sympathy, cortisol, and autonomic responses in new mothers and nonpostpartum women. *Parenting: Science and practice, 1,* 71–100.

Stark, R. E., Rose, S. N., & McLagen, M. (1975). Features of infant sounds: The first eight weeks of life. *Journal of Child Language, 2,* 205–221.

Steinberg, L. (1981). Transformations in family relations at puberty. *Developmental Psychology, 17,* 833–840.

Steinberg, L. (2001). We know things: Adolescent-parent relationships in retrospect and prospect. *Journal of Research on Adolescence, 11,* 1–19.

Steinberg, L., Elmen, J., & Mounts, N. (1989). Authoritative parenting, psychosocial maturity, and academic success among adolescents. *Child Development, 60,* 1424–1436.

Steinberg, L., & Silk, J. S. (2002). Parenting adolescents. In M. H. Bornstein (Ed.), *Handbook of parenting: Vol. 1. Children and parenting* (2nd ed.) (pp. 103–133). Mahwah, NJ: Erlbaum.

Steiner, H., & Lock, L. (1998). Anorexia nervosa and bulimia nervosa in children and adolescents: A review of the past 10 years. *Journal of the American Academy of Child and Adolescent Psychiatry, 37,* 352–359.

Steinglass, P. (1976). Experimenting with family treatment approaches to alcoholism, 1950–1975: A review. *Family Process, 15,* 97–123.

Stevens, D., Kiger, G., & Riley, P. J. (2001). Working hard and hardly working: Domestic labor and marital satisfaction among dual-earner couples. *Journal of Marriage and Family, 63,* 514–526.

Stevenson, M. B., Ver Hoeve, J. N., Roach, M. A., & Leavitt, L. A. (1986). The beginning of conversation: Early patterns of mother-infant vocal responsiveness. *Infant Behavior and Development, 9*, 423–440.

Stice, E., Barrera, M., & Chassin, L. (1993). Relation of parental support and control to adolescents' externalizing symptomatology and substance use: A longitudinal examination of curvilinear effects. *Journal of Abnormal Child Psychology, 21*, 609–629.

Strack, S., & Coyne, J.C. (1983). Social confirmation of dysphoria: Shared and private reactions to depression. *Journal of Personality and Social Psychology, 44*, 798–806.

Strage, A. (1998). Family context variables and the development of self-regulation in college students. *Adolescence, 33*, 17–31.

Strage, A., & Brandt, T. S. (1999). Authoritative parenting and college students' academic adjustment and success. *Journal of Educational Psychology, 91*, 146–156.

Straus, M. A., Gelles, R., & Steinmetz, S. (1980). *Behind closed doors: Violence in the American family*. Garden City, NY: Doubleday.

Straus, M. A., & Gelles, R. (1986). Societal change and change in family violence from 1975 to 1985 as revealed by two national surveys. *Journal of Marriage and the Family, 48*, 465–479.

Straus, M. A., & Sweet, S. (1992). Verbal/symbolic aggression in couples: Incidence rates and relationships to personal characteristics. *Journal of Marriage & the Family, 54*, 346–357.

Strauss, R., & Goldberg, W. A. (1999). Self and possible selves during the transition to fatherhood. *Journal of Family Psychology, 13*, 244–259.

Strazdins, L., & Broom, D. H. (2004). Acts of love (and work): Gender imbalance in emotional work and women's psychological distress. *Journal of Family Issues, 25*, 356–378.

Strober, M., & Lampert, C., Morell, W., Burroughs, J., & Jacobs, C. (1990). A controlled family study of anorexia-nervosa: Evidence of familial aggregation and a lack of shared transmission with affective disorders. *International Journal of Eating Disorders, 9*, 239–253.

Study finds that for young men, family comes first. (2004, May 4). *Harvard University Gazette*. Retrieved July 18, 2005, from www.news.harvard.edu/gazette/2000/05.04/radcliffe.html

Sturgess, W., Dunn, J., & Davies, L. (2001). Young children's perceptions of their relationships with family members: Links with family setting, friendships, and adjustment. *International Journal of Behavioral Development, 25*, 521–529.

Substance Abuse and Mental Health Services Administration. (2003, June 2). *Children living with substance-abusing or substance-dependent parents*. Retrieved October 26, 2004 from http://oas.samhsa.gov/2k3/children/children.htm

Substance Abuse and Mental Health Services Administration. (2004a, February 13). *Alcohol dependence or abuse among parents with children living in the home*. Retrieved October 26, 2004 from http://oas.samhsa.gov/2k4/ACOA/ACOA.htm

Substance Abuse and Mental Health Services Administration. (2004b, October 15). *Adolescent treatment admissions: 1992 and 2002*. Retrieved October 26, 2004 from http://oas.samhsa.gov/2k4/ACOA/ACOA.htm

Substance Abuse and Mental Health Services Administration. (2004c, October 22). *Delayed alcohol use linked to fewer problems with abuse or dependence as adults*. Retrieved October 26, 2004 from http://162.99.3.50/news/newsreleases/041022nr_delayed_alcohol.htm

Surra, C. A., Gray, C. R., Cottle, N., & Boettcher, T. M. (2004). Research on mate selection and premarital relationships: What do we really know? In A. Vangelisti (Ed.), *Handbook of family communication* (pp. 53–82). Mahwah, NJ: Erlbaum.

Tarter, R. E., Laird, S. B., & Moss, H. B. (1990). Neuropsychological and neurophysiological characteristics of children of alcoholics. In M. Windle & J. S. Searles (Eds.), *Children of alcoholics: Critical perspectives* (pp. 73–98). New York: Guilford Press.

Testa, M., Quigley, B. M., & Leonard, K. E. (2003). Does alcohol make a difference? Within-participants comparison of incidents of partner violence. *Journal of Interpersonal Violence, 18,* 735–743.

Testimony of Barbara Dafoe Whitehead, Ph.D, Co-Director, National Marriage Project, Rutgers, the State University of New Jersey, Before the Committee on Health, Education, Labor and Pensions, Subcommittee on Children and families, U.S. Senate. (2004, April 28). Retrieved August 2, 2005, from http://marriage.rutgers.edu/Publications/Pub%20Whitehead%20Testimony%20Apr%2004.htm

Thibaut, J., & Kelley, H. (1959). *The social psychology of groups.* New York: Wiley.

Thiriot, T. L., & Buckner, E. T. (1992). Multiple predictors of satisfactory post-divorce adjustment of single custodial parents. *Journal of Divorce and Remarriage, 17*(1/2), 27–48.

Thompson, L. (1991). Family work: Women's sense of fairness. *Journal of Family Issues, 12,* 181–196.

Timmer, S. G., & Orbuck, T. L. (2001). The links between premarital parenthood, meanings of marriage, and marital outcomes. *Family Relations, 50,* 178–185.

Ting-Toomey, S. (1983). An analysis of verbal communication patterns in high and low marital adjustment groups. *Human Communication Research, 9,* 306–319.

Tomlinson, P. S. (1987). Spousal differences in marital satisfaction during the transition to parenthood. *Nursing Research, 36,* 239–243.

Tweed, S. H., & Ryff, C. D. (1991). Adult children of alcoholics: Profiles of wellness amidst distress. *Journal of Studies on Alcohol, 52,* 133–141.

Twenge, J. M. (1997). Changes in masculine and feminine traits over time: A meta-analysis. *Sex Roles, 36,* 305–325.

Umberson, D., Williams, K., & Anderson, K. L. (2002). Violent behavior: A measure of emotional upset? *Journal of Health and Social Behavior, 43,* 189–203.

U.S. Bureau of Labor Statistics, (2004, May). *National occupational employment and wage estimates.* Retrieved June 24, 2005, from http://www.bls.gov/oes/current/oes_nat.htm

U.S. Census Bureau. (1992). *Current Population Reports, Series P-20, No. 458, Household and Family Characteristics: 1991.* Washington, DC: Government Printing Office.

U.S. Census Bureau. (1993). No 78. Children living with biological, step, and adoptive married-couple parents, by race and Hispanic origin of mother: 1980–1990. In *Statistical abstract of the United States, 1992* (113th ed., p. 62). Washington, DC: Government Printing Office.

U.S. Census Bureau. (1999). *Marital status and living arrangements: March 1998* (Current Population Reports, Series P60-207). Washington, DC: Government Printing Office.

U.S. Census Bureau. (2000). *Marital status by sex, unmarried households, and grandparents as caregivers: 2000* (Quick Table QT-P18). Retrieved July 18, 2005, from http://factfinder.census.gov/servlet/QTTable?_bm=y&-geo_id=01000US& -qr_name=DEC_2000_SF3_U_QTP18&-ds_name=DEC_2000_SF3_U&- _lang=en&-_sse=on

U.S. Census Bureau. (2001). *America's families and living arrangements: Population characteristics: 2000* (Current Population Reports, Series P-20, No. 537). Washington, DC: Government Printing Office.

U.S. Census Bureau. (2002). *Current population survey (CPS): Definitions and explanations.* Retrieved July 1, 2005, from www.census.gov/population/www/ cps/cpsdef.html

U.S. Census Bureau. (2003a). *Children's living arrangements and characteristics: March 2002* (Current Population Reports, Series P-20, No. 547). Washington, DC: Government Printing Office.

U.S. Census Bureau. (2003b). *Married-couple and unmarried partner households: 2000.* Retrieved July 18, 2005, from www.census.gov/prod/2003pubs/censr-5.pdf

U.S. Census Bureau. (2004, July 19). *Facts for features & special editions.* Retrieved July 18, 2005, from www.census.gov/Press-Release/www/releases/archives/facts _for_features_special_editions/002265.html

U.S. Department of Health and Human Services. (2004, March 12). *Summary: Child maltreatment 2002.* Retrieved November 2, 2004, from www.acf.dhhs.gov/ programs/cb/publications/cm02/summary.htm

Vaillant, C. O., & Vaillant, G. E. (1993). Is the U-curve of marital satisfaction an illusion? A 40-year study of marriage. *Journal of Marriage and the Family, 55,* 230–239.

Vakalahi, H. F. (1999). Adolescent substance use in Utah: The influence of family-based risk and protective factors. *Dissertation Abstracts International Section A: Humanities and Social Sciences, 59(8-A),* 3214.

Valenza, E., Simion, F., Cassia, V. M., & Umilta, C. (1996). Face preference at birth. *Journal of Experimental Psychology: Human Perception and Performance, 22,* 892–903.

Van den Oord, E. J. C. G., Rispens, J., Goudena, J. P. P., & Vermande, M. (2000). Some developmental implications of structural aspects of preschoolers' relations with classmates. *Journal of Applied Developmental Psychology, 21,* 619–639.

Van Egeren, L. A., & Barratt, M. S. (2004). The developmental origins of communication: Interactional systems in infancy. In A. Vangelisti (Ed.), *Handbook of family communication* (pp. 287–310). Mahwah, NJ: Erlbaum.

Vangelisti, A. L. (1994a). Family secrets: Forms, functions and correlates. *Journal of Social and Personal Relationships, 11,* 113–135.

Vangelisti, A. L. (1994b). Messages that hurt. In W. R Cupach & B. H. Spitzberg (Eds.), *The dark side of interpersonal communication* (pp. 53–82). Hillsdale, NJ: Erlbaum.

Vangelisti, A. L. (2001). Making sense of hurtful interactions in close relationships: When hurt feelings create distance. In V. Manusov & J. H. Harvey (Eds.), *Attributions, communication behavior, and close relationships* (pp. 38–58). Cambridge, UK: Cambridge University Press.

Vangelisti, A. L. (2002). Interpersonal processes in romantic relationships. In M. L. Knapp & J. A. Daly (Eds.), *Handbook of interpersonal communication* (pp. 643–679). Thousand Oaks, CA: Sage.

Vangelisti, A. L., & Banski, M. A. (1993). Couples' debriefing conversations: The impact of gender, occupation, and demographic characteristics. *Family Relations, 42,* 149–157.

Vangelisti, A. L., Caughlin, J. P., & Timmerman, L. (2001). Criteria for revealing family secrets. *Communication Monographs, 68,* 1–27.

Vangelisti, A. L., & Crumley, L. P. (1998). Reactions to messages that hurt: The influence of relational contexts. *Communication Monographs, 65,* 173–196.

Vangelisti, A. L., & Daly, J. A. (1997). Gender differences in standards for romantic relationships. *Personal Relationships, 4,* 203–219.

Vangelisti, A., L., & Huston, T. L. (1994). Maintaining marital satisfaction and love. In D. J. Canary & L. Staffor (Eds.), *Communication and relational maintenance* (pp. 165–186). New York: Academic Press.

Vangelisti, A. L., & Young, S. L. (2000). When words hurt: The effects of perceived intentionality on interpersonal relationships. *Journal of Social and Personal Relationships, 17,* 393–424.

Verbrugge, L. M. (1979). Marital status and health. *Journal of Marriage and the Family, 41,* 267–285.

Vettese, L.C., & Mongrain, M. (2000). Communication about the self and partner in the relationships of dependents and self-critics. *Cognitive Therapy and Research, 24,* 609–626.

Visher, E. B., & Visher, J. S. (1988). *Old loyalties, new ties: Therapeutic strategies with stepfamilies.* New York: Brunner/Mazel.

Vuchinich, S. (1987). Starting and stopping spontaneous family conflicts. *Journal of Marriage and the Family, 49,* 591–601.

Waddan, A. (2003). Redesigning the welfare contract in theory and practice: Just what is going on in the USA? *Journal of Social Policy, 32,* 19–35.

Wade, T. D., & Kendler, K. S. (2000). The relationship between social support and major depression: Cross-sectional, longitudinal, and genetic perspectives. *Journal of Nervous and Mental Disease, 88,* 251–258.

Wagner, H. L., Buck, R., & Winterbotham, M. (1993). Communication of specific emotions: Gender differences in sending accuracy and communication measures. *Journal of Nonverbal Behavior, 17,* 29–53.

Waite, L. J., & Gallagher, M. (2000). *The case for marriage: Why married people are happier, healthier, and better off financially.* New York: Doubleday.

Waite, L. J., & Lillard, L. A. (1991). Children and marital disruption. *American Journal of Sociology, 96,* 930–953.

Walker, J. P., & Lee, R. E. (1998). Uncovering strengths of children of alcoholic parents. *Contemporary Family Therapy, 20,* 521–538.

Walker, L. (1979). *The battered woman.* New York: Harper & Row.

Warren, C. (1992). Perspectives on international sex practices and American family sex communication relevant to teenage sexual behavior in the United States. *Health Communication, 4,* 121–136.

Waters, E., Wippman, J., & Stroufe, L. A. (1979). Attachment, positive affect, and competence in the peer group: Two studies in construct validation. *Child Development, 50,* 821–829.

Watzlawick, P., Beavin, J. H., & Jackson, D. D. (1967). *Pragmatics of human communication.* New York: Norton.

Weatherman, K. A. (2003). The role of injury experience on maternal beliefs, attitudes, and knowledge of unintentional injuries in preschool children. *Masters Abstracts International, 41*, 194.

Weiss, R. L. (1980). Strategic behavioral marital therapy: Toward a model for assessment and intervention (pp. 229–271). In J. P. Vincent (Ed.). *Advances in family intervention, assessment and theory* (Vol. 1, pp. 229–271). Greenwich, CT: JAI Press.

Weiss, R. L., & Heyman, R. E. (1990). Observation in marital interaction. In F. D. Fincham & T. N. Bradbury (Eds.), *Psychology of marriage* (pp. 87–117). New York: Guilford Press.

Weiss, R. L., & Tolman, A. O. (1990). The Marital Interaction Coding System-Global (MICS-G): A global companion to the MICS. *Behavioral Assessment, 12*, 271–294.

Wekerle, C., & Wall, A. M. (Eds.). (2002). *The violence and addiction equation: Theoretical and clinical issues in substance abuse and relationship violence.* New York: Brunner-Routledge.

Wells, J. W., & Kline, W. D. (1987). Self-disclosure of homosexual orientation. *Journal of Social Psychology, 127*, 191–197.

Werner, L. J., & Broida, J. P. (1991). Adult self-esteem and locus of control as a function of familial alcoholism and dysfunction. *Journal of Studies on Alcohol, 52*, 249–252.

West, R., & Turner, L. H. (1995). Communication in lesbian and gay families: Developing a descriptive base. In T. Socha & G. Stamp (Eds.), *Parents, children, and communication* (pp. 147–170). Mahwah, NJ: Erlbaum.

Whitaker, D. J., & Miller, K. S. (2000). Parent-adolescent discussions about sex and condoms: Impact on peer influences of sexual risk behavior. *Journal of Adolescent Research, 15*, 251–273.

Whitbeck, L. B., Conger, R. D., & Kao, M. Y. (1993). The influence of parental support, depressed affect, and peers on the sexual behavior of adolescent girls. *Journal of Family Issues, 14*, 261–278.

White, L. K., Booth, A., & Edwards, J. N. (1986). Children and marital happiness: Why the negative correlation? *Journal of Family Issues, 7*, 131–147.

White, L. K., & Reidmann, A. (1992). When the Brady Bunch grows up: Step, half and full sibling relationships in adulthood. *Journal of Marriage and the Family, 54*, 197–208.

Wilson, S. R. (2002). *Seeking and resisting compliance: Why people say what they do when trying to influence others.* Thousand Oaks, CA: Sage.

Wilson, S. R., & Morgan, W. M. (2004). Persuasion and families. In A. Vangelisti (Ed.), *Handbook of family communication* (pp. 447–471). Thousand Oaks, CA: Sage.

Wilson, S. R., & Whipple, E. E. (1995). Communication, discipline, and physical abuse. In T. Socha & G. Stamp (Eds.), *Parents, children, and communication* (pp. 299–317). Mahwah, NJ: Erlbaum.

Windle, M. (1996). On the discriminative validity of a family history of problem drinking index with a national sample of young adults. *Journal of Studies on Alcohol, 57*, 378–386.

Windle, M., & Searles, J. S. (Eds.). (1990). *Children of alcoholics: Critical perspectives.* New York: Guilford Press.

Winkler, A. E., McBride, T. D., & Andrews, C. (2005). *Wives who outearn their husbands: A transitory or persistent phenomenon for couples?* Retrieved July 18, 2005, from www.umsl.edu/~ecoawink/DemographyR&R-Jan31-2005final.pdf

Wolfe, D. A., Crooks, C. V., Lee, V., McIntyre-Smith, A., & Jaffe, P.G. (2003). The effects of children's exposure to domestic violence: A meta-analysis and critique. *Clinical Child and Family Psychology Review, 6,* 171–187.

Wonderlich, S. A., Brewerton, T. D., Jocic, Z., Dansky, B. S., & Abbott, D. W. (1997). Relationship of childhood sexual abuse and eating disorders. *Journal of the American Academy of Child and Adolescent Psychiatry, 36,* 1107–1115.

Xie, Y., Raymo, J. M., Goyette, K., & Thornton, A. (2003). Economic potential and entry into marriage and cohabitation. *Demography, 40,* 351–367.

Yelsma, P. (1996). Affective orientations of perpetrators, victims, and functional spouses. *Journal of Interpersonal Violence, 11,* 141–161.

Yingling, J. (1995). The first relationship: Infant-parent communication. In T. J. Socha & G. H. Stamp (Eds.), *Parents, children, and communication: Frontiers of theory and research* (pp. 23–41). Mahwah, NJ: Erlbaum.

Yogman, M. W. (1994). Observations on the father-infant relationship. In S. H. Cath, A. R. Gurwitt, & J. M. Ross (Eds.), *Father and child: Developmental and clinical perspectives* (pp. 101–122). Hillsdale, NJ: Analytic Press.

Young Pistella, C. L., & Bonati, F. A. (1998). Communication about sexual behavior among adolescent women, their family, and peers. *Families in Society: The Journal of Contemporary Human Services, 79,* 206–211.

Youniss, J., & Smoller, J. (1985). *Adolescent relations with mothers, fathers, and friends.* Chicago: University of Chicago Press.

Zill, N., Morrison, D. R., & Coiro, M. J. (1993). Long-term effects of parental divorce on parent-child relationship, adjustment, and achievement in young adulthood. *Journal of Family Psychology, 7,* 91–103.

Zinn, M. B., & Eitzen, D. S. (2002). *Diversity in families* (6th ed.). Boston, MA: Allyn & Bacon.

Index

Women, in labor force, 31-32.
    See also Mothers; Nurturer(s)
Wonderlich, S. A., 225
Wood, J. T., 114
Woodall, W. G., 13, 15, 85-86
Workforce. *See* Labor force
Working models, 94
Workload, increases in, 115-122.
    See also Division of household
    labor
Worthman, C., 123
Wright, J., 107
Wright, P., 221
Wu, L. C., 227
Wynkoop, T. F., 221

Xie, Y., 59, 243

Yau, J., 148
Yelsma, P., 212
Yingling, J., 62, 159
Yogman, M. W., 150
Young, R. M., 219
Young, S. L., 189, 195, 255
Young Pistella, C. L., 152
Youniss, J., 148

Zach, U., 123
Zahn-Waxler, C., 155
Zamostny, K. P., 114
Zaya, N., 7
Zentall, S. R., 151-152
Zhao, J. Z., 105
Zill, N., 48, 252
Zinn, M. B., 38, 104, 177, 182, 204

About the Author

Beth Le Poire is Professor of Communication at the University of California, Santa Barbara. Her interests are in family communication and nonverbal communication, substance abuse, attachment, and stigma. She has published 45 articles and chapters, with recent publications in *Human Communication Research, Communication Monographs,* and the *Journal of Applied Communication Research,* and is coediting a volume on socially meaningful applied research in interpersonal communication. She received her PhD from the University of Arizona.

LIBRARY, UNIVERSITY OF CHESTE